Dreamweaver® MX For Dummies

KT-429-783

Cheat Sheet

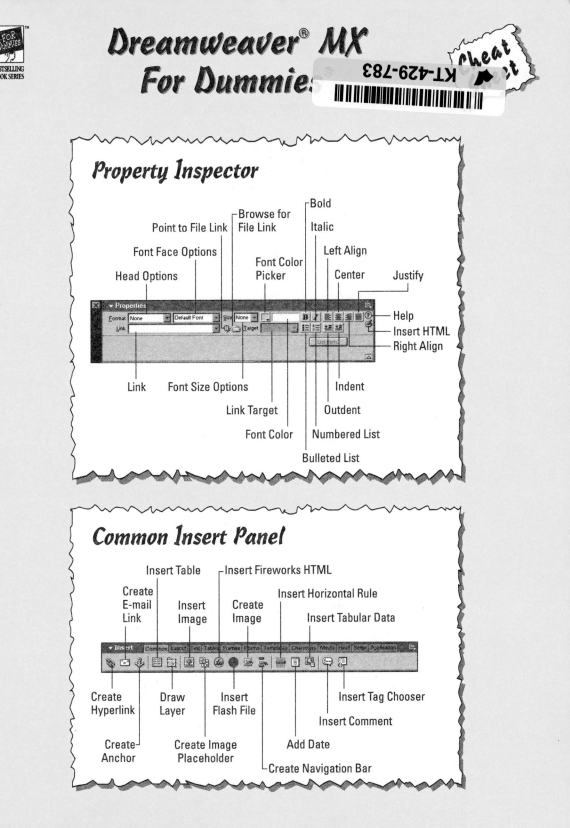

Property Inspector

- Bold
- Italic
- Left Align
- Center
- Justify
- Browse for File Link
- Point to File Link
- Font Color Picker
- Font Face Options
- Head Options
- Help
- Insert HTML
- Right Align
- Link
- Font Size Options
- Link Target
- Font Color
- Indent
- Outdent
- Numbered List
- Bulleted List

Common Insert Panel

- Insert Table
- Insert Fireworks HTML
- Create E-mail Link
- Insert Image
- Create Image
- Insert Horizontal Rule
- Insert Tabular Data
- Create Hyperlink
- Draw Layer
- Insert Flash File
- Insert Tag Chooser
- Insert Comment
- Create Anchor
- Create Image Placeholder
- Add Date
- Create Navigation Bar

Dreamweaver® MX For Dummies®

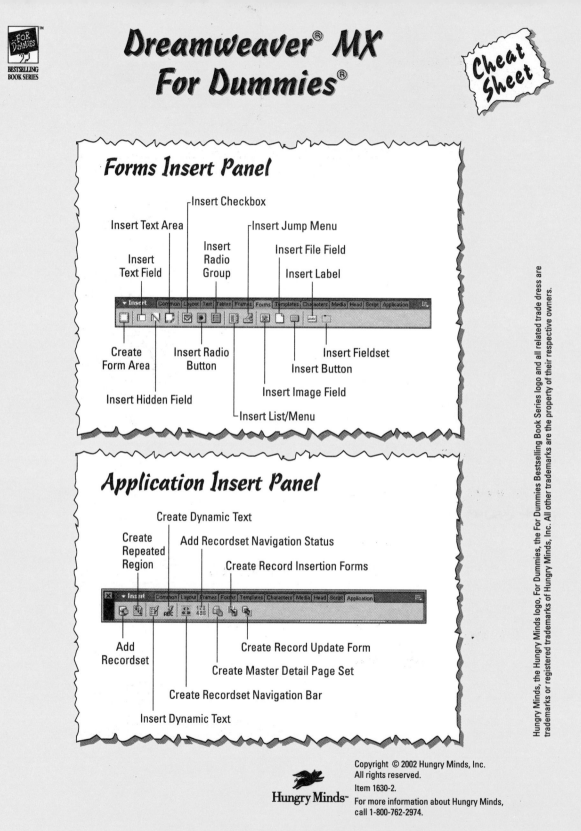

Forms Insert Panel

Insert Checkbox

Insert Text Area

Insert Jump Menu

Insert Text Field

Insert Radio Group

Insert File Field

Insert Label

Create Form Area

Insert Radio Button

Insert Fieldset

Insert Button

Insert Hidden Field

Insert Image Field

Insert List/Menu

Application Insert Panel

Create Dynamic Text

Create Repeated Region

Add Recordset Navigation Status

Create Record Insertion Forms

Add Recordset

Create Record Update Form

Create Master Detail Page Set

Create Recordset Navigation Bar

Insert Dynamic Text

Hungry Minds™

For Dummies: Bestselling Book Series for Beginners

Dreamweaver® MX FOR DUMMIES®

by Janine Warner and Ivonne Berkowitz

Hungry Minds™

Best-Selling Books • Digital Downloads • e-Books • Answer Networks • e-Newsletters • Branded Web Sites • e-Learning

New York, NY ◆ Cleveland, OH ◆ Indianapolis, IN

Dreamweaver® MX For Dummies®

Published by
Hungry Minds, Inc.
909 Third Avenue
New York, NY 10022
www.hungryminds.com
www.dummies.com

Library of Congress Control Number: 2002103274

ISBN: 0-7645-1630-2

Printed in the United States of America

10 9 8 7 6 5 4 3 2 1

1B/SV/QW/QS/IN

Distributed in the United States by Hungry Minds, Inc.

Distributed by CDG Books Canada Inc. for Canada; by Transworld Publishers Limited in the United Kingdom; by IDG Norge Books for Norway; by IDG Sweden Books for Sweden; by IDG Books Australia Publishing Corporation Pty. Ltd. for Australia and New Zealand; by TransQuest Publishers Pte Ltd. for Singapore, Malaysia, Thailand, Indonesia, and Hong Kong; by Gotop Information Inc. for Taiwan; by ICG Muse, Inc. for Japan; by Intersoft for South Africa; by Eyrolles for France; by International Thomson Publishing for Germany, Austria and Switzerland; by Distribuidora Cuspide for Argentina; by LR International for Brazil; by Galileo Libros for Chile; by Ediciones ZETA S.C.R. Ltda. for Peru; by WS Computer Publishing Corporation, Inc., for the Philippines; by Contemporanea de Ediciones for Venezuela; by Express Computer Distributors for the Caribbean and West Indies; by Micronesia Media Distributor, Inc. for Micronesia; by Chips Computadoras S.A. de C.V. for Mexico; by Editorial Norma de Panama S.A. for Panama; by American Bookshops for Finland.

For general information on Hungry Minds' products and services please contact our Customer Care Department within the U.S. at 800-762-2974, outside the U.S. at 317-572-3993 or fax 317-572-4002.

For sales inquiries and reseller information, including discounts, premium and bulk quantity sales, and foreign-language translations, please contact our Customer Care Department at 800-434-3422, fax 317-572-4002, or write to Hungry Minds, Inc., Attn: Customer Care Department, 10475 Crosspoint Boulevard, Indianapolis, IN 46256.

For information on licensing foreign or domestic rights, please contact our Sub-Rights Customer Care Department at 212-884-5000.

For information on using Hungry Minds' products and services in the classroom or for ordering examination copies, please contact our Educational Sales Department at 800-434-2086 or fax 317-572-4005.

For press review copies, author interviews, or other publicity information, please contact our Public Relations Department at 317-572-3168 or fax 317-572-4168.

For authorization to photocopy items for corporate, personal, or educational use, please contact Copyright Clearance Center, 222 Rosewood Drive, Danvers, MA 01923, or fax 978-750-4470.

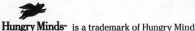

Hungry Minds™ is a trademark of Hungry Minds, Inc.

About the Authors

Janine Warner serves a broad range of clients from Internet companies to bricks-and-mortar businesses in the United States and abroad. Her expertise in media, technology, and cross-cultural business has taken her on consulting assignments from Miami to Mexico and speaking engagements from New York to New Delhi.

Janine is the author of several books about the Internet including *Managing Web Projects For Dummies* and *Dreamweaver 4 For Dummies*, both published by Hungry Minds. A syndicated newspaper columnist, Janine's business column, "Web Strategies That Work," appears in several publications including *The Miami Herald*. She is also a part-time faculty member at the University of Miami, where she teaches for the School of Communication.

Janine is a founding board member of the Miami Internet Alliance and a member of the board of the South Florida chapter of Women in Technology International (WITI). From 1998 to 2000, she worked for *The Miami Herald,* first as their Online Managing Editor and later as Director of New Media, managing a team of designers, programmers, journalists, and marketing staff for *The Miami Herald*, *El Nuevo Herald*, and Miami.com. She also served as Director of Latin American Operations for CNET Networks, an international technology media company.

From 1994 to 1998, Janine ran Visiontec Communications, a Web design business in Northern California, where she worked on such diverse projects as the corporate intranet for Levi Strauss & Co., an extranet sales site for AirTouch International, and e-commerce solutions for many small- and medium-size businesses.

An award-winning former reporter, she earned a degree in journalism and Spanish from the University of Massachusetts, Amherst, and worked for several years in Northern California as a reporter and editor. She speaks fluent Spanish.

To learn more, visit www.janinewarner.com.

Ivonne Berkowitz is the Web Services Coordinator for PBS&J, a top-ranking engineering firm in South Florida. She also consults for ModernMethod, a Web design firm that has worked on projects for numerous clients including The Orange Bowl, TeRespondo, and Metabolic Nutrition. Ivonne's strengths include graphic design for the Web, Web site planning, Flash animation, and logo design.

In 1998, Ivonne left a promising career in the Miami public relations arena to enter the unfamiliar world of Web design to satisfy a curiosity and cure her creative burnout. Little did she know that in short time, it would become her life's passion and the beginning of a great new career. After a year of fooling around with free online HTML editors and evaluation copies of Photoshop and Photo-Paint, Ivonne felt confident enough to find a job as a Web designer and in 1998, joined TigerDirect.com as a team designer. Deriving inspiration from the mantra "Fake it until you make it," it was there that she mastered Photoshop, Dreamweaver, and Flash. Ivonne's Web design talents also landed her consultancy positions with major corporations such as Knight Ridder, PBS&J, and several dotcoms from South Florida to California.

Her experience, design talent, and almost-unhealthy attention to detail have also ushered a flurry of freelance clients her way, including such names as The New York Post Online Store, Florida Counseling Association, photographer Robin Hill, photographer/illustrator Philip Brooker, forensic psychologist Dr. Charles Winick, and the popular South Florida cult horror store, Oh! The Horror.

Ivonne lives in Miami Springs, Florida, where she a spends her free time (if she gets any!) working out, vegging in front of the TV, working obsessively on home improvement projects, and writing "the big novel" in the form of an e-journal.

Dedication

Janine Warner: I dedicate this book to all those who have a message to share with the world. May Dreamweaver provide the tool you need to publish your ideas on the Web, and may this book make it easier to master this powerful program so that you may focus your time on your words and your dreams.

Ivonne Berkowitz: To Yanier, my partner in love and life.

Authors' Acknowledgments

Janine Warner: I have to start by thanking my new co-author, Ivonne Berkowitz, who came through to help me cover some of Dreamweaver's newest and most advanced features for creating dynamic, database-driven Web sites. Ivonne is a talented writer and Web developer, and her gracious and understated style make her a joy to work with. While I'm at it, I want to thank her partner in love and work, Yanier Gonzalez, for bringing his technical knowledge and vast Web experience to serve as tech editor on this book. Some of his beautiful Web sites appear in Chapter 17, and you can see them all live on the Web by visiting at his company's site www.modernmethod.com.

Special thanks to Andrea Boucher, my favorite editor ever (and I've worked with many). Andrea, your experience and attention to detail make this book better with each revision, and your encouragement, flexibility, and sense of humor have kept me sane and made this book much more fun to work on. Thanks also to Hungry Minds acquisition editor Bob Woerner for shepherding this book through the acquisition and development process, and to my wonderful agent, Margot Maley at Waterside, for making it happen in the first place.

I always thank my wonderful parents; my mother, Malinda McCain, who is a talented copyeditor (www.sharewords.com/copyedit/), and her witty and wonderful partner Janice Webster, who is finally getting to enjoy retirement after a great career as a scientist and academic; my father, Robin Warner, who has become quite a techie himself but still finds time for planting a forest in his backyard and ballroom dancing all over the world, and his delightful and creative wife, Helen Welford.

I also appreciate the support and love I receive from my brother Kevin Warner, his generous and ever-positive wife, Stephanie, their beautiful daughter, Mikayla, and the new one on the way. Love to my brother Brian, wherever life may take him, and to my aunt Margaret Warner, whose work in client-centered therapy and teaching I have always admired.

Other members of my wonderful family include my creative uncle, Tom McCain, and his energetic wife, Mindy, whose Web design work is featured at www.crittur.com; John, Gail, Ian, and Kate, as well as all of the Davids too numerous to mention; and in memory, our wonderful Grandma McCain, who finally learned to check e-mail in her eighties.

I always like to thank my journalism professors from the University of Massachusetts, Amherst, for teaching me so much about writing and viewing the world as an observer as well as a participant. My thanks to Howard Ziff for creating the department and giving us such a great excuse to throw alumni parties, Karen List for being the mentor I so needed in college, Norm Sims for heading the department and granting me the freedom to express my perspective in his classroom (even when his featured guests disagreed), and Madeline Blaise for inspiring us with her Pulitzer Prize and coming back to Miami on all of her book tours.

Thanks to so many dear friends: Ken "Doll" Milburn for always being there when I want to procrastinate and for helping me feel good about myself, anyway; Bob "Bobbins" Cowart, whose humor, music, and great business sense will always have my admiration; Madan Rao for introducing me to India and helping me appreciate the global power of the Internet; John Van Zwieten for helping me improve my management skills, especially in the most challenging moments; Victoria Usherenko, who has become a great ally in my efforts to find jobs for my friends; Francis Pisani, whose multicultural perspective of the world is broadening my views; Shari Witkoff, whose quick wit and intelligence are only part of the reason she's my favorite dentist; David Mitchell, publisher of the Pulitzer Prize-winning *Point Reyes Light,* who gave me my first job out of college and has supported me in countless ways ever since; Victor Reyes, for helping me improve far more than my Spanish; and many other dear friends in Miami, California, and Boston (especially the PINHEADs), who have made me feel loved and at home everywhere I have lived.

Ivonne Berkowitz: I always believed my work would someday be published and mass distributed as a book — I just always believed it would be as some kind of memoir or fiction loosely based on my horribly normal life. I never expected it to be in the form of a tech book! This has been an incredible learning experience, one that I will not soon forget. As this is the first time that I get to see my name on a book, I don't think I've gotten over the initial emotions and feelings that accompany such an accomplishment: honor, shock, success, self-criticism, pride, and happiness. Above all, gratefulness.

I am grateful first and foremost to Janine, who invited me to co-author this book with her. In the time that we've known each other, you have served as a friend, mentor, and sounding board. A big sister. A career counselor. A psychotherapist. A nutritionist. Janine, thank you for your thoughtfulness, generosity, friendship, and vote of confidence, and thank you for this wonderful opportunity. I don't know that I'll ever be able to give you back what you've given me.

I also want to thank Andrea Boucher, the editor of this fine book. Thank you for making my very first authoring experience so smooth and painless! Working with you has been a pleasure, and I hope this won't be the last time our paths cross. You've spoiled me for any other editor that I may work with in the future. Andrea, you have been amazing.

Yanier Gonzalez, who acted as technical editor, also played a key role in getting this book done. Yanier, you are not only a phenomenal technical editor, but also my best friend. You helped me keep my sanity through all the crazy-tight deadlines and coached me on technicalities I might have otherwise missed. Without your love, knowledge and patience, I might have given up on so many things. Thanks for sticking by me and cheering me on. I love you.

One of the greatest driving forces in my life has always been my family. My parents, Silvia and Emilio Berkowitz: Gracias Mami y Papi por todo el amor, apoyo y fe que me ofrecen cada dia de mi vida. Es por ustedes que mas yo me esfuerzo por salir adelante. My little brother Emilio (who's really not so little at all): You are my life-long sidekick and best friend. My older brother, Jorge: though our lives and thoughts may often be worlds apart, you are dear to me in the way only a brother can be. To my "other" family, Heriberto and Mari Gonzalez, Lilly and Benny and baby Julian — los quiero mucho!

Many other people have touched my life in one way or another, and just for that, I want to thank them:

My bosses at PBS&J, Marty Brown and Olga Acosta, and my bosses from the past, Kim Marcille at Knight-Ridder Digital and Howard Miller of Howard R. Miller Communications: your guidance, support, and friendship have never gone unnoticed or under-appreciated. Bosses like you are not common, and I want to take this opportunity to let you know how much I respect and appreciate you. Thank you for being so special, so caring, and so human. It is because of people like you that I still have faith in the corporate world.

The whole gang in Technology Operations at PBS&J, Miami — Jenna, Jesus, Carmen, Dedra, Cathy, Alan, David, Margie, Lisa, George, Glen, Andy, Alex, Amauris, Albert, Fernando and Martina — I couldn't ask for a better set of co-workers. Thank you. The staff "downstairs" — the PBS&J Media Group (Rick DeCamp, Scott Coventry, Tilky Fernandez, Pablo Illarramendi, Cathy Lisanti, and the rest of the folks down there) — thanks a trillion for always helping me out at the drop of a dime! My fellow ModernMethod-ites, with their unique and quirky personalities, also deserve some major love. Yanier, Tommy (Tlack) Lackner, Raul Cordoba, Robert (Jahmon) Murray, Franco Sabri, Kat Rhames — you're all awesome for working so hard to "keep the dream alive."

My all-time favorite college professors, Dr. Don Stacks and Dr. Donn Tilson at the University of Miami School of Communication and Dr. Maureen Kenny at the FIU College of Education: Of all the professors that have come and gone in my life, the three of you will always be the ones I think of most fondly and with utmost respect. I have always admired you for your guidance, dedication, and genuine concern for your students, both in their personal and academic lives. Thank you for doing your best to impart some of your wisdom on little ol' me.

Friends and folks who have left a mark on my life by sharing with me their friendship and bits of wisdom (whether they know it or not): Vanessa Amil-Zaila, Cristy Delgado, Lissis Ramos, Herminio Amil, Nery Dorsey, Sef Gonzalez, Raquelle Santiago-Argote, Barbara Santiago, Karina Hernandez (soon to be Karina Rubiera!), Tommy Chang, Carlos and Jose Bueno, Jesse Hurt and the rest of the Hurt family, Karla Haynes, Francisco Rivera, Robbie Adams, Philip Francis, Lucien Volmar, Cristina Perez, Rob Graney, Fabian De la Flor, Renee McEachern, Rob Hendricks, Sixto and Cindy Monroy, Osvaldo and Mio Fiallo, Martha and Josh Matias, Elena and Aida Rodriguez, Vera Ores (my babushka), Herminia and Julio Machado, Vicky and Jorge Nichar, Rolando Astudillo, Tony Speranza Jr., Pam Howard, Andrew Naylor, Robin and Cindy Hill, Nick Lomangino, Elkin Pabon, The Guerreros and Gaby Lorenzana at the United Academy of Tae Kwon Do, and so many other people, who I just can't name individually because I think the editors are going to smack me if I don't stop writing now! Thanks to everyone who has walked into my life and shared a piece of theirs.

Publisher's Acknowledgments

We're proud of this book; please send us your comments through our Hungry Minds Online Registration Form located at www.dummies.com.

Some of the people who helped bring this book to market include the following:

Acquisitions, Editorial, and Media Development

Project Editor: Andrea C. Boucher

Acquisitions Editor: Bob Woerner

Technical Editor: Yanier Gonzalez

Editorial Manager: Constance Carlisle

Permissions Editor: Laura Moss

Media Development Specialist:
Megan Decraene

Media Development Manager:
Laura Carpenter VanWinkle

Media Development Supervisor:
Richard Graves

Editorial Assistant: Amanda Foxworth

Production

Project Coordinator: Erin Smith

Layout and Graphics: Beth Brooks,
Stephanie D. Jumper, Barry Offringa,
Brent Savage, Betty Schulte,
Jeremey Unger, Mary J. Virgin, Erin Zeltner

Proofreaders: John Greenough,
Andy Hollandbeck, Susan Moritz,
Sossity R. Smith

Indexer: TECHBOOKS Production Services

General and Administrative

Hungry Minds Technology Publishing Group: Richard Swadley, Vice President and Executive Group Publisher; Bob Ipsen, Vice President and Group Publisher; Joseph Wikert, Vice President and Publisher; Barry Pruett, Vice President and Publisher; Mary Bednarek, Editorial Director; Mary C. Corder, Editorial Director; Andy Cummings, Editorial Director

Hungry Minds Manufacturing: Ivor Parker, Vice President, Manufacturing

Hungry Minds Marketing: John Helmus, Assistant Vice President, Director of Marketing

Hungry Minds Production for Branded Press: Debbie Stailey, Production Director

Hungry Minds Sales: Michael Violano, Vice President, International Sales and Sub Rights

Contents at a Glance

Cartoons at a Glance

By Rich Tennant

page 61

page 199

page 349

page 295

page 9

page 123

Cartoon Information:
Fax: 978-546-7747
E-Mail: richtennant@the5thwave.com
World Wide Web: www.the5thwave.com

Table of Contents

Introduction

*I*f you're working on a Web site, you probably don't have time to wade through another thick book while you're racing against a tight deadline. Neither do any other Web designers I know. That's why I wrote this book to serve as a quick reference. It's also why I choose Dreamweaver for all my Web design work. Dreamweaver enables you to work faster and more efficiently. And *Dreamweaver MX For Dummies* helps you get the most out of this comprehensive Web design program by making it easy and fast to find the answers you need.

Macromedia Dreamweaver has clearly emerged as the top Web design program on the market for anyone serious about Web design work. Its ease of use and high-end features make it an ideal choice for professional Web designers, as well as for those new to working on the Internet. And the new features in version MX make it better than ever!

I've been reviewing Web design programs since the first ones hit the market in 1994, and I can assure you that Dreamweaver is the best one I've ever worked with. But don't take my word for it — Dreamweaver has already won a slew of awards over the years, including Best of Show at Internet World, the prestigious five-mouse rating from *Macworld*, and Best Web Authoring Tool in the Readers Choice Awards by *PC Magazine*.

The best Dreamweaver features include its clean HTML code and sophisticated support for the latest HTML options (such as Dynamic HTML and Cascading Style Sheets). Dreamweaver MX adds many new high-end features for creating database-driven Web sites as well. These features used to be sold separately in Dreamweaver UltraDev, but with the release of Dreamweaver MX, you'll get the full package in one greatly enhanced program.

You'll also find a state-of-the-art integrated text editor and a JavaScript debugger, so switching back and forth between Dreamweaver and a text editor is a breeze. If you're a developer who still likes to work with raw HTML code at least part of the time, you'll appreciate this best-of-both-worlds solution.

If you've never written HTML before, don't be intimidated by these fancy features. The Dreamweaver graphical design environment uses sophisticated palettes and windows to enable beginners to create high-end Web sites that include such features as animations, interactive forms, and even e-commerce solutions, even if you don't know HTML. And enhancements to Dreamweaver's interface make MX even easier to work with.

My co-author, Ivonne Berkowitz, is also an experienced Web designer who still appreciates what it is like to be new to the Web. Her creative contributions make this an even stronger book and serve to beef up the more technical sections for those who want to get into the really cool stuff. Ivonne and I split up the chapters; I wrote more than half the book, but Ivonne contributed the three new chapters on how to create database-driven sites. She also worked on the two chapters about images because she's a more talented designer. In each chapter, we decided to stick with the personal pronoun *I* because we're generally referring to our own experiences; however, the book truly benefits from our combined talents.

Dreamweaver MX For Dummies is for anyone who wants to build sophisticated Web pages that are easy to create and maintain. Whether you're a professional or a novice, this book can get you up and running quickly with the best Web design program on the market today.

About This Book

I designed *Dreamweaver MX For Dummies* to make your life easier as you work with this Web program. You don't have to read this book cover to cover and memorize it. Instead, each section of the book stands alone, giving you easy answers to particular questions and step-by-step instructions for specific tasks.

Want to find out how to change the background color on a page, create a nested table, build HTML frames, or get into the really cool stuff like style sheets and layers? Then jump right in and go directly to the section that most interests you. Oh, and don't worry about keeping all those new HTML tags in your head. You don't have to memorize anything. The next time you need to do one of these tasks, just go back and review that section. Feel free to dog-ear the pages, too — I promise they won't complain!

Conventions Used in This Book

Keeping things consistent makes them easier to understand. In this book, those consistent elements are *conventions*. Notice how the word *conventions* is in italics? That's a convention I use frequently. I put new terms in italics and then define them so that you know what they mean.

When I type URLs (Web addresses) or e-mail addresses within regular paragraph text, they look like this: www.janinewarner.com. Sometimes, however, I set URLs off on their own lines, like this:

www.janinewarner.com

That's so you can easily spot them on a page if you want to type them into your browser to visit a site. I also assume that your Web browser doesn't require the introductory `http://` for Web addresses. If you use an older browser, remember to type this before the address.

Even though Dreamweaver makes knowing HTML code virtually unnecessary, you may have to occasionally wade into HTML waters. So I set off HTML code in the same monospaced type as URLs:

```
<A HREF="http://www.janinewarner.com">Janine's Web Site</A>
```

(That's the HTML code that makes a URL a link on a Web page.)

When I introduce you to a set of features, such as options in a dialog box, I set these items apart with bullets so that you can tell that they're all related. When I want you to follow instructions, I use numbered steps to walk you through the process.

What You're Not to Read

Don't read anything in this book that doesn't interest you. Some of the material here is for people just starting out in Web design. If you've been at this for a while, this material may be too basic for you. On the other hand, some of this information may be too advanced. For example, if you are working on a basic Web site, you don't need all the high-powered database features covered in Chapters 14, 15, and 16.

If you're a graphics guru or you don't care about design issues, skip over the chapters on design and image creation. Just pick and choose the information that you want to work with. Don't feel that you have to read everything to get the most out of it. Use this book as the reference that I intended it to be. Your time is more important than reading stuff that you don't need to know about!

Foolish Assumptions

When Macromedia developed Dreamweaver, it set out to make a professional Web development program and identified the target audience as anyone who spends more than 20 hours a week doing Web design. Fortunately for the rest of us, they also created a powerful program that's intuitive and easy to use.

Macromedia assumes that you're a *professional* developer; I don't. Even if you're new to Web design, this program can work for you, and this book can make Dreamweaver easy to use. In keeping with the philosophy behind the *For Dummies* series, this book is an easy-to-use guide designed for readers with a wide range of experience. It helps if you're interested in Web design and want to create a Web site, but that desire is all that I expect from you. In the chapters that follow, I show you all the steps you need to create Web pages, and in the glossary on the CD-ROM, I give you all the vocabulary you need to understand the process. You'll also find a bonus HTML chapter on the CD. If you're new to Web design or want a refresher course in the HyperText Markup Language, that bonus information is for you.

If you're an experienced Web designer, *Dreamweaver MX For Dummies* is an ideal reference for you because it will get you working quickly with this program, from basic Web page development to the more advanced features. If you're new to Web design, this book can get you started and walk you through all you need to create a Web site.

How This Book Is Organized

To ease you through the learning curve associated with any new program, I organized *Dreamweaver MX For Dummies* to be a complete reference. You can read it cover to cover (if you want), but you may find it more helpful to jump to the section most relevant to what you want to do at that particular moment. Each chapter walks you through the features of Dreamweaver step by step, providing tips and helping you understand the vocabulary of Web design.

The following sections provide a breakdown of the parts of the book and what you'll find in each one.

Part I: Fulfilling Your Dreams

This part introduces you to Dreamweaver and covers getting started with the basics. In Chapter 1, I give you a handy reference to toolbars and menu options, and I also describe the new features in version MX. And then in Chapter 2, I start you on the road to creating your first Web site, including setting up your site, importing an existing site, creating new Web pages, applying basic formatting to text, and even placing images and setting links on your pages.

Part II: Looking Like a Million (Even on a Budget)

Planning the design of your Web site is perhaps the most important part of Web site development — it can save you plenty of reorganizing time later. In Chapter 3, I start you out on the right foot with tips on Web site management, the principles of good design, and strategies that can save you countless hours. I also introduce you to Dreamweaver's site-management features. If you work with a team of designers, you'll be especially interested in Dreamweaver's check-in and check-out features for version control and integrated e-mail for communicating with other team members. In Chapter 4, I introduce you to some of my favorite Dreamweaver features, including sophisticated template capabilities, Library items, Tracing images, the Quick Tag Editor, Design Notes, and the History palette.

In Chapter 5, Ivonne introduces you to Web graphics and shows you how to integrate graphic elements to your pages. She also suggests tools and strategies that can help you create the best Web graphics for your pages and includes tips on where to find free images or buy graphics that are already optimized for the Web.

Part III: Advancing Your Site

In Part III, I show you how to use Dreamweaver with some of the more advanced HTML features. In Chapter 6, you discover how to use HTML tables to create complex page layouts that work in the most common Web browsers. A highlight of this chapter is the Table Layout View, which makes it easier than ever to create complex Web designs. In Chapter 7, you find all you need to know about designing a site with HTML frames. (This chapter helps you decide when you should and shouldn't use frames and gives you plenty of step-by-step instructions for creating HTML frames in Dreamweaver.)

Chapter 8 provides an overview of Cascading Style Sheets: how they work and how they can save you time. You'll find description of all the style definition options available in Dreamweaver and instructions for how to create and apply styles.

Part IV: Making It Cool

Now for the really fun stuff. In this part, you go for a walk on the wild side of HTML. In Chapter 9, I take you further into the Dynamic HTML features, such as layers and behaviors, which allow precise design control and new levels of interactivity. In Chapter 10, I introduce you to the Timeline, and show you how to create animations and even more complex designs. In Chapter 11, Ivonne introduces you to Fireworks, the Macromedia image program for the Web, and shows you how to take advantage of the Dreamweaver integration with Fireworks to create complex images.

In Chapter 12, I help you use Dreamweaver to add multimedia to your Web pages and show you how to link a variety of file types — from Flash to Java to RealAudio — to your Web pages. Then in Chapter 13, I address HTML forms and how you can use Dreamweaver to add interactive elements, such as search engines, online discussion areas, and e-commerce systems, to your pages.

Part V: Working with Dynamic Content

In Part V, Ivonne adds three powerful new chapters to this book to cover the newest and most advanced features in Dreamweaver MX. She starts in Chapter 14 by helping you understand how database-driven Web sites work and why they have become so important on the Web. Then in Chapter 15, she shows you how to add dynamic content to your pages, define data sources, and display record sets. In Chapter 16, she pulls it all together, showing you how to build master pages, create pages to search databases, and test your work with a live connection.

Part VI: The Part of Tens

In the Part of Tens, you discover ten great Web sites that were created with Dreamweaver, find ten great Web design ideas, and ten tips that can save you substantial time and make your sites work better when you're using Dreamweaver MX.

And finally, the "About the CD" appendix. In this appendix, you find a guide to the CD-ROM and all the great software that accompanies this book. On the CD-ROM you can also find a glossary of all the terms that you need to know when you're working with Dreamweaver — and then some! And you get a bonus HTML Chapter that introduces you to the HyperText Markup Language and helps you appreciate what's happening behind the scenes in Dreamweaver.

Icons Used in This Book

This icon signals technical stuff that you may find informative and interesting but isn't essential for using Dreamweaver. Feel free to skip over this stuff.

This icon indicates a tip or technique that can save you time and money — and a headache — later.

This icon reminds you of an important concept or procedure that you'll want to store away in your memory banks for future use.

This icon points you toward valuable resources on the World Wide Web.

This icon warns you of any potential pitfalls — and gives you the all-important information on how to avoid them.

When I want to point you toward something on the CD that accompanies this book, I use this icon.

This icon tunes you into information in other *For Dummies* books that you may find useful.

This icon alerts you to features of the Macromedia image editor Fireworks or topics dealing with the Dreamweaver integration with Fireworks.

Where to Go from Here

Turn to Chapter 1 to dive in and get started with Dreamweaver. You find a great overview of the program designed to get you up and running quickly, as well as a handy reference to all the new features in version MX. If you're already familiar with Dreamweaver and want to learn a specific trick or technique, jump right to the section you need; you won't miss a beat as you work to make those impossible Web design deadlines. And most of all, have fun!

Part I
Fulfilling Your Dreams

The 5th Wave — By Rich Tennant

"What do you mean you're updating our Web page?"

In this part . . .

Stay awake for Part I, and I'll show you that you're not dreaming as I introduce you to the wonders of this powerful Web design program. I give you a quick guide to the new features of Dreamweaver MX, and then I take you on a tour of the toolbars, menus, and panels that give Dreamweaver much of its power. In Chapter 2, you dive right into creating your first Web page.

Chapter 1

Introducing Your New Best Friend

● ●

In This Chapter

▶ Introducing the new features of Dreamweaver MX

▶ Examining your Web site objectives

▶ Finding your way around in Dreamweaver

● ●

*W*elcome to the wonderful world of Dreamweaver. If you're an experienced Web designer, you're going to love the power and sophistication of this HTML editor. If you're new to Web design, you will appreciate its simplicity and intuitive interface. Either way, this chapter starts you on your way to making the most of Dreamweaver by introducing you to the menus and panels that make this program so useful.

Dreamweaver can help you with every aspect of Web development, from designing simple pages, to fixing links, to publishing your pages on the World Wide Web. Dreamweaver can handle the simplest HTML, as well as some of the most complex and advanced features possible on the Web like Cascading Style Sheets and Dynamic HTML (see Chapters 8, 9, and 10 for more information on these features). It also integrates a powerful HTML text editor into its easy-to-use *what-you-see-is-what-you-get* (WYSIWYG) design environment. (Don't completely understand WYSIWYG? Then check out the glossary on the accompanying CD-ROM. You can find definitions for this term and many others.)

If you already work in another Web design program, don't worry — you can use Dreamweaver to modify existing Web pages and continue to develop your Web site without losing all the time you've already invested. All Web design programs create HTML pages and those pages can be opened in any other Web design program. So, for example, if you've been working in a program such as Microsoft FrontPage or Adobe GoLive, you can still change to Dreamweaver to edit and develop your site further. At the end of this chapter, you find tips about some of the challenges in the section called "Working on Web Pages Created in Another Web Design Program."

In this chapter, I introduce you to the new features in Dreamweaver MX, take you on a tour of the desktop, and give you an overview of what makes Dreamweaver such a powerful Web design program.

So, What's New in Dreamweaver MX?

And now to the good stuff. The following list gives you a quick overview of some of the new features you'll find in version MX:

- The Integrated Windows™ User Interface is a dramatic change in the Dreamweaver's workspace, which features customizable panels and tabbed document windows. Although you still have the option to use the floating panels — the only option in Dreamweaver's previous versions — Macromedia recommends (and I recommend) that you choose the new interface. You're given the option when you first turn on the program, and if you choose the new interface, you can expand and collapse panels as needed and even move them around to create a work environment that's best for you. Throughout this book, all the screenshots and instructions have been updated to reflect the new interface.

- Enhanced Dream Templates make it even easier to create complex designs with sophisticated rules. Template inheritance capabilities and editable regions enable more customized layout control and greater flexibility. Templates are covered in detail in Chapter 4.

- The new Site Setup Wizard enables you to quickly and easily configure Dreamweaver with all your site structure and FTP information, whether you are setting up a new site or importing an existing one. You find detailed steps for setting up your site in Chapter 2.

- The Customizable Insert Panel (located at the top of the workspace) provides easy access to objects and behaviors, and it's completely extensible, making it easy to add new behaviors and objects that you download for other Web sites, receive from other developers, or want to share with other programmers. Each of the object and panel tabs can be displayed or hidden depending on the type of document you are working on, and whether you are using the HTML or WYSIWYG view.

- The New File Explorer is built into the Site panel enabling you to browse for assets and files on your computer — or anywhere on a network you are connected to — without having to use the file explorer of your operating system.

- Enhanced Table Editing provides even greater layout control and has been optimized to create leaner tables that work well across many different kinds of browsers. Using the Layout view, table design is as easy as clicking and dragging boxes on the page, and they can easily be adjusted and edited further in Standard view. You find out all about creating HTML Tables (the best way to create complex designs for the Web) in Chapter 6.

- If you were frustrated by trying to print your code pages in the past, you'll be pleased to find out that Dreamweaver MX now enables source code to be printed with all the formatting.

✔ High-end database development is now possible with Dreamweaver MX, thanks to the integration with features previously available only in Dreamweaver UltraDev. Macromedia no longer calls it UltraDev, but you'll appreciate how these features enable you to create more complex Web sites, linking Web pages to a database and providing a wide range of interactive features, such as dynamic Web page creation. This enhancement is so significant, you'll find three completely new chapters in this book to walk you through the basics of creating Dynamic Web sites and working with databases on the Web. These chapters are Chapters 14, 15, and 16.

So, what's the big deal about Dreamweaver?

Dreamweaver has gotten great reviews and attracted considerable attention because it solves common problems found in other Web programs. Many Web designers complain that WYSIWYG design tools create sloppy HTML code, alter the code in existing pages, and make manually customizing pages difficult. Most of these problems stem from the fact that people who know how to write HTML code manually are used to having total control over their HTML pages. Unfortunately, many Web design programs force you to give up that control in order to have the convenience and ease of a WYSIWYG tool.

Dreamweaver gives you both control and convenience by packaging an easy-to-use WYSIWYG tool with a powerful HTML text editor, and in Dreamweaver MX, the built-in text editor is even more powerful. Then Dreamweaver goes a step farther with a feature Macromedia calls Roundtrip HTML. With Roundtrip HTML, you can create your HTML pages in any program, open them in Dreamweaver, and not have to worry about your original HTML code being altered.

Dreamweaver respects your HTML code. A big problem with many other WYSIWYG editors is that they can dramatically change HTML code if it doesn't conform to their rules. Unfortunately, the rules on the Web constantly change, so many designers like to break the rules or at least add their own variations to the theme. If you create a page with custom HTML code in a text editor and then open it in a program such as Microsoft FrontPage, you run the risk that FrontPage may change your design when it tries to make your code fit the limited rules of FrontPage.

Dreamweaver promises never to alter your code, which is one of the reasons it's becoming a best friend to so many professional designers, but even Dreamweaver is not perfect, especially if you use the Clean Up HTML feature on custom code or special scripts. If you're a programmer creating advanced features, you may want to turn off some of Dreamweaver's automatic code rewriting features by choosing Edit ⇨ Preferences ⇨ Code Rewriting.

The challenge was in figuring out how to display the HTML code created in a text editor in the WYSIWYG side of the program without ever changing the code, even if Dreamweaver has never seen your unique HTML code before. The success that Macromedia has had in solving this problem is a big part of the reason why Dreamweaver has gotten so much attention, won so many awards, and attracted the loyalty of even the most die-hard HTML coders.

Visualizing Your Site

Before you launch into building Web pages, take some time to plan your site and think about its structure and organization. Begin thinking about the following questions. Some of them you may not fully understand at this point and can't answer. But it's best to have answers to all these questions before you begin actually building your Web site:

- What do you want to accomplish with your Web site? (What are your goals and objectives?)
- Who is your target audience?
- Who will be working on your site? How many developers do you have to manage?
- How will you create or collect the text and images you'll need for your site?
- How will you organize the files in your site?
- Will you include multimedia files, such as Flash or RealAudio?
- Will you want interactive features, such as a feedback form or chat room?
- What other software will you need for specialized features (for example, Macromedia Flash for animations)?
- What kind of navigation system will you have for your site (that is, how can you make it easy for visitors to move from one area of your Web site to another)?
- How will you accommodate growth for the site?

In Chapter 2, you find out about site-management features and start creating your first Web pages, adding and formatting text, inserting images, and creating links. In Chapter 3, you find tips and suggestions for planning your site as you answer questions like these. Taking the time to get clear on your goals and objectives can set the tone for successful Web development.

Introducing the Many Components of Dreamweaver

Dreamweaver can seem a bit overwhelming at first. It has so many features that all the panels, toolbars, and dialog boxes can be confusing when you start poking around. In the next few sections, I introduce you to the basic functions and some of the terminology of Dreamweaver. I also show you where to find various features and explain, in general terms, the function of the buttons and menu options. I cover all these features in more detail later in the book.

The Workspace

Creating a basic Web page in Dreamweaver is remarkably easy. When you launch Dreamweaver, a blank page — called the *Workspace* — appears automatically, much like a blank document does when you open a program like Microsoft Word. You can type text directly into the Workspace and apply basic formatting, such as bold and italics, simply by selecting Text⇨Style⇨Bold or Text⇨Style⇨Italics.

You build your Web pages in the Workspace, which consists of a main window that shows the HTML page that you're working on and a number of floating panels and windows that provide tools that you can use to design and develop your pages (see Figure 1-1). The Dreamweaver Workspace consists of four basic components: the document window, floating panels, menu bar, and Status Bar.

The document window

The big, open area on the Workspace is the document window. It's essentially a blank page, but if you look at the HTML code behind it, you see that it's a simple HTML file. The document window is where you edit and design your Web page, and it is the document window that displays images, text, and other elements in much the same way that a Web browser displays them.

Figure 1-1:
The main Workspace in Dream- weaver includes a document window, menu bar, Status Bar, and various docking panels that can be expanded and collapsed when needed.

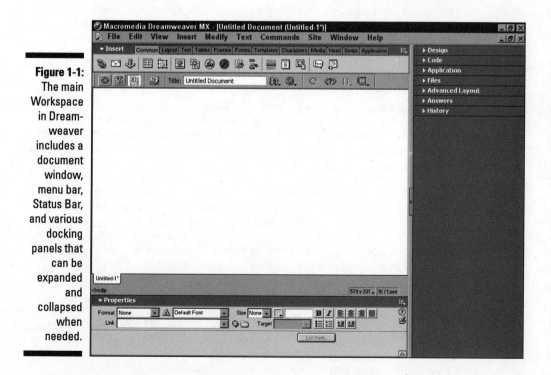

Pages viewed on the World Wide Web may not always look exactly the way they do in the document window in Dreamweaver because not all browsers support the same HTML features or display them equally. For best results, always test your work in a variety of Web browsers and design your pages to work best in the browsers that your audience most likely uses. Fortunately, Dreamweaver includes features that help you target your page designs to specific browsers. (For more information on browser differences, check out Chapter 10.)

The docking panels

The docking panels in Dreamweaver provide easy access to many of the program's features. You can move the panels around the screen by selecting them and using drag-and-drop to reposition them. If you find that having all these panels open distracts you from your ability to focus on your design, you can close any or all of them by clicking the small icon (which looks like three bullet points with lines next to them with a little arrow underneath) in the top right of any panel and selecting Close Panel from the pull-down menu. You can access all the panels through the Window menu. If you want to open a panel — the CSS Styles panel, for example — choose Window➪CSS Styles and it expands to become visible on your screen.

The panels are integral parts of this program, so I include a lot more information about them throughout the book. Check out the Cheat Sheet at the front of this book for a handy reference to these panels. In Chapter 2, I cover some of the most common features, such as inserting images (the icons for the images are provided in the Insert Common Objects panel at the top of the page).

The Insert panel

The Insert panel contains tabs across the top and buttons in the second row that can be used to create a variety of HTML elements, such as HTML forms, templates, and special characters. You also find icons for inserting images, plug-in files, and other objects. Dreamweaver uses the term *object* to mean any element that you can put on an HTML page, from a table to an image to a multimedia file.

The Insert panel has the following nine tabs or *subpanels* that offer separate sets of buttons for various functions: Common, Layout, Forms, Templates, Characters, Media, Head, Script, and Application. Dreamweaver generally refers to these subpanels with the full name, such as the Insert Forms panel or the Insert Media panel. You find more information on each of these panels in their relevant chapters. For example, the Forms panel is covered in detail in Chapter 13, Templates are covered in Chapter 4, Multimedia is covered in Chapter 12, and Application is covered in Chapters 14, 15, and 16.

To switch from displaying the buttons on one subpanel to showing the buttons for one of the other subpanels, select the tab. Figure 1-2 shows the nine panel options with the Forms panel selected. You can close this panel by clicking the icon in the top right of the panel and choosing Close Panel

Group. To reopen the Insert panel, choose Window⇨Insert. To change the icon display, choose Edit⇨Preferences, and select the Panels option.

Figure 1-2:
The various views (or subpanels) of the Insert panel provide quick access to options for frames, tables, images, and more.

The Property Inspector

The Property Inspector is docked at the bottom of the page in Dreamweaver MX so it no longer overlaps the work area. The Property Inspector displays the properties of a selected element on the page. A *property* is a characteristic of HTML — such as the alignment of an image or the size of a cell in a table — that you can assign to an element on your Web page. If you know HTML, you'll recognize these as HTML *attributes*.

When you select any element on a page (such as an image), the Inspector changes to display the properties, or attributes, for that element, such as the height and width of an image or table. You can alter those properties by changing the fields in the Property Inspector. You can also set links and create image maps using the Property inspector.

In Figure 1-3, the image in the upper-left corner has been selected, so the Property Inspector reveals the characteristics for that image: its height and width, its alignment, and the *URL* (Uniform Resource Locator or, more simply, Web address) to which it links.

At the bottom-right corner of the Property Inspector, you can see a small arrow. Click this arrow to reveal additional attributes that let you control more advanced features.

Figure 1-4 shows the Property Inspector when a table is selected. Notice that the fields in the Inspector have changed to reflect the attributes of an HTML table, such as the number of columns and rows. (See Chapter 6 to find out more about HTML tables.)

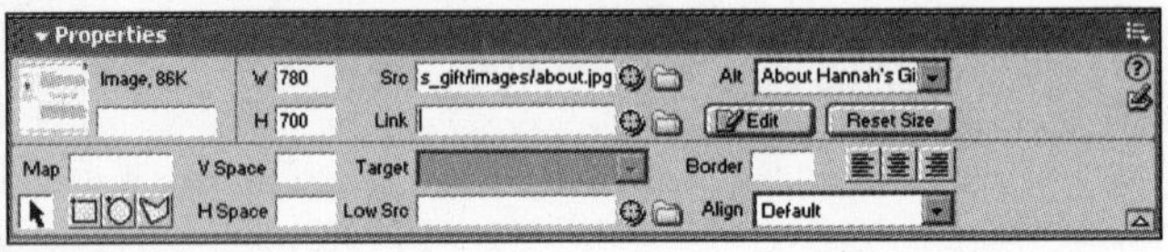

Figure 1-3:
The
Property
Inspector
displays the
attributes of
a selected
element,
such as the
image
shown here.

Figure 1-3:
The
Property
Inspector
displays the
attributes of
a selected
element,
such as the
image
shown here.

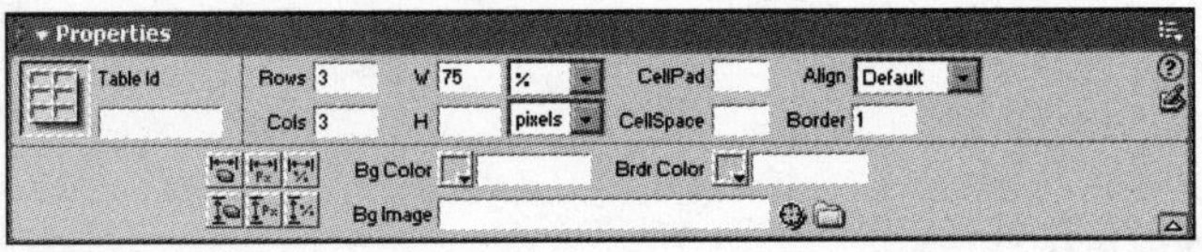

Figure 1-4:
The
Property
Inspector
displays the
attributes of
the selected
HTML table.

The Launcher bar (your way to the best goodies)

The Launcher bar, shown in Figure 1-5, is now located across the bottom of the work area (although you can move it). The Launcher bar contains information about the size and estimated download time for a site, as well as a list of shortcuts to Site features, Assets, CSS *(Cascading Style Sheets)*, Behaviors, History, Data Bindings, Server Behaviors, Components, and Databases. You can edit the preferences for panel options to change the shortcuts and specify if the icons should be visible.

Figure 1-5:
The
Launcher
bar provides
easy access
to various
Dream-
weaver
features.

The following list offers a description of the elements that you can access through the Launcher bar.

- ✔ **Site panel:** Shown in Figure 1-6, the Site tab in the Files panel lists all the folders and files in a Web site and helps you manage the structure and organization of the site. The Site panel is also where you access FTP *(file transfer protocol)* capabilities. You can use the Connect button at the top of this dialog box to dial quickly into your server. The Get and Put buttons enable you to transfer your pages back and forth between your computer and the server. (See Chapter 2 to find out more about the Site panel.)

- ✔ **Assets panel:** The new Assets panel in Dreamweaver MX provides easy access to images, colors, external links, multimedia files, scripts, Templates, and Library items. The Library panel, shown in Figure 1-7, enables you to store items in a central place so that you can easily add them to multiple pages. After an element is stored in the Library (you store an item simply by dragging the element onto the Library panel), you can then drag that element from the Library onto new pages. The Library is ideal for elements that are used throughout a Web site, as well as those that you must update frequently. The other parts of the Assets panel work in much the same way, providing easy access to related elements.

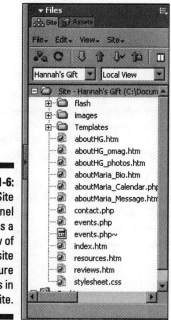

Figure 1-6:
The Site
panel
provides a
view of
the site
structure
and files in
your site.

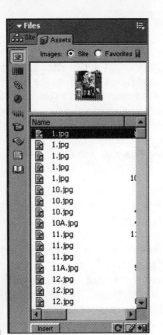

Figure 1-7:
The Assets
panel stores
items in a
central
place,
making it
easy to
place the
same
element,
such as a
navigation
row, on
multiple
pages.

These features work only if you've defined your site using the Site Definition dialog box, available by selecting Site➪Define Sites. If you find that the Library options aren't available to you, go to Chapter 2 and follow the steps for defining a site. (For more information on the Library feature, see Chapter 6.)

✔ **CSS Styles panel:** This box enables you to define styles by using Cascading Style Sheets (CSS). CSS styles are similar to style sheets used in desktop publishing programs such as QuarkXPress and Adobe PageMaker. You define a style and name it, and the style is then included in the CSS Styles panel, which is accessible through the tab at the top of the panel (see Figure 1-8). The CSS Styles panel provides access to the Style Definition panel, shown in Figure 1-8, where you can specify the type, size, and formatting of the style. After you define a style, you can apply it to text or other elements on a page. Style sheets are a big time-saver because they let you set several attributes simultaneously by applying a defined style. (For more information about CSS, see Chapter 8.)

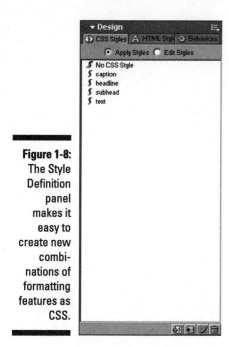

Figure 1-8:
The Style
Definition
panel
makes it
easy to
create new
combi-
nations of
formatting
features as
CSS.

✔ **Behaviors panel:** In Dreamweaver, *behaviors* are scripts (usually written
  in JavaScript) that you can apply to objects to add interactivity to your
  Web page. Essentially, a behavior is made up of a specified event that,
  when triggered, causes an action. For example, an event may be a visitor
  clicking an image or section of text, and the resulting action may be that
  a sound file plays. Figure 1-9 shows the Behaviors dialog box with the
  plus sign (+) selected to reveal the drop-down list of behaviors. The left
  pane displays events; the right pane displays the actions triggered by
  those events. (Chapters 9 and 10 provide more information on creating
  and applying behaviors.)

✔ **History panel:** The History panel, shown in Figure 1-10, keeps track of
  every action you take in Dreamweaver. You can use the History panel to
  undo multiple steps at once, to replay steps you performed, and to automate tasks. Dreamweaver automatically records the last 50 steps, but you
  can increase or decrease that number by choosing Edit➪Preferences➪
  General, and changing the Maximum Number of History Steps.

✔ The Data Bindings, Server Behaviors, Components, and Databases
  options in the launcher are only used if you are working with a database.
  These options are described in more detail in Chapter 14.

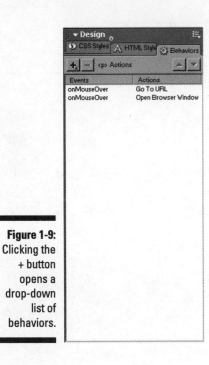

Figure 1-9:
Clicking the
+ button
opens a
drop-down
list of
behaviors.

Figure 1-10:
The History
panel keeps
track of all
your actions
in Dream-
weaver,
making it
easy to
undo or
replay
steps.

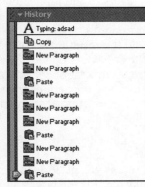

Code Inspector

The Code Inspector in Dreamweaver is the best-integrated HTML text editor
of any Web design program, and it's been improved for Dreamweaver MX —
now you can print code with formatting. Notice that in Figure 1-11, the highlighted text in the WYSIWYG area is also highlighted in the HTML Code
Inspector. Changes made in one immediately appear in the other. This integration makes moving back and forth between writing HTML code manually
and creating it in the graphical editing environment nearly seamless.

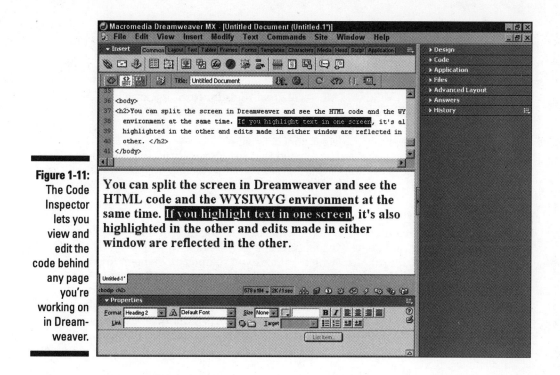

Figure 1-11:
The Code
Inspector
lets you
view and
edit the
code behind
any page
you're
working on
in Dream-
weaver.

The menu bar

At the top of the screen, the Dreamweaver menu bar provides easy access to all the features that you find in the floating panels, as well as a few others that are available only from the menu. (See the following sections for more on these menu features.)

The File menu

Under the File menu, you find many familiar options, such as New, Open, and Save. You also find a Revert option, which is similar to the Revert feature in Adobe Photoshop. This sophisticated "undo" feature enables you to return your page quickly to its last-saved version if you don't like the changes you've made. Dreamweaver automatically keeps track of the your 50 actions, but you can increase or decrease that number by choosing Edit⇨Preferences⇨ General and changing the Maximum Number of History Steps.

The File menu also includes access to Design Notes, a unique feature that associates private notes with HTML and other files. Take a look at Chapter 4 for more information about Design Notes and other Dreamweaver features that make collaboration easier.

Under the File menu, you can also find features that are useful for checking your work in Web browsers. Most Web design programs include some way of previewing your work in a browser. Dreamweaver takes this feature two steps farther by enabling you to check your work in a number of browsers and even test the compatibility of your pages in different versions of different browsers.

Figure 1-12 shows the Check Page options, which have been expanded in Dreamweaver MX to include Check Links, Check Target Browsers, Validate Markup, and Validate XML — all great tools for testing your work. The Check Target Browsers option enables you to specify a browser and version, such as Netscape 3.0 (still a widely used browser on the Web) or Internet Explorer 3.0. When you do a browser check, Dreamweaver generates a report listing any HTML features you have used that the chosen browser doesn't support. The biggest limitation of this feature is that it doesn't include Mac browsers, which are often more sensitive to things like Javascript and Table behaviors.

The Edit menu

The Edit menu contains many features that you may find familiar, such as Cut, Copy, and Paste. One feature that may be new to you is the Edit with External Editor option, which enables you to open an element in another program, such as an image editor, and make changes without ever leaving Dreamweaver.

You also find the Preferences settings under the Edit menu. Before you start working with a new program, it's always a good idea to go through all the Preferences options to ensure that the program is set up the best way for you.

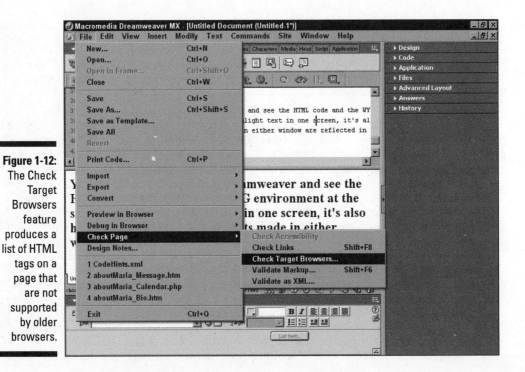

Figure 1-12: The Check Target Browsers feature produces a list of HTML tags on a page that are not supported by older browsers.

The View menu

The View menu provides access to some helpful design features, such as grids and rulers. The Visual Aides option in the View menu gives you the option of turning on or off the borders of your HTML tables, frames, and layers, as well as controlling visibility of image maps and other invisible elements. This option is useful because you often want to set the border attribute of these HTML tags to zero so that they're not visible when the page displays in a browser. However, while you work on the design of your page in Dreamweaver, seeing where elements like tables and layers start and stop can be very useful. Checking the frame options in the View menu lets you see the borders in Dreamweaver even if you don't want them to be visible to your site's visitors.

The Insert menu

As shown in Figure 1-13, the Insert menu offers access to a number of features unique to Web design. From this menu, you can insert elements like a horizontal rule, a Java applet, a form, or a plug-in file.

Dreamweaver offers extra support for inserting Flash or Shockwave Director files, both of which are products from Macromedia. (You can find out lots more about using multimedia files, such as Shockwave and RealAudio, in Chapter 12.)

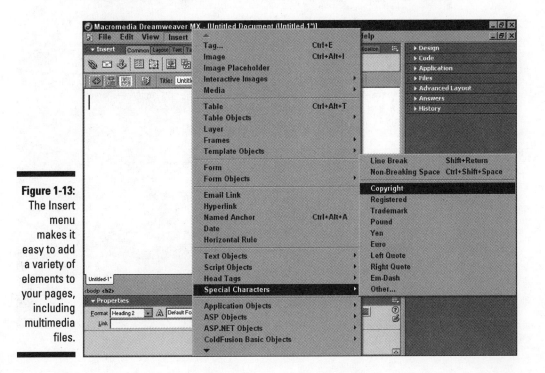

Figure 1-13: The Insert menu makes it easy to add a variety of elements to your pages, including multimedia files.

The Modify menu

The Modify menu is another place where you can view and change object properties, such as the table attributes shown in Figure 1-14. The properties (usually called *attributes* in HTML) let you define elements on a page by setting alignment, height, width, and other specifications.

Note that you can also set nearly all these attributes using the Property Inspector. One exception to this is the Page Properties option under the Modify menu. Changing page properties (see Figure 1-15) enables you to set link and text colors for the entire page and specify the background color or image.

The Text menu

You can easily format text with the Text menu by using simple options, such as bold and italic, as well as more complex features, such as font styles and custom style sheets. Text formatting options have evolved dramatically on the Web. Just a couple of years ago, you didn't even have the option of specifying a particular font style or controlling leading and spacing. Today, although these options aren't yet universally supported, you have more control than ever over the look of your Web pages.

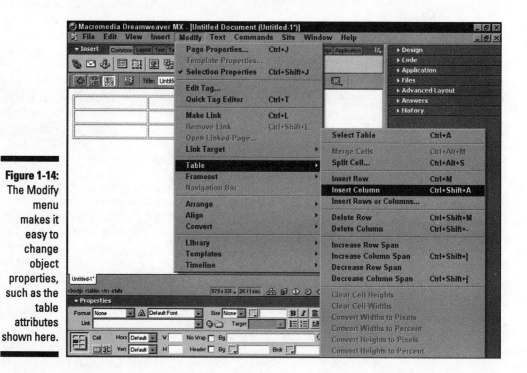

Figure 1-14: The Modify menu makes it easy to change object properties, such as the table attributes shown here.

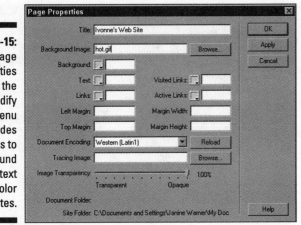

Figure 1-15:
The Page
Properties
option in the
Modify
menu
provides
access to
background
and text
color
attributes.

For example, if you choose a particular font for your text, that font must be available on the user's computer for the text to display properly. Because of this limitation, HTML enables you to specify several font possibilities to improve your odds that a font you want can be displayed. The browser searches the user's computer for one of these fonts in the order in which you list them. Dreamweaver recognizes the importance of specifying more than one font and the safety of using the more popular fonts.

The Commands menu

The Commands menu, shown in Figure 1-16, gives you access to a host of new options in Dreamweaver. These options include the Start and Play Recording features, which let you quickly save a series of steps and then repeat them. To use this feature, choose Command⇨Start Recording, perform whatever actions you want to record — for example, adding a table with three rows and two columns — and then choose Stop Recording. Then to perform that action again, choose Play Recording and a second, identical table will be created. You can download an action by choosing Command⇨Get More Commands, a feature that automatically launches a browser and takes you to the Macromedia Web site. Once there, you can download new commands to add functionality to Dreamweaver.

The Clean Up HTML option on the Commands menu helps you correct bad HTML code, and the Clean Up Word HTML feature is designed especially to correct the common problems caused by the Save As HTML feature in Microsoft word.

The Add/Remove Netscape Resize Fix option on this menu inserts or removes a JavaScript script that is designed to help correct a Netscape bug by automatically reloading the page when users resize their browser windows.

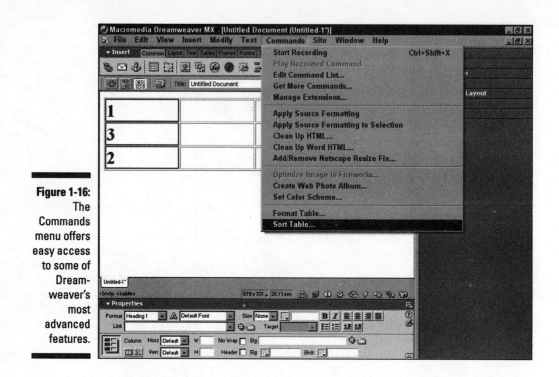

Figure 1-16:
The
Commands
menu offers
easy access
to some of
Dream-
weaver's
most
advanced
features.

Another great feature under the Commands Menu is the Set Color Scheme Command. This option includes a list of background and text colors that are specially designed to work well together on the Web.

The Site menu

The Site menu provides access to the options you need to set up your site, a process required before many of the other Dreamweaver features will work properly. (This process is covered in detail in Chapter 2.) The Site menu also gives you easy access to Check In and Check Out, which are options that can help you keep a team of designers from overwriting each others work. (Chapter 2 also talks about this feature.)

The Window menu

The Window menu lets you control the display of panels and dialog boxes, such as Insert, Properties, and Behaviors. To turn these features on, select the panel name so that a check mark appears next to the feature you want to display; to turn the feature off, click again to remove the check mark. Other panels and dialog boxes, such as CSS Styles and HTML Code Inspector, are also listed in the Window menu for easy access.

The Help menu

The Help menu provides easy access to help options that can assist you in figuring out many features of Dreamweaver. You also find access to the Dreamweaver template and example files under Help. Templates and examples provide visual samples of common HTML designs, such as tables and frames, and provide design ideas and great shortcuts for creating complex layouts.

The Status Bar

The Status Bar appears at the very bottom-left of the Dreamweaver screen. On the right end of the Status Bar, you can see shortcuts to all the features available in the Launcher bar. On the left end, you find HTML codes that indicate how elements on your page are formatted. If you run your mouse pointer over text that is centered, for example, the Status Bar displays <center>. This feature makes double-checking the kind of formatting applied to any element on your page easy. To turn the display of the Status Bar on or off, choose View⇨Status Bar. You can also use the Status Bar to identify a section on your page. For example, if you click the name of a tag in the Status Bar, the section of your page where that tag is applied will be highlighted. This makes it easier to select certain sections of a page, such as a table.

Working on Web Pages Created in Another Web Design Program

In theory, all Web design programs should be compatible because HTML files are, at their heart, just ASCII (or plain-text) files. You can open an HTML file in any text editor, including Macintosh SimpleText and Windows Notepad. However, HTML has evolved dramatically over the years and different Web programs follow different standards, which can cause serious conflicts when a page created in one program is opened in another.

One of the reasons Dreamweaver is so popular is because it creates very clean code and is considered more accurate and more respectful of HTML standards than other programs. Dreamweaver is also better at creating pages that work in different browsers and on different platforms, but importing files created in another Web program can be challenging.

To help with the transition, Dreamweaver includes some special features, such as the Clean Up Word HTML option, designed to fix some of the common problems with Microsoft Word's HTML code.

Before you start working on a site that has been developed in another program, you need to import the site into Dreamweaver. I recommend you make a backup of the site first so you have a copy of all the original pages. You find step-by-step instructions for importing an existing Web site in Chapter 2.

The following sections describe the most popular HTML editors and what you need to know if you're moving files from one of these programs to Dreamweaver.

Microsoft FrontPage

Microsoft FrontPage is one of the most popular HTML editors on the market, in large part because Microsoft office is so popular. FrontPage also offers some powerful features as well as an attractive bundle of programs for Web developers, including Image Composer, a bundled graphics program designed for creating images for the Web. FrontPage also includes *Web components* that you can use to add interactive features, such as a simple search engine or a discussion area, to your Web site. Web components work only if their corresponding programs reside on the Web server that you use, but many commercial service providers now offer FrontPage Web components.

If you are migrating a site from FrontPage to Dreamweaver, first make note of any FrontPage Web components that you've used, such as search engines or forms. Dreamweaver doesn't offer these built-in features, and you won't be able to continue editing them in Dreamweaver the way you did in FrontPage. Though the components should still work, thanks to the Dreamweaver Roundtrip HTML, which respects unique code, you'll be sacrificing some of the convenience of FrontPage's built-in components for Dreamweaver's more standard approach to creating code. If you've used a number of components, have gotten used to the way they work in FrontPage, and feel that you can't live without them, you may be better off sticking with FrontPage for awhile.

If you've used the Dynamic HTML features in FrontPage, you need to pay special attention to those features as you convert your site to Dreamweaver. Microsoft FrontPage isn't as good as Dreamweaver at creating DHTML features that work in both Netscape Navigator and Microsoft Internet Explorer, so you probably want to improve your DHTML code if you expect viewers to use any browser other than Internet Explorer. Because DHTML is much more complex than HTML, you probably don't want to edit this code manually — converting from other editors to Dreamweaver can get pretty tricky. You may find that the simplest solution is to delete the DHTML features that you created in FrontPage and re-create them in Dreamweaver. (For more on DHTML, check out Chapters 9 and 10.)

Microsoft Word

Although Microsoft Word is a word processor and is not considered an HTML editor per se, it does have HTML output capabilities. As a result, you're likely to encounter pages that have been output from Microsoft Word at some point. The problems you find in HTML code generated from Word are similar to the problems generated from FrontPage: They both tend to output verbose and redundant code that deviates from HTML standards. Because Word-generated HTML is so common, Dreamweaver includes a special Clean Up Word HTML command. To use this feature, choose Commands⇨Clean Up Word HTML and then specify the code you want altered in the Clean Up Word HTML dialog box.

NetObjects Fusion

If you've been working in NetObjects Fusion, you face a more dramatic transition to Dreamweaver than you would coming from almost any other HTML editor discussed in this section. That's because Fusion took a unique approach to Web design and HTML code output. This program is no longer available, but there are still many Web sites out there that were created with it.

The biggest challenge with Fusion sites is that Fusion used complex HTML tables and a transparent graphic to control spacing. The down-to-the-pixel design control enticed many graphic designers because they could create complex layouts with less effort, but those designs were not well supported by all browsers — meaning that the designs didn't work well for broad audience sites.

The problem if you are importing a Web site created with Fusion is that it will have very complex code that doesn't lend itself easily to further editing in any other program. Unfortunately, if you want the cleanest HTML code possible, which speeds up download time and makes editing pages easier in the future, your best bet is to re-create your designs from scratch. I'm sorry to break this to you, but if you're importing a site created in Fusion, you should probably start over with Dreamweaver; the transition process is just too daunting to be worth it. Move all of your images into new image directories, set up a new site in Dreamweaver, and start over with your design work.

Adobe GoLive

Previously called GoLive CyberStudio, GoLive is now Adobe's flagship HTML editor, replacing the earlier PageMill program. GoLive offers some great features for easy page design and a lot of similarities with Dreamweaver, but it also brings many of the same problems as pages created in NetObjects Fusion (see preceding section). GoLive uses a grid to provide down-to-the-pixel layout control in much the same way that Fusion did. So, like Fusion, GoLive often outputs very complex code that is difficult to edit in other programs.

Because you can see the alignment grid in GoLive, you may be more aware of the complex table that GoLive creates in the background. The grid feature in GoLive is optional, and if the site you are importing was created without this feature, converting your pages to Dreamweaver should be a much easier task. If the site was created using the grid, you may find that re-creating your pages from scratch in Dreamweaver is your best option. The code used to create the complex HTML tables that GoLive uses in its grids is extremely difficult to edit outside of GoLive. If you're working with people who use GoLive, try to get them to avoid using the Layout Grid feature when designing their pages and you'll have an easier time working on the site with Dreamweaver.

If you've added any JavaScript actions to your pages in GoLive, you won't be able to edit them in Dreamweaver, either, but the actions should still work. Likewise, Dynamic HTML features and animations created in GoLive can't be edited in Dreamweaver without working with the coding manually. If your page contains any actions or DTHML features, you may find it easiest to re-create the page in Dreamweaver.

Other HTML editors

A few years ago there were lots of different visual HTML editors being used. Today there are only a few major ones left. The few that I discuss here seem to have captured most of the market. Still, you may find yourself inheriting sites built in older visual editors such as Adobe PageMill, Claris HomePage, or Symantec VisualPage, to name a few. Each of these should present fewer problems than either Fusion or GoLive, which tend to be the hardest to work with. In any case, as you consider how best to convert your work into Dreamweaver, pay special attention to unusual code output, non-standard rules about HTML tags and syntax, and sophisticated features such as Dynamic HTML and CGI scripts. These are the elements of an HTML page that are most likely to cause problems when you import them into Dreamweaver.

For the most part, you can open any HTML page with Dreamweaver and continue developing it with little concern. If you run into problems, remember that you always have the option of re-creating the page from scratch in Dreamweaver — a sure way to get rid of any unwanted code. You may also want to use Dreamweaver's Clean Up HTML feature to identify potentially problematic code. To use this feature, choose Commands⇨Clean Up HTML and then select the elements you want to alter in the Clean Up HTML dialog box.

Also be careful if you use Adobe ImageReady to automatically output HTML with images, for example, if you use the slicing feature to break up a large image into smaller images arranged in an HTML table. ImageReady also relies heavily on the transparent image trick for alignment and makes heavy use of the COLSPAN attribute in Tables. Both of these tricks can be problematic if you change the table width values. If you are having trouble getting your images to align the way you intend, you may again be better off deleting the original page and re-creating the table in Dreamweaver.

Chapter 2

Setting Up a Web Site with Dreamweaver

*I*f you're ready to dive in and start building your Web site, you've come to the right place. In this chapter, you find out how to work on an existing Web site — or create an entirely new site.

Before you start creating or editing individual pages, you need to set up your site using the site-management features in Dreamweaver. Whether you're creating a new site or working on an existing site, follow the steps in the next section to get Dreamweaver ready to manage the site for you. The site management features enable Dreamweaver to keep track of the elements in your site, automatically create links, update your server, and even manage a team of developers. With the enhancements in this latest version, all these features are even more powerful and easy to use.

You can use Dreamweaver without doing the initial site setup explained in the following section, but some of the features — such as the Library, which enables you to store elements for easy use throughout your site — won't work.

Setting Up a New or Existing Site

To create a new site in Dreamweaver, you first create a folder on your hard drive in which you save all the pages and other elements of your site. During the site setup process, you identify that folder as the location of your site on your local computer so that Dreamweaver can keep track of the structure and files as you create your site.

If you're working on an existing site, you follow the same steps, but instead of creating a new folder, you direct Dreamweaver to a folder that contains the existing site.

The site setup process is important because when you finish your site and upload it to your Web server, the individual pages, images, and other elements must remain in the same relative location to each other on the Web server as they are on your hard drive. The site-management features in Dreamweaver are designed to ensure that things work properly on the server by making certain that you set links and other features correctly when you create them. If you don't use the site management features, you risk breaking links between pages when you upload your site to your Web server. The site setup process also gets you ready to use Dreamweaver's FTP capabilities, which facilitate the transfer of your site from your local computer to your Web server and manage updates any time you make changes to your site.

Note: FTP *(File Transfer Protocol)* is used for copying files to and from servers elsewhere on a network, such as the Internet. FTP is the protocol you use to send your Web site to your server when you're ready to publish it on the Web. (For a glossary of this and other terms, see the CD-ROM.)

Defining a site

The following steps walk you through the process of using the Site Definition dialog box to define your site. This is an important first step to your Web design work because this is where you identify your site structure, which enables Dreamweaver to set links and effectively handle many of the site-management features explained in later chapters.

If you are opening an existing Web site, skip to Step 2. Just make sure that the entire Web site directory — a single folder containing the entire contents of your Web site — is on your hard drive. If you want to work on an existing site that is on a remote server, follow the steps in the section called "Downloading an Existing Web Site."

To define a site using the Site Definition dialog box, follow these steps.

1. **In Windows Explorer or the Macintosh Finder, depending on the system you use, create a new folder for your Web site. This is where you store all the files, images and other elements of your site.**

   In Windows Explorer, the command is File⇨New⇨Folder.

   In the Macintosh Finder, the command is File⇨New Folder.

   You can call this folder anything you like; it's just a container that represents the server space where your Web site will reside later. All the files, subfolders, and images for your Web site should go in this folder.

2. Choose Site⇨New Site.

The Site Definition dialog box appears, as shown in Figure 2-1. Make sure that the Local Info category is selected in the left side of the dialog box.

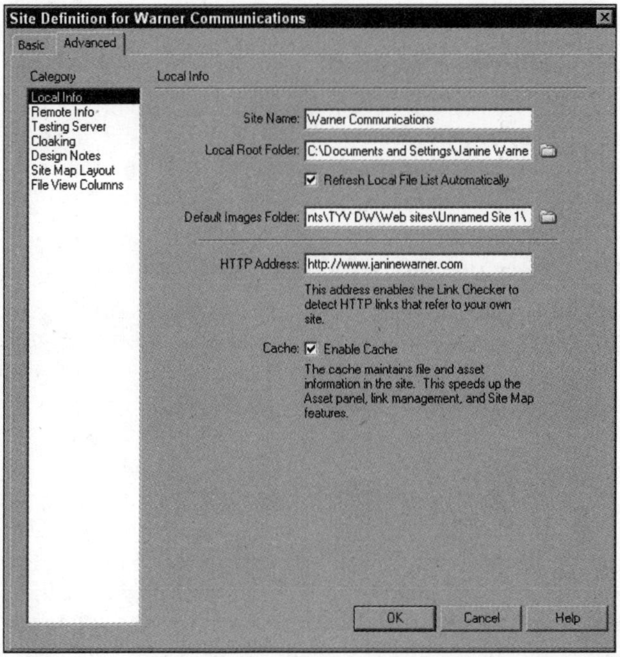

Figure 2-1:
The Site
Definition
dialog box
enables you
to set up a
new or
existing
Web site in
Dream-
weaver.

3. In the Site Name text box, type a name for your site.

You can call your site whatever you like. After you name it here, the name appears as an option on the drop-down list in the Site dialog box. You use this list to select the site you want to work on when you open Dreamweaver, which is especially helpful if you're working on multiple Web sites.

4. Use the Browse button (it resembles a file folder) next to the Local Root Folder text box to locate the new folder on your hard drive that you created in Step 1 to hold your Web site.

If you're working on an existing site, follow the same step to locate the folder that holds the site you want to start working on in Dreamweaver.

5. If Refresh Local File List Automatically isn't already selected, click to place a check mark in the box next to this option if you want Dreamweaver to automatically update the list of all the new pages you add to your site.

6. **Under Link Management Options, type the URL of your Web site in the HTTP Address text box.**

    The HTTP Address is the URL, or Web address, that your site will have when it is published on a Web server. If you do not yet know the Web address for your site or you do not plan to publish it on a Web server, you can leave this box blank.

7. **Check the Enable Cache option.**

    Dreamweaver creates a local cache of your site to be able to quickly reference the location of files in your site. The local cache speeds up many of the site management features of the program and takes only a few seconds to create, unless you have a really content-heavy site or a very slow computer.

8. **Click OK to close the Site Definition dialog box.**

    If you haven't checked the Enable Cache option, a message box appears asking whether you want to create a cache for the site. Figure 2-1 shows what the Site Definition dialog box should look like when all the areas in the Local Info tab are filled in.

Setting up Web server access

To make your life simpler, Dreamweaver incorporates FTP capability so that you can easily upload your pages to a Web server. Integrating this feature also enables Dreamweaver to help you keep track of changes you make to files on your hard drive and ensure that they match the files on your Web server.

You enter information about the Web server where your site will be published on the Remote Info page of the Site Definition dialog box. You access this page by selecting Remote Info in the Category box on the left side of the Site Definition dialog box. The Remote Info page opens on the right side of the box, as shown in Figure 2-2.

If you aren't going to publish your site on a server, choose None from the Remote info drop-down list. If you're going to send your site to a server on a network, choose Local/Network from the Server Access drop-down list; then use the Browse button to specify that server's location on your network. The other two options, Source Safe Database and WebDAV, enable a version control system and help you to keep track of changes when a team of developers is working on a site. You find more on these Dreamweaver features in Chapter 3.

The most common way to publish a Web site after you develop it is to use FTP to send it to a remote server, such as those offered by commercial Internet service providers. If that is how you're going to publish your site, the step-by-step instructions that follow walk you through the process.

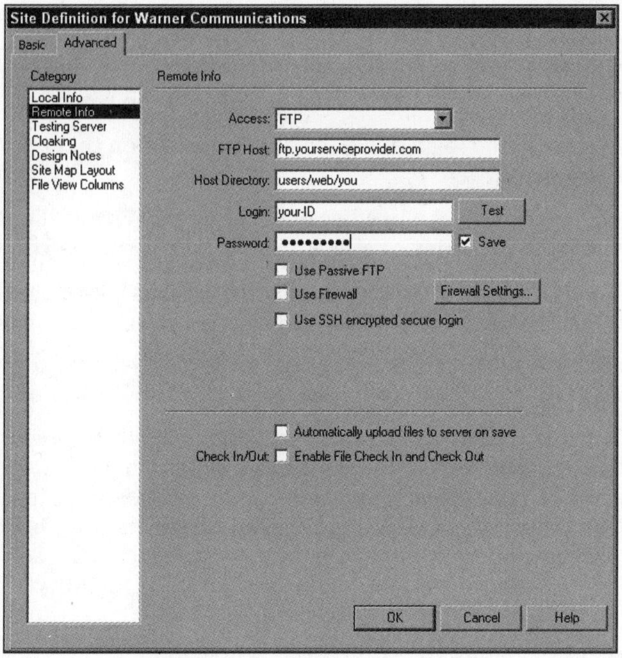

Figure 2-2:
The Site
Definition
dialog box
specifies
the access
information
for a remote
Web server.

If you're using a remote server, such as an Internet service provider, ask your provider for the following information:

> FTP host name
>
> Path for the host directory
>
> FTP login
>
> FTP password

Choose FTP from the Server Access drop-down list in the Remote Info page of the Site Definition dialog box and follow these steps:

1. In the FTP Host text box, type the hostname of your Web server.

It should look something like `ftp.host.com` or `shell.host.com` or `www.host.com`, depending on your server.

2. In the Host Directory text box, type the directory on the remote site in which documents visible to the public are stored (also known as the *site root*).

It should look something like `public/html/` or `www/public/docs/`. Again, this depends on your server.

3. **In the text box next to Login and Password, type the login name and password required to gain access to your Web server. If you check the Save box, Dreamweaver stores the information and automatically supplies it to the server when you connect to the remote site.**

   This is your unique login and password information that provides you access to your server.

4. **Put a check mark in the Use Passive FTP or Use Firewall options only if your service provider or site administrator instructs you to do so.**

   If you aren't on a network and use a commercial service provider, you shouldn't need to check either option.

5. **If you don't want to check any other settings, click OK to save your Web Server Info settings and then close the Site Definition dialog box.**

   If you want to continue reviewing the settings in other categories, choose Check In/Out, Site Map Layout, or Design Notes from the Category box on the left side of the screen (I explain each of these settings in the following sections). Then continue with the applicable instructions in one of the following three subsections. Otherwise, skip ahead to the section "Creating New Pages" so you can jump right into creating your Web site.

Using Check In/Out

The Check In/Out category was designed to keep people from overwriting each other's work when more than one person is contributing to the same Web site (a valuable feature if you want to keep peace on your Web design team). When a person working on the Web site "checks out" a file, other developers working on the site are unable to make changes to that page. When you check out a file, you see a green check mark next to the filename. If someone else has checked out a file, you see a red check mark.

To use the Check In/Out feature, check the box next to Check In/Out at the bottom of the Remote Info box. The Check In/Out section expands when you check it to expose other options. If you want files checked out whenever they are opened, put a check in the Check Out Files When Opening box (see Figure 2-3).

Using this feature, you can track which files a particular person is working on. If you're the only person working on a Web site, you shouldn't need this feature, but if you want to use this tracking mechanism, check the box next to Check Out Files When Opening and then fill in the name you want associated with the files (presumably your name or nickname if you prefer) in the Check Out Name field and then include your Email Address in that field. (The Email Address field is needed for Dreamweaver's integration with e-mail, which facilitates communication among developers on a site. You find more information about integrated e-mail in Chapter 3.)

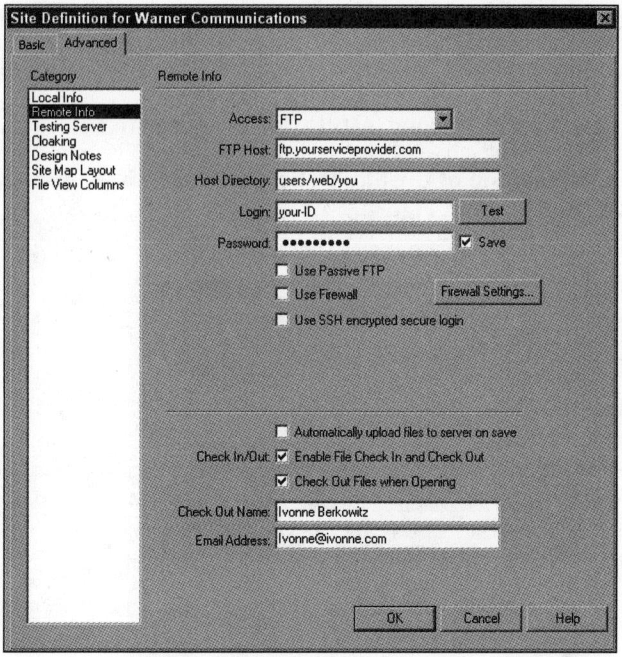

Figure 2-3:
The Check
In/Out
feature
helps you
keep track
of develop-
ment when
more than
one person
is working
on the site.

Site Definition for Warner Communications

Basic | Advanced

Category
Local Info
Remote Info
Testing Server
Cloaking
Design Notes
Site Map Layout
File View Columns

Remote Info

Access: FTP

FTP Host: ftp.yourserviceprovider.com

Host Directory: users/web/you

Login: your-ID   Test

Password: •••••••••   ☑ Save

☐ Use Passive FTP
☐ Use Firewall   Firewall Settings...
☐ Use SSH encrypted secure login

☐ Automatically upload files to server on save

Check In/Out: ☑ Enable File Check In and Check Out
☑ Check Out Files when Opening

Check Out Name: Ivonne Berkowitz

Email Address: Ivonne@ivonne.com

OK   Cancel   Help

Using the Application Server

The Application Server option enables you to specify a development server, a necessary step if you are creating a Web site using Dreamweaver's UltraDev features with a database. You find more information about how to do this in Chapters 14, 15, and 16. If you are not creating a site linked to a database, you don't need to make any changes to this dialog box.

Cloaking options

Dreamweaver's new Cloaking option enables you to exclude any specified folder or files from all site operations, meaning they can't be altered or uploaded to the live site. This feature is handy if you have sections of a site that you want to save but don't want visible to your viewers. For example, if you have a special Christmas section that you don't want visible during the rest of the year, you can use the Cloaking feature to save it, with the assurance that no one can alter, delete, or publish the files until you uncloak them.

Make sure you remove the files from your live server if you don't want them visible to your users.

You can also use cloaking to exclude certain file types from site operations. For example, you can cloak all your multimedia files so that they are not uploaded to your site every time up update your work to the server.

To use Dreamweaver's Cloaking feature, follow these steps:

1. **In the Cloaking tab of the Site Definition dialog box, select Enable Cloaking as shown in Figure 2-4.**

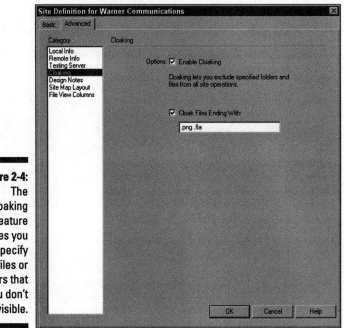

Figure 2-4:
The Cloaking feature enables you to specify files or folders that you don't want visible.

2. **If you want to Cloak files of a certain type, select the Cloak Files Ending With box and enter the extension(s) in the text field below it.**

   For example, if you want to cloak all your JPEG and GIF files, you would enter those extension in this dialog box. Separate each file extension with a space. Do not use a comma or other delimiter.

3. **Click OK to close the Site Definition dialog box and then click Done in the Define Sites dialog box to close it.**

4. **In the Site tab of the Files dialog box located in the right-hand area of the development area, select the files or folders you want to cloak (see Figure 2-5).**

5. **Right-click (Windows) or Ctrl+click (Mac) and select Cloaking ⇨Cloak.**

   To uncloak files or folder, repeat Steps 4 and 5 and select Uncloak. You can also use these steps to uncloak all the files in your current site, disable Cloaking in the site, and change Cloaking Settings.

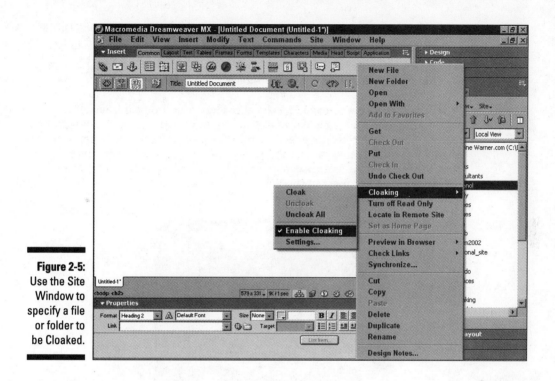

Figure 2-5:
Use the Site
Window to
specify a file
or folder to
be Cloaked.

Using Design Notes

If you sometimes forget the details of your work or neglect to tell your colleagues important things about the Web site you're all working on, the Dreamweaver Design Notes feature may save you some grief.

Design Notes enable you to record information and associate it with a file or folder. They work like the HTML comment tag, which lets you add text to a page that won't display in a browser, so you can make notes in the code. But Design Notes takes this concept a step further, enabling you to add comments to any element, including images, multimedia files, and even folders. And unlike the comment tag, which is embedded directly in the HTML code of a page, visitors can't see Design Notes when they view your Web site — even if they look at the HTML source code. You can choose to upload Design Notes so that they are available to others with access to your server, or you can prevent them from ever being loaded to your public site.

To access the Design Notes page, choose Design Notes from the Category box in the Site Definition dialog box (see Figure 2-6). The settings on this page let you control how Dreamweaver uses Design Notes:

✔ **Maintain Design Notes:** Click to place a check mark in this box to ensure that the Design Note remains attached to the file when you upload it, copy it, or move it.

> ✔ **Upload Design Notes for Sharing:** Choose this option to include Design Notes when you send files to the server via FTP.
>
> ✔ **Clean Up:** This button enables you to delete Design Notes that are no longer associated with files or folders in your site.

When you create graphics in Macromedia Fireworks, you can save a Design Note for that file that is also available in Dreamweaver. To use this integrated feature, save the Fireworks image to your local Web site folder. When you open the file in Dreamweaver, the Design Note is displayed when you right-click the image. This feature is a great way for graphic designers to communicate with other members of the Web development team.

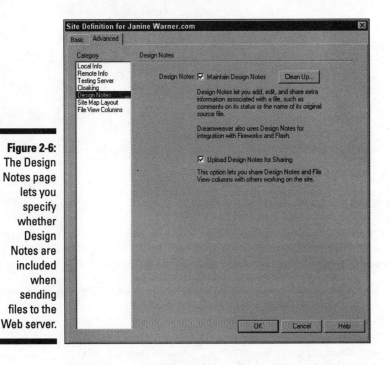

Figure 2-6:
The Design Notes page lets you specify whether Design Notes are included when sending files to the Web server.

Activating Site Map Layout

If you have trouble keeping track of all your files and how they are linked in your site, you're not alone. As Web sites get larger and larger, this task becomes increasingly daunting. Dreamweaver includes a Site Map Layout feature to help you keep track of your Web pages and the hierarchy of your site. This is not a Site Map like those you often see on Web sites that's visible to visitors of your site and provides links to all or many of the pages in the site. Dreamweaver's Site Map Layout is a site management feature in that you can use it to visually manage the files and folders that make up your site. To access the settings for the Site Map Layout feature, choose Site Map Layout from the Category box in the Site Definition dialog box. The Site Map Layout page opens on the right side of the box, as shown in Figure 2-7.

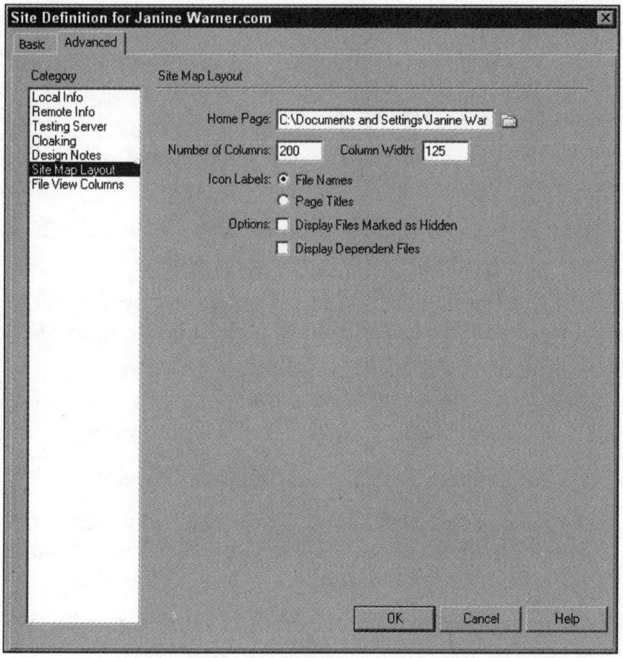

Figure 2-7:
The Site Map Layout page enables you to specify how the Site Map navigation window appears.

You can use this feature to automatically create a site map of all the pages in your Web site. This is a useful management tool because it gives you a visual reference of the hierarchy of your Web site and all of its links.

To create a site map from the Site Map Layout page of the Site Definition dialog box, follow these steps:

1. **In the Home Page text box, type the path to the main page of your site or use the Browse button (the icon that resembles a file folder) to locate it. If you have already filled out the Local Info page, this field should automatically be filled in.**

   This text box specifies the home page for the site map and provides Dreamweaver with a reference for where the Web site begins. If you don't specify a home page and Dreamweaver cannot find a file called index.html or index.htm (the most common names for a home page), Dreamweaver prompts you to select a home page when you open the site map.

2. **Set the Number of Columns field to the number of pages you want displayed per row in the site map.**

   If you're not sure what you want for these settings, the default values are a good place to start. You can always come back and change these settings later if you don't like the spacing of the icons in your site map.

3. **Set the Column Width, in pixels, to represent how wide you want the site map.**

   Again, the default is a good place to start if you're not sure how wide you want this to display.

4. **In the Icon Labels section, click either the File Names option or the Page Titles option if you want the filename or page title of each page to be displayed in the site map.**

   You can manually edit any filename or page title after you generate the site map.

5. **In the Options section, you can choose to hide certain files, meaning that they won't be visible in the Site Map window.**

   If you select the Display Files Marked as Hidden option, files you have marked as hidden are displayed in italic in the site map.

   If you select the Display Dependent Files option, all dependent files in the site's hierarchy are displayed. A *dependent file* is an image or other non-HTML content that the browser loads when it loads the main page.

6. **When you have adjusted all the settings, click OK.**

   A message window appears asking if you want to create a cache file for the site. This helps Dreamweaver keep your links up to date and improves the performance of the Site Map.

7. **Click Create to generate a cache file and launch the site map process.**

   Dreamweaver scans all the files in your site and creates a cache, which helps make things work faster in the program.

8. **Click Done in the Edit Sites dialog box when you are finished.**

9. **To view a site map, select the Expand/Collapse icon in the right-hand side of the Site panel. Then select the Site Map icon in the top left of the expanded display window and choose Map Only from the pull-down menu. Alternatively, you can select Map and Files to display the site map on the left of the screen and the files list on the right, as shown in Figure 2-8.**

Downloading an existing Web site

If you want to work on an existing Web site and you don't already have a copy of it on your local computer's hard drive, you can use Dreamweaver to download any or all of the site so that you can edit the current pages, add new pages, or use any of Dreamweaver's other features.

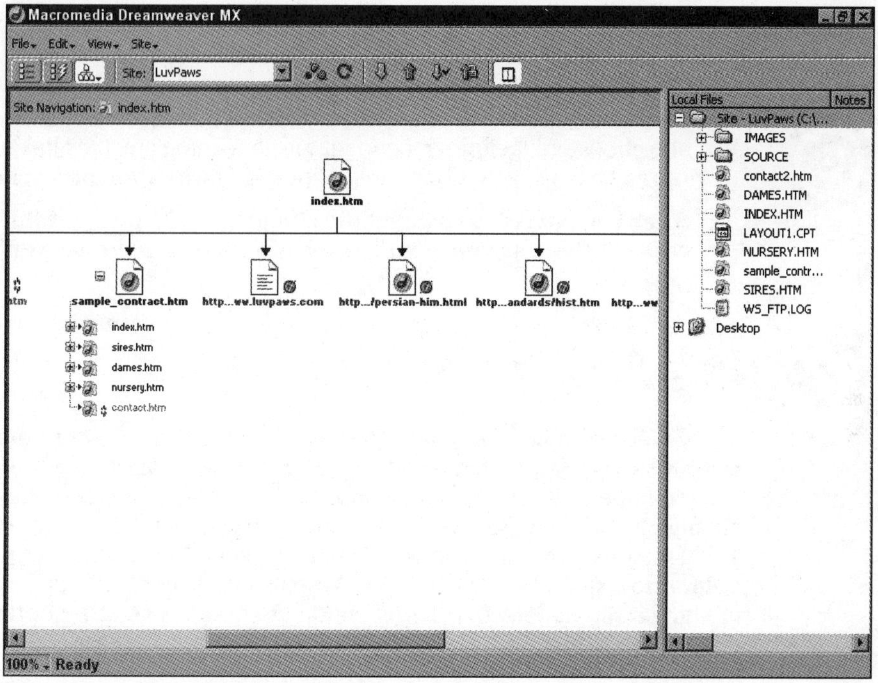

Figure 2-8:
The Site Map provides a quick visual reference to the locations of pages and links in your site structure.

To download an existing Web site, follow these steps.

1. **Create a new folder on your computer that you will use to store the existing site.**

2. **Specify this folder as the local root folder for the site using Dreamweaver's site set up features described in the section "Defining a site," earlier in this chapter.**

3. **Set up the Remote Info dialog box as explained in the "Setting up Web server access" section earlier in this chapter.**

4. **Connect to the remote site by clicking the Connects to Remote Host button in the Site window (located in the Files panel to the right of Dreamweaver's work area).**

5. **Select Get to download the entire site to your local disk.**

   If you only want to download specific files or folders from the site, select those files or folders in the Remote pane of the Site window, and click Get File(s). Dreamweaver automatically duplicates some or all of the remote site's structure, meaning the folders in the site but not all of the files within them, to place the downloaded file in the correct part of the site hierarchy. Recreating the folder structure on your local computer is important because Dreamweaver needs to know the location of the files as they relate to other parts of the site in order to set links properly. The safest option is to download the entire site, but if you are working on a really large Web project, downloading a part and duplicating the structure enables you to work on a section of the site without downloading all of it.

If you are working on only one page or section of a site, you should generally choose to include dependent files, meaning any files linked to those pages, to ensure that links are set properly when you make changes.

6. **After you have downloaded the site or specific files or folders, you can edit them as you would any other file in Dreamweaver.**

Creating New Pages

Every Web site begins with a single page. The front page — or *home page* — of your site is a good place to start. Dreamweaver makes it easy: When the program opens, it automatically creates a new page. To create another page, simply choose File⇨New⇨Category Item Basic Page⇨Basic Page Item HTML. You'll find many other options in Dreamweaver's New Document dialog box, but for now, don't worry about all of those. In this chapter, you start off by creating a simple HTML file. You'll find out about those other options in later chapters.

Creating a new page to start a Web site may seem obvious, but consider this: You may want to create a bunch of new pages before you get too far in your development, and you may even want to start organizing the new pages in subdirectories before you have anything on them. Doing so enables you to organize your pages before you start setting links. After all, you can't set a link to a page that doesn't exist. So if you plan to have five links on your front page to other pages in your site, go ahead and create those other pages, even if you don't put anything on them yet.

Dreamweaver MX includes a wealth of ready-to-use Web Components. You'll find these in the New Document dialog box when you choose File⇨New. These components can help you get your site designed quickly, using sample layouts, Dream Templates, framesets, and many other goodies.

When I first start building a Web site, I often create a bunch of pages with nothing but a simple text headline across the top of each. I make a page like this for each area of my site and often place them in subdirectories. For example, if I were creating a site for my department at a big company, I might have a page about my staff, another about what we do, and a third with information about the resources that we provide. At this initial stage, I'd create four pages — one for the front page of the site and three others for each of the subsections. With these initial pages in place, I benefit from having an early plan for organizing the site, and I can start setting links among the main pages right away. See Chapter 3 for more tips about Web site planning and organization. Chapter 4 guides you through the use of templates, a great way to develop multiple pages with similar designs.

Designing your first page

Before you get too far into design or organization, I want to give you a general idea about how to do basic tasks in Dreamweaver, such as formatting text and setting links.

If you're ready to plunge right in, click to insert your cursor at the top of a blank page in Dreamweaver and type some text. Type anything you like; you just need something that you can format. If you have text in a word processor or another program, you can copy and paste that text from the other program into your Dreamweaver page. After you enter the text on your page, dive into the following sections to find out how to play around with formatting your text.

You can collapse the panels on the right side of the work area by clicking the small tab on the right side of the panel set. In the following figures, I've collapsed the panels to create more room in the design area.

Creating a headline

Suppose that you want to center a headline and make it big and bold, like the one shown in Figure 2-9. To create a new page in Dreamweaver, choose File➪ New➪Category item Basic Page➪Basic Page item HTML.

To create a headline, follow these steps:

1. **Highlight the text you want to format.**

2. **Choose <u>T</u>ext➪<u>S</u>tyle➪<u>B</u>old.**

   The heading becomes bold. You can also use the Property Inspector at the bottom of the page and select the B icon to make the selected text bold.

3. **With the text still selected, choose <u>T</u>ext➪<u>A</u>lign➪<u>C</u>enter.**

   The text automatically centers. You can also use the Property Inspector at the bottom of the page and select the center icon.

4. **With the text still selected, choose <u>T</u>ext➪<u>S</u>ize➪<u>6</u>.**

   The text changes to HTML Font size 6 and you should have a headline at the top of your page that looks something like the headline shown in Figure 2-9. You can also use the Property Inspector at the bottom of the page and 6 from the pull-down menu next to Size, as shown in Figure 2-9.

In general, I find the Property Inspector the easiest way to apply basic formatting, but some people prefer using the drop-down menus from the menu bar. Both achieve the same results.

Figure 2-9:
The
Property
Inspector
provides
easy access
to common
formatting
features,
such as
alignment
and heading
sizes.

Indenting text

Type a little more text after your headline text. A single sentence is enough. To indent that text, follow these steps:

1. **Highlight the text you want to indent.**

2. **Choose Text⇨Indent.**

    The text automatically indents. Alternatively, you can use the Text Indent and Text Outdent icons in the Property Inspector.

If you want to continue adding text and you don't want it to be indented, choose Text⇨Outdent to transition back to plain text mode without the indent. You can also use the Indent and Outdent icons in the Property Inspector.

If you just want to indent a line or two, the Indent option in the Text menu is ideal. If, however, you want to create the effect of a narrower column of text on a page, you may find that putting your text in an HTML table is a better option because it enables you to control the width of the column. You can find information about creating HTML tables in Chapter 6.

Adding images

Adding an image to your Web page is simple with Dreamweaver. The challenge is to create a good-looking image that loads quickly in your viewer's browser. You'll need another program, such as Photoshop or Fireworks, to create and edit images. Use Dreamweaver to place the images on your page. For more information on finding and creating images, as well as keeping file sizes small, see Chapters 5 and 11. For now, I'm going to assume that you have a GIF or JPEG image file ready, and just walk you through the steps to link your image to your page. (The only image formats you can use on your Web page are GIF and JPEG, which can be shortened to JPG.) If you don't have an image handy, you can find a few GIF and JPEG files on the CD-ROM included at the back of this book. You can use any image on your Web site, as long as it's in GIF or JPEG format.

You need to do two important things before inserting an image on a Web page. First, save your HTML page in your Web site's folder on your hard drive. This step is important because Dreamweaver can't properly set the link to your image until it can identify the relative locations of the HTML page and the image. Until you save the page, Dreamweaver doesn't know what folder the page will be in.

For this same reason, you need to make sure that the image file is where you want to store it on your Web site. Many designers create a folder called *images* so that they can keep all their image files in one place. If you are working on a very large site, you may want an images folder within each of the main folders of the site. An important thing to remember is that if you move the page or image to another folder after you place the image on your page, you risk breaking the link between the page and the image, and an ugly broken image icon appears when your page is viewed in a browser. If you move files or folders around in Dreamweaver's Site panel, it automatically fixes the links, but if you move them outside of Dreamweaver, the link is broken. If for some reason you do end up breaking an image link, simply click the broken image icon that appears in its place, and use the browse icon to find the correct image to replace it.

Follow these steps to place an image to your Web page:

1. **Click the Image icon located in the Common tab of the Insert panel at the top of the work area. (Still not sure where the Image icon is? Look for the cursor in Figure 2-10.)**

   The Image dialog box opens.

2. **Click the Select button.**

   A dialog box opens, displaying files and folders on your hard drive.

3. **Navigate to the folder that has the image you want to insert.**

Figure 2-10:
The Image
Property
Inspector
provides
easy access
to common
image
attributes,
such as
alignment
and
spacing.

4. Double-click to select the image you want.

The image automatically appears on your Web page.

If you haven't already saved your page, a warning box appears to tell you that Dreamweaver cannot properly set the link to the image until you save the page. You see this message because Dreamweaver needs to know the location of the HTML page relative to the image to create the link. If you see this box, cancel the step, save your page by choosing File➪Save, and then repeat the preceding steps. Similarly, if the image is not located within your designated root folder, a dialog box opens asking if you want to copy the image to that folder. Click Yes if you want Dreamweaver to automatically copy the image to your root folder (this helps ensure the image is transferred to your server correctly when you upload your site to your server).

5. Click the image on your Web page to display the image options in the Property Inspector at the bottom of the page.

Use the Image Property Inspector to specify image attributes, such as alignment, horizontal and vertical spacing, and alternative text. (The image properties are visible in the Property Inspector in Figure 2-10.)

The Image Property Inspector dialog box enables you to specify many attributes for images that you use in your Web site. Table 2-1 describes those attributes. If you don't see all the attributes that are listed in the table, click the triangle in the bottom-right corner of the Image Property Inspector to reveal all the image options.

Although you can resize an image in Dreamweaver by clicking and dragging on the edge of the image or by changing the Height and Width values, you're almost always better off using an image editor to change the physical size of an image. If you use Dreamweaver to resize an image, you risk distorting the image, using a bigger file size than necessary, and/or loosing image quality.

Table 2-1		Image Attributes
Abbreviation	*Attribute*	*Function*
Image	N/A	Specifies the file size.
Image Name	Name	Identifies image in scripts.
Hotspot tools	Image map coordinates	Use the Rectangle, Oval, and Polygon icons to create image map hotspots on an image. (See Chapter 8 to find out how to create an image map.)
W	Width	Dreamweaver automatically specifies the width of the image based on the actual size of the image file.
H	Height	Dreamweaver automatically specifies the height of the image based on the actual size of the image file.
Src	Source	The *source* is the link or the filename and path to the image. Dreamweaver automatically sets this when you insert the image.
Link	Hyperlink	This field shows the address or path if the image links to another page. (For more about linking, see "Setting Links" later in the chapter.)
Alt	Alternate Text	The words you enter here are displayed if the image doesn't appear on your viewer's screen because the viewer either has images turned off or can't view images. Special browsers for the blind also use this text and convert it to speech with special programs, such as screen readers.
Edit	N/A	The Edit button can be used to launch an image editor, such as Fireworks, but you must first specify the editor you want to use in Dreamweaver's Preferences dialog box, available by selecting Edit ⇨ Preferences and then choosing the File Types/Editors Category.

(continued)

Table 2-1 (continued)

Abbreviation	Attribute	Function
Reset Size	N/A	The Reset Size button enables you to automatically reset the actual image size. This is handy if you change the size of the image by clicking and dragging on the edge of the image and then want to reset it.
Map	Map Name	Use the Map name text box to assign a name to an image map. All image maps require a name.
Map Tools	N/A	The three icons below the Map Name area enable you to draw out the areas of an image map where you will set the links. (You'll find instructions for creating image maps in Chapter 5.)
V Space	Vertical Space	Measured in pixels, this setting inserts blank space above and below the image.
H Space	Horizontal Space	Measured in pixels, this setting inserts blank space to the left and right of the image.
Target	Link Target	Use this option when the image appears in a page that's part of an HTML frameset. The Target specifies the frame into which the linked page should open. I cover creating frames and how to set links in frames in Chapter 7.
Low Src	Low Source	This option enables you to link two images to the same place on a page. The Low Source image loads first and is then replaced by the primary image. You may find this option especially useful when you have a large image size because you can set a smaller image (such as a black-and-white version) as the Low Source, which displays while the main image downloads. The combination of two images in this way can also create the illusion of a simple animation.
Border	Image Border	Measured in pixels, this attribute enables you to put a border around an image. I nearly always set the image border to 0 (zero) when linking an image to get rid of the colored border that automatically appears around a linked image.
Align	Alignment	This option enables you to align the image. Text automatically wraps around images that are aligned to the right or left. The other options, including Baseline, Top, and Middle, control how text or other elements align next to the image.

Setting Links

Dreamweaver is truly a dream when it comes to setting links. The most important thing to keep in mind is that a link is essentially an address (URL) that tells a viewer's browser what page to go to when the viewer selects the text or image with the link.

If that page is within your Web site, you want to create a *relative link* that includes the path that describes how to get from the current page to the linked page. A relative link shouldn't include the domain name of the server. Here's an example of what the code looks like when you create a relative link:

```
<A HREF="staff/boss.html">The boss</A>
```

If you link to a page on a different Web site, you want to create an *absolute link*. An absolute link does include the full Internet address of the other site. Here's an example of the code behind an absolute link:

```
<A HREF="http://www.janinewarner.com/books">Janine's
        Books</A>
```

If all that HREF code stuff looks like Greek to you, don't worry. The following section shows you how Dreamweaver makes it possible for you to set links without even knowing what the code means.

If you want to know more about all that "Greek stuff," you'll find an introduction to HTML on the CD-ROM that accompanies this book.

Linking pages within your Web site

Linking from one page in your Web site to another — known as an *internal link* — is easy. The most important thing to remember is to save your pages in the folders that you want to keep them in before you start setting links and make sure that all your files are in the root folder, as described in the section "Defining a site," earlier in this chapter.

Here's how you create an internal link:

1. **In Dreamweaver, open the page on which you want to create a link.**

2. **Select the text or image that you want to serve as the link (meaning the text or image that when a user clicks it, will open the new page).**

3. **Click the folder icon to the right of the Link text box in the Property Inspector.**

    The Select File dialog box opens.

4. **From the Select File dialog box, click the page that you want your image or text to link to, and then click the Select button.**

   Alternatively, you can double-click the image or text to select it.

   The link is automatically set and the window closes. If you haven't already saved your page, a message box opens, explaining that you can create a relative link only after you save the page. Always save the page you're working on before you set links.

If the page is part of a frameset, use the Target field in the Property Inspector to specify which frame the linked page should open into. (You find out more about setting links in frames in Chapter 7.)

Setting links to named anchors within a page

If you like to create really long pages, using anchor links to break up navigation within the page is a good idea. A *named anchor link,* often called a *jump link,* enables you to set a link to a specific part of a Web page. You can use a named anchor to link from an image or text string on one page to another place on the same page, or to link from one page to a specific part of another page. To create a named anchor link, you first insert a named anchor in the place that you want to link to, and then use that anchor to direct the browser to that specific part of the page when a viewer follows the link.

Suppose that you want to set a link from the word *Convertible* at the top of a page to a section lower on the page that starts with the headline *Convertible Sports Cars.* You first insert a named anchor at the *Convertible Sports Cars* headline. Then you link the word *Convertible* from the top of the page to that anchor.

To insert a named anchor and set a link to it, follow these steps:

1. **Open the page on which you want to insert the named anchor.**

2. **Click to place your cursor next to the word or image that you want to link to on the page.**

   You don't need to select the word or image; you just need a reference point that is displayed when the link is selected. For this example, I would place the cursor to the left of the headline *Convertible Sports Cars.*

3. **Choose Insert⇨Named Anchor.**

   The Insert Named Anchor dialog box appears.

4. **Enter a name for the anchor.**

   You can name anchors anything you want; just make sure that you use a different name for each anchor on the same page. Then be sure that

you remember what you called the anchor, because you have to type
the anchor name to set the link. (Unlike other Web design programs,
Dreamweaver doesn't automatically enter the anchor name.) In this
example, I would choose *Convertible* as the anchor name because it
would be easy for me to remember.

5. **Click OK.**

    The dialog box closes, and a small anchor icon appears on the page
    where you inserted the anchor name. You can move an anchor name by
    clicking the anchor icon and dragging it to another location on the page.

    If you're curious about what this named anchor looks like in HTML,
    here's the code that appears before the headline in my example:

    ```
    <A NAME=convertible></A>
    ```

6. **To set a link to the named anchor location, click to select the text or
    image that you want to link from.**

    You can link to a named anchor from anywhere else on the same page or
    from another page. In my example, I would link from the word *Convertible*
    that appears at the top of the page to the anchor I made next to the
    headline.

7. **In the Property Inspector, type the pound sign (#) followed by the
    anchor name.**

    You can also select the text and drag a line from the "point to file" icon
    (next to the link text box) to the anchor icon. The anchor name automat-
    ically appears in the link box, saving you typing the name again.

    In my example, I would type **#convertible** in the Link text box. The
    HTML code for this line looks like this:

    ```
    <A HREF="#convertible">Convertible</A>
    ```

    If you wanted to link to an anchor named *Convertible* on another page with
    the filename coolcars.html, you would type **coolcars.html#convertible** in
    the Link text box.

Linking to pages outside your Web site

Linking to a page on another Web site — called an *external link* — is even
easier than linking to an internal link. All you need is the URL of the page to
which you want to link, and you're most of the way there.

To create an external link, follow these steps:

1. **In Dreamweaver, open the page from which you want to link.**

2. **Select the text or image that you want to act as a link.**

3. **In the Link text box in the Property Inspector, type the URL of the page you want your text or image to link to (see Figure 2-11).**

The link is automatically set.

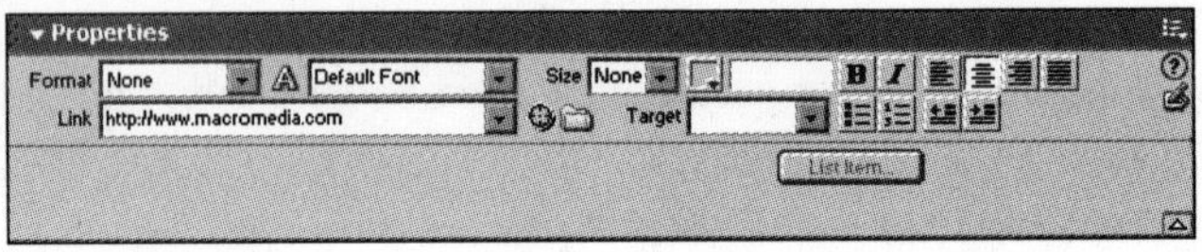

Figure 2-11:
To set a link to another Web site, highlight the text or image and type the URL in the Link text box in the Property Inspector.

Although you don't have to type the http:// at the beginning of a Web site address to get to a site in most browsers, you should use the full URL, including the http:// when you create an external link. Otherwise, the browser may think that the www.whatever.com is the name of a folder on your Web server instead of an external site address and will result in a 404, Page Not Found Error. (See Figure 2-11 for an example of how you would set a link to Macromedia's Web site, using their full URL.)

Setting a link to an e-mail address

Another common link option goes to an e-mail address. E-mail links make it easy for visitors to send you messages. I always recommend that you invite visitors to contact you because they can point out mistakes in your site and give you valuable feedback about how you can further develop your site.

Setting a link to an e-mail address is almost as easy as setting a link to another Web page. Before you start, you need to know the e-mail address to which you want to link. The only other thing you need to know is that e-mail links must begin with the code mailto:. Here's an example of the full line of code behind an e-mail link:

```
<A HREF="mailto:editor@janinewarner.com">Send a message to
        the Janine</A>
```

To create an e-mail link in Dreamweaver, follow these steps:

1. **In Dreamweaver, open the page on which you want to create a link.**

2. **Select an image or highlight the text that you want to act as the link.**

3. **Choose <u>W</u>indow⇨<u>P</u>roperties to open the Property Inspector, if it's not already open.**

4. **In the Link text box, type** mailto:, **followed by the e-mail address, as shown in Figure 2-12.**

   The link is automatically set. Even if the page is part of a frameset, you don't need to specify a target for an e-mail link. (To find out more about framesets and targets, see Chapter 10.) When a visitor clicks an e-mail link, the browser automatically opens an e-mail message window where the user can type a subject and message before sending it.

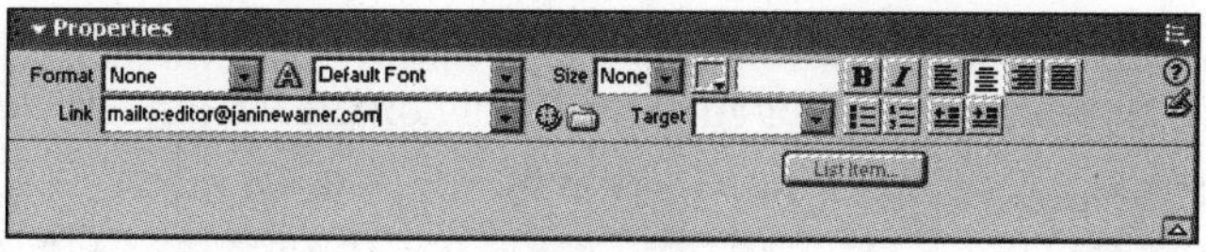

Figure 2-12:
To specify
an e-mail
link, type
mailto: and
the e-mail
address in
the Link
text box.

Changing Page Properties

Dreamweaver provides access to many of the elements you can change across an entire page in the Page Properties dialog box. These include background colors, link and text colors, and the page title (the text that appears at the very top of the browser, next to the browser name, and is also the text that is saved in a users bookmarks list. You'll find some other options in this dialog box, such as the Tracing Image feature, which is covered in Chapter 4, and the Background Image feature, covered in Chapter 5. For now, let's keep things simple and just change the background and text colors.

To change the Background and Text Colors on a page, follow these steps:

1. **Choose <u>M</u>odify⇨<u>P</u>age Properties.**

   The Page Properties dialog box appears, as shown in Figure 2-13.

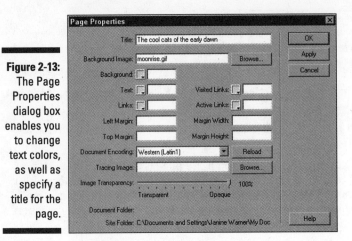

Figure 2-13:
The Page
Properties
dialog box
enables you
to change
text colors,
as well as
specify a
title for the
page.

2. **Click the color swatch box next to Background to reveal the color palette. Choose any color you like. (Just make sure it will look good with the text color you select and that your text will still be readable.)**

   The color you selected fills the color swatch box. The color does not fill the background until you click the Apply or OK button.

3. **Click the color swatch box next to Text to reveal the color palette. Choose any color you like, (But again, make sure it will be readable against your background color. In general, a light background color works best with a dark text color and vice versa.)**

4. **Click Apply to see how the colors look on your page. Click OK to finish.**

Putting Your Web Site Online

In the section "Setting Up a New or Existing Site" earlier in this chapter, I tell you how to set up a site and enter the address, login name, and password for your server. In this section, I show you how to put pages on your server and retrieve them by using the built-in FTP capabilities of Dreamweaver.

To transfer files between your hard drive and a remote server, follow these steps:

1. **First, make sure you have defined your site, as described in the "Setting Up a New or Existing Site" section in the beginning of this chapter and make sure that that the site you've set up is open. You can open an existing site by selecting Site⇨Open Site⇨and selecting the site from the drop-down menu.**

If you have done this properly, the files and folders of your site will be visible in the Site tab of the Files panel on the right side of the work area. (See Figure 2-14.)

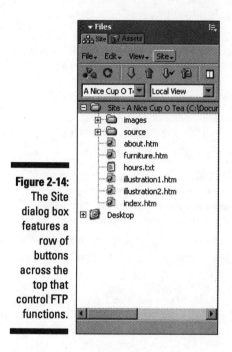

Figure 2-14: The Site dialog box features a row of buttons across the top that control FTP functions.

2. Click the Connects to Remote Host button.

If you're not already connected to the Internet, the Connect button should start your dial-up connection. If you have trouble connecting this way, try establishing your Internet connection as you usually do to check e-mail or surf the Web; then return to Dreamweaver and choose Connect. After you're online, Dreamweaver should have no trouble establishing an FTP connection with your host server.

If you still have trouble establishing a connection to your Web Server, refer to the section "Setting up Web server access" earlier in this chapter and make sure that the server information is specified correctly. If you still have trouble, contact your service provider or site administrator to ensure you have all the correct information for connecting to your server. It can be tricky to get all this information set up correctly the first time and each service provider is different. The good news is that once you get this right, Dreamweaver saves your settings so it connects automatically the next time.

After you establish the connection, the directories on your server appear in the Files Site panel, distinguished by the small heading that says Remote Site. The files on your local hard drive will be visible again if you select the Local button in the panel. To be sure you are looking at your local files, look for the small heading that says Local Files.

3. **To *upload* a file (that is, transfer a file from your hard drive to your Web server), select the file from the Local Files panel (which shows the files on your hard drive) and click the Put Files icon (the up arrow) in the Site panel.**

   The files are automatically copied when you transfer them. You can select multiple files or folders to be transferred simultaneously and you can test your work by using a Web browser to view them on the server.

4. **To *download* files or folders (that is, transfer files or folders from your Web server to your hard drive), select the files or folders from the Remote Files panel (which shows the files on your server) and click the Get Files icon (the down arrow) in the Site panel.**

   The files are automatically copied when you transfer them. When the transfer is complete, you can open the files on your hard drive.

 If you're not happy with the FTP capabilities in Dreamweaver, you can use a dedicated FTP program, such as Fetch for the Macintosh or Cute_FTP for Windows. If you're a more advanced user, you may prefer Leech FTP for Windows. It's not very intuitive to use but is very powerful and doesn't demand much from your system resources. You can download these shareware programs from www.shareware.com and www.download.com.

Part II
Looking Like a Million (Even on a Budget)

The 5th Wave   By Rich Tennant

"Games are an important part of my Web site. They cause eye strain."

In this part . . .

No matter how great the content is on your Web site, the first things viewers always notice are the design and the images. This part helps you get organized and introduces you to the design rules of the Information Superhighway so that you can make your pages look great, even if you're new to the Web.

Chapter 3

Designing a Well-Planned Site

● ●

In This Chapter

▶ Building a new site

▶ Changing and fixing links

▶ Synchronizing your site

▶ Setting the tone for your site

▶ Testing your site with the Dreamweaver's Site Report feature

● ●

*O*ne of the most common mistakes new Web designers make is plunging into developing a site without thinking through all of their goals, priorities, budget, and design options. The instinct is to simply start creating pages, throw them all into one big directory, and then string stuff together with links. Then, when they finally test it out on their audience, they're often surprised when users say the site is hard to navigate and users can't find the pages they want to use.

Do yourself a favor and save yourself some grief by planning ahead. By having a plan, you also stand a much better chance of creating an attractive Web site that's easy to maintain and update. In this chapter, you discover many of the common planning issues of Web design. You also find out how Dreamweaver makes it easier to manage a team of developers and how to get the most out of the site management features, such as site synchronization and integrated e-mail. If you do find yourself in the unfortunate predicament of trying to fix broken links, you may also appreciate how Dreamweaver makes that task easier, too.

Preparing for Development

One of the first things I recommend is that you hold a brainstorming session with a few people who understand the goals you have for your Web site. The purpose of this session is to come up with possible features and elements for your Web site. A good brainstorming session is a nonjudgmental free-for-all — a chance for everyone involved to make all the suggestions that they can think of, whether realistic or not.

Not discrediting ideas at the brainstorming stage is important. Often an unrealistic idea can lead to a great idea that no one may have thought of otherwise. And if you stifle one person's creative ideas too quickly, that person may feel less inclined to voice other ideas in the future.

After the brainstorming session, you should have a long list of possible features to develop into your site. Now the challenge is to edit that list down to the best and most realistic ideas and then plan your course of development to ensure they all work well together when you're done.

Developing a New Site

In a nutshell, building a Web site involves creating individual pages and linking them to other pages. You need to have a home page (often called the *front page*) that links to pages representing different sections of the site. Those pages, in turn, can link to subsections that can then lead to additional subsections. A big part of Web site planning is determining how to divide your site into sections and deciding how pages link to one another. Dreamweaver makes it easy to create pages and set links, but how you organize those pages is up to you.

If you're new to this, you may think you don't need to worry much about expandability in your Web site. Think again. All good Web sites grow, and the bigger they get, the harder they are to manage. Planning the path of growth for your Web site when you get started makes a tremendous difference later. Neglecting to think about growth is probably one of the most common mistakes among new designers. They jump right into the home page, add a few pages, and then add a few more, throwing them all into one directory. Before they know it, they're working in chaos.

Managing your site's structure

Managing the structure of a Web site has two sides: the side that users see, which depends on how you set up links, and the behind-the-scenes side that depends on how you organize files and folders.

What the user sees

The side that the user sees is all about navigation. When users arrive at your home page, where do you direct them from there? How do they move around your site? A good Web site is designed so that users can navigate easily and intuitively and create their own path to the information most relevant to them. As you plan, make sure that users can access key information easily from more than one place in the site. Make sure that they can move back and forth between pages and sections and return to main pages and indexes in one step. Setting links is easy in Dreamweaver; the challenge is to make sure that they're easy for visitors to follow.

What you see

The second side to managing your Web site structure happens behind the scenes (where your users can't see the information, but you want some kind of organizational system to remember what's what). Before you get too far into building your site with Dreamweaver, spend some time thinking about the management issues involved in keeping track of all the files you create for your site. By *files,* I mean all the images, HTML pages, animations, sound files, and anything else you put in your Web site. As you create pages for your Web site, it's best to organize them in separate folders or directories.

I've seen many Web developers get 20 or 30 pages into a growing Web site and then realize that having all of their files in one folder was a mistake. In fact, it's more than a mistake; it's a mess. And to make matters worse, if you start moving things into new folders after the site grows, you have to change all the links. Not realizing this, some people start moving files around and then find that they have broken links and don't remember where things are supposed to go. Fortunately, Dreamweaver includes site management tools that automatically fixes links when you move pages around or create new folders, but starting out with a good plan is still better than having to clean up the structure later.

Before you build those first few pages, think about where you're likely to add content in the future. After you've put together a list of the key elements you want in your site, you're ready to create a storyboard or outline. Use the list and outline to create logical sections of a site that anticipate growth. For example, you may start with one page that lists all of your staff; however, after they see how cool it is, staff members may want to develop their own pages. In that case, you may want a separate folder dedicated to staff pages. If you're providing information for your sales team, you may find that you want a separate section for each product. As you add new sections, such as the ones I mention here, create new sub-directories or sub-folders to store their respective files. Creating sub-directories also makes it easier to manage a site that's built by multiple people. If each subsection has a separate folder, then each developer can better manage his or her own files.

Naming your site

Dreamweaver lets you call your files any name that works on your operating system, even something like `don't forget this is the photo the boss likes.htm`, but be aware that your Web server may use a different operating system that's more restrictive. Many of the servers on the Web are run on UNIX machines, which are not only case-sensitive, but they also don't allow spaces or special characters, except for the underscore (_). So coming up with names that work and that you — and everyone else on your site development team — can remember can be difficult. For example, `staff stuff.htm` is not a good file name because it has a space in it, but `staff_stuff.htm` is fine, because the underscore will work on any server, and you still have a break between the words to make them easier to read.

Under construction? No hard hats here!

All good Web sites are under construction — always. It's the nature of the Web. But build your site in such a way that you can add pages when they're ready instead of putting up placeholders. Don't greet your viewers with a guy in a yellow hat who seems to say, "You clicked this link for no good reason. Come back another day, and maybe we'll have something for you to see." Instead of creating "Under Construction" placeholders, create directory structures that make adding new pages later easy. You can let readers know that new things are coming by putting notices on pages that already have content — a message like "Come here next Thursday for a link to something even cooler" is a great idea. But never make users click a link and wait for a page to load, only to find that nothing but a guy with a hard hat is waiting for them.

Keeping track of the information on the pages in your Web site is much easier if you develop a naming structure that makes sense to everyone working on the project. For example, say your Web site is a newsletter that includes articles about the happenings in your town. Simple names like fire.html and truck.html may make sense to you this week because you're familiar with the top stories. But six months from now, if you're looking for that article on the big vehicle accident, you may not remember that you called it truck.html. Adding dates to the end of filenames can help you identify the files that you may need months — or even years — down the road. Remember that you can't use spaces, but you can use the underscore. So a good filename may be, `fire8_12_2002.html` or `truck8_19_2002.html` to help you remember that these articles were added in August of 2002.

Another option is to create a folder for each new update and name it with a date. For example, a folder named `stories8_2002` could contain all the stories from the August, 2002 issue. Then you can put `truck.html` and any other stories from that issue in the stories8_2002 folder, and you can find them by date as well as by filename. Talk to other people who may work on the site and make sure that you create a system that makes sense to everyone and is easy to explain if a new person joins the team. Whatever you do, don't name files randomly and throw them all in one directory. You should also consider documenting your naming system. Printing out a list of all the filenames in your site can also provide a handy reference if you're looking for a particular file.

Organizing images and handling links

Before I go on, I want to make a few points about organizing images in a Web site. I've heard many HTML teachers and consultants suggest that you place all of your images in a single folder at the top level of the directory structure and call it Images or Graphics. You may also find that some other HTML authoring tools require you to keep all of your images in one folder. Dreamweaver doesn't require an images folder, but it does let you specify one when you set up your site (for more on that, see Chapter 2.)

The advantage of keeping all of your images in one folder is that the path to all of your images can be the same, and you only have to go one place to look for them. However, the problem with using just one folder is that if all of your images are in one place, you're likely to end up with a long list of image files, making it easy to lose track of which image is which if you want to change one later.

A good alternative is to store your images in multiple image folders within the sub-folders that hold the HTML files where those images appear. For example, keep all of your staff photos for your staff pages in an images folder within a sub-folder called staff. If you have images that link throughout the site — a logo, for example — you may want to create an images folder at the top level of your directory structure for those images so they are easy to find from any folder in the site.

Dreamweaver makes no distinction between a folder called images and a folder by any other name, so you can call these folders whatever you like, including my personal favorite: Goofy_pictures.

Managing links

From the Site dialog box in Dreamweaver, you can move or rename local files, and Dreamweaver automatically adjusts all related links. This feature can save you tons of time, especially if you're trying to organize a large, haphazard site and have decided to add new folders and move pages into them for better organization.

One thing to note, however, is that this feature works only on local files. In order to rearrange files and automatically correct corresponding links, you need to have your entire site, or a self-contained section of it, stored on your local hard drive. You can use the FTP features in Dreamweaver to download a site before you work on it. Before this feature will work, you have to turn on the link-management options in Dreamweaver.

To turn on the Dreamweaver link-management options in Preferences, follow these steps:

1. **From the Dreamweaver menu bar, choose Edit⇨Preferences.**

   The Preferences dialog box opens.

2. **Select the General Category from the left side of the Preferences dialog box.**

3. **Choose Always, Never, or Prompt from the Update Links When Moving Files pop-up menu. (It's the fourth option in the dialog box.)**

   Choose Always to automatically update all links to and from a selected document whenever you move or rename it. Choose Prompt to first view a dialog box that lists all the files affected by the change. Choose Never if you don't want Dreamweaver to automatically update links.

If you choose Prompt, you are given the following two options whenever you move or rename a file: Update, to update the links in the file(s), or Don't Update, to leave the file(s) unchanged.

4. **Click OK to save your changes and exit the Preferences dialog box.**

If Check In/Out is enabled, Dreamweaver automatically attempts to check out the file before making any changes.

Changing and moving links

After you enable link-management options in the Preferences dialog box, you can use the Site panel to rename or rearrange files and folders with drag-and-drop ease.

To rename or rearrange files, follow these steps:

1. **Make sure the site you want to work on is selected. You can do this by selecting the site name from the pull-down menu at the top of the Site panel and choosing the site you want to work on from the list.**

   If you are working on only one site, you should already have your site selected. After a site is selected, the folders and files of that site are displayed in the Files Site panel on the right side of Dreamweaver's work area.

2. **Use the plus (+) and minus (–) signs to open and close folders in the Site panel.**

3. **Click to select a file or folder in the Site panel you want to change.**

4. **Drag that file or folder anywhere in the window to move it. For example, you can move a file into a folder and Dreamweaver will automatically change all of the related links.**

   This window works just like the Explorer window on a PC or the Finder on a Mac, except Dreamweaver tracks and fixes links when you move files through the Site panel, but if you move or rename files or folders in the Finder or Explorer, you risk breaking the links. For example, in Figure 3-1, I simply dragged a file from one into another folder in the site. The Update Files dialog box appears with a list of links that need to be updated because I chose Prompt in the Preferences dialog box.

5. **To rename a file in the Site dialog box, select the file, right-click (Windows) or Ctrl+click (Mac), and type the new name.**

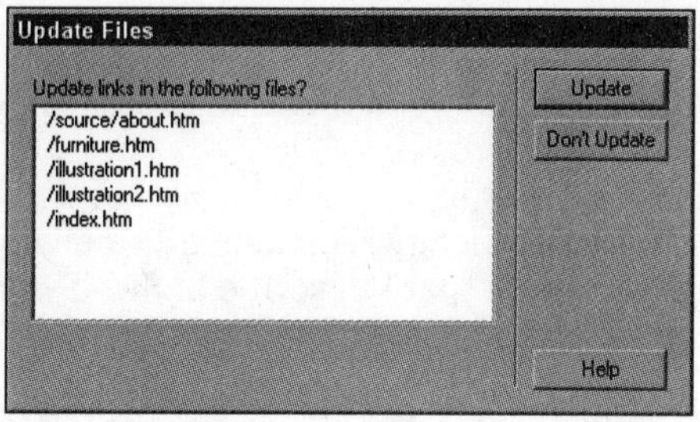

Figure 3-1:
The Update
Files dialog
box shows
you which
links will be
changed
when you
move or
rename a
file in the
Site
Window.

Update Files

Update links in the following files?

/source/about.htm
/furniture.htm
/illustration1.htm
/illustration2.htm
/index.htm

Update

Don't Update

Help

Making global changes to links

If you want to globally change a link to point at a new URL or to some other page on your site, you can use the Change Link Sitewide option to enter the new URL and change every reference automatically. You can use this option to change any kind of link, including mailto, ftp, and script links. For example, if the e-mail address that you list at the bottom of every page on your site changes, you can use this feature to fix it automatically — a real timesaver. You can also use this feature when you want a string of text to link to a different file than it currently does. For example, you could change every instance of the words *Enter this month's contest* to link to /contest/january.htm instead of /contest/december.htm throughout your Web site.

To change all links from one page on your site to another using the Change Link Sitewide feature, follow these steps:

1. **Make sure the site you want to work on is selected. You can do this by selecting the site name from the pull-down menu at the top of the Site panel and choosing the site you want to work on from the list.**

   If you double-click on a file name in the Files Site Panel, the page opens in Dreamweaver's work area, but it's not necessary to have any page selected or to have the page open to make global changes.

2. **Choose Site⇨Change Link Sitewide.**

3. **In the Change Link Sitewide dialog box that appears, use the Browse button to locate another filename or type a filename and relative path into the Into Links To box.**

   For example, if you are changing a link from one page on your site to another, type in or browse to find the old file name in the first text box, labeled Change All Links To.

4. **Type in the new filename or browse to find the page you want to change the links to and enter the name of that file in the Into Links To text box. (See Figure 3-2.)**

5. **Click OK.**

Dreamweaver updates any documents that link to the selected file.

Remember that these changes occur only on the local site until you change them on the remote server. To automatically reconcile these changes, use the Dreamweaver Synchronize Files option that I describe in the "Synchronizing Local and Remote Sites" section later in this chapter.

To change an e-mail link or a link to a remote URL, follow these steps:

1. **Make sure the site you want to work on is selected. You can do this by selecting the site name from the pull-down menu at the top of the Site panel and choosing the site you want to work on from the list.**

   If you are working on only one site, you should already have your site selected. After a site is selected, the folders and files of that site are displayed in the Files Site panel on the right side of Dreamweaver's work area.

2. **From the options in the Site panel, choose Site➪Change Link Sitewide.**

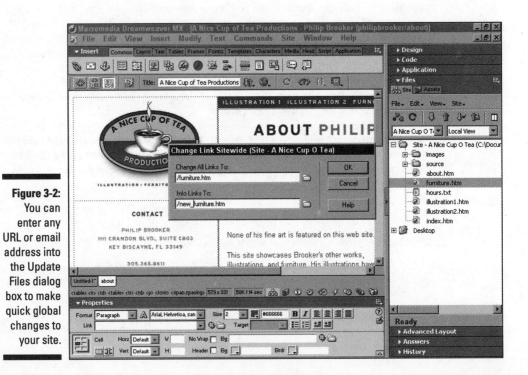

Figure 3-2:
You can enter any URL or email address into the Update Files dialog box to make quick global changes to your site.

3. **In the Change Link Sitewide dialog box that appears, type the URL or e-mail link that you want to change in the top text box, labeled Change All Links To.**

4. **In the second text box labeled Into Links To, type the new URL or e-mail address that you want to use. (Note that if you are entering an e-mail address, you need to include *mailto:* before the address. For example, mailto:editor@janinewarner.com.)**

5. **Click OK.**

   If you selected Prompt in the Link Update Preferences (described at the beginning of this section), Dreamweaver displays the Update Files dialog box listing all the places where the change will be made. Choose Update to make the change to all of the files listed; choose Don't Update to cancel. If you chose Always in the Link Update Preferences, Dreamweaver automatically executes the changes, updating all documents that contain the specified URL or e-mail address as soon as you choose OK.

Again, remember that these changes will not be reflected on the live site until you FTP the changes to your server. The best way to do this is to use the Dreamweaver Synchronize Files option described later in this chapter.

Finding and Fixing Broken Links

If you're trying to rein in a chaotic Web site, or if you just want to check a site because you fear that it may have broken links, you'll be pleased to discover the Check Links feature. You can use Check Links to verify the links in a single file or an entire Web site, and you can use it to automatically fix all the referring links at once.

Here's an example of what Check Links can do. Assume that someone on your team (because you would never do such a thing yourself) has changed the name of a file from new.htm to old.htm without using the Dreamweaver automatic link update process to fix the corresponding links. Maybe this person changed the name using another program or simply changed the name in the Finder on the Mac or in the Explorer in Windows. Changing the filename was easy, but what this person may not have realized is that if he or she didn't change the links to the file when the file was renamed, the links are now broken.

If only one page links to the file your clueless teammate changed, fixing it isn't such a big deal. As long as you remember what file the page links from, you can simply open that page and use the Property Inspector to reset the link the same way you would create a link in the first place. (You can find out all the basics of link creation in Chapter 2.)

But many times, a single page in a Web site is referred to by links on many other pages. When that's the case, fixing all the link references can be time-consuming, and it's all too easy to forget some of them. That's why Check Links is so helpful. First, it serves as a diagnostic tool that identifies broken links throughout the site (so you don't have to second-guess where someone may have changed a filename or moved a file). Then it serves as a global fix-it tool. You can use the Check Links dialog box to identify the page a broken link should go to, and then you can have Dreamweaver automatically fix all links referring to that page. The following section walks you through the process.

If you are working on a dynamic, database-driven site or if your site was altered with programming that was done outside of Dreamweaver, the Check Links feature may not report every bad link. For example, some sites use scripts that generate links, like the new story links posted on a news sites. If I'm trying to find `news_fire0216.htm` and my function reads `response.write 'news_' + $stories + '.htm"` where `"fire0216"` or it is stored in a variable elsewhere on the page or in a database, Dreamweaver will not be able to make the correction.

Checking for broken links

To check a site for broken links, follow these steps:

1. **Make sure the site you want to work on is selected. You can do this by selecting the site name from the pull-down menu at the top of the Site panel and choosing the site you want to work on from the list.**

   Link checking works only for sites listed in the Dreamweaver Site dialog box. For more information about the Site dialog box and how to set up a new site or import an existing one, see Chapter 2.

2. **From the Site panel, choose Site⇨Check Links Sitewide.**

   The Check Links Sitewide dialog box opens at the bottom of the page, just under the Property Inspector, as shown in Figure 3-3. The dialog box displays a list of filenames with broken links, as well as any pages, images or other items that are not linked to any other pages in the site. This is handy if you want to clean up old images or other elements you are no longer using on the site.

Most service providers limit the amount of space on your server and charge extra if you exceed that limit. Deleting unused files can help you save valuable server space, especially if they are image or multimedia files. But remember, just because you delete them from your hard drive, doesn't mean they are off the server. Dreamweaver should remove them when you use the Synchronize option described later in this chapter, but it's always good to double check.

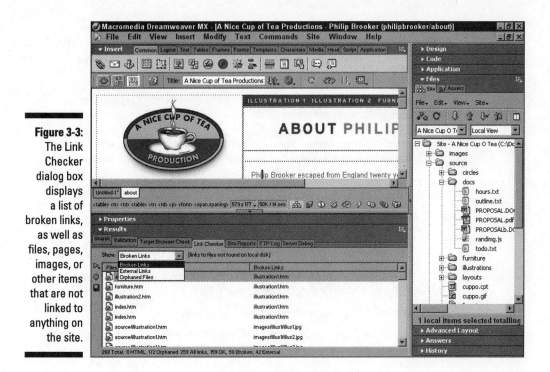

Figure 3-3:
The Link
Checker
dialog box
displays
a list of
broken links,
as well as
files, pages,
images, or
other items
that are not
linked to
anything on
the site.

Be very careful of Dreamweaver's Synchronize option if you have special administrative pages, such as stats files, which are often added to your server space by your service provider to track traffic on your site. Remember, any files that are on your server that are not on your local computer may be deleted when you synchronize. The best way around this is to download those files before you synchronize so Dreamweaver knows you want to keep them. To be completely safe, consider using another method for sending your files to your server. (You'll find a couple of FTP program recommendations at the end of this chapter that you can use as alternatives.)

If you find broken links, the next section, "Fixing broken links," shows you how Dreamweaver automatically updates multiple link references to make fixing them fast and easy.

Fixing broken links

Broken links are one of the most embarrassing problems in Web design. After you identify a broken link in your site, you should feel compelled to fix it immediately. Nothing can turn your users off faster than clicking a link and getting a "File Not Found" error page (also known as a *404 error* because that's usually the message viewers see if they click a broken link). Fortunately, Dreamweaver makes fixing broken links simple by providing quick access to files with broken links and automating the process of fixing multiple links to the same file.

After using the Link Checker, described in the preceding section, to identify broken links, follow these steps to use the Results panel to fix them:

1. **With the Results panel open at the bottom of the page, double-click a filename that Dreamweaver has identified as a broken link.**

   The page and its corresponding Property Inspector open. The Results panel should remain visible.

2. **Select the broken link or image on the open page.**

   In the example in Figure 3-4, I've selected a broken image and I'm fixing the link by using the Property Inspector to find the correct image name.

3. **In the Property Inspector, click the folder icon to the right of the Src text box to identify the correct image file.**

   The Select Image Source dialog box appears.

   If you already know the location of the file that you want to link to, you can type the correct filename and path in the text box or browse to find the image. The correct image must be in the site's root folder.

   You fix links to pages just like you fix links to images, except you type the name of the correct file into the Link text box or click the folder icon next to it to find the file in your site folder.

4. **Click the filename and choose the Select button; then click OK.**

   The link automatically changes to reflect the new filename and location. If you're replacing an image, the image file reappears on the page.

If the link that you correct appears in multiple pages, Dreamweaver prompts you with a dialog box asking if you want to fix the remaining broken link references to the file. Click Yes to automatically correct all other references. Click No to leave other files unchanged.

Figure 3-4:
Use the
Select
Image
Source
dialog box
to fix broken
image links.

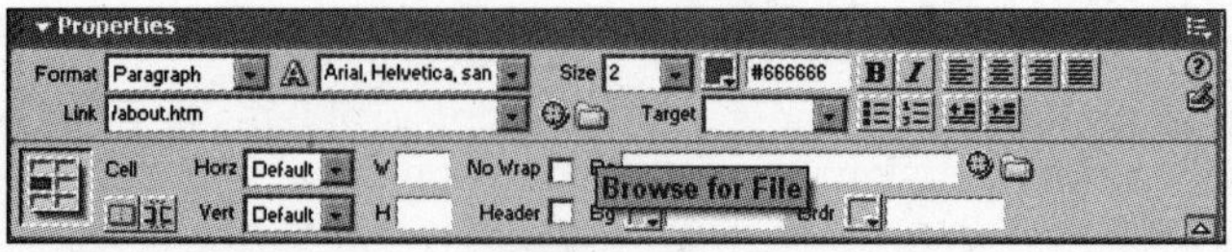

Using the Site Reporting Feature to Test Your Work

Before you put your site online for all the world to see, it's a good idea to check your work using Dreamweaver's Site Reporting feature. You can create a variety of reports, and even customize them, to identify problems with external links, redundant and empty tags, untitled documents and missing Alt text. These are all easy things to miss — especially when you're working on a tight deadline — and they can cause real problems for your viewers if you leave them unfixed. Before Dreamweaver added this great new feature, finding these kinds of mistakes was a tedious and time-consuming task. Now you can run a report that identifies these errors for you and use Dreamweaver to fix mistakes across your entire site automatically.

Follow these steps to produce a Site Report of your entire Web site:

1. **Make sure the site you want to work on is selected. You can do this by selecting the site name from the pull-down menu at the top of the Site panel and choosing the site you want to work on from the list.**

   See Chapter 2 for step-by-step instructions for defining your site if you haven't done it already.

2. **From the Site panel, choose Site⇨Reports.**

   The Reports dialog box appears (see Figure 3-5).

3. **From the Report On pull-down menu, choose Entire Local Site (see Figure 3-5).**

   You can also choose to check only a single page by opening the page in Dreamweaver and then choosing Current Document from the Report On pull-down menu. You can also run a report on Selected Files or on a particular Folder. If you choose Selected Files, you must have already selected the pages you want to check in the Files Site panel.

4. **Select the type of report you want by putting check marks next to the report names in the Select Reports section of the Reports dialog box.**

   Table 3-1 describes the kind of report you get with each option. You can select as many reports as you want.

The Workflow options are available only if you have already selected Check In/Out in the Remote Info section of Site Definition panel and selected Maintain Design Notes in the Design Notes section of the Site Definition Panel.

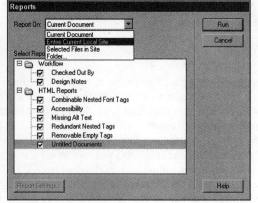

Figure 3-5:
You can
select any
or all of the
options in
the Reports
dialog box
to run simul-
taneously.

Table 3-1	Site Report Options
Report Name	**Results**
Check Out By	Produces a list of files that are checked out of the site and identifies the name of the person who has checked them out.
Design Notes	Produces a list of Design Notes (see Chapter 4 for more on how to use Design Notes).
Combinable Nested Font Tags	Produces a list of all instances where nested tags could be combined. For example, `<font color="#00000"><font size="2">Great Web Sites You Should Visit</font></font>` would be identified because you can simplify the code by combining the two font tags into: `<font color="#00000" size="2">Great Web Sites You Should Visit</font>`.
Missing Alt Text	Produces a list of all the Image tags that do not include Alt text. *Alt text* is used to add alternative text to an image tag. If the image isn't displayed for some reason (many people choose to surf with images turned off), the Alt text appears in place of the image. Alt text is also important to the blind because special browsers that "read" pages to site visitors can't interpret text that is part of an image, but can "read" the Alternative text included in the image tag.
Redundant Nested Tags	Produces a list of all places where there are redundant nested tags. For example, `<center>Good headlines <center>are harder to write</center> than you might think</center>` would be identified because you could simplify the code by removing the second center tag to make the code look like this: `<center>Good headlines are harder to write than you might think</center>`.

Report Name	Results
Removable Empty Tags	Produces a list of all of the empty tags on your site. These often occur if you delete an image or text section without deleting all the tags associated with it.
Untitled Documents	Produces a list of filenames that don't have a title or have duplicate titles. The title tag is easy to forget because it does not display in the body of the page. The title tag contains the text that appears at the very top of the browser window and is also the text that appears in the favorites list when someone saves your page in their browser. And if that's not enough, a good title tag is key to getting good placement in many search engines, as well.

5. **Click Run to create the report(s).**

   If you haven't already done so, you may be prompted to save your file, define your site, or select a folder (see Chapter 2 for more information on defining a site in Dreamweaver.)

   The Results dialog box opens (see Figure 3-6 displaying a list of problems found on your site). You can sort the list by different categories by clicking the column heading. You can also sort by filename, line number, and description. If you run several reports at the same time, you can keep all the results windows open at the same time.

6. **Select any item in the Results dialog box to see a detailed description of the problem, as shown in Figure 3-6.**

7. **Double-click any item to open the corresponding file in the Document window.**

8. **Use the Property Inspector or other Dreamweaver feature to fix the identified problem and then save the file.**

   Remember that your changes aren't applied to your live site until you update your server. Use the Synchronize feature, described in the next section of this chapter, to update all of your changes at once.

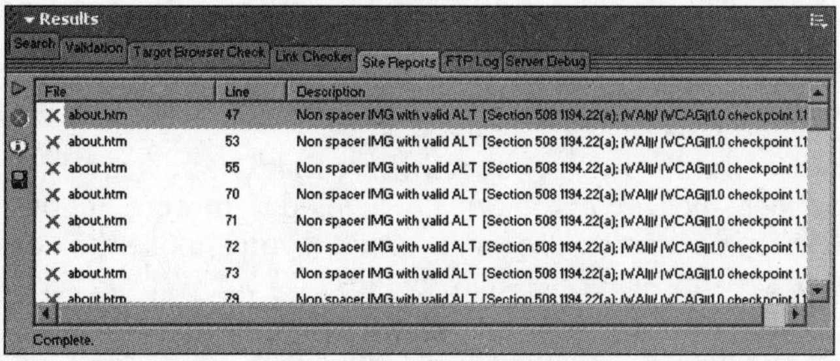

Figure 3-6:
The Results dialog box displays a list of problems found on your site.

Synchronizing Local and Remote Sites

After you've done all of this cleanup and organization on the local copy of your Web site, you want to make sure that those changes are reflected on the live site on your Web server. Fortunately, Dreamweaver makes that easy, too, by including a feature that automatically synchronizes the files in both places. Before you synchronize your sites, you can use the Site FTP dialog box to verify which files you want to put on or get from your remote server. Dreamweaver also confirms which files are updated after you've completed the synchronization.

Follow these steps to synchronize your Web site:

1. **Make sure the site you want to work on is selected. Do this by choosing Site⇨Open Site and selecting the name of the site you want to work on.**

   See Chapter 2 for step-by-step instructions for defining your site if you haven't done it already.

2. **Select the Connects To Remote Host button to log on to your remote site.**

   Chapter 2 shows you how to set up this feature for your site.

3. **Choose Site⇨Synchronize.**

   A pop-up menu appears.

4. **From the pop-up menu, choose to make your local site the master.**

   You also have the option to make the remote site the master. This choice may be useful if multiple people are working on the same site from remote locations.

5. **Choose which option you want to use to copy the files:**

   • **Put Newer Files to Remote:** This option copies the most recently modified files from your local site to the remote site.

   • **Get Newer Files from Remote:** This option copies the most recently modified files from your remote site to the local site.

   • **Get and Put Newer Files:** This option updates both the local and remote sites with the most recent versions of all the files.

6. **Select whether or not you want to delete the files on your local or remote site.**

   Be aware that if you don't specify here that Dreamweaver should *not* delete files, files are automatically deleted if they are not on the site you designated as master. That means that if you choose the local site as the master, Dreamweaver deletes any files on your Web server that do not exist in the local version on your hard drive. If you choose the remote site as the master, Dreamweaver deletes any files in your local site that do not exist on the remote site.

7. Click OK.

The Site FTP dialog box displays the files that are about to be changed.

This is your last chance before files are deleted! In the Site FTP dialog box, you have the option to verify the files you want to delete, put, and get. If you don't want Dreamweaver to alter a file, deselect it now or forever live with the consequences.

8. Click OK.

All approved changes are automatically made, and Dreamweaver updates the Site FTP dialog box with the status.

9. A dialog box appears, and you can choose to save the verification information to a local file.

Choose to save or not save the verification information. Having the option to save this information can be handy later if you want to review your changes.

Chapter 4

Coordinating Your Design Work

Strive for consistency in all your designs — except when you're trying to be unpredictable. A little surprise here and there can keep your Web site alive. But, generally, most Web sites work best, and are easiest to navigate, when they follow a consistent design theme. Dreamweaver offers several features to help you develop and maintain a consistent look and feel across your site, whether you're working on a Web site by yourself or you're coordinating a team of developers.

In this chapter, you discover three of my favorite Dreamweaver features — templates, Library items, and the Tracing image — and find out how they combine to make your work faster and easier to manage. I also introduce you to Design Notes, the History panel, and the Quick Tag Editor.

Templating Your Type

Many Web design programs boast about their HTML templates. But what they really mean is that they include some ready-made page designs with the program. Dreamweaver takes this concept a few leaps farther by providing template design features that enable you to create the basic design of a page and then limit the sections other developers can and can't alter. This is a valuable feature if you are working with a team of people with varying skill levels. For example, if you're building a site for a real estate company and you want to let the employees update the sales listings without being able to mess up the page design, a template can be the perfect solution.

When you create a template, you essentially create the outline of what the page should look like. Usually a template represents a design with placeholders but no actual content. You can use templates to create documents for your site that have a common structure and appearance. And here's a great bonus: When you're ready to redesign your site, simply go back and edit the template itself, and then you can automatically apply the changes to every page on the site that uses that template (for example, if you change the logo for your company or add a new navigation element that you want to appear on every page in a section).

Templates are best used when you are creating a number of pages that share certain characteristics, such as background color or image placement. Rather than setting the correct properties for every new page or making the same changes on page after page, you can use a template to make changes to several pages at once. For example, if you have a section with all the bios of your staff, you can create a template and just replace the image and text on each page.

Dreamweaver MX includes a wealth of ready-to-use Web Components. You'll find these in the new document dialog box when you choose File⇨New. These components can help you get your site designed quickly, using sample layouts, Dream Templates, framesets, and many other goodies.

Typing your template

One of the greatest advantages in using the Dreamweaver template feature is that you can specify which areas of the template can be changed. This is especially useful if you're working with people who have various skill levels in Web development, and you want a more advanced designer to create a page that a less experienced person can't mess up later. With that goal in mind, a template has editable regions and locked (noneditable) regions. Use *editable regions* for content that changes, such as a product description or events in a calendar. Use locked regions for static, unchanging content, such as a logo or site navigation elements.

For example, if you're publishing an online magazine, the navigation options may not change from page to page, but the titles and stories do. To indicate the style and location of an article or headline, you can define *placeholder text* (an editable region, with all the size and font attributes already specified). When you're ready to add a new feature, you simply select the placeholder text and either paste in a story or type over the selected area. You do the same thing to create a placeholder for an image. By default, templates are locked. You can add content to the template, but when you save the template, all content is marked noneditable automatically. If you create a document from such a template, Dreamweaver warns you that the document will not contain any editable regions. To make a template useful, you must create editable regions or mark existing content areas as editable. (The step-by-step instructions in the following section, "Creating templates," walk you through the process.)

You can modify a template even after you've used it to create documents. Then when you update documents that use the template, the noneditable sections of those documents are updated to match the changes you made in the template.

While you're editing the template itself, you can make changes to any part of the file, be it the editable or locked regions. While editing a document made from a template, however, you can make changes only to the editable regions of the document. If you go back and change a template after it is created, Dreamweaver gives you the option of having those changes reflected in all the pages you've created with that template or only the page you are currently editing.

Creating templates

Creating a template is as easy as creating any other file in Dreamweaver, as you can see in the following steps. You can start with an existing HTML document and modify it to suit your needs, or you can create a completely new document. When you save a file as a template, the file is stored automatically in the Templates folder of the main folder for the Web site. Templates must be saved in this common folder for the automated features in Dreamweaver to work properly. If you don't already have a Templates folder in your Web site, Dreamweaver automatically creates one when you store your first template.

The Template features work only if you have defined your Web site in Dreamweaver. If you aren't sure how to do this, refer to Chapter 2.

All elements in a template are locked by default, except the document title section, which is indicated by the <TITLE></TITLE> tags. For the template to be of any use for building new pages, you must make other areas of the page editable as well. Remember that you can always return to the template and make more areas editable or remove the capability to edit certain areas later. To create a template with editable regions, follow these steps:

1. **From the Files panel, choose the Assets tab and then select the Templates icon (see Figure 4-1).**

   The Templates panel in the Files Assets panel opens in the right side of your screen.

2. **In the Templates panel, click the icon that is an arrow with dots in the top-right corner and choose New Template from the drop-down menu that opens.**

   A new, untitled template is added to the list of templates in the panel.

3. **With the template still selected, type a name for the template just as you would name any file in the Finder on a Mac or the Explorer on a PC.**

   The new template is added to the Templates for Site list, as shown in Figure 4-2.

Figure 4-1:
The
Templates
panel
makes it
easy to
create and
organize
templates.

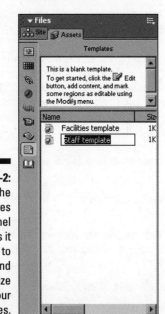

Figure 4-2:
The
Templates
panel
makes it
easy to
access and
organize
your
templates.

4. After you name the new template, double-click the name to open it.

The template page opens in Dreamweaver as any other HTML page would, except that the filename ends with the extension .dwt.

You can now edit this page as you would any other HTML page, inserting images, text, tables, and so on.

5. Choose Modify⇨Page Properties to specify background, text, and link colors.

Again, this works just like it would in any other Dreamweaver document.

6. To make an image or text area editable, select the image or text and choose Modify⇨Templates⇨Make Attribute Editable (shown in Figure 4-3).

The Editable Tag Attributes dialog box opens. The image or text that you select as editable becomes an area that can be changed in any page created with the template. Areas that you don't mark as editable will become locked and can be changed only if you modify the template itself.

7. From the Attribute pull-down list, choose the attribute that you want to be editable.

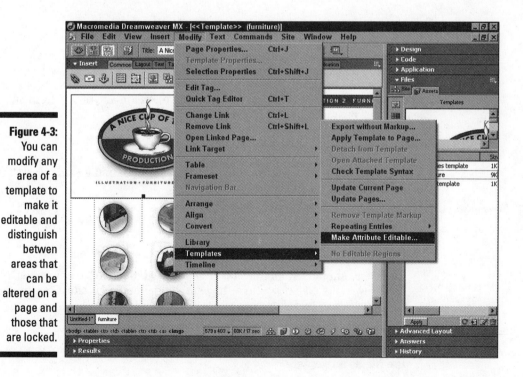

Figure 4-3:
You can modify any area of a template to make it editable and distinguish betwen areas that can be altered on a page and those that are locked.

8. **Click the Make Attribute Editable box and fill in the options.**

   The attribute options will vary depending on whether you selected an image, text, or other element on the page to make an editable region. These options enable you to control not only if an image can be changed, but which attributes of the image tag may be altered when the template is used.

9. **To make other images or text areas editable, repeat Steps 6 and 7.**

10. **Save your template and close the file when you're finished.**

You can make an entire table or an individual table cell editable, but you can't make multiple cells editable all at once, unless you have merged them first. You have to select each cell one at a time if you want to make some of the cells in a table editable, but not others. (For more about creating HTML tables, see Chapter 6.) Layers and layer content are also treated as separate elements, but they can also be modified to be editable. Making a layer editable enables you to change the position of that layer. Making layer content editable means that you can change the content of the layer, such as the text or image in the layer. (For more information about layers, see Chapter 9.)

Saving any page as a template

Sometimes you get partway through creating a page before it occurs to you that it would be better to make the page a template. Other times, you may have a page that someone else created, and you decide that you want to make it into a template. Either way, it's as easy to create a template from an existing page as it is to create a new one.

To save a page as a template, follow these steps:

1. **Open the page that you want to turn into a template the same way that you open any other file in Dreamweaver.**

2. **Choose File⇨Save as Template.**

   The Save As Template dialog box appears.

3. **Use the drop-down menu next to the Site text box to select a site.**

   The menu should list all the sites that you've defined in Dreamweaver. If you're working on a new site or haven't yet defined your site, Chapter 2 shows you how to define your site.

4. **In the Save As text box, type a name for the template.**

5. **Click the Save button in the top-right corner of the dialog box to save the file as a template.**

6. **Make any changes that you want and choose File⇨Save to save the page. Follow the steps in the earlier section, "Creating templates," to make areas editable.**

   Notice that the file now has the .dwt extension, indicating that it's a template. You can now make changes to this template the same way you edit any other template.

7. **Choose File⇨Close to close the file.**

Using Templates

After you create all these great templates, you'll want to put them to use. You can use templates to create or modify all the pages in your Web site or just use them for specific areas or sections. Using a template to create a new page is similar to creating any other HTML page.

To use a template to create a page, follow these steps:

1. **Choose File⇨New.**

2. **Select the Templates tab.**

   The Template dialog box opens. In this newest version of Dreamweaver, the New dialog box provides access to all of the file formats you can create in Dreamweaver.

3. **From the Templates section in the Category panel on the left, choose the Template collection you want to use. (Dreamweaver now includes several ready-made templates.)**

4. **Open any template by double-clicking its name.**

5. **Choose File⇨Save and name the new file as you would any other HTML page.**

6. **You can now edit any of the regions of the page that are editable using Dreamweaver's regular editing features.**

   Note: Dreamweaver's Convert Layers to Tables feature is not available on pages created with templates.

Remember that only the editable regions of the template can be altered when you use a template to create a page. If you want to change a locked region of the page, you have to either remove the template association from the file or open the template and change that area of the file to make it editable by revising the template itself.

You can remove the template association from a file by selecting Modify➪Templates➪Detach From *templatename*.dwt. This action makes the file fully editable again, but changes you make to the template are not reflected on a detached page. To edit the template itself, choose Modify➪Templates➪Open Attached Template. Alternatively, you can select Modify➪Templates➪Remove Template Markup to remove all template code from a page.

You can also apply a template to an existing page. When you apply a template to an existing document, the content in the template is added to the content already in the document. If a template is already applied to the page, Dreamweaver attempts to match editable areas that have the same name in both templates and to insert the contents from the editable regions of the page into the editable regions in the new template.

You can apply a template to an existing page by using any one of the following techniques:

✔ Choose Modify➪Templates➪Apply Template to Page and then double-click the name of a template to apply it to the page.

✔ Drag the template from the Template panel to the Document window.

✔ Select the template in the Template panel and choose Apply from the pull-down list available through the arrow at the top-right corner of the Template panel.

Making Global Changes with Templates

The greatest advantage of using templates is that you can apply changes to all the pages that use a template all at once. Suppose that you redesign your logo or want to change the positioning of key elements in a section of your site. If you've built those elements into a template, you can make the change and update all the places they are used on the site automatically — a real time saver. You can use the template update commands to update a single page or to update all the places that template has been used in the entire site.

To change a template and update the current page, follow these steps:

1. **Open a document that uses the template that you want to change.**

2. **Choose Modify➪Templates➪Open Attached Template.**

   The template opens.

3. **Modify the template as you would edit a new template.**

   For example, to modify the template's page properties, choose Modify➪Page Properties.

4. **When you're finished making changes to the template, choose Modify➪Templates➪Update Current Page.**

   The page you have open changes to reflect the changes you've made to the template.

   If you save a template after making changes, the Update Pages dialog box opens automatically, prompting you to choose the page or pages you want to update. Choose All to update all pages at once, or select one or more pages to update them individually. You can also choose Don't Update if you aren't ready to apply the changes.

To change a template and update all the files in your site that use that template at once, follow these steps:

1. **Open an existing template and make the changes that you want to apply.**

2. **Choose Modify➪Templates➪Update Pages.**

   The Update Pages dialog box appears.

3. **From the Look In drop-down list, choose one of the following options:**

   • **Entire Site:** Select the site name to update all pages in the selected site to all the corresponding templates.

   • **Files That Use:** Select the template name to update all pages in the current site that use that template.

   Make sure that Templates is selected in the Update option.

4. **Click Start to run the update process.**

   When the update process is completed, the Updated Pages dialog box opens with a report on which pages were altered.

Reusing Elements with the Library Feature

The Library feature is not a common feature in other Web design programs, so the concept may be new to you even if you've been developing Web sites for a while. The more experienced you are, however, the more likely you are to appreciate the value of this feature and the time it can save you.

The Dreamweaver Library feature was designed to automate the process of inserting and changing elements that appear on multiple pages in a Web site. You can save any element as a Library item — for example, a logo or a navigation row of images and links. You can then insert that element (or collection of elements) on any page by simply dragging it from the Library to the new page.

Even better, if you ever need to change the Library element (by adding a link or image, for example), you can change the element in the Library and let Dreamweaver automatically update the change throughout the site. Libraries are not shared among sites, so each site you define must have its own Library.

A *Library item* is a snippet of code that can contain image references and links. Like templates, Library items are a great way to share the work of your best designers with less experienced ones. For example, one designer could create a logo and another the navigation elements, and then these could be placed in the Library and made available to the rest of the team. However, you have more flexibility with Library items because they are elements that can be placed anywhere on any page, even multiple times.

Library items can be any element from the body of a document, such as text, tables, forms, images, Java applets, and plug-in files. Library elements are efficient because Dreamweaver stores the snippet of code like a document in the Library folder and then updates the links to it from wherever the Library element is applied, which makes it easy to store one image in one place and use it all over your site. Library items can also contain behaviors, but there are special requirements for editing the behaviors in Library items.

Library items cannot contain timelines or style sheets because the code for these elements is part of the Head area of an HTML file. (For more information on behaviors and timelines, see Chapter 10; for more on style sheets, see Chapter 8.)

Creating and using Library items

The following sections lead you through the steps for creating a Library item, adding one to a page, and editing a Library item when an element changes. For these steps to work appropriately, you must do them carefully, in sequential order. Before creating or using Library items, you must first define a site or open an existing site. If you're not sure how to do this, see Chapter 2.

Creating a Library item

To create a Library item that you can use on multiple pages on your site, follow these steps:

1. **Open any existing file that has images, text, or other elements on the page.**

   A navigational row with images and links that are used throughout your Web site is an ideal use of the Library feature.

2. **From this page, select an element that you want to use as a Library item, such as an image.**

3. **From the Files panel, choose the Assets tab and then select the Library icon (see Figure 4-4).**

4. **Name the element as you name any file in the Finder on a Mac or in Explorer on a PC.**

   When you name a Library item, you automatically save it to the Library, so you can then easily apply it to any new or existing page in your site. All Library items are listed in the Library section of the Assets panel shown in Figure 4-4.

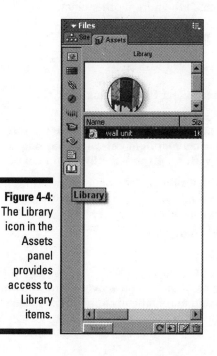

Figure 4-4:
The Library icon in the Assets panel provides access to Library items.

Adding a Library item to a page

You can take elements out of the Library as easily as you put them in. When you add a Library item to a page, the content (or a link to it) is inserted in the document.

To add a Library item to a page, follow these steps:

1. **Create a new document in Dreamweaver or open any existing file.**

2. **From the Files panel, choose the Assets tab and then select the Library icon.**

   The Library panel opens in the Assets panel on the right side of the work area.

 3. **Drag an item from the Library panel to the Document window.**

 Alternatively, you can select an item in the Library panel and click the Insert button.

 The item automatically appears on the page. After you've inserted a Library item on a page, you can use any of Dreamweaver's formatting features to position it on the page.

Highlighting Library items

Library items are highlighted to distinguish them from other elements on a page. You can customize the highlight color for Library items and show or hide the highlight color in Highlighting preferences.

To change or hide Library highlighting, follow these steps:

 1. **Choose Edit⇨Preferences and then select Highlighting from the Category section on the left.**

 2. **Click the color box to select a color for Library items. Check the box next to Show to display of the Library highlight color on your pages. Leave the box blank if you don't want to display the highlight color.**

 For the Library highlight color to be visible in the Document window, you must also be sure that the Show Library Items box is checked in the Highlighting section of the Preferences dialog box.

 3. **Click OK to close the Preferences dialog box.**

Changing a Library item

One of the biggest timesaving advantages of the Dreamweaver Library feature is that you can make changes to items and automatically apply those changes to multiple pages. First, you edit the original Library item file; then you can choose to update the edited item in any one or all the documents in the current site.

To edit a Library item and then update one or all the pages on which you use that item, follow these steps:

 1. **From the Files panel, choose the Assets tab and then select the Library icon.**

 The Library panel opens in the Assets panel on the right side of the work area.

 2. **Select any item listed in the Library panel and double-click to open the item.**

 Dreamweaver opens a new window for editing the Library item.

 Notice that the background of the Library item is gray. Because the Library item is just a snippet of code, there is no <BODY> tag in which to specify a background color. Don't worry over this — the Library item will have the same background color or image as the page where you use the Library item.

3. **Using the editing functions, make any changes you want to the Library item.**

   For example, you can redirect the link of text items or images, edit the wording or font, or add images or text.

4. **Choose File⇨Save to save changes to the original item or choose File⇨Save As and give it a new name to create a new Library item.**

   The Update Library Items dialog box opens, displaying a list of all pages where the Library item appears.

5. **Select the page or pages you want to update and choose Update. To cancel without making changes, choose Don't Update.**

   Because Library items can contain only Body elements, but no Body attributes, the Style panel and the Timeline Inspector are unavailable when you are editing a Library item. Timeline and style sheet code are parts of the Head area of a Web page. The Behavior Inspector is also unavailable because it inserts code into the Head as well as the Body.

Making Library items editable

As I say at the beginning of this chapter, you should strive for design consistency in *almost* all things. If you find that you want to alter a Library item in just one place, however, or make just a couple of exceptions, you can override the Library feature by breaking the link between the Library and the item in the document.

Remember that after you've broken that connection, you cannot update the Library item automatically.

To make a Library item editable, follow these steps:

1. **Open any file that contains a Library item and double-click the Library item.**

   The Property Inspector displays the Library item options.

2. **Choose the Detach from Original button.**

   A warning message appears, letting you know that if you proceed with detaching the Library item from the original, it will no longer be possible to update this occurrence of it when the original is edited.

3. **Click OK to detach the Library item.**

Using a Tracing Image to Guide Your Layout

Macromedia's Tracing Image feature is unique in the world of Web design tools, although the concept dates back to the earliest days of design. The Tracing Image feature enables you to use a graphic as a guide to your page design, much like you would put thin paper over an existing image to re-create it by tracing over it.

The Tracing Image feature is ideal for people who like to first create a design in a program such as Photoshop or Fireworks and then model their Web page after it. By using the Tracing Image feature, you can insert an image into the background of your page for the purpose of "tracing" over it. Then you can position layers or create table cells on top of the Tracing image, making it easier to exactly re-create your design in HTML. You can use JPG, GIF, or PNG format images as tracing images, and you can create them in any graphics application that supports these formats.

Although the tracing image appears in the background of a page, it doesn't take the place of a background image and is never displayed in a browser.

To add a tracing image to your page, follow these steps:

1. **Create a new page or open any existing page in Dreamweaver.**

2. **Choose View➪Tracing Image➪Load.**

   The Select Image Source dialog box opens.

3. **Double-click the filename or highlight the image that you want to use as a Tracing image; then choose Select.**

   The Page Properties dialog box opens and the image name and its path are displayed in the Tracing Image text area.

   Alternatively, you can choose Modify➪Page Properties and use the Browse button next to the Tracing Image text area to select a Tracing image.

4. **Use the Transparency slider to set the opacity for the Tracing image. I set it at 44%, as shown in Figure 4-5.**

   Lowering the transparency level causes the Tracing image to appear faded, making it easier to distinguish between the Tracing image and editable elements on the page. You can set the transparency level to suit your preferences, but somewhere around 50 percent seems to work well with most images.

5. **Click OK.**

   A tracing image appears in the document window.

Figure 4-5:
The Tracing
Image
feature lets
you place
an image
behind your
pages that
you can use
to "trace"
your design
in HTML.

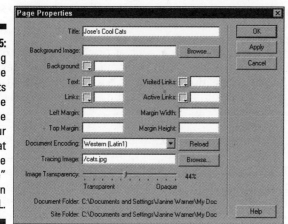

If a tracing image doesn't appear, make sure that you have a check next to Show when you choose View➪Tracing Image➪Show.

A Tracing image doesn't replace a background image. The Tracing image itself is visible only when you're editing the page in the document window; it never appears when the page is loaded into a browser.

You have a few other options with the Tracing Image feature. Select View➪ Tracing Image to reveal the following options:

- ✔ **Show:** Hides the tracing image if you want to check your work without it being visible but don't want to remove it.

- ✔ **Align with Selection:** Enables you to automatically line up the tracing image with a selected element on a page.

- ✔ **Adjust Position:** Enables you to use the arrow keys or enter X, Y coordinates to control the position of the tracing image behind the page.

- ✔ **Reset Position:** Resets the tracing image to 0, 0 on the X, Y coordinates.

Keeping in Touch with Design Notes

Design Notes are ideal for communicating with other developers who are working on your site. This Dreamweaver feature works like the comment tag, but with a lot more privacy because only those with password access to your site will ever see them. Many developers use *comment tags* — HTML code that enables you to embed text in a page that won't display in a browser — to share information with each other. But anyone who views the source of your documents can see a comment tag, so it's not a very secure way to share information.

If you want to hide sensitive information, such as pricing structures or creative strategies, yet still be able to share it with other members of your development team, use Design Notes. Information saved as a Design Note in Dreamweaver can travel with any HTML file or image, even if the file is transferred from one Web site to another or from Fireworks to Dreamweaver.

To activate the Design Notes feature, follow these steps:

1. **Choose Site⇨Edit Sites.**

   The Edit Sites dialog box opens.

2. **Click to select the site you want to work on and then click Edit.**

   The Site Definition dialog box opens.

3. **In the Category list at the left, choose Design Notes.**

   The Design Notes page appears.

4. **If it's not already selected, click to select the Maintain Design Notes option.**

   With this option selected, whenever a file is copied, moved, renamed, or deleted, the associated Design Notes file is also copied, moved, renamed, or deleted with it.

5. **If you want your Design Notes to be sent with your files when they are uploaded to your server, click to select the Upload Design Notes for Sharing option.**

   If you're making notes only to yourself and don't want them to be associated with the page when you upload them to the server, deselect this option and Design Notes will be maintained locally but not uploaded with your files.

6. **Click OK in the Site Definition dialog box; then click Done in the Define Sites dialog box.**

   The Site dialog box opens.

7. **You can now add Design Notes to your files by choosing File⇨Design Notes to open the Design Notes dialog box.**

To add Design Notes to a document, follow these steps:

1. **Open the file you want to add a Design Note to and choose File⇨Design Notes.**

   The Design Notes dialog box opens (see Figure 4-6).

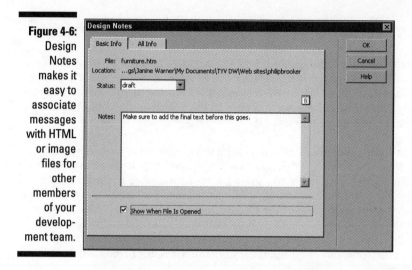

Figure 4-6:
Design Notes makes it easy to associate messages with HTML or image files for other members of your development team.

2. **Choose the status of the document from the Status drop-down list box.**

   Your options are Draft, Revision 1, Revision 2, Revision 3, Alpha, Beta, Final, and Needs Attention. You can choose any status, and you should set a policy with your design team about what each status means and how you will use these options to manage your development.

3. **Type your comments in the Notes text box.**

4. **Click the date icon (just above the Notes text box) if you want to insert the current local date.**

   The current date is inserted automatically.

5. **In the All Info tab, you can add other information that may be useful to developers of your site. For example, you can name a key designer (in the Name field) and define the value as the name of that person or the priority of the project (in the Value field). You also may define a field for a client or type of file that you commonly use.**

   Click the plus (+) button to add a new key; click the minus (–) button to remove a key.

6. **Click OK to save the notes.**

   The notes you entered are saved to a subfolder named *notes* in the same location as the current file. The filename is the document's filename, plus the extension .mno. For example, if the filename is art.htm, the associated Design Notes file is named art.htm.mno. Design Notes are indicated in the Site View by a small yellow icon that looks like a cartoon bubble. They are also visible in the directory that you can see on your hard drive.

Staying in Touch with Integrated E-Mail

Dreamweaver features integrated e-mail as another handy tool for collaborative Web design. This is not a new application in Dreamweaver, but a feature that enables you to use Dreamweaver in conjunction with any e-mail program you already use and to have easy access to the e-mail address of other members of your team when you need it.

When you're working on a site with a team of people, it's not uncommon that the page you want to work on has already been checked out by someone else, making it impossible for you to do the work you need to do on it. In Dreamweaver's Site Definition dialog box, you can associate an e-mail address with each developer's name in the Check In/Check Out feature. Then when you find that someone else has the page you need, you can easily fire off an e-mail telling that person to check it back in so you can work on it. (Sometimes threats work, but I find offering chocolate or other bribes is usually more effective.)

Developers on your team can use the following steps to associate their e-mail address with their version of Dreamweaver as part of the Check In/Check Out set up:

1. **Choose Site⇨Edit Sites.**

   The Edit Sites dialog box opens.

2. **Click to select the site you want to work on and then click Edit.**

   The Site Definition dialog box opens.

3. **In the Category list at the left, choose Remote Info.**

   The Remote Info page appears.

4. **If it's not already selected, click to select the Enable File Check In/Check Out (see Figure 4-7).**

TIP

Keeping the peace with version control

Version control systems enable you to better manage changes made by different team members and prevent them from overwriting each other's work. If you already use these programs, you'll be glad to know that you can now integrate both Visual Source Safe and systems that use the Web DAV protocol with Dreamweaver, which makes it possible to take advantage of the Dreamweaver site management features and still protect your code development process. If you don't know about these programs, visit the Microsoft site (www.microsoft.com) to learn more about Visual SourceSafe, or visit www.ics.uci.edu/pub/ietf/webdav/ to learn more about WebDAV protocols.

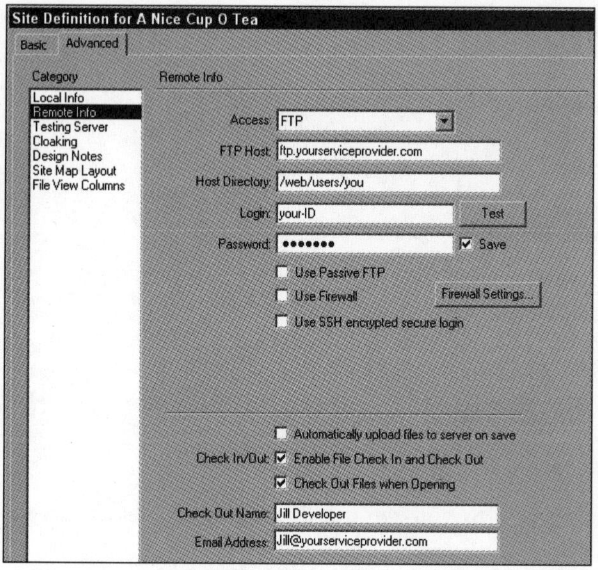

Figure 4-7:
You can
associate
your e-mail
address
with the
Check In/
Check Out
feature to
make it easy
for other
developers
to send you
messages.

5. **Click to select Check Out Files When Opening.**

6. **Enter your name in the Check Out Name text box. (Nicknames are okay as long as everyone on the team knows your silly name.)**

7. **Enter your e-mail address in the Email Address text box.**

8. **Click OK to save your changes.**

Remembering Your History

You can keep track of what you've been doing and even replay your steps with the History panel. The History panel also lets you undo one or more steps and create commands to automate repetitive tasks.

To open the History panel, shown in Figure 4-8, choose Window⇨Others⇨ History. As soon as you open the History panel, it starts automatically recording your actions as you do work in Dreamweaver. You can't rearrange the order of steps in the History panel, but you can copy them, replay them, and undo them. Don't think of the History panel as an arbitrary collection of commands; think of it as a way to view the steps you've performed, in the order in which you performed them. This is a great way to let Dreamweaver do your work for you if you have to repeat the same steps over and over again. It's also a lifesaver if you make a major mistake and want to go back one or more steps in your development work.

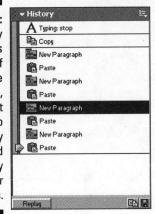

Figure 4-8:
The History
panel keeps
track of
what you've
done,
making it
easy to
undo any
move and
repeat any
or all your
steps.

Here's a rundown of how you can put the History panel to use:

- **To copy steps you've already executed:** Use the Copy Steps option as a quick way to automate steps you want to repeat. You can even select steps individually, in case you want to replay some, but not all, of your actions exactly as you did them.

- **To replay any or all the steps displayed in the History panel:** Highlight the steps you want replayed and click the Replay button in the bottom of the History panel.

- **To undo the results of the replayed steps:** Choose Edit⇔Undo.

- **To apply steps to a specific element on a page:** Highlight that element in the document window before selecting and replaying the steps. For example, if you're applying bold and italic formatting to just a few words on a page, you can replay the apply bold and italics steps to selected text.

You can also set the number of steps that are displayed in the History panel by choosing Edit⇔Preferences and selecting General from the Category list on the left. The default is 50, more than enough for most users. The higher the number, the more memory the History panel uses.

Using the Quick Tag Editor

If you're one of those developers who likes to work in the Dreamweaver WYSIWYG editing environment but still wants to look at the HTML tags once in a while, you'll love the Quick Tag Editor.

The Quick Tag Editor, as the name implies, lets you modify, add, or remove an HTML tag without opening the HTML Source Window. That means that while you're in the middle of working on a page, you can quickly bring up the tag you are working on without leaving the document window. You can use the Quick Tag Editor to insert HTML, edit an existing tag, or wrap new tags around a selected text block or element.

The Quick Tag Editor opens in one of three modes — Edit, Insert, or Wrap — depending on what you have selected on a page. Use the keyboard shortcut Ctrl+T (Windows) or ⌘+T (Macintosh) to change modes while the Quick Tag Editor is open.

You can enter or edit tags in the Quick Tag Editor, just as you would in the Document Source Window, without having to switch back and forth between the text editor and WYSIWYG environment.

To enter or edit tags in the Quick Tag Editor, follow these steps:

1. **With the document you want to edit open, select an element or text block.**

   If you want to add new code, simply click anywhere in the file without selecting text or an element.

2. **Choose Modify⇨Quick Tag Editor.**

   You can also press Ctrl+T (Windows) or ⌘+T (Macintosh).

   The Quick Tag Editor opens in the mode that is most appropriate for your selection. For example, if you click an image or formatted text, it opens to display the code so that you can edit it. If you don't select anything, or if you select unformatted text, the Quick Tag Editor opens with nothing in it, and you can enter the code you want to add.

   If you want to edit an existing tag, go to Step 3. If you want to add a new tag, skip to Step 4.

3. **If you selected an element that is formatted with multiple HTML tags or a tag with multiple attributes, press Tab to move from one tag, attribute name, or attribute value to the next. Press Shift+Tab to move back to the previous one.**

   If you aren't sure about a tag or attribute, pause for a couple of seconds and a drop-down list appears automatically, offering you a list of all the tags or attributes that are available for the element you are editing. If this "hints" list doesn't appear, choose Edit⇨Preferences⇨Quick Tag Editor Preferences and make sure that the Enable Tag Hints option is selected.

4. **To add a new tag or attribute, simply type the code into the Quick Tag Editor.**

   You can use the Tab and arrow keys to move the cursor to the place you want to add code. You can keep the Quick Tag Editor open and continue to edit and add attribute names and values as long as you like.

5. **To close the Quick Tag Editor and apply all your changes, press Enter (Windows) or Return (Mac).**

Chapter 5

Adding Graphics

• •

In This Chapter

▶ Creating images

▶ Using royalty-free images

▶ Choosing a graphics program

▶ Keeping file sizes small

▶ Inserting images

▶ Using image maps

• •

*N*o matter how great the writing may be on your Web site, the graphics are always what gets people's attention first. And the key to making a good first impression is to use images that look great, download quickly, and are appropriate to your Web site.

If you're familiar with using a graphics editing program to create graphics, you're a step ahead. If not, I'll give you some pointers and show you how to use pre-existing graphics on your Web site. In this chapter, you can find out how to bring graphics into Dreamweaver and work with some of the more popular image editing programs. I also include information about choosing other image editing programs, working with clip art, keeping image file sizes small, and working with graphics for the Web. Lastly, you can discover how to place and align images on your pages, create image maps, and set a background image using Dreamweaver.

Getting Great Graphics

You want your Web graphics to look good, but where do you get them? If you have any design talent at all, you can create your own images with Fireworks or any of the other image programs that I describe in "Creating your own images" later in this chapter. If you're not an artist, you may be better off gathering images from *clip art collections* (libraries of ready-to-use image files) and using royalty-free or stock photography, as I describe in this section. If you have a scanner, you can also scan in existing photographs or logos to use.

Unfortunately, Dreamweaver doesn't have any image creation or editing capabilities of its own, so you have to use a different program if you want to create or edit images. If you bought the Dreamweaver/Fireworks Studio, however, you're in luck; you have everything you need to create and edit images for your Web site. Otherwise, you'll need a separate program to create and edit your images. Dreamweaver integrates well with almost any other image-editing program, and many designers use Photoshop, Image Ready, or other programs to create images for the Web.

Buying royalty-free clip art and photographs

If you don't want the hassle of creating your own images (or, like me, you lack the artistic talent), you may be happy to find many sources of clip art available. Royalty-free images, which include clip art and photographs, are generally sold for a one-time fee that grants you all or most of the rights to use the image. (Read the agreement that comes with any art you purchase to make sure that you don't miss any exclusions or exceptions.) You can find a wide range of CD-ROMs and Web sites full of clip art, photographs, and even animations that you can use on your Web site. Speaking of animations, nowadays you can even find Web sites that sell Flash files, animations, buttons, and other artistic elements that you can edit and integrate into your Web site. For more on creating a multimedia Web site, see Chapter 12. Many professional designers buy clip art images and then alter them in an image program — such as Macromedia Fireworks, Adobe Illustrator, or Adobe Photoshop — to tailor them for a specific project or to make an image more distinct. Here are some clip art suppliers:

- **Artville** (www.artville.com): Artville is an excellent source of quality illustrations and a great place to find collections of artistic drawings and computer-generated images that can provide a theme for your entire Web site.

- **Eyewire** (www.imageclub.com and www.eyewire.com): One of the world's largest sources of clip art, Eyewire includes illustrations as well as photographs.

- **PhotoDisc, Inc.** (www.photodisc.com): PhotoDisc is one of the leading suppliers of royalty-free digital imagery, specializing in photographs of a wide variety of subjects.

- **Stockbyte** (www.stockbyte.com): Stockbyte is a great source for international royalty-free photos.

- **Flash Kit** (www.flashkit.com): Flash Kit is mainly an open-source Web site where you can download pre-made, fully-editable Flash source files to enhance your existing Flash animations or to use as a starting point for new animations.

- ✔ **We're Here Forums** (www.werehere.com): We're Here Forum also provides Flash source files for download and use. This site offers sound loops and links to other Flash resources as well.

- ✔ **Web Promotion** (www.webpromotion.com): A great source for animated GIFs and other Web graphics. Artwork on this site is free provided you create a link back to Web Promotion on your Web site, or you can buy the artwork for a small fee.

Creating your own images

The best way to get original images is to create your own. If you're not graphically talented or inclined, consider hiring someone who can create images for you. If you want to create your own images for use in Dreamweaver, Fireworks is a good one to start with because of its tight integration with Dreamweaver and overall "dummy-proof" features — no pun intended! Fireworks is a perfect tool for making Web graphics and is easy to learn because it shares a common interface with Dreamweaver. However, you can use any other image-editing programs on the market either separately or in unison with Fireworks. The following list of image-editing programs shows you a little of what's out there. Most of these programs also allow you to scan photographs and logos using a scanner.

The last few years have seen a tremendous advancement in the features and capabilities of specialized Web graphics programs as well as increased competition between application vendors, especially the heavyweights like Adobe and Macromedia. Consequently, the current "best of the crop" graphics program is a toss-up between Macromedia's Fireworks and Adobe's Photoshop. One of these two programs will come out on top of almost any comparison of features and ability to produce the smallest Web graphics. If you're serious about Web graphics, I highly recommend getting one of these two programs — they're the cream of the crop and can easily pay for themselves by giving you the most professional and efficient results on your Web projects.

However, if you don't have the budget or the time to learn more complex programs, you may be better off with a more limited photo-editing program such as Adobe PhotoDeluxe, which is a capable yet far less expensive option, costing only around $49. For creating buttons, banners, and other Web graphics on a budget, consider Jasc Paint Shop Pro, MicroFrontier Color It!, or Microsoft Image Composer.

Unless otherwise indicated, all of these programs are available for both Mac and Windows:

✔ **Macromedia Fireworks** (www.macromedia.com/software/fireworks): Fireworks was one of the very first image-editing programs designed specifically to create and edit Web graphics. Fireworks gives you everything you need to create, edit and output the best-looking Web graphics, all in one well-designed product. Besides sharing a common interface with Dreamweaver, Fireworks also integrates extremely well with Dreamweaver to speed up and simplify the process of building a Web site. In Chapter 11, I cover some of the special features of Fireworks and Dreamweaver that help you to work together with these two programs.

✔ **Adobe Photoshop** (www.adobe.com/products): Adobe calls Photoshop the "camera of the mind." This is unquestionably the most popular image-editing program on the market and a widely-used standard among graphics professionals. With Photoshop, you can create original artwork, correct color in photographs, retouch photographs and scanned images, and do much more. Photoshop has a wealth of powerful painting and selection tools in addition to special effects and filters to create images that go beyond what you can capture on film or create with classic illustration programs. The latest versions of Photoshop also add a wealth of features for creating and editing Web graphics, putting it on par with Fireworks in this department.

✔ **Adobe Photoshop LE and PhotoDeluxe** (www.adobe.com/products): For novices or users who don't need all the bells and whistles offered in the full-blown version of PhotoShop, Adobe offers two products that provide just the basic features — PhotoShop LE and PhotoDeluxe. One or the other often comes bundled with a scanner or printer. While you can still accomplish a lot with PhotoShop LE, it's not great for preparing Web images. However, PhotoDeluxe *is* geared for Web graphics output and is very easy to learn and use.

✔ **Adobe Illustrator** (www.adobe.com/products): Illustrator is one of the industry standards for creating illustrations. You can drag and drop illustrations that you create in Illustrator right into other Adobe programs, such as Photoshop or PageMaker. Illustrator also comes with an export feature that enables you to export your illustrations in GIF or JPEG format with a browser-friendly palette of colors so that your illustrations look great on the Web.

✔ **Corel Photo-Paint** (www.corel.com): Widely-used, though definitely not an industry standard, Corel Photo-Paint offers almost all the same features and capabilities as Adobe PhotoShop, for a fraction of the price. Photo-Paint comes with a generous clip art and royalty-free photography collection. One of the best things about Photo-Paint is that for about fifty dollars less than PhotoShop, you can get the complete Corel Draw Graphics Suite, which includes Photo-Paint, Draw and RAVE 3D. Undoubtedly, this is a great set for home users who want professional-grade graphics and page layout capabilities at a more affordable price.

✔ **Equilibrium DeBabelizer** (www.equilibrium.com/debab): DeBabelizer, by Equilibrium Technologies, is a graphics-processing program capable of handling almost every image format ever used on a computer. This one probably isn't the best program to use for creating images from scratch, but it does excel at some of the highly specialized tasks of preparing and optimizing images for the Web. One of the best features of DeBabelizer is its capability to convert images from just about any format to just about any other. If you have a bunch of images to convert, you can use DeBabelizer's *batch convert* feature, which enables you to automatically convert hundreds of photographs into JPEGs or convert many graphics into GIFs all at once without having to open each file separately. Be aware, though, that DeBabelizer has a pretty steep learning curve and isn't recommended for someone just starting out in creating Web graphics.

✔ **Jasc Paint Shop Pro** (www.jasc.com): Paint Shop Pro, by Jasc Software, is a fully featured painting and image-manipulation program available only for Windows. Paint Shop Pro is very similar to Photoshop, but on a more limited scale because it doesn't offer the same range of effects, tools, and filters. However, it costs less than Photoshop and may be a good starter program for novice image-makers. You can also download an evaluation version for free from the Jasc Web site.

✔ **Macromedia Freehand** (www.macromedia.com/software/freehand): Macromedia Freehand is an illustration program used widely both on the Web and in print. Freehand has many excellent Web features, including support for Web file formats such as GIF89a, PNG, and JPEG, as well as vector formats such as Flash (.SWF) and Shockwave FreeHand (.FHC). Thirty-day trial versions are available for free on the Macromedia Web site.

✔ **MicroFrontier Color It!** (www.microfrontier.com): This low-cost, easy-to-use graphics program is available only for the Macintosh and is a great tool for beginners, as well as those on a tight budget. Although it's much more limited than many of the other programs in this list, it provides enough features to create basic banners and buttons for a small business Web site. A demo version is available for free from the MicroFrontier Web site.

✔ **Microsoft PhotoDraw 2000** (www.microsoft.com/office/photodraw): PhotoDraw 2000 is Windows-only and comes bundled with Office 2000 to offer photo-editing and drawing tools for easily making Web graphics. This product is an adequate starting point for creating and editing images for use on the Web.

Understanding the Basics of Web Graphics

Because having a basic understanding of graphics formats and how they work on the Web is so important, I include the following sections to give you an overview of what you need to know about graphics as you create them or place them on your pages.

The most important thing to keep in mind when placing images on a Web page is that you want to keep your file sizes as small as possible. You may ask, "How small is *small?*" In fact, this is one of the most common questions people ask about Web graphics. The answer is largely subjective — remember that the larger your graphics files are, the longer people have to wait for them to download before they can see them. You can have the most beautiful picture of Mount Fuji on the front page of your Web site, but if it takes forever to download, most people aren't going to be patient enough to wait to see it. Also remember that when you build pages with multiple graphics, you have to consider the cumulative download time of all the graphics on the page. So smaller is definitely better. Most Web pros consider anything from about 40K to 60K a good maximum *cumulative* size for all the graphics on a given page. With the increasing popularity of DSL and cable modems, however, many Web sites are starting to become a bit more graphics-heavy. However, anything over 100K is definitely a no-no if you expect people with dial-up modems (56K and under) to stick around long enough to view your pages. To make it easy to determine the total file size of the images on your page, Dreamweaver includes this information in the status bar of the current document window, as shown in Figure 5-1. This number indicates the total file size of all the images and HTML on your page as well as the expected download time at a given connection speed (you can set your own connection speed by choosing Edit⇨Preferences⇨Status Bar⇨Connection Speed).

Achieving small file sizes requires using compression techniques and color reduction, tasks that can be achieved using any of the graphics programs mentioned in the preceding section. Whatever program you use, you should understand that image sizes can be reduced to varying degrees and that the challenge is to find the best balance between small file size and good image quality. If you really want to find out the best ways to create graphics for the Web, read *Web Design For Dummies* by Lisa Lopuck. It has a fantastic section on designing Web graphics.

One of the most common questions about images for the Web is when you use GIF and when you use JPEG. The simple answer:

Figure 5-1:
The Dream-
weaver
Status Bar
(in the
bottom-right
corner of
the screen)
indicates
the total
download
size of the
page,
including
graphics
and HTML,
as well
as the
estimated
download
time.

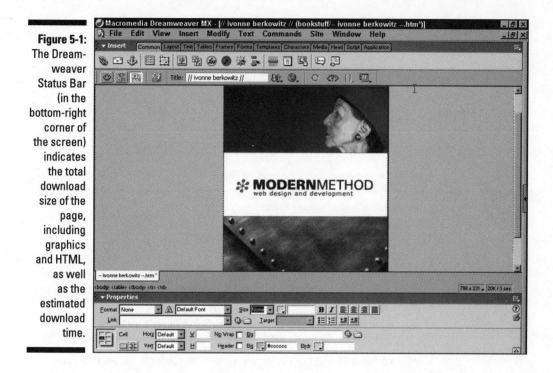

Use	For
GIF	Line art (such as one- or two-color logos), simple drawings, and basically any image that has no gradients or blends
JPEG	Colorful, complex images (such as photographs), images containing gradients or color blends, and so on

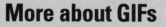

TECHNICAL STUFF

More about GIFs

GIFs, aside from the barely-supported PNG format, is the only file format widely accepted that can have an invisible color to create a transparency effect. GIFs can also have multiple frames, so you can create small animated loops with this format. Ads on the Web, generally referred to as *banners,* are almost always made in GIF.

Designers frequently create a GIF that just consists of words because it lets us use non-standard fonts with perfect anti-aliasing and whatever colors and effects we want without worrying about whether the end user has the font. GIF is the ideal format for this because it offers transparency, where JPG compression can make the small lines and curves in text fuzzy. This technique is referred to as making "GIFtext."

That said, sometimes the best thing to do is just experiment with both formats and see which yields the best results. In time, you'll get a knack for which is the best format to use depending on the type of image you're working with.

Inserting Images on Your Pages

Dreamweaver makes placing images on your Web pages easy.

Before inserting any images into your page, it's important to save your page because Dreamweaver must know the directory location of the page so that it can properly create the image links.

To place an image in a new file, follow these steps:

1. **Choose File⇨New to start a new page.**

2. **Choose File⇨Save to Name and save the new HTML file in the folder of your choice.**

3. **If the Objects panel and Property Inspector aren't already visible, choose Window⇨Objects and Window⇨Properties to open them.**

4. **Click the Insert Image icon in the Common Objects panel (the first icon in the upper-left corner).**

   The Select Image Source dialog box appears, as shown in Figure 5-2.

5. **In the Select Image Source dialog box, browse your local drive in order to locate the image you want to place.**

   Alternatively, you can insert images simply by choosing Insert⇨Image, which brings up the same dialog box, or by dragging and dropping image files from any open directory right into your Dreamweaver document, provided that they are in a valid Web graphics file format such as GIF or JPEG.

   Remember that when you work with images in Dreamweaver, as with any Web authoring tool, it's best to maintain the same directory structure on your local hard drive as you intend to use on your server when you upload your files. Starting out with all of your images and HTML files in one common folder on your computer makes them easier to track. Within this common folder, you can subdivide your images and HTML folders however you like. Mirroring the structure of your server on your local machine vastly simplifies uploading, tracking, and maintaining your site structure throughout the development cycle as well as later on when you want to update your site.

6. **Highlight the image to insert and double-click it or click once and then click the Select (or Open) button.**

   The image automatically appears on your page.

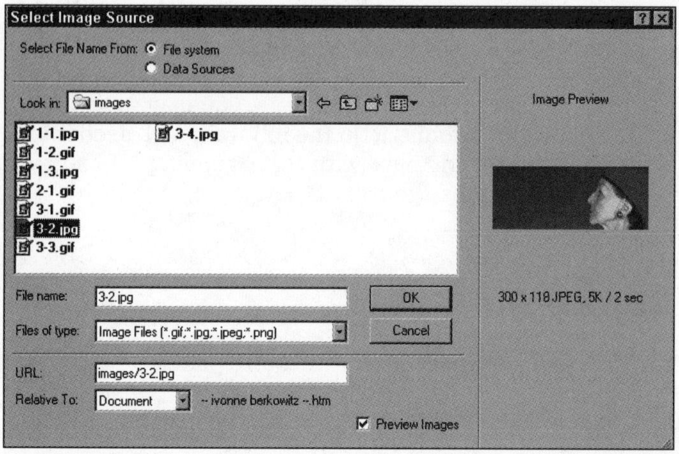

Figure 5-2:
Clicking the
Insert Image
icon opens
up a dialog
box in which
you can
locate and
preview the
image you
want to
place.

```
Select Image Source                                                    ? X
Select File Name From:  ● File system
                        ○ Data Sources
Look in: [📁 images        ▼]  ← ⤴ 📁 📰▼              Image Preview

📄 1-1.jpg        📄 3-4.jpg
📄 1-2.gif
📄 1-3.jpg
📄 2-1.gif
📄 3-1.gif
📄 3-2.jpg
📄 3-3.gif

File name:     [3-2.jpg                    ]   [  OK  ]
Files of type: [Image Files (*.gif;*.jpg;*.jpeg;*.png) ▼] [ Cancel ]   300 x 118 JPEG, 5K / 2 sec
URL:           [images/3-2.jpg            ]
Relative To:   [Document ▼]  ~ ivonne berkowitz ~.htm
                                    ☑ Preview Images
```

How an image appears on a Web page

The HTML tag that you use to place images on a Web page is similar to the link tag that you use to create hyperlinks between pages. Both tags instruct the browser where to find something. In the case of the link tag, the path to the linked page instructs the browser where to find another URL. In the case of an image tag, the path in the tag instructs the browser to find a GIF or JPEG image file. The path describes the location of the image in relation to the page on which it appears. For example, /images/baby.gif is a path that instructs a browser to look for an image file called baby.gif in the /images directory. This path also implies that the /images directory is in the same directory as the HTML file containing the link. Whenever you see a forward slash in HTML, it signifies a directory (or folder) that contains other files or folders.

Trying to determine the path can get a little complicated. Fortunately, Dreamweaver sets the path for you, but you need to take care of two important steps before Dreamweaver can do this properly:

1. Save your page.

   When you save a page, Dreamweaver automatically remembers the exact location of the page in relation to the image. Saving the file is essential because the path always indicates the location of an image relative to the page containing the link (this is called a *relative link*). If you forget to save your file beforehand, Dreamweaver always prompts you to save the file before completing the link. If you don't save the file, Dreamweaver inserts an absolute link that references the image's location on your hard disk, but this link isn't valid on any other machine or when you upload your Web site. An *absolute link* to your hard drive works on your machine, but not on your Web server — or any other machine, for that matter.

2. Make sure that your images and pages stay in the same relative locations when you're ready to go public with your site and move them all to a server.

Aligning Images on a Page

After you place an image on your Web page, you may want to center or align it so that text can wrap around it. In the following two sections — "Centering an image" and "Aligning an image with text wrapping" — I show you the steps to accomplish both of these goals.

Centering an image

To center an image on a page, follow these steps:

1. **Click to select the image that you want to center.**

   The Property Inspector changes to display the image properties.

2. **From the icons for alignment options in the Property Inspector, shown in Figure 5-3, click the Center Alignment icon.**

   The image automatically moves to the center of the page.

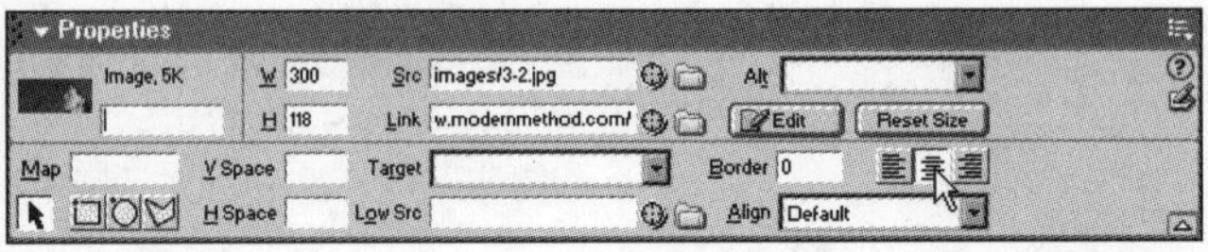

Figure 5-3:
Use the alignment icons in the Property Inspector to center an image.

Aligning an image with text wrapping

To align an image to the right of a page and wrap text around it on the left, follow these steps:

1. **Insert the image immediately to the left of the first line of the text (see Figure 5-4).**

   The easiest way to do this is to place the cursor before the first letter of text; then select Insert⇔Image.

   Don't put spaces or line breaks between the image and the text.

2. **Select the image.**

   The Property Inspector changes to display the image attribute options.

3. **In the Property Inspector, choose Left from the Align drop-down list, as shown in Figure 5-5.**

   The image aligns to the left and the text automatically wraps around it.

To align the image to the right of the page with text wrapping around on the left, follow Steps 1 and 2, and then in Step 3, choose Right from the Align drop-down list instead of Left.

To prevent text from "sticking" to an image, click the image, find V and H spacing on the Property Inspector, and enter a numerical value for the amount of pixels you'd like spaced. Ten is typically a safe number.

Creating complex designs with images

The alignment options available in HTML enable you to align your images vertically or horizontally, but you can't do both at once. Also, the alignment options don't really enable you to position images in relation to one another or in relation to text with much precision. The way to get around this limitation is to create HTML tables and use the cells in the table to control positioning, as shown in Figure 5-6.

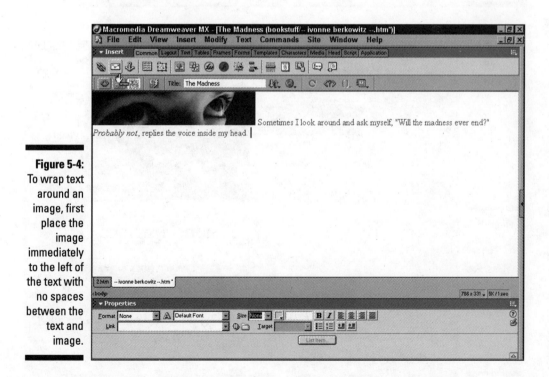

Figure 5-4:
To wrap text around an image, first place the image immediately to the left of the text with no spaces between the text and image.

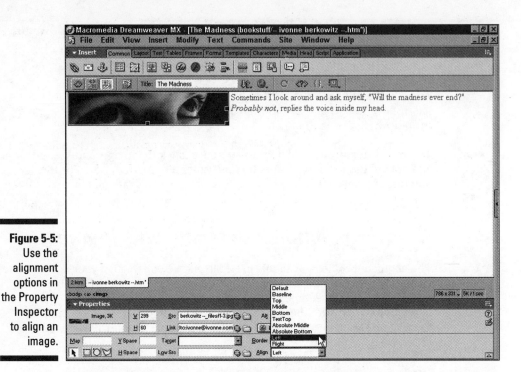

Figure 5-5:
Use the alignment options in the Property Inspector to align an image.

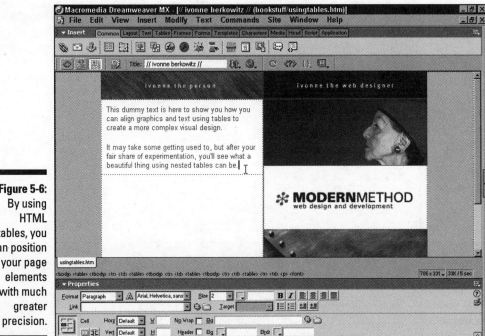

Figure 5-6:
By using HTML tables, you can position your page elements with much greater precision.

This sounds complex at first, but with a little experimentation, you can create almost any page layout using tables. Chapter 9 shows how to use tables to create more complex Web page designs.

Using the transparent GIF trick

You may find it strange that I would suggest you place an invisible image on a Web page, but that's exactly what I show you how to do in this section. A small, transparent GIF is a powerful element in Web page design because you can use it to control the exact position of other elements on a page. You'll notice that some other programs, such as Fireworks, also utilize transparent GIFs to "force" other page elements into compliance. These GIFs are automatically generated, and you can often recognize them because they use names such as shim.gif, dot clear.gif, or clear.gif. Regardless of the name, they all perform the same function.

When you create a sliced image in Adobe ImageReady, it often uses the transparent GIF trick on the far-most right-hand column to ensure that each table cell is the right size.

If you're not sure how to make a clear GIF, don't worry — I include one on the CD-ROM that accompanies this book. You can do whatever you like with it. I always name this image clear.gif, and I use one on nearly every Web site I work on. See the appendix for more information about what's on the CD.

If you want to make your own transparent GIF, just create a small, solid-color image, save it as a GIF, and designate the color you use as transparent. You can make a color transparent in most good graphics programs, including Adobe Photoshop, Fireworks, and Microsoft Image Composer. You can find descriptions of a number of graphics programs that provide this feature earlier in this chapter.

HTML enables you to specify any height and width for an image, regardless of its actual size. Thus, you can use a small transparent GIF with a corresponding small file size (for quick download) and then alter the image attributes for height and width to create exact spaces between other visible elements on your page. Many Web designers recommend that you create a single-pixel graphic for this purpose, but I've found that a 10 x 10 pixel image works best because some older browsers have trouble displaying a GIF that's only one pixel. Remember, even if the clear GIF is 10 x 10 pixels, you can still set the height and width to a smaller size.

Dreamweaver makes it easy to use the transparent GIF trick because it provides easy access to the height and width attributes in the Property Inspector. You may also need to specify the alignment of the image to achieve the desired effect.

You can also use a transparent GIF to control spacing around text. This method is handy when you want more than just a break between lines of text or other elements, but not as much as you get with the paragraph tag. This is also an ideal way to create larger spaces between elements with down-to-the-pixel design control.

To use a transparent GIF between images, text, or other elements on a page, follow these steps:

1. **Insert the image in the space where you plan to use it, whether it is between two images or within text.**

2. **Click OK.**

   The transparent GIF is inserted on your page and automatically selected.

3. **With the clear.gif image still selected, type** 20 **in the text box next to the W in the Property Inspector and** 20 **in the text box next to the H in the Property Inspector.**

   This sets the height and width of the image to 20 pixels each.

   I use a value of 20 pixels just for demonstration — you can set the height and width to any values you want.

If you click clear.gif, you can see the outline of the image while it's selected. Notice that as soon as you deselect the image, it becomes invisible in Dreamweaver. You can always reselect it by clicking in the area until the cursor highlights it. If you're working with a very small GIF, say one that's only 1 pixel high by 1 pixel wide, you may have difficulty selecting it by clicking after it's been deselected. For this reason, I recommend resizing the GIF as soon as it's been placed on the page and is still highlighted.

Creating a Background

Background images can bring life to a Web page by adding color and fullness. Used cleverly, a background image can help create the illusion that the entire page is one large image while still downloading quickly and efficiently. The trick is to use a small background image that creates a dramatic effect when it *tiles* (repeats) across and down the page (see Figures 5-7 and 5-8).

Beware, though, that certain backgrounds can make it hard to read text that's placed on top of them (such as the one shown in Figure 5-9). Choose your background images carefully and make sure there is plenty of contrast between your background and your text — it's hard enough to read on a computer screen as it is.

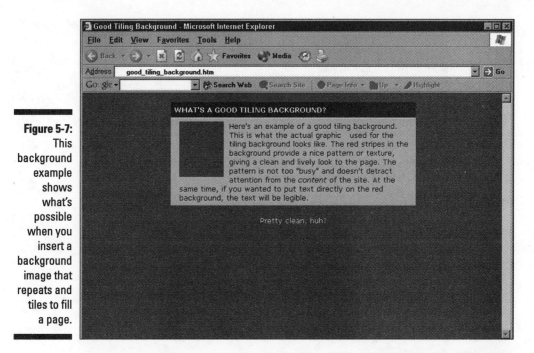

Figure 5-7:
This background example shows what's possible when you insert a background image that repeats and tiles to fill a page.

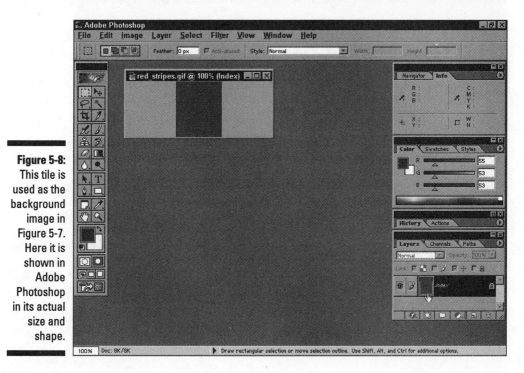

Figure 5-8:
This tile is used as the background image in Figure 5-7. Here it is shown in Adobe Photoshop in its actual size and shape.

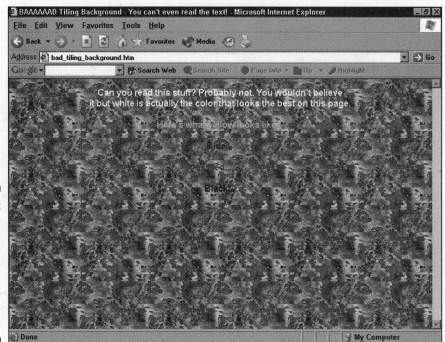

Figure 5-9:
Using the wrong background will make the text on your Web page illegible.

When you set an image as the background for your Web page, the browser repeats it across and down the page, as you see in Figure 5-7. This is why background images are often called *tiles,* because they repeat like tiles across a kitchen floor. However, if you use a long, narrow image as a background or a large image that's small in file size, you can create many effects beyond a repeating tile.

In the event that you don't want a background image to tile, your only option is to use an image that is larger than the maximum size of the largest monitor you expect people to view your site with. That way, they'll never see the next tile because it will always be out of view. Sometimes I create a background image that is something like 1200 x 1600 pixels in size. The key here is that you must be careful to keep your image file size very small. Background images of these dimensions work well only if you are using GIFs with very limited numbers of colors in them, never with JPEG images. Because GIFs can use only a couple of colors, their files sizes stay small even though their physical dimensions are huge. A GIF that size with no more than eight solid colors takes up only a few kilobytes of space. Use fewer colors, and it takes up even less space.

To set a background on a Web page, follow these steps:

1. **Choose Modify⇨Page Properties.**

   The Page Properties dialog box appears, as shown in Figure 5-10.

2. **Click the Browse button to the right of the text box next to Background Image.**

   The Select Image Source dialog box opens.

3. **Browse to find the image that you want to use as your background image.**

   When you insert an image in your Web site, you want to make sure that the image is in the same relative location on your hard drive as it is on your server. If you plan to use your background tile throughout your site, you may want to store it in a common images folder where it is easy to link to from any page in your site.

4. **Click the filename of your background image to select it.**

   The Select Image Source dialog box disappears.

5. **Click OK in the Page Properties dialog box to finish.**

   Note that if you click the Apply button, you see the effect of the background tile being applied to the page before you click OK to close the dialog box.

Figure 5-10:
The Page
Properties
dialog box
enables you
to set a
background
image, as
well as a
background
color, text,
and link
colors.

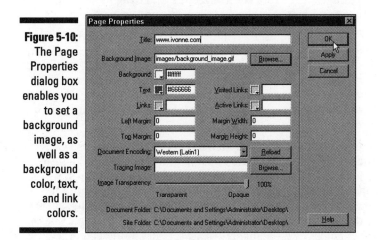

Creating Image Maps

Image maps are popular on the Web because they enable you to create hot spots in an image and link them to different URLs. A common use of an image map is a geographic map, such as a map of the United States, that links to different locations depending on the section of the map selected. For example, if you have a national bank and want to make it easy for customers to find a local branch or ATM machine, you can create hot spots on an image map of the United States and then link each hot spot to a page listing banks in that geographic location. Dreamweaver makes creating image maps easy by providing a set of simple drawing tools that enable you to create hot spots and set their corresponding links.

To create an image map, follow these steps:

1. **Place the image you want to use as an image map on your page.**

2. **Click the Properties Inspector to view the image properties if it's not already open; then highlight the image.**

   With the Property Inspector visible, click the image so that the image properties display in the Property Inspector window.

3. **To draw your hot spot, choose a shape tool from the Image Map tools in the lower-left of the Property Inspector (see Figure 5-11).**

   The shape tools include a rectangle, an oval, and an irregular polygon that allow you to draw regions on your images, called *hot spots,* each with a specific link.

   For this exercise, select the rectangle shape.

4. **With the rectangle shape tool selected, click and drag over an area of the image that you want to make *hot* (link to another page).**

   As you click and drag, a light blue highlight appears around the region that you're making hot; this highlighted area indicates the active region. Position this region so that it covers the area that you want. If you need to reposition the hot area, select the arrow tool from the lower-left corner of the Property Inspector and then select and move the region to the location you want. You can also resize it by clicking and dragging any of the corners.

   If you want to make a shape other than a rectangle, you can use either the oval or polygon hot spot tools. The polygon tool functions a little bit differently; to make a polygon selection (such as one of the state of California in a U.S. map), you click the tool once for each point of the polygon shape you want to draw. Then, to close the shape, click again on the first point you drew after you finish drawing all the other points.

5. **To link a selected hot area, click the Folder icon next to the Link text box (at the top of the Property Inspector).**

   The Select HTML File dialog box opens.

6. **Browse to find the HTML file that you want to link to the hot spot on your image.**

7. **Double-click the file to which you want to link.**

   The hot spot links to the selected page and the Select HTML File dialog box automatically closes. You can also type the path directly into the link field if you know it, saving you from having to find it on your hard drive.

8. **To add more hot spots, choose a shape tool and repeat Steps 4 through 7.**

9. **To give your map a name, type a name in the text field next to Map, just above the shape tools.**

   Giving your map a name helps to distinguish it in the event that you have multiple image maps on the same page. You can call the map anything you want.

   When you are finished, you see all your image map hot spots indicated by a light blue highlight.

You can go back at any point and re-edit the image map by clicking and highlighting the blue region on your image and dragging the edges to resize the image or by entering a new URL to change the link.

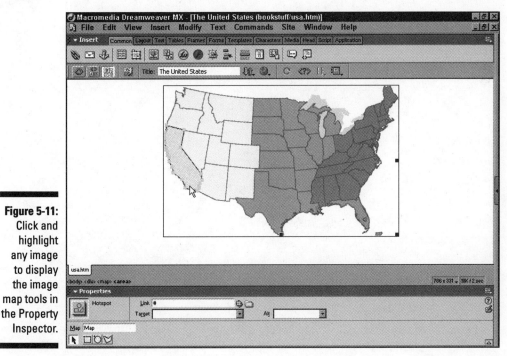

Figure 5-11:
Click and
highlight
any image
to display
the image
map tools in
the Property
Inspector.

Part III
Advancing Your Site

The 5th Wave   By Rich Tennant

"Give him air! Give him air! He'll be okay. He's just been exposed to some raw HTML code. It must have accidently flashed across his screen from the server."

In this part . . .

1f you want to create compelling designs within the confines of the rules of HTML, you need to use HTML tables, frames, and Cascading Style Sheets (CSS). This part walks you through the maze of nested tables and merged cells, split pages framed with links, and the power and design control that you can achieve only with CSS.

Chapter 6

Coming to the HTML Table

• •

• •

Designers often get frustrated when they learn that they can't just put an image wherever they want it on a page by dragging it into place. They get annoyed when they learn they don't have line spacing control in text and many of the other design features common in print. As HTML evolves, it's becoming possible to create designs precisely the way you want them using DHTML features — such as layers — that enable the placement of elements anywhere on a page. The problem is, DHTML is not universally supported by browsers, so what you gain in easy design control, you lose with the risk that someone using an old browser won't be able to view your work as you intended it.

For now, my best advice for achieving the best design control with the most universally recognized HTML is to use HTML tables — a trick good designers have been using on the Web for years, and one that still works today.

If you've ever used a desktop publishing program such as QuarkXPress or Adobe PageMaker, you've probably used text and image boxes to lay out pages. DHTML layers work much like this, but tables can be used to achieve a similar effect. You use the table cells (the "boxes" created at the intersection of each row and column in a table) to control the placement of text and images. Because you can make the borders of the table invisible, your viewers don't see the underlying structure of your table when they look at your Web page in a browser. For example, you can use a table to align elements side by side on a page and create columns of text. You still won't get the design control you're used to in a desktop publishing program, but with a little ingenuity, you can create the same effects.

This chapter is designed to show you how to use HTML tables for everything from columnar data to complex page designs. You explore a wide range of uses for HTML tables and find step-by-step instructions for how to create a variety of designs for your Web pages.

Creating Simple Tables in Layout View

Tables are made up of three basic elements: rows, columns, and cells. If you've ever worked with a spreadsheet program, you're probably familiar with what tables are all about. Tables in HTML differ from spreadsheet tables mainly in that they are used for more complex alignment of data, which requires lots of merging and splitting cells. Back in the days when you had to design Web pages in raw HTML code by hand, even simple tables were difficult to create. The code behind an HTML table is a complex series of <TR> and <TD> tags that indicate table rows and table data cells. Figuring out how to type in those tags so that they create a series of little boxes on a Web page was never an intuitive process. If you wanted to merge or split cells to create uneven numbers of rows or columns, you really faced a challenge.

Thank the cybergods that you have Dreamweaver to make this process easier. If you've ever written HTML code manually, you can appreciate how much simpler Dreamweaver makes it to quickly create tables, merge or split cells, change a background color, or specify the width of a border. Using the Layout View mode, the easiest way to work with tables in Dreamweaver, you can quickly and easily create the most complex tables simply by clicking and dragging table cells around on the screen. When your basic table structure is complete, you can then use the Property Inspector to specify a wide range of table attributes, such as border size, alignment, colors, and so on. Using Layout View, a special feature of Dreamweaver designed to make it easier to create tables, you can easily drag cell borders around to alter the size and positioning of cells, move the contents of cells around your page, and ulti- mately get around one of the great pitfalls of table design: changing your mind about how you want the table to look after you've built it. As you switch back and forth between Standard View and Layout View, you'll see that some of the table edit features are not available in Layout View. You find more information about when it's best to use each view in the "Understanding Table Options" section that follows.

Using Dreamweaver, it's possible to modify both the appearance and the structure of a table. You can add any type of content to a cell, such as images, text, and multimedia files. You can also add color to the background or border and change the alignment of elements within a cell.

The easiest way to work with tables in Dreamweaver is to switch to Layout View and use the special Layout Cell and Layout Table tools (see the following steps to do this). With these tools, which are available only in Layout View, Dreamweaver makes table creation much more intuitive. You can even switch between the two modes, Standard View and Layout View. You're already used to working in Standard View in Dreamweaver because that's the default for working on documents. Layout View provides a special view mode designed to assist in constructing and editing of tables that enables you to draw cells anywhere on a page and drag the edges of a table to change the size. Figures 6-1 and 6-2 show the same table in Layout View and Standard View.

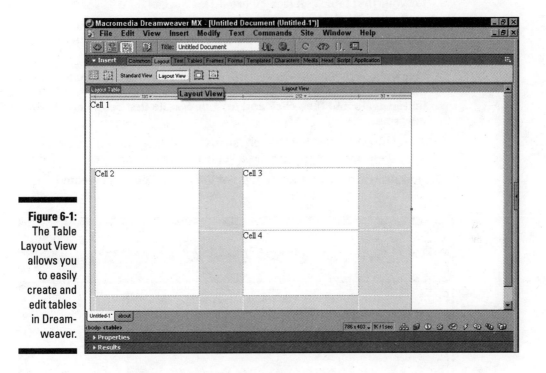

Figure 6-1:
The Table Layout View allows you to easily create and edit tables in Dreamweaver.

To create a table in Layout View with a long cell across the top and two smaller cells below it (like the table shown in Figures 6-1 and 6-2), create a new HTML page and follow these steps:

1. **Switch to Layout View by selecting Layout Tab in the Insert Panel and then clicking the Layout View button.**

   You can also switch to Layout View by selecting View⇨Table View⇨ Layout View, but the Layout Tab in the Insert Panel makes it easier to access other table options.

You may see a message describing how to use the Layout Table and Layout Cell buttons when you select first this option. Click "Don't show me this message again" to avoid seeing it next time and then click OK to close it.

2. **Click the Draw Layout Cell button.**

   The cursor changes to a crosshair when you move the mouse over the document area, indicating you're ready to draw a table cell.

3. **Click the mouse on the document and while holding down the mouse button, drag to draw a rectangular shape across the top of the page for your first table cell (see Figure 6-1).**

   The cell is drawn and its surrounding table structure is automatically generated. A grid representing the table structure appears with the current cell shown in white.

4. **Below the cell you just drew, draw another cell of approximately half the size of the top cell. To do this, select the same Draw Layout Cell button again and then click and drag under the first cell to create the new cell.**

   As you draw, notice that the cell "snaps" into place along the guidelines in the table grid. Use the grid as a guide in lining up your cells.

5. **Now draw a third cell to the right of the second one you created.**

Figure 6-2:
The same table viewed in Standard View, which mimics the browser view more closely. Tables can also be created and edited in this mode.

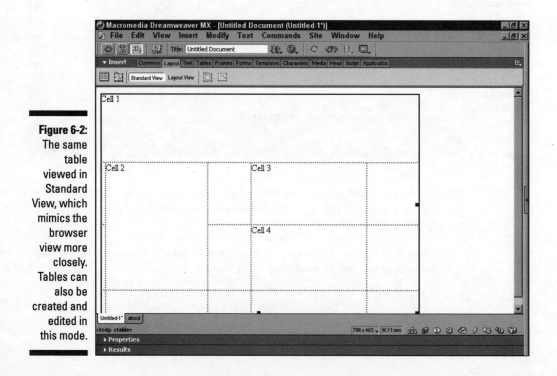

6. **Click your mouse in the first cell you drew and type some text; then repeat that for the other two cells.**

   You can type any text you want. This is just to show you that you can enter text into a cell as easily as you can anywhere else on the page. In the example shown in Figures 6-1 and 6-2, I typed *Cell #1*, *Cell #2*, and *Cell #3* to help you appreciate the order I suggested creating these cells.

7. **Switch to Standard View by clicking the Standard View or selecting View⇨Table View⇨Standard View to see how your table looks.**

Depending on where you started drawing your table cells, Dreamweaver may create table cells around the cells you created to maintain their position on the page. For example, in the table shown in Figures 6-1 and 6-2, although I've created three new cells, Dreamweaver has filled in the gaps by automatically creating more cells, so there are actually seven cells in this final table. Normally a table defaults to the top left corner of a page, so the first cells in the table are close to the top left margin. However, using Layout View, you can draw cells wherever you want them on a page, and Dreamweaver automatically generates the other cells that are needed to keep the positioning you created in Layout View. Remember, HTML won't allow you to place things anywhere on a page unless you use table cells to control their placement. Empty cells that Dreamweaver creates to fill space in a table merely act as *spacer cells* and don't show up in the browser, giving the illusion that various page elements are positioned independently on any part of the page.

Designers often wonder how wide they should make their tables. My best advice is to design your pages for an 800 x 600 screen resolution because that's the most common size in use today on the Web. If you are creating a table that will cover the entire display area, a safe bet is to make your table 760 pixels wide and center it in the middle of the page because that leaves a little room on each side to avoid sideways scrollbars appearing.

Editing Tables in Layout View

One of the really wonderful things about working with tables in Layout View is that you can use the layout grid to edit, move, and resize any of the rows, columns, and cells in the table, which allows you to really use the grid as a design guide for creating any kind of layout you want. Normally, the only way to create complicated layouts in HTML is by meticulously building complex tables. But in Layout View, you can move table cells around on the grid using drag-and-drop to precisely position text or images without having to manually create spacer cells to do the job. You also have the flexibility to create *nested* tables (tables drawn within tables) for even more control over your layout. To create a nested table, simply click the Draw Layout Table button and begin drawing a new table inside an existing table cell. For more information on nested tables see the section titled "Using nested tables: Tables within tables" later in this chapter.

Understanding Table Options

Layout View works best for creating and editing the overall *structure* of your table. When you're ready to start editing the *contents* of the table and its individual cells, it's best to work in Standard View. In Layout View, you can change some of the table attributes, but in Standard View, you can change all the HTML table attributes, including the number of rows and columns, as well as height, width, border size, and spacing. When you select a table or cell, the attributes are displayed in the Property Inspector, which is located at the bottom of the work area. Click the border of any table to select it, and the Property Inspector displays the table options shown in Figure 6-3. To view all the options, click the expander arrow in the lower-right corner of the Property Inspector.

You can also insert elements such as text, images, and multimedia files into cells by clicking to place your curser in the cell and typing text or by using the Insert Common Objects Panel options to insert images, multimedia files, and other elements.

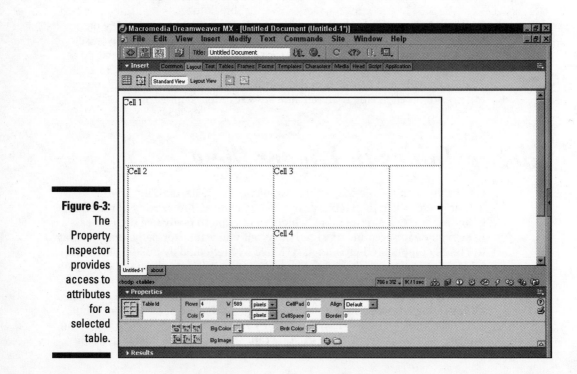

Figure 6-3:
The
Property
Inspector
provides
access to
attributes
for a
selected
table.

Sometimes selecting a table with the mouse can be a bit tricky. Here are a couple of tips for selecting a table more easily. In Standard View, you can access table properties by clicking directly on top of the border of the table, which works best for simple tables. For nested tables where there are many confusing borders touching each other, try clicking inside of any cell that belongs to the table you want to select and then right click and choose Table⇨Select Table. Use the HTML tag selector in the document's Status Bar at the bottom-left edge of the work area to select an entire table easily. You can click your mouse anywhere in your table to display the HTML tags in the status bar; then click the <TABLE> tag in the tag selector to select the entire table.

The Property Inspector gives you access to the following table options for customizing the appearance of your table:

- **Rows:** Displays the number of rows in the table. You can alter the size of the table by changing the number. Be careful, though: If you enter a smaller number, Dreamweaver deletes the bottom rows — contents and all.

- **Columns:** Displays the number of columns in the table. You can alter the size of the table by changing the number. Be careful, though: If you enter a smaller number, Dreamweaver deletes the columns on the right side of the table — contents and all.

- **W (Width):** Displays the width of the table. You can alter the width by changing the number. The width can be specified as a percentage or a value in pixels. Values expressed as a percentage increase or decrease the table's size relative to the size of the user's browser window.

- **H (Height):** Displays the height of the table. You can alter the height by changing the number. The height can be specified as a percentage or a value in pixels. Values expressed as a percentage increase or decrease the table's size relative to the size of the user's browser window. This table attribute is only recognized by version 4.0 browsers and above.

- **CellPad:** Specifies the space between the contents of a cell and its border.

- **CellSpace:** Specifies the space between table cells.

- **Align:** Controls the alignment of the table. Options are left, right, and center.

- **Border:** Controls the size of the border around the table. The larger the number, the thicker the border. If you want the border to be invisible, set the border to 0.

- **Clear and Convert:** The icons the bottom left of the Property Inspector (click the expander arrow in the bottom-right to view them), provide the following formatting options:

- **Clear Row Heights** and **Clear Column Widths** enable you to remove all the height and width values at once, leaving the table to adjust to the available browser window.

- **Convert Table Heights to Pixels** and **Convert Table Heights to Percents**, and **Convert Table Widths to Pixels** and **Convert Table Widths to Percents** enable you to automatically change Height and Width settings to pixels, which specify a fixed width or a percent, that automatically adjusts to the specified percentage of the browser display area.

Table dimensions expressed as a percentage enable you to create a table that changes in size as the browser window is resized. If you want a table to always take up 75 percent of the browser window no matter how big the user's monitor or display area, percentages are a good way to specify table size. If you want a table to always take up a specific number of pixels — that is, to remain the same size regardless of the browser window size — choose pixels instead of percentages for your table dimensions.

✔ **Bg Color:** Controls the background color. Click the color square next to this label and select a color from the box that appears. When you click the color square, the cursor changes to an eyedropper, enabling you to pick up a color from anywhere on the page by clicking the color. You can apply this option to a single cell or to the entire table.

✔ **Bg Image:** Enables you to select a background image. Specify the file-name or click the folder icon to locate it. You can apply this option to a single cell or to the entire table. Note that many older browsers do not support background images in single cells so the image will not display for all viewers.

✔ **Brdr Color:** Controls the border color. Click the color square next to this label and select a color from the box that appears. When you click the color square, the cursor changes to an eyedropper, enabling you to pick up a color from anywhere on the page by clicking the color. You can apply this option to a single cell or to the entire table.

Dreamweaver limits the actual colors to those best supported on the Web. As a result, if you sample a color from a 16-bit color (or higher) image, you may not get exactly the color you wanted. (I've had light greens replaced as grays, for example.) If this happens, you can tweak the color after using the eye-dropper tool with the "system color picker" button within the Properties box.

For die-hard designers who dream in Pantone: If you insist on a 100 percent match from your design, you can create a small (10 x 10 pixel), one-color GIF with an image editor and use a background image to ensure an exact color match. Because background images tile by default, the cell will appear filled in with the GIF's color even if the cell is bigger than the GIF.

Controlling Cell Options

In Standard View, in addition to controlling the table options in the Property Inspector, you can control options for the individual cells within the table. When you select a cell by clicking the cursor inside the cell area, the Property Inspector changes to display the individual properties for that cell (see Figure 6-4), allowing you to change the options for specific cells. You can also change multiple cells at the same time. Say you want to have some, but not all, of the cells in your table take on a certain color background and style of text. You can apply the same properties to multiple cells at the same time by holding down the Shift key while clicking adjacent cells to select multiple cells at once. If you want to select multiple cells that are not adjacent, hold down the Ctrl key (Command key on the Mac) and click each cell that you want to select. Any properties you changed in the Property Inspector are applied to all selected cells. If you are having trouble selecting a cell because it contains an image, click the image and then use either side arrow key on your keyboard to move the curser and deselect the image, which activates the Property Inspector and displays the options for that cell.

When one or more cells are selected, the top half of the Property Inspector controls the formatting of text and URLs within table cells. The bottom half of the Property Inspector provides the following options (see Figure 6-4):

- **Merge Cell Icon:** Merges two or more cells. To merge cells, you must first select two or more cells by clicking and dragging or by holding down the Shift or Ctrl keys while selecting multiple cells.

- **Split Cell Icon:** Splits one cell into two. When you select this option, a dialog box lets you specify if you want to split the Row (meaning split the cell horizontally) or the Column (meaning split the cell vertically). You can then specify the number of Columns or Rows, which controls how many times the cell will be divided. Note that the Split Cell option can be applied to only one cell at a time.

- **Horz:** Controls the horizontal alignment of the cell contents.

- **Vert:** Controls the vertical alignment of the cell contents.

- **W:** Controls the width of the cell.

- **H:** Controls the height of the cell.

- **No Wrap:** Select No Wrap to prevent word wrapping within the cell. The cell will widen to accommodate all text as you type or paste it into a cell. (Normally the text would just move down to the next line and increase the height of the cell.)

- **Header:** Use to format a cell's contents using a Header style, which makes the text bold and centered.

    ✔ **Bg (Image):** Allows you to specify a background image for the cell.

    ✔ **Bg (Color):** Allows you to specify a background color for the cell.

    ✔ **Brdr (Color):** Allows you to change the border color of the cell.

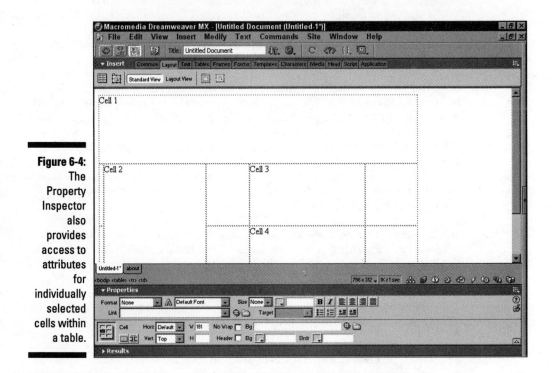

Figure 6-4:
The
Property
Inspector
also
provides
access to
attributes
for
individually
selected
cells within
a table.

Using the Format Table Feature

One of the best reasons for using tables is to present lots of data in a clear
and structured way. Tables accomplish this because the use of rows and
columns allows the reader to follow along easily when there is a lot of data to
represent. One of the ways to make your data even more presentable and
attractive is to colorize the rows and columns in the table. In the previous
section, I show you how to change the attributes of individual cells. In this
section, I show you a really great Dreamweaver feature that allows you to
select predefined table formats with great color schemes to enhance your
presentation. Figure 6-5 shows a sample of the Format Table feature that lets
you do this.

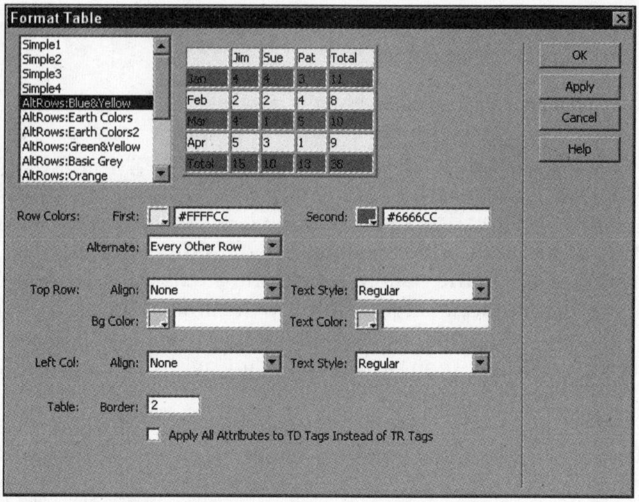

Figure 6-5:
The Dream-
weaver
Format
Table
feature
provides a
variety of
previously
created
color
schemes to
enhance the
look of your
tables.

Format Table						
Simple1		Jim	Sue	Pat	Total	OK
Simple2						Apply
Simple3	Jan	4	4	3	11	Cancel
Simple4	Feb	2	2	4	8	Help
AltRows:Blue&Yellow	Mar	4	1	5	10	
AltRows:Earth Colors	Apr	5	3	1	9	
AltRows:Earth Colors2	Total	15	10	13	38	
AltRows:Green&Yellow						
AltRows:Basic Grey						
AltRows:Orange						

Row Colors: First: [ ] #FFFFCC   Second: [ ] #6666CC
Alternate: [Every Other Row ▼]

Top Row: Align: [None ▼]   Text Style: [Regular ▼]
Bg Color: [ ]   Text Color: [ ]

Left Col: Align: [None ▼]   Text Style: [Regular ▼]

Table: Border: [2]
☐ Apply All Attributes to TD Tags Instead of TR Tags

To use the Format Table feature, create a new HTML page, insert a simple table of any size, and follow these steps.

1. **Select an existing table in the document.**

2. **Make sure you're in Standard View.**

   The Standard View icon in the Layout Tab of the Insert panel should be selected.

3. **Choose Commands⇨Format Table.**

   The Format Table dialog box appears.

4. **Select one of the schemes by scrolling the list or modify any of the parameters to create your own scheme.**

5. **Click OK.**

   The color scheme is applied to the table.

These color schemes were created by professional designers so you can be sure they'll look good on your Web page. You can also modify any of the attributes in the Format Table dialog box and create your own color schemes.

Using low-contrast color schemes in tables is considered the most effective way to present content in a table. (Just look at Intuit's Quicken software, E-Trade, Amazon, and so on for real-life examples.) High contrast colors in tables are usually reserved for site menus and submenus or other elements you want to call more attention to.

Formatting Multiple Columns in a Table

When you're working with lots of cells in a table, you may want to format multiple cells in the same way. Dreamweaver makes it easy to do that, whether you want to align numbers, make the headings bold, or change the color scheme. But before you start planning how to line up all of your numbers perfectly, be aware that you don't have as much control in HTML as you have in a program such as Excel, where you can align numbers to the decimal point. You can, however, align the content of columns left, right, or center. Thus, if you use the same number of digits after the decimal point in all your numbers, you can get them to line up. For example, if one price is $12.99 and another is $14, express it as $14.00; then, when you align right, the numbers will line up properly.

In the following steps, I show you how to create a table of financial data in Standard View and align all the data cells on the right so that the numbers align. You can also use these steps to align the contents of table cells to the left, center, or top, or to apply other formatting options, such as bold or italic. In these steps, I insert the data into the table after I create it in Dreamweaver.

If you want to import data from a table that you've created in a program such as Word or Excel, see the section, "Importing Table Data from Other Programs," later in this chapter. If you're working with a table that already has data in it and just want to format or align the cells, go directly to Step 7.

To create a table of financial data and align the data, create a new blank HTML page and follow these steps:

1. **Make sure you're in Standard View. (The Standard View icon in the Layout Tab of the Insert panel should be selected.)**

2. **Click to place your cursor where you want to create a table.**

3. **Click the Insert Table icon from the Insert panel.**

   Alternatively, you can choose Insert⇨Table. The Insert Table dialog box appears.

4. **In the appropriate boxes, type the number of columns and rows you want to include in your table.**

   For this example, I specified four rows and four columns.

5. **Specify the width, border, and Cell Padding and Spacing; then click OK.**

   I set my table to 75 percent so that it doesn't fill the entire page. You can set the width to whatever is most appropriate for your design. I also set the Border to 1 because I want the border to be visible for this table, and I left the Cell Padding and Spacing options set to 0 so there isn't any extra spacing in the cell.

When you click OK, the table automatically appears on the page.

6. Click to place your cursor in a cell, and then type the data that you want in each cell.

As you can see in Figure 6-6, I entered the heading information across the top row of cells. Then I listed several CD titles and entered the data for each CD in the rest of the table.

7. Select the column or row for which you want to change the alignment.

Place your cursor in the first cell in the column or row that you want to align; then click and drag your mouse to highlight the other columns or rows that need to be changed.

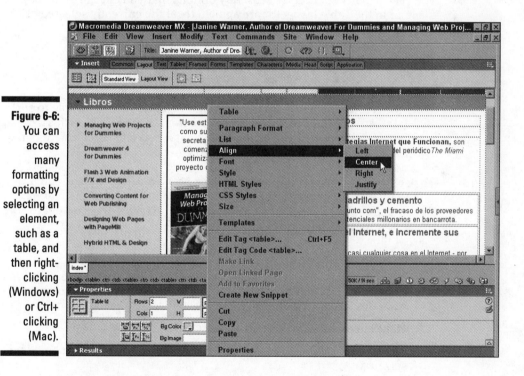

Figure 6-6: You can access many formatting options by selecting an element, such as a table, and then right-clicking (Windows) or Ctrl+ clicking (Mac).

8. Right-click (Windows) or Ctrl+click (Mac) on any cell in the high-lighted column or row.

A pop-up menu appears (as shown in Figure 6-6). Alternatively, you can also use the Property Inspector to change selected items.

9. From the pop-up menu, choose Alignment Left, Center, or Right.

This option enables you to change the alignment of all the highlighted cells in the column or row at once. If you're working with financial data, the Align Right option often produces the best alignment for numbers. You can also apply other formatting options to selected cells in this way by selecting the option from the pop-up menu or from the Property Inspector. Notice that all the headings across the top of the table in Figure 6-6 are bold. This was done the same way, except I selected Bold from the Property Inspector instead of choosing Align⇨Center.

If you want to format one cell in a column or row differently from the others, click to place your cursor in just that cell and then click one of the formatting options in the Property Inspector. You can also choose to align multiple cells that aren't contiguous (meaning they don't touch each other) by pressing and holding down the Ctrl key in Windows while you click the cells that you want to select. On the Mac, you press and hold down the Command key (⌘) while you click to select particular cells. Any options that you change in the pop-up menu or in the Table Inspector are applied to all the currently selected cells.

Using the Sort Table Feature

When you are working with lots of columnar data, it's nice to be able to sort that data, like you would in a spreadsheet program such as Excel. In this newest version of Dreamweaver, you can now sort data even after it's formatted in HTML (something that wasn't easily done before).

To use the Sort Table Data feature, create a new blank HTML page, add a table with several rows and columns, and add some content. You may want to use an existing table with columnar data so you have some content to sort, and follow these steps.

1. **Select two or more cells.**

   Place your cursor in the first cell in the column or row that you want to align; then click and drag your mouse to highlight the other columns or rows that need to be changed.

2. **Make sure you're in Standard View.**

   The Standard View icon in the Layout Tab of the Insert panel should be selected.

3. **Choose Commands⇨Sort Table**

   The Sort Table dialog box appears as shown in Figure 6-7.

4. **Specify which column you want to sort by; then choose Alphabetically or Numerically, Ascending or Descending. You can set up two sorts to happen simultaneously and can opt to include the First Row and to keep the TR (Table Row) attributes with a sorted Row.**

5. **Click OK**

   The selected cells are sorted, just like they would be in Excel. (Pretty cool, huh?)

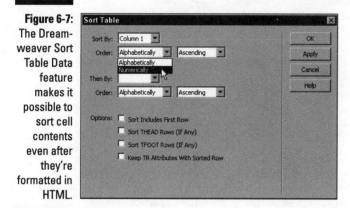

Figure 6-7:
The Dream-
weaver Sort
Table Data
feature
makes it
possible to
sort cell
contents
even after
they're
formatted in
HTML.

Importing Table Data from Other Programs

Manually converting financial data or other spreadsheet information can be tedious. Fortunately, Dreamweaver includes a special feature that enables you to insert table data created in other applications such as Microsoft Word or Excel. To use this feature, the table data must be saved from the other program in a *delimited* format, which means that the columns of data are separated either by tabs, commas, colons, semicolons, or another delimiter. Most spreadsheet and database applications, as well as Microsoft Word, enable you to save data in a delimited format, often called CSV because that's the file extension they are given. Consult the documentation for the application you are using to find out how to do this. After the data is saved in a delimited format, it can be imported in Dreamweaver.

To import table data into Dreamweaver after it has been saved in a delimited format in its native application, create a new blank HTML page and follow these steps:

1. **Choose File⇨Import⇨Table Objects⇨Tabular Data or choose Insert⇨Import Tabular Data.**

   The Import Tabular Data dialog box appears. (See Figure 6-8.)

2. **In the Import Tabular Data text box, type the name of the file that you want to import or use the Browse button to locate it.**

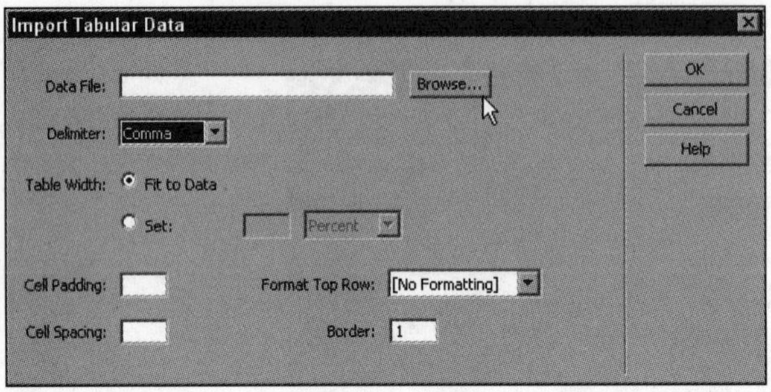

Figure 6-8:
You can
import
tabular data
in Dream-
weaver
from other
programs,
such as
Excel.

3. **From the Delimiter drop-down list, select the delimiter format you used when you saved your file in the other application.**

   The delimiter options are Tab, Comma, Semicolon, Colon, and Other. You should have made this choice when you exported the data from the original program you created it in, such as Excel. If you don't remember what you chose, you can always go back and do it again. You must select the correct option in order for your data to import correctly.

4. **Select the Table Width.**

   If you choose Fit to Data, Dreamweaver automatically creates the table to fit the data being imported. If you choose Set, then you must specify a Percent or Pixel size.

5. **Specify the Cell Padding and Spacing only if you want extra space around the data in the table that is created.**

6. **Choose an option from the Format Top Row option only if you want to format the data in the top row of the Table. Your options are Bold, Italic, or Bold Italic.**

7. **Specify the Border size. The default is 1, which puts a small border around the table. Choose 0 if you don't want the border to be visible. Choose a larger number if you want a thicker border.**

8. **Click OK to automatically create a table with the imported data.**

Dreamweaver also enables you to export data from a Table into a delimited format. This is useful if you want to export data from a Web page so that you can import it into another program, such as Word, Excel, or a database program, such as FileMaker or Access. To export data from Dreamweaver, place

your curser anywhere in the table and select File⇨Export⇨Table.
In the Export Table dialog box, choose from the options in the Delimiter pull-down menu (you can choose Tab, Space, Comma, Semicolon, or Colon). In the Line Breaks pull-down menu, specify the operating system (you can choose Windows, Mac, or UNIX).

Using Tables for Spacing and Alignment

As you get more adept at creating Web pages, you may find that HTML tables are a crucial part of creating almost any design that requires more than basic alignment of elements on a page. Using tables, you can get around many of the limitations of basic HTML and accomplish some of the following design feats:

- Evenly spaced graphic bullets (little GIFs that can take the place of bullets) next to text
- Text boxes and fields properly aligned in a form
- Images placed wherever you wan them on a page
- Columns of text that don't span the entire page
- Myriad intricate layouts that are impossible to accomplish with HTML alone

In the rest of this chapter, I show you how to use tables to create a variety of page designs, including a few of the ones I just listed.

When you use a table for design control, you'll want to turn off the border so that it's not visible in the design. You do that by typing 0 in the Border text box of the Table Property Inspector while the table is selected.

Using tables to design forms

Creating text boxes and pull-down menus for HTML forms is easy in Dreamweaver, but you need to use tables to make them look good. In Chapter 13, you can find lots of information about creating forms; but for now, I assume that you've already created a form and that you want to align the text boxes evenly. I use a guest book form — a common, yet simple, form — as an example, but you can use this technique to align other form elements.

To use a table to align text boxes evenly on your form, create a new blank HTML page and follow these steps:

1. **Open a page that has an HTML form on it (or create an HTML form by using the steps provided in Chapter 13).**

2. **Click to place your cursor where you want to start formatting your form.**

3. **Choose Insert⇨Table.**

   The Insert Table dialog box appears.

4. **Type the number of columns and rows you want in your table.**

   I set the table to two columns and three rows.

5. **Set the Width to whatever is most appropriate for your design and click OK.**

   I set the width to 100 percent. When you click OK, the table automatically appears on the page.

6. **Enter 0 for the Border.**

   When you set the border to 0, the edges of your table change from solid lines to dotted lines so that you can still see where the borders are while you're working in Dreamweaver. When you view the page in a browser, as shown in Figure 6-9, the border of the table is invisible.

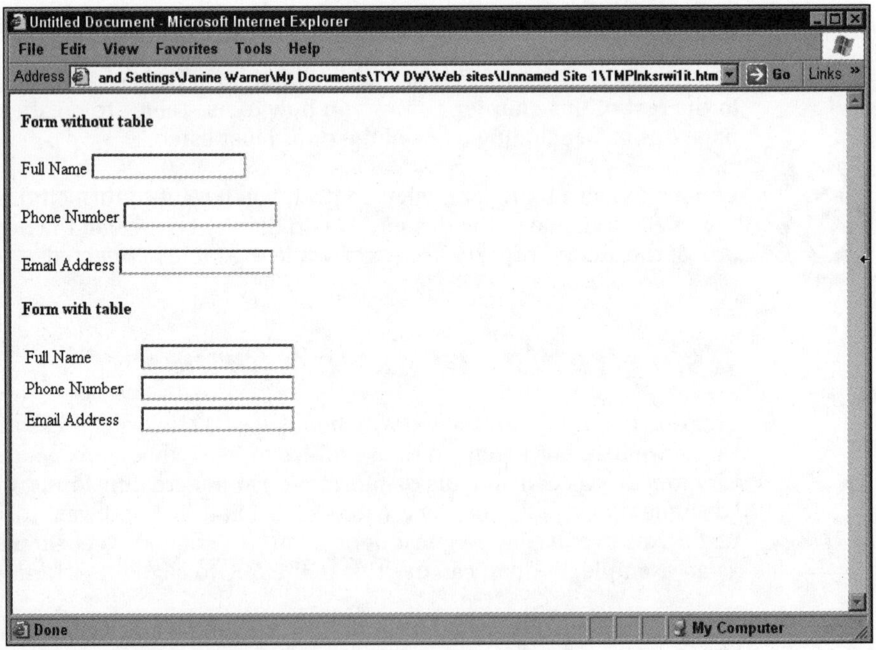

Figure 6-9:
When displayed in the browser, the form fields in the table line up evenly with no visible border.

7. **Now you need to copy the data from your form into the table. Using the Copy and Paste commands from the Edit menu, copy the text preceding the form's first text field and paste it into the cell at the top-left corner of the table.**

Alternatively, you can click and drag the text and form elements into each table cell.

In my example in Figure 6-10, this means copying the words *First Name* and pasting them into the first table cell.

8. **Select the first text field (the empty box where users would type their names) and copy and paste (or click and drag) it into the top-right cell of the table.**

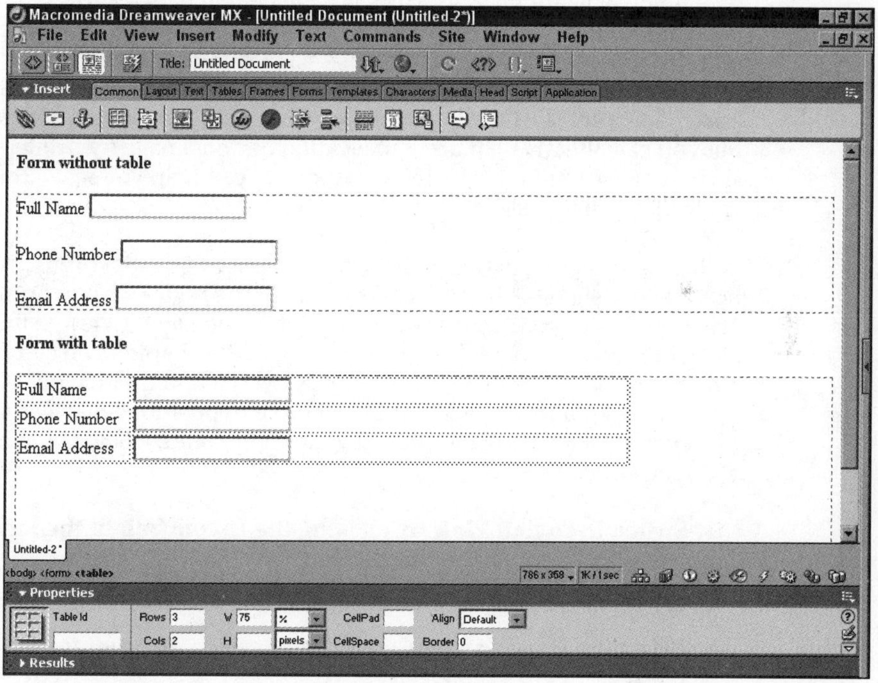

Figure 6-10:
You can use a table to better align form data and elements.

9. **Repeat Steps 6 and 7 for the rest of the form until you've moved all the form elements into table cells.**

10. **Click the vertical column divider line between the first and second columns and drag it to the left or right to create the alignment desired for your form.**

If you are designing a site with the latest in HTML, you can choose to use HTML Layers instead of Tables. *Layers* enable precise pixel placement of elements in your designs, but they are not supported by older versions and are not supported consistently even in newer browsers. If you do decide to use Layers on your site, you may want to create an alternate page for older browsers using the Layers to Table conversion feature described in Chapter 9. This feature is not perfect, especially if the layers overlap, but it will help you work around some of the limitations of Layers, which are covered in detail in Chapter 9.

Aligning a navigation bar

A common element on Web pages is a *navigation bar* — a row of images or text with links to the main sections of a Web site. Navigation bars are usually placed at the top, bottom, or side of a page where users can easily access them but where they're out of the way of the main part of the page design. Designers often use HTML frames (see Chapter 7) to insert a navigation bar, but you can effectively place a navigation bar on a page by using tables. The sidebar "Why use tables instead of frames?" can help you make the right choice for your Web site.

In the last example, in the section "Using tables to design forms," I show you how to create a table in Standard View with the regular table tools. In this example, I show you how to use the table tools in Layout View to build a table, similar to the way you did at the beginning of the chapter. You can really use either view mode for creating a table, but you'll find that Layout View often-times makes it a lot easier. To create a table to position a navigation bar on the left side of a Web page using Layout View, create a new blank HTML page and follow these steps:

1. **Switch to Layout View by clicking the Layout Tab in the Insert panel.**

2. **Select the Draw Layout Table button and create a table by clicking in the top left of the display area and dragging to fill the entire page.**

3. **Select the Draw Layout Cell button to select the tool for drawing table cells.**

   Visualize how you want your table to be structured as you begin drawing cells in the next step. The structure is dictated by the shape and size of your navigation bar and other elements that need to be on the page. (See Figure 6-11 to visualize what you'll be creating in this exercise.)

4. **Click and drag your mouse on the page to draw the size and shape of cells you need to contain your navigation bar and other page elements.**

Figure 6-11 shows how I created a table with three large cells, one down the left side of the page for the navigation elements, one at the top that would be well suited for a banner or title, and one that fills the rest of the display area for the content of the page.

Even while you're drawing cells, Dreamweaver automatically creates a table to enclose the cells you draw. To continue drawing cells without having to go back each time and reselect the Draw Layout Cell tool, hold down the Ctrl key (⌘ on Mac) while you draw cells to retain the tool.

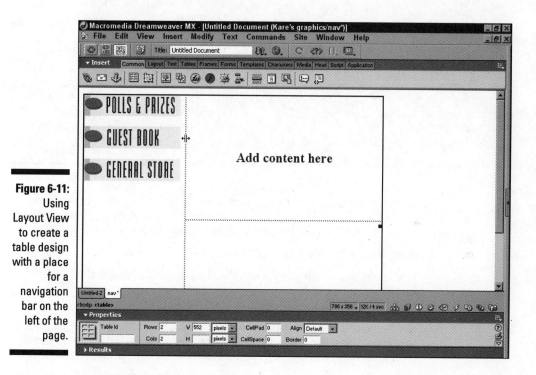

Figure 6-11:
Using
Layout View
to create a
table design
with a place
for a
navigation
bar on the
left of the
page.

5. **When you're done setting up the table, click the Standard View icon to return to Standard View.**

6. **Click to place your cursor in the table cell in which you want to insert your navigation bar.**

To provide an example, I placed several images that combine to create a navigation bar on the left side of this page. Even if you want your navigation bar somewhere else, you probably want to create a table with cells to divide the elements on your page.

Why use tables instead of frames?

Some people don't like frames because they can be difficult to create and confusing for users to navigate, and some older browsers can't display frames. So tables provide a more universally accessible design element.

Frames can save a little time because the entire page doesn't have to reload every time a user clicks a link; only the new frame has to load. With a navigation bar, for example, the images and text of the navigation bar stay in their own frame while new material appears in another frame. If you design your page carefully with tables, you can achieve a similar effect (as shown in Figure 6-11) and the download time can be minimal. If you use text links instead of

images, they load so quickly that it doesn't matter. And if you use the same graphics on every page (as most people do in a navigation bar), the linked images reload quickly because they're *cached* (stored in temporary memory on the visitor's computer) the first time the user visits the page.

You can create very similar designs using tables or frames, so you should make your choice based on your goals and your audience. If you want to make sure that the largest possible audience can see your page, use tables; if you want to change only part of a page and keep some of your page elements visible at all times, use frames.

---

7. **To insert images for a navigation bar, click to place the curser in the left table cell and choose Insert⇨Image. Use the Browse button to locate the image that you want to insert into the table cell.**

8. **Double-click the filename of the image.**

   The image automatically appears in the table cell. Repeat this step to insert multiple images.

   As you can see in Figure 6-11, I am using a series of images that I insert one beneath the other, separated by breaks, to create a row of buttons that runs down the left side of the page. You can also use text by simply typing the names of each element of the navigation bar into the table cell.

   Make sure you put paragraph returns or breaks between each image or you risk them lining up end to end if the cell ever displays wider than the images. It's a little more work, but you will have greater design control if you place each image in a separate table cell because you can better adjust the spacing between images that way.

9. **Select the table and make sure the Border is set to 0 in the Property Inspector. This makes your table invisible so the border won't display in a browser.**

Merging and splitting table cells

Sometimes the easiest way to modify the number of cells in a table is to *merge* cells (combine two or more cells into one) or *split* cells (split one cell into two or more rows or columns). This technique makes it possible to vary the space in table sections and customize their structure. For example, you may want a long cell space across the top of your table for a banner and then multiple cells underneath it so that you can control the spacing between columns of text or images. The following two sets of steps show you how to merge and split cells in a table:

Merging and splitting cells can be done only in Standard View.

To merge cells, create a new HTML page and follow these steps:

1. **Choose Insert⇨Table and create a table with four rows and four columns, width 75 Percent, and border 1. Click OK, and the table appears on the page.**

2. **Highlight two or more adjacent cells by clicking and dragging the mouse from the first cell to the last.**

   You can only merge cells that are adjacent to one another.

3. **Click the Merge Selected Cells icon in the bottom left of the Property Inspector to merge the selected cells into a single cell.**

   The cells are merged into a single cell using the span attribute. The span attribute is an HTML attribute that makes a single cell merge with adjacent cells by spanning extra rows or columns in the table.

To split a cell, follow these steps:

1. **Click to place your cursor inside the cell you want to split.**

2. **Click the Split Selected Cell icon in the bottom left of the Property Inspector.**

   The Split Cell dialog box appears.

3. **Select Rows or Columns in the dialog box, depending on how you want the cell to be divided.**

   A cell can be split into however many new rows or columns you want.

4. **Type the number of rows or columns you want to create.**

   The selected cell is split into the number of rows or columns you entered.

Using nested tables: Tables within tables

Placing tables within tables, called *nested tables,* can help you create the most complex designs. You create nested tables by inserting a table within a cell of another table. In the days when you had to write your own code, this was a daunting task. Today, Dreamweaver makes nesting tables easy, enabling you to create complex designs without ever looking at the HTML code.

Nested tables can get pretty messy. As with all design tricks, don't get carried away and overuse nested tables just because Dreamweaver makes them easy to create. The best Web designs are those that communicate the information to your audience in the most elegant and understandable way. Try to avoid nesting your tables too many levels deep. A table within a table within a table is nested three levels deep. Anything more than that gets a bit hairy. Pages that use nested tables take longer to download because browsers have to interpret each table individually before rendering the page. For some designs, the slightly longer download time is worth it, but in most cases, you're better off adding or merging cells in one table, as I explain in the section "Merging and splitting table cells," earlier in this chapter.

One situation that makes a nested table worth the added download time is when you want to place a table of financial or other data in the midst of a complex page design.

To place a table inside another table, follow these steps:

1. **Click to place your cursor where you want to create the first table.**

2. **Choose Insert⇨Table.**

   The Insert Table dialog box appears.

3. **Type the number of columns and rows that you need for your design.**

   In this case, I created two columns and three rows.

4. **Set the Width to whatever is appropriate for your design, and click OK.**

   The table is automatically sized to the width you set. I used 80 percent.

5. **Click to place your cursor in the cell in which you want to place the second table.**

6. **Repeat Steps 2 through 4, specifying the number of columns and rows that you want and the width of the table.**

   The new table appears inside the cell of the first table.

7. **Type the information that you want in the nested table cells as you would enter content into any other table.**

Chapter 7

Framing Your Pages

• •

• •

*N*o one wants to be "framed," whether that means being falsely accused of a crime or trapped in the HTML frameset of a Web site with no escape. That's why it's important to appreciate not only the best way to create frames, but the best way to use them to enhance site navigation and not leave viewers feeling stuck in your pages.

To help you make the most of this HTML design feature, I demonstrate not only how to build HTML framesets in Dreamweaver, but also discuss when frames are most useful and when they should be avoided. Frames add a wide range of design possibilities, but they can also create confusing navigation systems and can be very frustrating to viewers. As you go through this chapter, consider not only how to create frames, but also if they are really the best solution for your Web site project.

Appreciating HTML Frames

Frames add innovative navigation control because they enable you to display multiple HTML pages in one browser window and control the contents of each framed area individually. Designers commonly use frames to create a page with two or more sections and then place links in one section that, when selected, displays information in another section of the same browser window.

Web pages that use frames, such as the one shown in Figure 7-1, are split into separate sections — or individual *frames*. All the frames together make up a *frameset*. Behind the scenes, each frame of the frameset is a separate HTML file, which makes a page with frames a little complicated to create, even with Dreamweaver. If you choose to create your frame files in a text editor, you have to juggle multiple pages, working on each frame one at a time, and you can see what you're creating only when you preview your work in a browser. The visual editor in Dreamweaver makes creating frames a lot easier because you can view all the HTML files that make up the frameset at the same time and can edit them while they are displayed in the way in which they appear in a browser.

As a navigational feature, frames enable you to keep some information constant, while changing other information on the same page. For example, you can keep a list of links visible in one frame and display the information each link brings up in another frame, as the site shown in Figure 7-1 does.

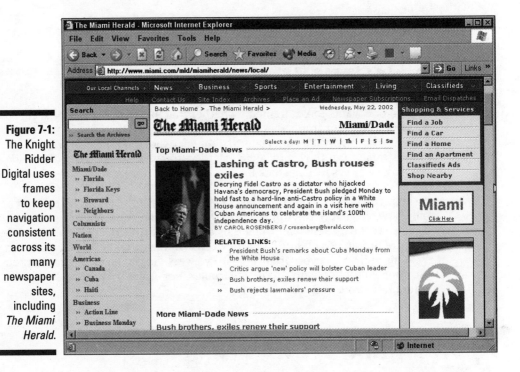

Figure 7-1: The Knight Ridder Digital uses frames to keep navigation consistent across its many newspaper sites, including *The Miami Herald*.

For example, you can create as many frames as you want within a browser window. Unfortunately, some people overuse them and create designs that are so complex and broken up that they're neither aesthetically appealing nor easily navigable. Putting too many frames on one page can also make a site hard to read because the individual windows are too small. This has led many Web surfers to passionately hate frames. And some sites that rushed to implement frames when they were first introduced have either abandoned them or minimized their use.

A more problematic aspect of frames is that they're not backward compatible for very old or purely text-based browsers, which means that if visitors use an older browser (older than Netscape 2.0 or Internet Explorer 3.0) that doesn't support frames, they won't see anything — that's right, they get a blank page — unless you use a special tag called the <NOFRAMES> tag to create an alternative page to supplement your framed page. Fortunately, Dreamweaver automatically inserts a <NOFRAMES> tag in all frameset pages and makes it very easy to add the alternative content for viewers with browsers that don't support frames. I show you how to do this in the "Creating Alternative Designs for Older Browsers" section at the end of this chapter. If you don't use the <NOFRAMES> tag, you're only excluding an esti-mated 5 percent of the Web's population. Just remember, those few people won't see anything on your Web pages.

If you want to see some good examples of frames on the Web, visit www.Lynda.com, follow the link to Inspiration, and look at the frames sites she features on her site.

Here's a list of guidelines to follow when using frames:

✔ **Don't use frames just for the sake of using frames.** If you have a com-pelling reason to use frames, then create an elegant and easy-to-follow frameset. But don't do it just because Dreamweaver makes it easy.

✔ **Limit the use of frames and keep files small.** Remember that each frame you create represents another HTML file. Thus, a frameset with three frames requires a browser to display four Web pages, and that can dramatically increase download time.

✔ **Turn off frame borders.** Newer browsers support the capability to turn off the border that divides frames in a frameset. If the section has to be scro-lable, the border is visible no matter what. But if you can turn the borders off, your pages look cleaner. Frame borders are thick and an ugly gray in color, and they can break up a nice design. Use them only when you feel that they're really necessary. I show you how to turn off frame borders in the "Changing Frame Properties" section toward the end of this chapter.

✔ **Don't use frames when tables are better.** Tables are easier to create than frames and can provide a more elegant solution to your design needs because they're less intrusive to the design. I include lots of infor-mation on creating tables in Chapter 6.

✔ **Don't place frames within frames.** The windows get too darned small to be useful for much of anything, and the screen looks horribly compli-cated. You can also run into problems when your framed site links to another site that's displayed in your frameset. The sidebar "Resist using frames when you link to other people's Web sites" later in this chapter provides many more reasons to limit using frames inside of frames.

✔ **Put in alternate <NOFRAMES> content.** The number of users surfing the Web with browsers that don't support frames becomes smaller every day. Still, it's a good idea to show them *something* other than a blank page. I usually put in a line that says "This site uses frames and requires a frames-capable browser to view."

Understanding How Frames Work

Frames are a bit complicated, but Dreamweaver helps to make the whole process somewhat easier. When you create a Web page with frames in Dreamweaver, you need to remember that each frame area is a separate HTML file, and you need to save each frame area as a separate page. You also want to keep track of which file is displayed in which section of the frame so that you can set links.

Figure 7-2 shows a simple frameset example with three frames, each containing a different HTML page and different text (*Page 1, Page 2,* and *Page 3*) so that I can clearly refer to them in the numbered steps that follow.

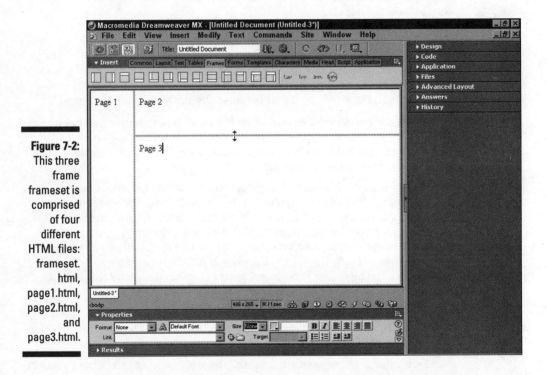

Figure 7-2:
This three frame frameset is comprised of four different HTML files: frameset. html, page1.html, page2.html, and page3.html.

In addition to the files that display in each frame, a separate HTML file needs to be created to generate the frameset. This page isn't visible in the browser, but it describes the frames and instructs the browser how and where to display them. This gets a little complicated, but don't worry. Dreamweaver creates these pages for you. I just want to give you a general understanding of all the files that you're creating so that the steps that follow make more sense.

To help you understand how this works, take a look at the example in Figure 7-2. In this document, you see three frames, each displaying a different HTML page. The fourth HTML file that makes up the frame page *contains* the other frames but doesn't show up in the browser, even though you see it in the title bar (it's called frameset.html). This file is the frameset file, and it describes how the frames should be displayed, whether they should be on the left side of the page or the right, the top or bottom, and how large they should be. The frameset file also contains other information, such as the <NOFRAMES> tag I mention earlier and the names assigned to each frame section. The name of each frame is used to set links so that you can specify which frame a new HTML file should *target,* or open into. I cover more about linking frames in the "Setting Targets and Links in Frames" section later in this chapter.

Creating a frame in Dreamweaver

When you create a frame page in Dreamweaver, it's important to realize that the file you are starting with is the *frameset* file — the file that doesn't show up in the browser but merely instructs the browser how to display the rest of the frames and which pages to use as content for each frame. When you edit the *content* of any of the frames in the frameset, you're not actually editing the frameset file, but the files that populate the framed regions within the frameset. Normally you'd have to edit the files separately, but Dreamweaver makes it a lot easier to design with frames by letting you edit the content of each frame in the *context* of the frameset as it looks in a browser. If you can grasp this concept, you've come a long way in understanding how frames work and how to use Dreamweaver to create and edit them. If it hasn't sunk in yet, read on, and it will.

Creating a frame by using the Split Frame command

You can create frames in two ways in Dreamweaver. The first way is achieved by splitting a single HTML file into two sections, which then become individual frames. When you do that, Dreamweaver automatically generates an untitled page with the <FRAMESET> tag and then additional untitled pages that are displayed in each of the frames within the frameset. Suddenly you're managing several pages, not just one. This is important to understand because you have to save and name each of these pages as a separate file, even though Dreamweaver makes it look like you're working on only one page that's broken into sections.

Always save your HTML files first before inserting anything into them; however, the opposite is true when you are working with frame files in Dreamweaver. Wait until after you've created all the frames in your frameset and *then* save them; otherwise, it gets a bit too complicated and confusing to track your files. I explain more in the section, "Saving files in a frameset," but first, I show you how to create a simple framed page.

To create a simple frameset in Dreamweaver, such as the one shown in Figure 7-2, follow these steps:

1. **Choose File⇨New⇨HTML Page.**

   A new page opens.

2. **Choose Modify⇨Frameset⇨Split Frame Left.**

   The page splits into two sections. You can also choose Split Frame Right, Up, or Down. Split Frame Left or Right divides the page vertically. Split Frame Up or Down divides the page horizontally.

3. **Click inside the right frame area to make it active.**

4. **Choose Modify⇨Frameset⇨Split Frame Up, Down, Left, or Right to divide the page again.**

   I chose Split Frame Up. The right frame divides into two sections.

5. **Click on any of the bars dividing the frames to select the bar and drag it until the page is divided the way you want.**

6. **To edit each section of the frameset, click inside the frame that you want to work on, but remember, you should always save your files before setting links or inserting images and other files.**

   You can type, insert images, create tables, and add any other features just as you would to any other page.

   To save your files, continue with the instructions in the section "Saving files in a frameset."

Creating a frame by using the Frames Insert panel

Another way to create frames is with the Frames Insert panel, shown at the top of Figures 7-2 and Figures 7-3. The Frames Insert panel (available by selecting the Frames Tab from the Insert Panel at the top of the work area) displays several predefined frames sets. You can create a frameset in Dreamweaver simply by clicking any of these icons or dragging and dropping the icon into your document. Figure 7-3 shows the Frames Insert panel with an icon selected and applied to a new document.

To create a framed page using the icons in the Frames panel, follow these steps:

1. **Choose File⇨New⇨HTML Page to create a new page.**

2. **From the Frames Insert panel, choose the frames icon that most closely approximates the type of frameset you want to build and drag it onto your page (you can also click the icon once to apply it).**

   Don't worry if it isn't exactly the design you want; you can alter it later. Figure 7-4 shows the results of dragging the selected frame option on the page.

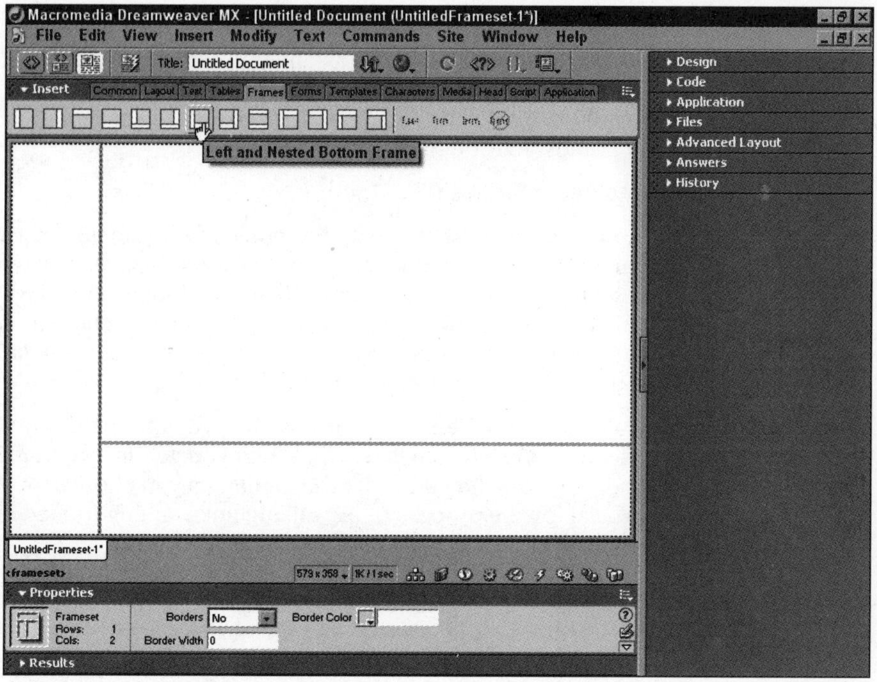

Figure 7-3:
The Frames
panel
contains
predefined
framesets
that you can
drag-and-
drop onto
your page.

3. Modify the frameset as needed.

You can further modify your frameset by clicking and dragging the borders of the frames to resize them, splitting frames as you did in the preceding set of steps, or dragging new frames icons into existing frames.

To save your files, continue with the instructions in the section "Saving files in a frameset."

Saving files in a frameset

As I mentioned earlier, you shouldn't save your frameset file until *after* you've added all of your frames; otherwise, keeping track of your files gets very complicated. Remember, frames in HTML consist of at least two or more HTML files, even if it appears as if you are only working on one file. When you are ready to save, Dreamweaver gives you multiple save options for saving all the files. You can either save everything all at once, or you can save each frame and frameset individually. The example in the previous section is composed of four separate HTML files, each of which needs to be named and saved to your hard drive. To save all the files in the frames document you just created, follow these steps:

1. **Choose File⇨Save All Frames.**

   A Save As dialog box appears, asking you to name the file and designate a folder to save it in. This is the first of several Save As dialog boxes you are prompted with. How many dialog boxes you see depends on how many frames your document contains.

2. **Enter a name for the file.**

   Dreamweaver suggests a name, but you can choose your own. Be sure to use an .htm or .html extension. The first file you save represents the *frameset* file (the file that holds all the other frames in place). You can tell this because if you look at the Dreamweaver document window behind the Save dialog box, the entire document has a thick dotted highlight around it representing the frameset.

   Carefully name the files that you save in a way that helps you keep them in order and know which is which. When you get into setting links in the next section, you may find that the filenames you choose for your frames are crucial for the process of organizing links among framed documents.

3. **Browse your hard drive to locate the desired folder for the HTML files and click Save.**

   The first frameset file is saved and a new Save dialog box appears for the next one. For each frameset file you'll need a distinct name. I like to name them things like frame1.html, frame2.html, or leftframe.html, rightframe.html. It doesn't matter, but it is helpful if you use names that help you distinguish them later. After you save all the frames, the Save dialog box disappears.

After you have saved and named your documents the first time, choosing Save All saves any and all of the files in your frameset without prompting you separately for each frame. Choosing Save All is a good way to make sure that all the pages in your frameset are saved whenever you edit a frames-based document.

Sometimes you may not want to save all the files at once. To save an individual frame displayed in a frameset without saving all the other frames, place your cursor in any of the frames and choose File⇨Save Frame just as you would save any other individual page. Dreamweaver saves only the file for the frame in which your cursor is located.

To save only the page that defines the frameset, choose File⇨Save Frameset. Remember that this page isn't displayed in any of the frames; it simply defines the entire display area, specifying which of the other pages displays in each frame, as well as the position and size of the frames.

As you continue to work on your frame page, remember that whenever you make a change in one of the content frames, you're editing content in a *different* file from the one you started with (the frameset file). You may get confused as to which file you need to save when working in this manner. Don't worry — this is what confuses a lot of people about using frames in Dreamweaver. When you edit the content in one of the frames, make sure that your cursor is still in that frame when you choose File⇨Save Frame so that you save the page that corresponds to the frame you are working on. To be safe, you can always choose File⇨Save All Frames in order to save all changes to all files in the frameset, including the frameset file itself. Save All is also useful when you've made changes to several of the frames and want to save all the changes with just one command.

Setting Targets and Links in Frames

One of the best features of frames is that you can change the contents of each frame separately within the Web browser. This feature opens a wide range of design possibilities that can improve navigation for your site. One very common way to use a frameset is to create a frame that displays a list of links to various pages of your site and then open those links into another frame on the same page. This technique makes it possible to keep a list of links constantly visible and can make navigation a lot simpler and more intuitive.

Resist using frames when you link to other people's Web sites

I understand that most people don't want to lose viewers to another site when they set a link, but that's the nature of the Web. If your site is designed well, you shouldn't have to worry about losing people. Instead, you should guide them around your informative site and then politely help them to other resources that they may find of interest — and let them go. Frames keep users captive and usually leave them annoyed with you for taking up part of their browser area with your site. By displaying content from other sites within one or more of the frames in your site, you do yourself more harm than good in trying to keep them.

If you insist on using frames when you link to another site, do so discretely by placing a small, narrow frame across the bottom of the screen or the left side — not a wide band across the top, and certainly not more than one frame that still contains information from your site. Not only is this rude and ugly, but it's gotten a few Web sites sued because the people they linked to felt that the designers were making it look like their content belonged to the site using the frames.

An additional reason not to use frames when you link to another site is that many other sites use frames, too. You can quickly create a mass of frames within frames that makes it difficult for users to find their way through information. Not everyone realizes that you can get out of frames. If you haven't figured it out yet as a user, within the browser, you can always right-click the link in Windows or click and hold on the link on a Mac to open the frame in a separate window. Now that you know this trick, you can get out of a framed situation — but don't count on your users knowing how to do this if they get annoyed.

Setting links from a file in one frame so that the pages they link to open in another frame is like linking from one page to another, and that's essentially what you're doing. What makes linking a frameset distinctive is that, in addition to indicating which page you want to open with the link, you have to specify which frame section it should *target* (open into).

But before you can set those links, you need to do a few things: First, you need to create some other pages that you can link to (if you haven't done so already). Creating new pages is easy. Choose File➪New➪HTML Page to create additional pages and then save them individually. If your pages already exist, you're more than halfway there; it's just a matter of linking to those pages.

The other thing you have to do before you can set links is to name each frame so that you can specify where the linked file should load. If you don't, the page will just replace the frameset altogether when someone clicks the link and defeat the purpose of using frames in the first place. Naming the *frame* is different from naming the *file* that the frame represents; the *frame name* is like a nickname that allows you to distinguish your frames from one another on a page and refer to them individually. The *filename* is the actual name of the HTML file for the frame. This makes more sense after you see how it works, as I show in the next section.

Naming frames

To specify the names of the frames in you frameset, create a new HTML page and follow these steps.

1. **Click to select the frameset icon on the far right of the Frames panel labeled Top and Nested Right Frame.**

   The frameset is automatically created.

2. **Choose File➪Save Frameset and save each file with a separate file-name.**

   This just saves the files — it's not what I mean by giving each frame a name for the purpose of targeting, which you'll do next.

3. **Choose Window➪Others➪Frames to open the Frames panel at the right of the work area.**

   The Frames panel is a miniature representation of the frames on your page that enables you to select different frames by clicking within the panel (see Figure 7-4).

4. **Click to place your cursor in the area of the Frames panel that corresponds to the frame that you want to name.**

   As displayed in Figure 7-4, you can see my cursor where I have selected the top frame. You can click to select any of the frames in the panel, and the Property Inspector displays the properties for that particular frame.

You can make any changes to the frame's properties by altering the properties in the Property Inspector after selecting the frame. You can also select the entire frameset by clicking the border around all the frames in the Frames panel window. The Frames panel allows you to select only one frame or frameset at a time.

5. **In the text box on the left side of the Property Inspector, type the name that you want to assign to the frame.**

Dreamweaver assigns names automatically when you save the files in a frameset. In the example shown in Figure 7-4, Dreamweaver assigned the names topFrame, mainFrame, and rightFrame. You can leave these names as is or change them to something else in the Property Inspector. I recommend naming frames with descriptive words such as Top, Left, Nav, Content, and so on, so that you can easily tell which frame is which by its name.

6. **Save each file after changing names.**

You can either save each frame individually or choose the Save All Frames command. Refer to the "Saving files in a frameset" section earlier in this chapter for more information on saving frames.

Now that you have identified or changed the names of your frames, you're ready to start setting links that target frames. Don't close these files yet — you'll want to use them to follow the steps in the next section to set links.

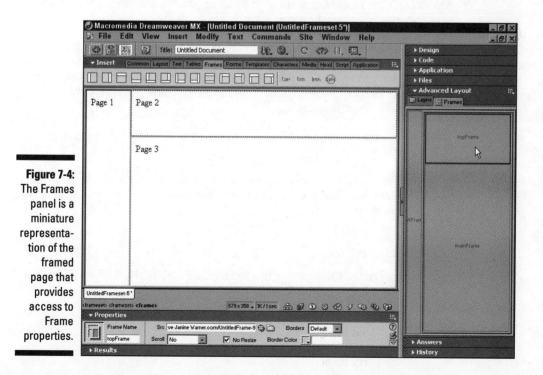

Figure 7-4: The Frames panel is a miniature representation of the framed page that provides access to Frame properties.

I like to save my work on a regular basis so that I never lose more than a few minutes of work if my system crashes or the power goes out. Beware, however, that when you work with frames, you need to save all of your pages to save your work. You can save each page separately choosing File⇨Save Frame to save only the frame that the cursor is currently located in. To save all of your pages at once, simple select File⇨Save All to save all the pages in the frameset.

Setting links to a target frame

Setting links in a frameset requires some preliminary work. If you jumped to this section without having created a frameset or naming your frames, you may want to refer to the sections earlier in this chapter. If you already have a frameset, have named the frames, and just want find out how to set links, this section is where you want to be.

Setting links in a frameset is like setting any other links between pages, except that you need to specify the target frame, meaning the frame where the link will be displayed. For example, if you want a link in the right frame to display in the main frame, you need to specify the main frame as the target in the link. If you don't specify a target, the link opens in the same frame the link is in. Because the most common reason to use frames is to keep navigation links in one frame and open them in another, you'll probably want to know how to target a frame when you set a link.

For the purposes of this exercise, I'm going to walk you through creating three text links in the right frame that open in the main frame, the left area of the frameset you created in the last exercise. If you're working on your own frameset, refer to Figures 7-4 and 7-5 to follow along and set the links as they correspond to your frameset.

If this seems confusing, don't fret. It's easier to understand after you try the following steps:

1. **Click to place the cursor inside the right frame and type the words** Cool Link #1, **followed by a return; then** Cool Link #2 **followed by a return; then** Cool Link #3.

   Refer to Figure 7-5 to see how this should look.

2. **Highlight the text link.**

   For this exercise, highlight the words *Cool Link #1*. Note that this works the same way if you want to link an image.

3. In the Property Inspector, type the URL http://www.macromedia.com.

This creates a link to the Macromedia Web site. If you want to create a link to another page in your Web site, select the file icon next to the link box and browse to find the link, just like you would to set any other link in your site.

4. From the drop-down list next to <u>T</u>**arget in the Property Inspector, choose the name of the frame that you want the link to open into.**

If you are following my exercise, select *mainframe*. If you've changed the names, choose the name that corresponds to the main frame on the page. Notice that Dreamweaver conveniently lists all the frames you named in your document in this drop-down list.

The result, as shown in Figure 7-6, is that when you click the linked text Cool Link #1 in the left frame, the Macromedia Web site is displayed in the main frame area. ***Note:*** You'll have to save your work before you preview it in a browser. Use F12 as a shortcut to save all files and open them in a browser automatically.

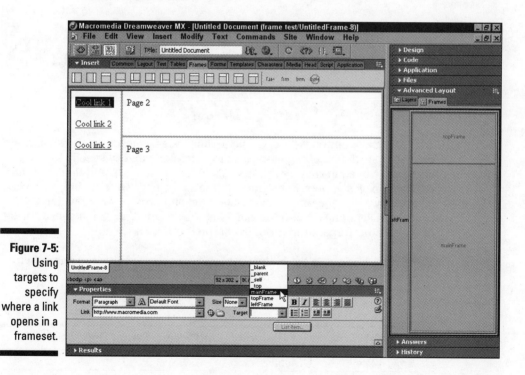

Figure 7-5:
Using
targets to
specify
where a link
opens in a
frameset.

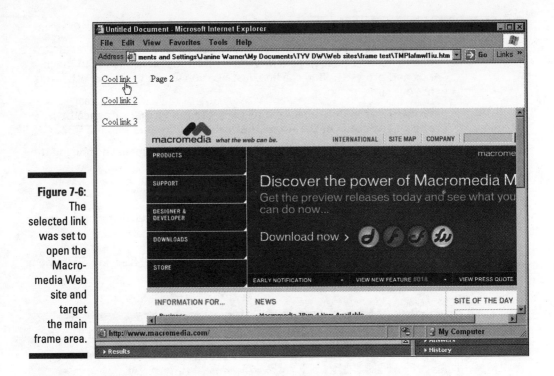

Figure 7-6:
The
selected link
was set to
open the
Macro-
media Web
site and
target
the main
frame area.

Comparing target options

You have many options when you target links in a frameset. As shown in the preceding section, "Setting links to a target frame," you can specify that a linked page open in another frame within your frameset. In addition, you can set linked pages to open in the same frame as the page with the link, to open a completely new page, and even to open a second browser window. Table 7-1 provides a list of target options and what they mean. You can find all of these options in the Target drop-down list of the Property Inspector.

The Target drop-down list in the Property Inspector is activated only when you select a linked image or section of text and specify the link in the page you want to link to in the link text box.

Table 7-1	Understanding Frame Target Options
Target Name	*Action*
_blank	Opens the linked document into a new browser window.
_parent	Opens the linked document into the parent frameset of the page that has the link. (The *parent* is the window that contains the frameset.)

Target Name	Action
_self	Opens the linked document in the same frame as the original link, replacing the current content of the frame.
_top	Opens the linked document into the outermost frameset, replacing the entire contents of the browser window.

Changing Frame Properties

As you get more sophisticated in using frames, you may want to further refine your frames by changing properties, which enables you to turn off frame borders, change the frame or border colors, limit scrolling, and so on. To access these options in Dreamweaver, choose Window⇨Frames, click inside the Frames panel in the area that corresponds to the frame that you want to change, and then use the Property Inspector to access the options I describe in the following four sections. Figure 7-7 shows the Property Inspector as it appears when you select a frame in the Frames panel.

If you don't see the margin height and width options, make sure that you click the expander arrow in the bottom-right corner of the Property Inspector. Clicking this arrow causes all available properties to be displayed for the selected item.

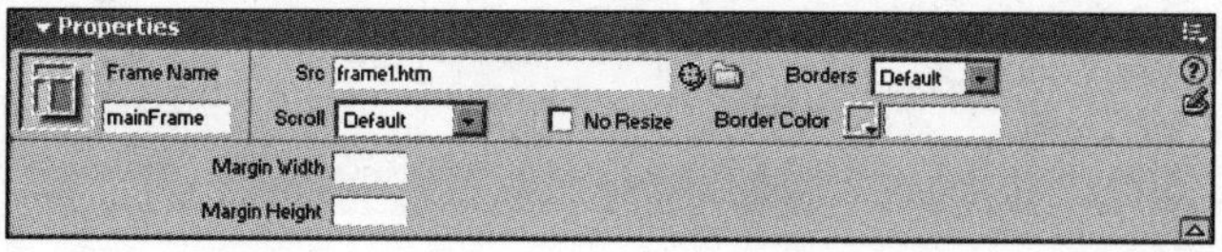

Figure 7-7: Use the Frames panel to select frames or framesets so that their properties are visible in the Property Inspector.

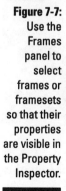

Changing frame borders

I think that the best thing that you can do with a frame border is to turn it off. In the example from Lynda Weinman's site in Figure 7-1, the site appears like a single document because the frame borders have been turned off. You can do the same by choosing No from the Borders drop-down list in the Property Inspector for either the frameset or any of the individual frames in the frameset. Your other options include Yes, which forces the borders to be visible, and Default, which usually means Yes. In case of individual frames, however, the Default option defaults to the settings for the parent frameset.

You can make global border settings by using the Property Inspector and applying the settings to the frameset. To select the frameset so that its properties are visible in the Inspector, click the border that encloses the frameset in the Frames panel. Figure 7-8 shows a frameset selected in the Frames panel and its corresponding properties displayed in the Property Inspector.

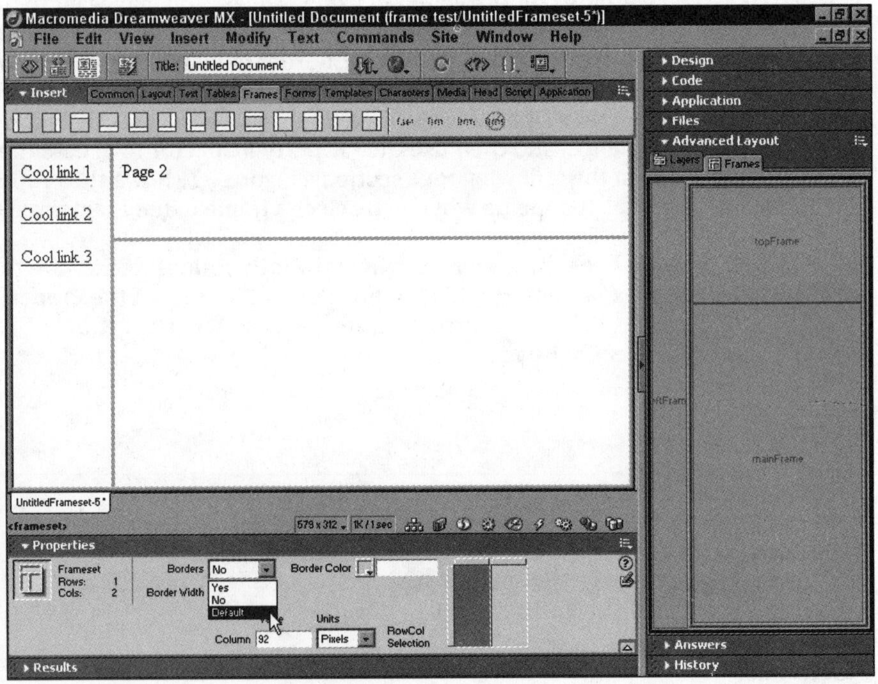

Figure 7-8: Changing the border settings on a frameset to make the borders invisible.

If you choose to keep your borders visible, you may want to customize the color by clicking the Border Color square and then choosing a color from the Dreamweaver palette.

If you select a specific border, the Property Inspector also enables you to specify the border width. Simply enter a value in pixels in the Border Width text field to change the width of the selected border.

Changing frame sizes

The easiest way to change the size of a frame is to select the border and drag it until the frame is the size that you want. When you select the border, the Property Inspector displays the size of the frame, enabling you to change the size in pixels or as a percentage of the display area by entering a number in the text area next to Row or Column. If you've specified 0 width for your frame borders, you may not be able to see them on the page in order to drag and resize them. If this is the case, you can view the borders by choosing View⇨Visual Aids⇨Frame Borders, and Dreamweaver indicates the borders with a thin gray line so that you can easily select them.

Changing scrolling and resizing options

Scrolling options control whether a viewer can scroll up and down or left and right in a frame area. As shown in Figure 7-9, the scrolling options for frames are Yes, No, Auto, and Default. As a general rule, I recommend leaving the scroll option set to Auto because a visitor's browser can then turn scrolling on if necessary. That is, if the viewer's display area is too small to see all the contents of the frame, the frame becomes scrollable. If all the contents are visible, the scroll arrows aren't visible.

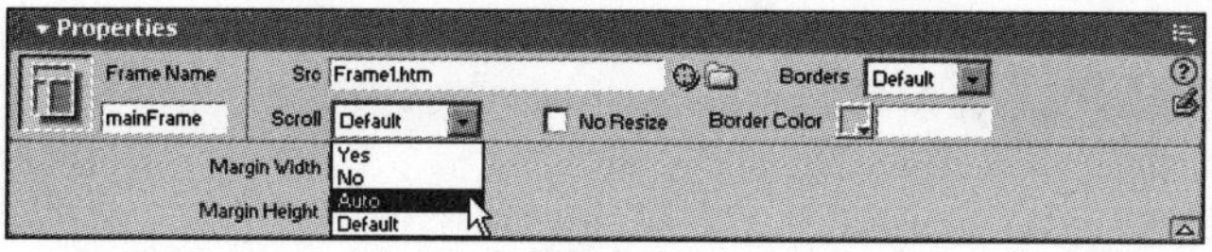

Figure 7-9: Use Scroll Options list in the Property Inspector to control frame-scrolling options.

If you set this option to Yes, the scroll arrows are visible whether they're needed or not. If you set it to No, they won't be visible, even if that means your viewer can't see all the contents of the frame — a sometimes dangerous proposition because there's no way to scroll. Default leaves it up to the browser. In most browsers, the Default option results in the same display as the Auto option, but Default can yield unpredictable results. As a general rule, it's best to use Auto so the scroll bar is visible only if needed.

Also notice the No Resize option in Figure 7-9. If you place a check mark in this box, a visitor to your site can't change the size of the frames. If you leave this box unchecked, your user can select the border and drag it to make the frame area small or larger, just as you can when you develop your frames in Dreamweaver. Generally, I like to give viewers control, but I often check the No Resize option because I want to ensure that my viewers don't alter the design, especially because some viewers may do so accidentally.

Setting margin height and width

The Margin Width and Margin Height options enable you to specify the amount of margin space around a frame. Normally in a browser window, there's always a small margin between the edge of the window and any content such as images or text. That's why you can't normally place an image on your page that is flush against the edge of the browser. With frames, though, you can actually control the size of the margin or even eliminate the margin altogether. I generally recommend that you set the margin to at least two pixels and make it larger if you want to create more space around your content. If you want to get rid of the margin altogether, set it to zero and any images or text in the frame appear flush against the edge of the frame or browser window if the frame touches the edge of the browser. If the frame touches another frame, you can use this technique to create the impression of seamless images across frames.

Creating Alternative Designs for Older Browsers

Frames provide some great navigational options, but they can also provide the worst possible navigation nightmare. Navigation problems exist because frames are not supported by very old browsers or by text-only browsers. For example, if you create a frameset on your site and visitors try to access your page with an old browser that doesn't support frames, they won't see the contents of any of your frames. In fact, if you don't provide an alternative, they won't see anything at all.

So what's the alternative? It's called the <NOFRAMES> tag, and Dreamweaver makes it easy to create this option for low-end users. The <NOFRAMES> tag enables you to create an alternative page that displays in browsers that don't support frames. The contents of the <NOFRAMES> tag are stored in the frameset file — that invisible file that describes how your frames look, but never shows up in the browser. A browser that supports frames ignores the contents of the alternative page because it knows not to display anything that appears in the <NOFRAMES> tag. A browser that doesn't support frames ignores the contents of the frameset because it doesn't understand the pointers within the <FRAMES> tag and displays all the content contained within the <NOFRAMES> tag instead.

If this all sounds a bit complicated, don't worry; it works like a charm. Fortunately, you don't have to know much about how it works; you just need to know that you should add the alternative content in Dreamweaver if you want to ensure that your pages look okay to people with older browsers.

To create an alternative page for older browsers by using the <NOFRAMES> tag, open any document that uses frames and follow these steps:

1. **Choose Modify⇨Frameset⇨Edit NoFrames Content.**

   A new Document window opens with NoFrames Content displayed at the top.

2. **Edit this page as you would any other page in Dreamweaver by inserting images, typing text, creating tables, and adding any other features that you want (except frames, of course).**

   Your goal is to create an alternative page that can be viewed by people using older browsers. The alternative page can be as simple as instructions for how viewers can get a newer copy of Microsoft Internet Explorer or Netscape Navigator or as complex as a copy of the page you created in frames that you've re-created as well as you can without frames.

   Your best bet is to keep your NoFrames page as simple as possible, using only text to ensure it displays well for the broadest possible audience.

3. **To close the window and return to your frameset, choose Modify⇨Frameset⇨Edit NoFrames Content again.**

   The check box next to the Edit NoFrames Content option disappears and the frames page replaces the NoFrames Content page in the document window.

If you create an alternative page, don't forget to update it when you make changes to your frameset.

Chapter 8

Formatting Text in HTML and CSS

• •

In This Chapter

▶ Formatting text on Web pages

▶ Creating HTML styles

▶ Creating CSS styles

▶ Applying CSS styles

• •

*T*ext is at the heart of nearly every Web page. In fact, HTML was originally developed as a way to exchange text-only files between scientists and researchers, not to design pretty pages. Graphics didn't come along until later. Before Dreamweaver, even formatting text for things like bold and italic required a pretty thorough knowledge of HTML tags, and there were lots of tags to memorize. With Dreamweaver, formatting and working with text is much easier, and you can accomplish a lot more than you could a few years ago, even if you were an HTML expert.

After you figure out how to work with text in Dreamweaver, you'll probably come to the conclusion that HTML doesn't give you a whole lot of typographic control over your page designs. Welcome to the world of HTML design. Fortunately, things in the HTML world have progressed a lot since the early days of Web design, and thanks to some new technologies, today's Web designers have a lot more control over type than they did even a few years ago.

The evolution of HTML text formatting means that today you can use specific font faces, control size and style more precisely, and even create style sheets. Cascading Style Sheets *(CSS)* are a kind of extended HTML that enable greater style control and the ability to specify formatting features for types of text, such as headlines, even across multiple pages. You find out how to use CSS in the second part of this chapter.

In this chapter, you also find out about HTML styles, a unique feature of Dreamweaver that provides an alternative to CSS and enables you to save and apply repetitive text attributes to documents — things like type size, color, bold, italic, and so on.

Formatting Text in Dreamweaver

Before you find out about HTML styles and CSS, this section makes sure you understand how to use the text formatting features, using the Property Inspector. In Chapter 2, you find the basics of entering and formatting text by using Dreamweaver. This section takes text formatting several more steps beyond what you find in Chapter 2 and ensures you have the basics down before you get into the more complex aspects of style sheets.

Understanding the <FONT> tag

HTML is really all about tags. Whenever you make changes to a type selection in Dreamweaver, you alter the contents of the HTML `<FONT>` tag or add additional tags that control things like bold and italic. Changing the contents of the `<FONT>` tag allows you to specify size, font face, color, and tells the browser how to display the type. All these options are attributes of the `<FONT>` tag, so you specify them in the Property Inspector in Dreamweaver. But before you start applying these options, you need to understand a little about how they work.

Regarding font sizes, HTML may be different from what you're used to if you've been formatting text in a word processor or graphics program. HTML only uses a limited list of sizes, which range from 1 to 7, with 7 being the largest. HTML can also specify font sizes relative to a given browser's default font size. The actual size of the default font varies from browser to browser and from platform to platform. In most browsers, the standard default size is HTML Font Size 3, but users can change the default to any font and size in the browser's preferences. If you're used to regular font sizes, 3 sounds like it's a really tiny font size. But, actually, it's about the same size as Times 12 point on the Mac and Times Roman 14 point on the PC. That's why the default size option in the Property Inspector in Dreamweaver is the equivalent of font size 3.

In addition to setting absolute font sizes, you can also set relative font sizes. *Absolute* font sizes keep their size no matter what; *relative* sizes adjust according to users settings, always keeping their relative size in relation to other sizes on the page. HTML gives you the option of setting the font size using +1 through +7 or –1 through –7. Using these options enables you to specify a font size relative to the default of the browser, even if it's something other than font size 3. For example, if you set the font size to +2, it is displayed at +2 larger than whatever the default font size is, even if the viewer made the default size in her browser the equivalent of Times 24 point. This enables you to create relative sizes in HTML so that you can ensure that one section of text is larger than another, even though you can't control the exact font size.

When you specify a font face in Dreamweaver, you override the default font of the browser (the default font and size can be changed in the browser's preferences). But for the font to be displayed, it must be available on the viewer's computer. If you specify that you want to use Helvetica but your viewer's computer doesn't have Helvetica, the browser reverts to the browser's default font.

To help get around the problem of specifying specific fonts, HTML lets you specify multiple font faces and then prioritize their use. For example, if you specify Helvetica, you may also specify a similar font, such as Arial, as your second choice. Then, if Helvetica isn't available, the browser looks for Arial. If Arial is on the viewer's hard drive, the browser uses it to display the text instead. You can even take this a step further and choose a family of fonts, such as serif or sans serif, as one of your options. Then the browser at least tries to use a font in the same family if none of the fonts you've chosen is available. (*Serif* fonts have the little curly edges, like Times Roman; *sans serif* fonts, such as Helvetica and Arial, don't have the curly edges.)

To help you specify multiple font choices, Dreamweaver provides a list of common fonts and families in the font drop-down list in the Property Inspector. These are organized into groups of three or four fonts that you can apply to text, and they include some of the most popular and useful combinations of font choices. You can also edit this list to add fonts and combinations of fonts of your own choosing. Figure 8-1 shows the drop-down list for font choices in the Property Inspector. In this example, I've chosen the Arial, Helvetica, Sans-Serif option. The browser that displays this text will try to display it first in Arial. If Arial isn't available on the computer, the text is displayed in Helvetica, and if that's not available, it will use the third option and display the text in any sans-serif font available on the user's computer.

HTML font sizes display differently when viewed on Macintosh and PC computer systems. A given font size viewed on the Mac usually appears about two point sizes smaller than the same font size viewed on a PC because of a difference in the display standards of the two systems. Unfortunately, this is not something you can control (unless you literally create two different pages, one for each system your visitors may use). Most designers choose to create their page for the Windows system, because that is the most commonly used system, but good designers also test their work on Mac systems to ensure the page looks good on both, even if it's not exactly the same.

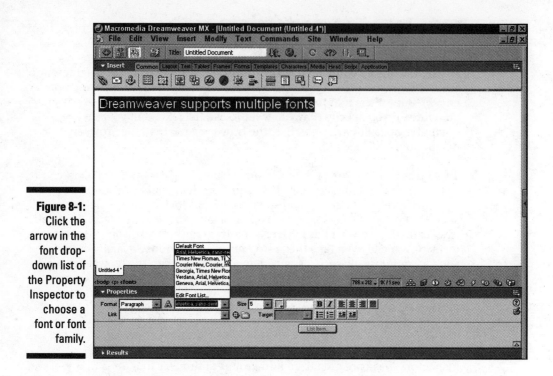

Figure 8-1:
Click the
arrow in the
font drop-
down list of
the Property
Inspector to
choose a
font or font
family.

The most important thing is to be sure to take this difference into considera-
tion, especially if you're designing a site on a Mac. Ideally, you should view
the results on both platforms during development of your site in order to find
a size that works best, knowing that the size you choose will look smaller on
a Mac or bigger on a PC.

Applying font attributes

With Dreamweaver, applying a font or combination of fonts and setting font
sizes and colors is easy.

To apply font attributes to text, follow these steps:

1. **Highlight the text that you want to change.**

2. **In the Property Inspector, choose a set of fonts from the font drop-
   down list (click the button to the right of where it says Default Font).**

   The font is automatically applied to the text. If you don't see the fonts
   you want to apply, you can create your own set by choosing Edit Font
   List from this drop-down list and adding fonts in the order you want
   them to display.

3. **With the text still highlighted, choose the size you want from the Size drop-down list in the Property Inspector (button to the right of the Size field in the Property Inspector).**

   You can choose a size from 1 to 7 or specify sizes relative to the default font size by choosing + or –1 through 7.

4. **With the text still highlighted, click the color square in the middle of the Property Inspector, just to the right of the Size text box.**

   When you click the color square, a pop-up color palette appears so that you can select a font color.

5. **Choose any color from the color palette (see Figure 8-2) by clicking the eyedropper over the appropriate color.**

   The color palette is limited to Web-safe colors (those that best display on both the Macintosh and Windows operating systems). The arrow in the top right of the color palette provides access to other color palette options, including those best suited to Mac, those best suited to PC, and grayscale. As a general rule, the Web-safe palette is your best option because it displays most consistently across different monitors and platforms.

   If you want to create a custom color, click the icon that looks like a rainbow-colored globe in the top-right corner of the color palette, just be aware that your custom color may not appear exactly as you created it because Dreamweaver converts RGB colors into hexadecimal codes. If you click the first icon, the square with a diagonal red line, the color reverts to the default text color for the page (the color specified as text color in Page Properties). You can also pick up a color from anywhere on the screen simply by dragging the eyedropper icon over any part of the screen and clicking over a desired color.

6. **You can also click Bold (B) or Italic (I) in the Property Inspector to change the font style accordingly.**

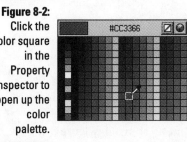

Figure 8-2:
Click the color square in the Property Inspector to open up the color palette.

Creating Your Own HTML Styles

Now that you know how to control font attributes, you'll probably find that making font changes throughout a site can become rather boring and repetitive, especially if you need to make the same changes over and over. If you want to save some time, you can easily save commonly used attributes as particular styles and then use them over and over again. This is what HTML styles are about. Don't confuse HTML styles with Cascading Style Sheets (discussed later in this chapter); HTML styles are simply a collection of <FONT> tag and other style attributes that you can save in Dreamweaver and then easily reuse.

HTML styles are convenient, and they are better suited to consistent display across different browsers, but they are more limited than Cascading Style Sheets. First of all, they only let you apply font attributes that are available as part of regular HTML. This means that you can't specify font sizes based on pixels, picas, or any other measurement other than the normal, very limited, HTML sizes. HTML styles also can't be shared among sites unless the other sites are also being edited in Dreamweaver. No other HTML program can use or modify Dreamweaver HTML styles.

Perhaps the greatest limitation of HTML styles compared with Cascading Style Sheets, however, is that if you format text to a certain style and later change the style definition, the text you formatted earlier doesn't update automatically to reflect the changes to the style. Still, in many cases, HTML styles can save time and increase productivity if your needs aren't that demanding and automatic updating isn't critical to your needs.

Here's an example of how you might use HTML styles. Say you want all the headlines on your site to be font face Arial, size 5, and bold. You can create a style called Headline and apply all of those formatting options at once when you use the Headline style. If you want different size headlines, you can create a style sheet that defines Headline 1 as one size and Headline 2 as a smaller size for sub heads.

To create a new HTML style, follow these steps:

1. **Choose Text⇨HTML Styles⇨New Style.**

   A submenu appears offering you a list of predefined styles, along with the New Style option.

2. **Choose New Style.**

   The Define HTML Style dialog box opens, as shown in Figure 8-3.

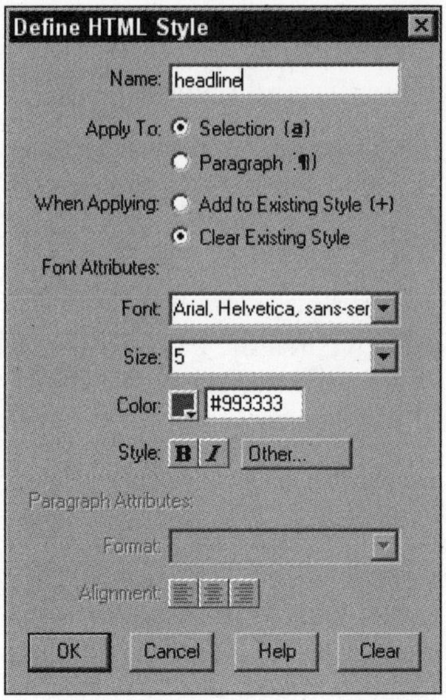

Figure 8-3:
Dream-
weaver lets
you define
and name
custom
HTML styles
to use
throughout
your page or
Web site.

3. Enter a name in the text box.

You can name the style anything you want. In this case, I've chosen to name a style Headline. The name you enter appears in the style menu after you create the style.

4. Specify if the style should be applied only to selected text elements or to all elements separated by the paragraph tag.

5. Specify the behavior of the style when it is applied.

If you want the style you create to be applied in addition to existing formatting, choose Add to Existing Style (+). If you want to clear any existing formatting before applying the new style, choose Clear Existing Style.

6. Select all formatting attributes, including font, size, color, style, and alignment, that you want to include in this style.

The Paragraph attributes are only available if you have selected Paragraph in the Apply To section at the top of the dialog box.

7. Click OK to save the style.

Your new style now appears in the submenu when you choose Text⇨HTML Styles. Any time you want to apply this style to a selected area of text, you can simply choose the style from the submenu and your text changes to reflect that style. When you quit Dreamweaver and start it up again, or even restart your computer, the HTML Style you created remains as an option in the HTML Styles menu until you remove it.

To apply an existing HTML style, follow these steps:

1. **Highlight the text you want to modify and choose <u>Text</u>➪HTML St<u>y</u>les.**

   A submenu appears offering you a list of predefined styles that ship with Dreamweaver or any custom styles that you have created.

2. **Click to select one of the styles from this list, and the style is applied to your selected text.**

HTML styles are stored on your hard drive in a file called styles.xml. This folder is located either in the site folder (in the Library subfolder) or in the Dreamweaver configuration folder if the site root folder has not been defined.

Working with Cascading Style Sheets

The addition of Cascading Style Sheets *(CSS)* to HTML has many people with graphic design backgrounds excited. Finally, you can have real design control on the Web and apply global style settings across multiple pages — or even an entire site.

If you're not familiar with the concept of style sheets, you're sure to appreciate the benefits. Cascading Style Sheets, more commonly referred to by the acronym *CSS,* enable you to define styles with multiple text formatting options in HTML. CSS goes a long way toward giving you real typographic control and a consistent look and feel throughout a Web site, as well as saving time in designing your Web page.

Before you get too excited, however, I have to warn you that CSS is not supported by many of the browsers still in use on the Web. Because CSS is a relatively new addition to HTML, older versions of Web browsers like Netscape and Internet Explorer won't display formatting that is designed as a CSS. Even newer browsers won't always display CSS the same way. (You find more on browsers in the following section, "Understanding the Differences among Browsers.")

As a result, most of the sites on the Web still use regular HTML formatting options, which you'll find explained earlier in this chapter.

The main reason to create CSS today is that the future benefits are so appealing. In another year or so, it will probably be safe to rely on CSS for most of your users. If you know that most of the people who are visiting your site have recent browsers, it may already be reasonable for you just use CSS today, but most general-audience sites are better off using regular HTML formatting or the HTML styles feature of Dreamweaver described in the previous section.

You should also know that Cascading Style Sheets are much more complex to create than basic HTML formatting. Dreamweaver makes it much easier than writing the codes by hand, but you'll still want to take some time to discover the best way to create CSS with the fonts, colors, styles, and other formatting you want in your styles.

Understanding the Differences among Web Browsers

The differences in the way that Netscape Navigator and Internet Explorer support Cascading Style Sheets can be extremely frustrating, to say nothing of the differences between different versions of the same browsers. The good news is that style sheets are great for design consistency and for making fast changes throughout a page and even an entire site. The bad news is that style sheets are one of the newer additions to HTML, and some older browsers don't support them. The worse news is that style sheets aren't *backward compatible,* meaning that if you use this cool new design feature and visitors view your site using an older browser, such as Netscape Navigator 3.0, they won't be able to see any of the formatting that you created with a style sheet. They will be able to see the text — and it'll just look like plain old HTML text.

Now for even worse news: Even if your viewers use the latest browser, they won't necessarily see the same formatting because Netscape and Microsoft haven't agreed on how to implement and support style sheets. Ironically, even Microsoft hasn't been able to get CSS to work consistently in Internet Explorer on both Mac and PC computers.

For example, in Internet Explorer 4 and 5, you can use JavaScript to change attributes, such as font color and size, after a page has loaded. This feature can add powerful effects to your site, such as changing the color of a link when a user moves the cursor over it. But this feature doesn't work the same way in Navigator because Navigator 4.0 doesn't support changes to attributes, though Navigator 6, the latest version from Netscape, does offer support. On the other hand, version 3.0 and above of both Internet Explorer and Netscape Navigator enable you to swap images, so you can create a similar effect by using two images of different colors. Fortunately, you don't have to know what browser supports what features. Dreamweaver takes care of that for you by enabling you to target browsers and limit design options to features supported by target browsers.

Dreamweaver works hard to try to solve these problems with browser differences. When you work with Dynamic HTML (DHTML), Dreamweaver creates complex code in the background that is designed to take best advantage of the features supported by each browser. If you look at the code, it may look a bit more complex than necessary sometimes, but that's because Dreamweaver creates these tags in ways that both browsers can interpret them. And this is true not only for DHTML. As I explain in Chapter 12, the best way to insert many multimedia files, such as Shockwave and Flash, is to use a combination of code that's designed to compensate for the differences between browsers.

Appreciating Cascading Style Sheets

CSS provides a whole new level of control over page design. CSS also makes it possible to do fancy stuff with Dynamic HTML, but for the rest of this chapter, you'll focus on how CSS relates to controlling the appearance of text. (In Chapters 9 and 10 you'll find out more about Dynamic HTML.)

By using CSS, Web page designers can gain control over such things as font type, sizing, spacing, and even exact positioning of page elements, in a way that is much more consistent across computer platforms. If you're sure your Web audience can view CSS and you want to learn how to do some really cool stuff with type, read on.

A Cascading Style Sheet is basically a list of rules defined in HTML. HTML already contains a bunch of rules of behavior, but you can neither see them (unless you read a very technical HTML manual) nor alter them — they're kind of like the grammar rules in a language. CSS, however, lets you create your own rules and override the rules of HTML, which are very limited in terms of page design. These new rules determine how the browser renders certain page elements. Imagine if you could invent a bunch of new words and grammar rules for the English language. Now imagine that everyone else can do that, too. What keeps the communication from breaking down is that every time you invent these new rules, you include a dictionary and a grammar guide to go along with each document. That's what CSS is all about.

The term *cascading* refers to the way in which the general CSS rules within a style are overridden by local rules. With CSS, you can create general rules or local rules. Because local rules override the general rules, they are referred to as cascading. This definition becomes clearer as you read on and become more familiar with how CSS operates.

Cascading Style Sheets are actually just one component of Dynamic HTML, which is covered in greater detail in Chapters 9 and 10. Cascading Style Sheets are a set of technologies that gives you enhanced capabilities over standard HTML, bringing a whole new level of interactivity and design control to Web page design, even beyond just typographic control. Dynamic HTML is made possible through scripting languages that utilize the Document Object Model to create dynamic effects and global styles. Think of Cascading Style Sheets as kind of like HTML on steroids. If this still seems a little confusing, don't worry. It makes more sense as you find out what you can do with these powerful new HTML features. For more on the Document Object Model, see the sidebar "What is the Document Object Model?"

Have you ever used a style sheet in a word processor or desktop publishing application? If so, you can appreciate how style sheets make life easier. CSS is a powerful tool because with it, you can define a set of formatting attributes and then apply them to as many elements on a page or throughout a Web site as you want.

The most powerful aspect of CSS is the ability to make global style changes across a site. Suppose, for example, that one fine day you decide that all your headlines should be purple rather than blue. You can change the style definition for Headline, and all the text on your page or site that you formatted with the Headline style changes from blue to purple. One simple change to the style can save you hours, even days, if you ever find yourself in a redesign (and believe me, every good site goes through periodic redesigns).

Creating CSS in Dreamweaver

When you get into creating and using Cascading Style Sheets, you use one of the most complex and advanced features of Dreamweaver. Consequently, creating style sheets takes a little more time to grasp than applying basic HTML

What is the Document Object Model?

If you want to impress your geek friends, start talking about the DOM (rhymes with *mom*). But first you may want to know a bit more about what it actually means. The Document Object Model (DOM), part of the World Wide Web Consortium's HTML 4.0 specification, strives to make every element on a page an identifiable object. The properties of that object are then readable and writeable, meaning that you can use a scripting language such as JavaScript to change, hide, or move the object's attributes. So for example, if the image on a page is an object, you can say "Take object #2 and move it over here." The DOM provides a method to refer to and control objects in your document.

By defining a standard DOM, a consistent method for interacting with page elements can be achieved across platforms and browsers. This capability makes most of the DHTML effects, such as dynamically changing text and images, possible.

Unfortunately, as with many standards in the world of HTML, there is still a great divergence in the way that the major browsers implement the DOM. This inconsistency has had the effect of limiting the practical usefulness of DHTML until the major browsers can more fully support the World Wide Web Consortium (W3C) standards. Still, the foundation is there for some very powerful additions to the current limited capabilities of HTML.

tags or using HTML styles. Still, Dreamweaver makes it much easier to define style sheets than to write them by hand — a task that is a lot closer to writing programming code than to creating HTML tags.

To help you get the hang of using Dreamweaver to create style sheets, I first walk you through the screens that define styles and give you an overview of your options as you create styles. After the following sections on each aspect of style sheet creation, you find specific numbered steps that walk you through the process of creating and applying your own CSS styles.

Understanding CSS style types

You can create two types of style sheets with CSS and Dreamweaver: internal style sheets and external style sheets. An *internal style sheet* stores its data within the HTML code of a page and applies styles to only that page. An *external style sheet* is a text file that you create and store outside of your HTML page. You then reference it as a link, much like you do any other HTML page on the Web. In this way, you can apply style sheets to an entire Web site or to any page that links to the external style sheet, which also means that you can have many different pages referencing the same style sheet. You create these two kinds of style sheets in much the same way, as you see in the following step-by-step exercises.

You can define two different kinds of CSS styles to use in either an internal or external style sheet: custom styles and redefined HTML tag styles. The difference is that a *custom style* is a completely new set of formatting attributes that you can apply to any text selection. Custom styles in CSS are referred to as *classes*. Don't worry about this too much because I get into it in more detail later in the chapter. For now, just know that when you define a custom style, you give it a class name and then you use that name to apply the style to any text block on the page. So you can call a custom style anything you want, you can create a new custom style any time you want, and the new style doesn't necessarily affect anything else on the page. Creating a custom style is a little bit like making up your own HTML tag, with formatting rules that you can define yourself.

In contrast, you create redefined HTML tag styles by *redefining* how *existing* HTML tags are rendered by the browser; you are changing existing rules instead of creating new ones. This means that you change how common HTML tags format text throughout your page — or throughout your Web site if you want to define it that way. The result is that if you redefine a tag, such as the <BLOCKQUOTE> tag, all the text already formatted with the <BLOCK-QUOTE> tag automatically changes to reflect your new style definition.

Suppose that you define the <BLOCKQUOTE> tag to render text in blue at 12-point italic. Normally, *blockquoted text* simply creates an indent on the right and left margins — great for setting off quoted text on a page. Because you've redefined the <BLOCKQOUTE> tag, it's going to also add the new attributes of blue and 12-point italic. But there's more. Because style sheets are cascading, any styles applied to tags *within* the <BLOCKQUOTE> tag override the <BLOCK-QUOTE> tags that enclose it. So, if you placed a set of <B> tags (that normally indicate bold text) inside the <BLOCKQUOTE> tag and defined the <B> tag as red text, any text falling inside the <B> tags would be red instead of blue, in addition to bold. The <B> tag would override the enclosing <BLOCKQUOTE> tags. This is true for any tag that you modify using CSS.

Creating a new CSS Style

To create a new CSS, open any HTML document or create a new file in Dreamweaver and choose Window⇨CSS Styles to open the CSS Styles panel at the right of the display area. In the lower-right corner of this panel you can see four small icons (really small). From left to right, these icons represent Attach Style Sheet, New Style, Edit Style Sheet, and Delete Style (resembles a trash can). Choose Text⇨CSS Styles⇨New CSS Style.

The New CSS Style dialog box, shown in Figure 8-4, opens, giving you the following options:

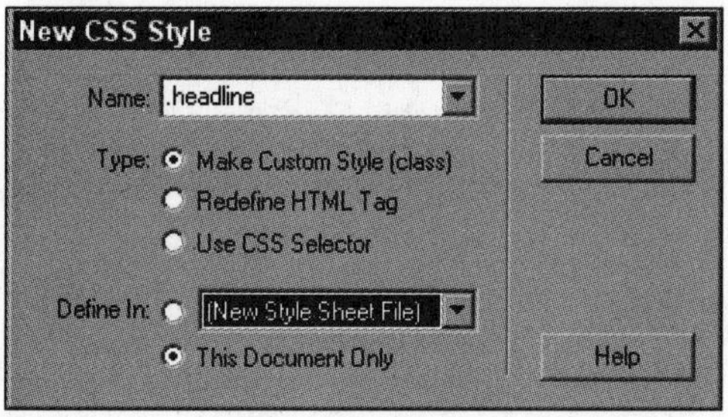

Figure 8-4:
The New
CSS Style
dialog box.

- **Name:** Although the first field in this box is titled Name, when you first bring it up, its title actually changes depending on which of the CSS types you select using the three radio buttons beneath it. Read the description for each of the CSS types in the following three bullets to see how to fill out this field.

- **Make Custom Style (class):** Enables you to define a new style that you can apply to any section of text on a page by using the class attribute. When you select this option, the first field asks for a name. All custom style names must begin with a period, which Dreamweaver automatically inserts as you name the style. This kind of style is also referred to as a *class*. If you choose this option, after clicking OK another dialog box appears, allowing you to define the different options for the style, which I explain in the section "Creating a custom style" later in this chapter.

✔ **Redefine HTML Tag:** Enables you to create a style that changes the formatting associated with an existing HTML tag. When you select this option, the first field asks for a tag name. Clicking the pop-up menu next to the tag field allows you to select from a huge list of HTML tags (the default one is the <BODY> tag). For more information on this option, see "Redefining HTML tags" later in this chapter.

✔ **Use CSS Selector:** Enables you to define a kind of pseudoclass that combines a custom style with a redefined HTML tag. CSS Selector styles apply only to the <A> tag and enable you to do things such as change the color of a link when the mouse hovers over it. When you select this option, the first field asks for the Selector name. Choices in the pop-up list are a:active, a:hover, a:link, and a:visited.

- A:active affects an active link, which is triggered while someone is actually clicking on the link.

- A:hover is triggered while the mouse is directly over the link.

- A:link is applied to any text link.

- A:visited affects links that have already been visited by the user.

Please note that CSS Selector styles work only in Internet Explorer 4 and above browsers.

✔ **Define In:** This option lets you choose whether your style sheet exists within the current page or in a separate file. When you select a new style sheet file, you're creating an external style sheet. If you select "This document only," you're creating an internal style sheet, meaning defined styles will be available only for the page you are working on.

Defining styles

When you choose to make a new style and select one of the three style options in the New CSS Style dialog box, the CSS Style Definition dialog box opens. This is where you decide how you want your style to look by selecting the attribute options. This dialog box includes eight categories, each with multiple options that you can use to define various style elements. In this section, I discuss each of these eight categories.

You don't have to make selections for all the options in each category. Any options that you leave blank remain at the browser's default. For example, if you don't specify a text color, the text is displayed as black or whatever the page's default color is.

Don't be frustrated by options in these categories that Dreamweaver doesn't display. If they don't display in Dreamweaver, they almost certainly won't work in any of the current browsers. The good news is that Macromedia is looking ahead and building these options into Dreamweaver so that they'll be ready when these features are supported. Keep an eye on the Macromedia

Web site at `www.macromedia.com` and Macromedia's DHTML information site at `www.dhtmlzone.com` for changes and updates to Dreamweaver, as well as for news about changing standards and support for these CSS features. Right now, Microsoft Internet Explorer 5 and above provide the most complete CSS support.

The Type category

After you name your style and specify the fields described in the earlier section, click OK and the CSS Style Definition dialog box appears (Figure 8-5). When you choose Type from the Category panel on the left, the Type options are visible, as shown in Figure 8-5, and you have the following formatting options:

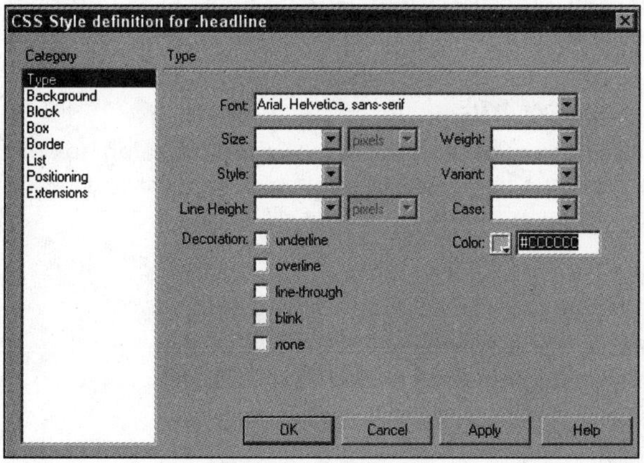

Figure 8-5: The Type page of the CSS Style Definition dialog box.

- ✔ **Font:** Specifies a font, font family, or series of families. You can add fonts to the list by selecting Edit Font List from the drop-down list.

- ✔ **Size:** Defines the size of the text. You can choose a specific point size or use a relative size, expressed as small, extra small, and so on.

- ✔ **Style:** Enables you to choose whether the text appears as Normal, Italic, or Oblique.

- ✔ **Line Height:** Enables you to specify the height of a line that the text is placed on (graphic designers usually call this *leading*). The 4.0 browsers don't support this feature, and it can cause problems in older browsers. So, for now, you should probably avoid this one.

- ✔ **Decoration:** Enables you to specify whether text is underlined, overlined (the line appears over the text instead of under it), or displayed with a strikethrough. You can also choose blink, which makes the text flash on and off.

  Use the Decoration options sparingly, if at all. Links are automatically underlined, so if you underline text that isn't a link, you risk confusing viewers. Overlined and strikethrough text can be hard to read. So use these options only if they enhance your design. And, by all means, resist the blink option; it's distracting and can make the screen difficult to read. (Overline and blink do not yet display in Dreamweaver.)

✔ **Weight:** Enables you to control how bold the text is displayed by using a specific or relative boldness option.

✔ **Variant:** Enables you to select a variation of the font, such as small caps. Unfortunately, this attribute is not yet supported.

✔ **Case:** Enables you to globally change the case of selected words, making them all uppercase or lowercase or with initial caps. Unfortunately, this attribute is not yet supported.

✔ **Color:** Defines the color of the text. You can use the color square icon to open a Web-safe color palette in which you can select predefined colors or create custom colors.

The Background category

The Background category of the CSS Style Definition dialog box (see Figure 8-6) enables you to specify a background color or image for a style. You can choose from the following options:

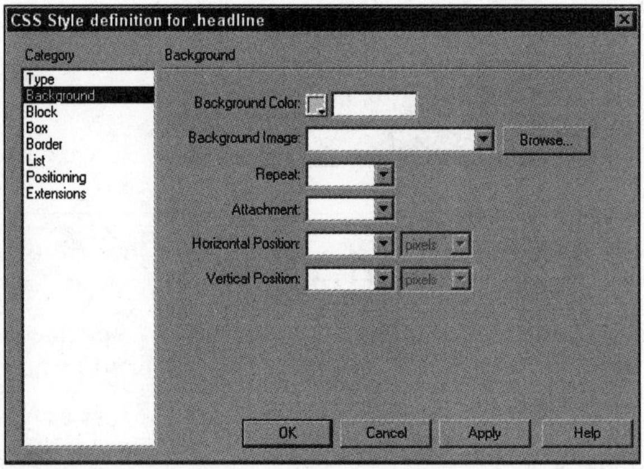

Figure 8-6: The Background page of the CSS Style Definition dialog box.

✔ **Background Color:** Specifies the background color of an element, such as a table.

✔ **Background Image:** Enables you to select a background image as part of the style definition.

✔ **Repeat:** Determines how and whether the background image tiles across and down the page. In all cases, the image is cropped if it doesn't fit behind the element.

The Repeat options are as follows:

- **No repeat:** The background is displayed once at the beginning of the element.

- **Repeat:** The background tiles repeat vertically and horizontally behind the element.

- **Repeat-x:** The background repeats horizontally, but not vertically, behind the element.

- **Repeat-y:** The background repeats vertically, but not horizontally, behind the element.

✔ **Attachment, Horizontal Position,** and **Vertical Position** options control alignment and positioning of the background image.

The Block category

The Block category (see Figure 8-7) defines spacing and alignment settings for tags and attributes. You can choose from the following options:

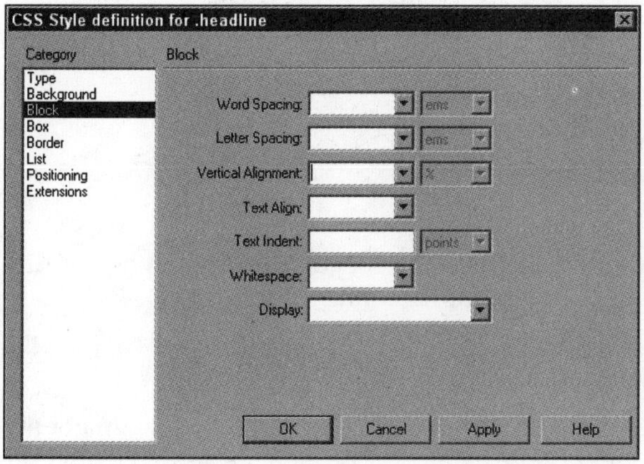

Figure 8-7:
The Block page of the CSS Style Definition dialog box.

✔ **Word Spacing:** Can be specified in points, millimeters (mm), centimeters (cm), picas, inches, pixels, ems, exs.

✔ **Letter Spacing:** Can be specified in points, millimeters (mm), centimeters (cm), picas, inches, pixels, ems, exs.

✔ **Vertical Alignment:** Works only with the <IMAGE> tag in Dreamweaver. It specifies the vertical alignment of an image, usually in relation to its parent.

✔ **Text Align:** Specifies how text aligns within an element.

✔ **Text Indent:** Specifies how far the first line of text indents.

✔ **Whitespace:** Options are normal, pre (for previous), and nowrap.

The Box category

The Box category (see Figure 8-8) defines settings for tags and attributes that control the placement of elements on the page. You can choose from the following options:

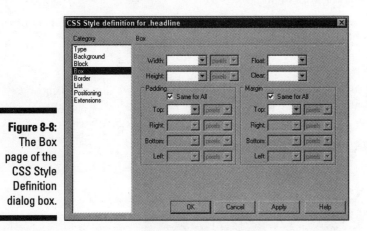

Figure 8-8:
The Box page of the CSS Style Definition dialog box.

✔ **Width, Height:** Enable you to specify a width and height that you can use in styles that you apply to images or layers.

✔ **Float:** Enables you to align an image to the left or right so that other elements, such as text, wrap around it.

✔ **Clear:** Sets the side (left or right) on which layers are not allowed to be displayed next to the element. The element drops behind the layer if the layer intersects the selected side. (Doesn't currently display in Dreamweaver.)

✔ **Padding:** Sets the amount of space between the element and its border or margin. (Doesn't currently display in Dreamweaver.)

✔ **Margin:** Enables you to define the amount of space between the border of the element and other elements on the page.

The Border category

The Border category defines settings, such as width, color, and style, for the borders of elements on a page. Options are Style, Width, and Color. (See Figure 8-9.)

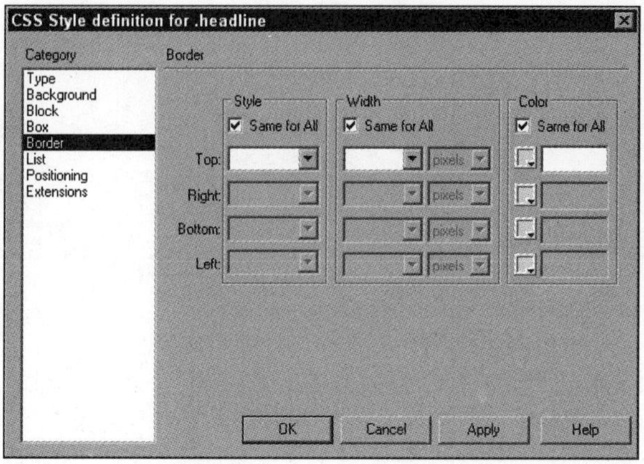

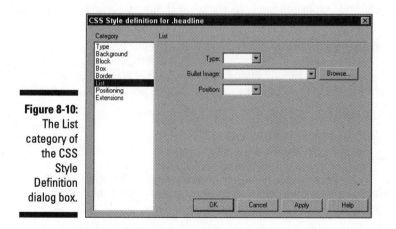

Figure 8-9:
The Border category of the CSS Style Definition dialog box.

The List category

The List category defines settings, such as bullet size and type, for list tags. You can specify if bullets are disc, circle, square, decimal, lower-roman, upper-roman, upper alpha, lower alpha, or none. If you want to use a bullet, you can use the Browse button to locate an image to be used as the bullet. You can also specify the Position inside or outside to control positioning. (See Figure 8-10.)

Figure 8-10:
The List category of the CSS Style Definition dialog box.

The Positioning category

The Positioning category (see Figure 8-11) enables you to change a tag or block of text into a new layer and specify its attributes. When applied, this style uses the tag specified for defining layers in the Layer preferences. The default in Dreamweaver for layers is the <DIV> tag. You can change this by editing the Layer preferences, but the <DIV> tag is the most universally supported, so you're best to stick with it. You can choose from the following options:

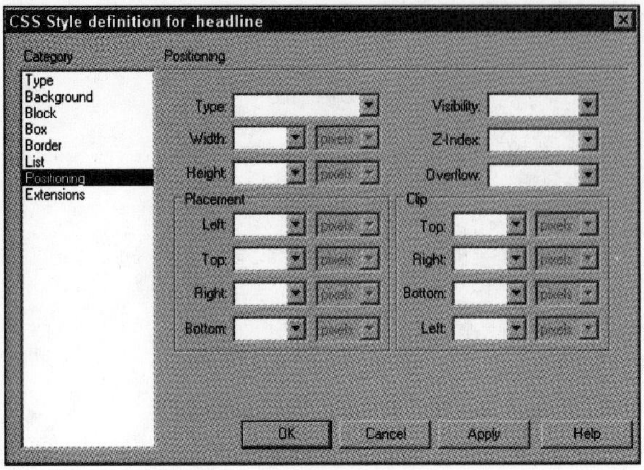

Figure 8-11:
The
Positioning
page of the
CSS Style
Definition
dialog box.

✔ **Type:** Enables you to specify the position of a layer as absolute, relative, or static.

- **Absolute:** This positioning uses the top and left coordinates entered in the Placement text boxes on this screen to control the position of the layer relative to the top-left corner of the Web page.

- **Relative:** This positioning uses a position relative to the current position of the layer instead of the top-left corner of the page.

- **Static:** This positioning keeps the layer in the place where you insert it on the page.

✔ **Visibility:** Enables you to control whether the browser displays the layer. You can use this feature, combined with a scripting language such as JavaScript, to dynamically change the display of layers. The default on most browsers is to inherit the original layer's visibility value.

- **Inherit:** The layer has the visibility of its parent.

- **Visible:** The layer is displayed.

- **Hidden:** The layer isn't displayed.

✔ **Z-Index:** Controls the position of the layer on the Z coordinate, meaning how it stacks in relation to other elements on the page. Higher-numbered layers appear above lower-numbered layers.

✔ **Overflow:** Tells the browser how to display the contents of a layer if it exceeds its size. (Doesn't currently display in Dreamweaver.)

- **Visible:** Forces the layer to increase in size to display all of its contents. The layer expands down and right.

- **Hidden:** Cuts off the contents of the layer that don't fit and doesn't provide any scroll bars.

- **Scroll:** Adds scroll bars to the layer regardless of whether the contents exceed the layer's size.

- **Auto:** Makes scroll bars appear only when the layer's contents exceed its boundaries. (Doesn't currently display in Dreamweaver.)

✔ **Placement:** Defines the size and location of a layer, in keeping with the setting for Type. The default values are measured in pixels, but you can also use pc (picas), pt (points), in (inches), mm (millimeters), cm (centimeters), or % (percentage of the parent's value).

✔ **Clip:** Enables you to specify which part of the layer is visible by controlling what part of the layer is cropped if it doesn't fit in the display area.

The Extensions category

Extensions (shown in Figure 8-12) include filters and cursor options, most of which aren't supported in any browser or are supported only in Internet Explorer 4.0 and above:

✔ **Pagebreak:** Inserts a point in a page where a printer sees a page break.

✔ **Cursor:** Defines the type of cursor that appears when a user moves the cursor over an element.

✔ **Filter:** Enables you to apply to elements special effects such as drop shadows and motion blurs.

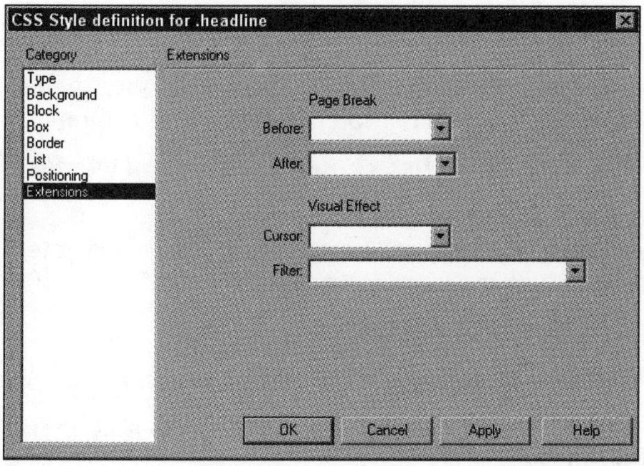

Figure 8-12:
The Extensions page of the CSS Style Definition dialog box.

Creating a custom style

The following steps tell you how to use Dreamweaver to create a custom style. In this example you define a style for headlines using CSS. If you want to create a style for another element, follow these same steps but change the specific attributes.

You can leave attributes unspecified if you don't want to use them. If you don't specify them, the browser uses its own default. For example, I don't recommend using any of the Decoration options because they can distract and confuse viewers.

To define a style for a headline, follow these steps:

1. **Choose Text➪CSS Styles➪New CSS Style.**

   The New CSS Style Sheet dialog box appears. The new style is automatically called .unnamed1.

2. **In the Name text box, type a new name for the style.**

   Dreamweaver gives you a default name that begins with a period (.) because class names must begin with a period. You can name the style anything you want as long as you don't use spaces or punctuation. Dreamweaver adds the initial period to the class name if you omit it.

3. **Next to Type select Make Custom Style (class).**

4. **Next to Define, select This Document Only to create an internal style sheet.**

5. **Click OK.**

   The CSS Style Definition dialog box opens.

6. **From the Font drop-down list, choose a font or font set.**

   If you want to use fonts that aren't on the list, choose the Edit Font List option from the drop-down list to create new font options.

7. **From the Size drop-down list, choose the size you want for your headline.**

   Large headlines are generally 24 or 36 point. You may prefer to choose a relative size, such as large or larger.

8. **From the Style drop-down list, choose a style.**

   Italic and Oblique are both good for making text stand out on a page.

9. **From the Weight drop-down list, choose Bold to make your headline thicker and darker.**

10. **Ignore Variant and Case because these attributes aren't well supported by current browsers.**

11. **Click the Color square and choose a color from the color well.**

    Sticking to the default color swatches in the color well is best because it ensures that you use a Web-safe color. You can also create a custom color by clicking the icon that looks like a rainbow-colored globe in the upper-right corner of the color well.

12. **Click OK when you're finished.**

    Your style is automatically added to the Styles list.

You can apply styles in the Styles list to any Web page or selected text block. After you create your style, it appears in the submenu under Text⇨CSS Styles. Any text that you apply it to takes on the formatting attributes you just specified. For more on how to use styles, read "Applying Styles" later in this chapter.

Redefining HTML tags

When you create a custom style, as I explained in the preceding section, you start a completely new style with its own unique name. When you redefine an HTML tag, however, you begin with an existing HTML tag, such as <B> (bold), <HR> (horizontal rule), or <TABLE> (table), and change the attributes associated with that specific tag. Any new attributes that you apply through CSS to an existing tag override the existing attributes.

To redefine a tag, start a New CSS Style, and select the Redefine HTML Tag option in the New CSS Style dialog box. When you choose this option, a list of tags appears at the top of the dialog box. Choose the tag that you want to change from the Tag drop-down list shown in Figure 8-13. Then define how you want to change it by altering the various categories and attributes in the CSS Style Definition dialog box. Be aware that when you redefine an existing HTML tag, any text that you've already formatted with that tag changes to reflect the new definition.

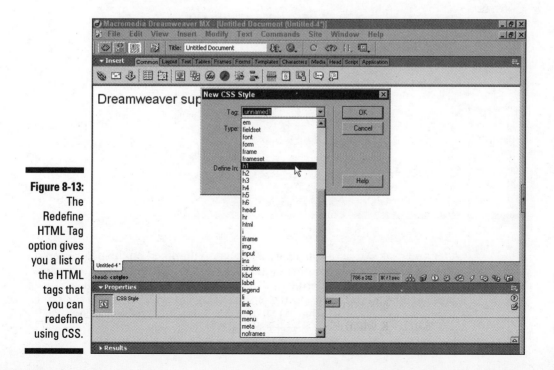

Figure 8-13:
The Redefine HTML Tag option gives you a list of the HTML tags that you can redefine using CSS.

Eliminating underlines from links

Now that you know how to redefine an HTML tag, here's your chance to put it into practice. One of the most commonly used HTML tag modifications involves disabling the underline for the anchor tag, <A>, so that hypertext links are no longer underlined in the browser. Many Web designers like to remove the underline because they think it detracts from the design and also because the cursor changes to a hand over any link, they consider the underline unnecessary. This technique works in both Netscape and Internet Explorer 4.0 (and above) browsers.

To disable underlining for hypertext links, follow these steps:

1. **Choose Text⇨CSS Styles⇨New CSS Style.**

2. **Select the Redefine HTML Tag option and choose the anchor tag <A> from the drop-down list.**

3. **Next to Define, select This Document Only.**

4. **Click OK.**

   The CSS Style Definition dialog box opens.

5. **Make sure that the Type category is selected; then check the none option under the Decoration section, as shown in Figure 8-14.**

6. **Click OK to apply the changes.**

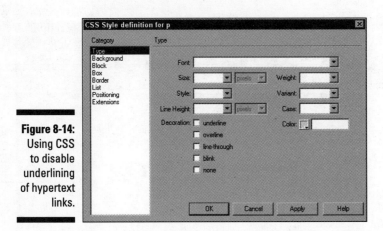

Figure 8-14:
Using CSS
to disable
underlining
of hypertext
links.

After you click OK, active links are no longer underlined on the page, even when displayed in a browser (as long as it's 4.0 or higher). In older browsers, the links appear with underlines, but otherwise are unaffected. You can make more modifications to the <A> tag in this manner, or you can apply the same principles to any of the other HTML tags available in the New CSS Style dialog box. Remember, any time you redefine an HTML tag using CSS, the changes are visible in your page only if those tags are actually used.

Conflicting styles

Be careful when you apply more than one style to the same text (something that is easier to do than you may realize). The styles may conflict, and because browsers aren't all consistent in the way in which they display styles, the results can be inconsistent and unexpected.

For the most part, Netscape Navigator 4.0 and above and Internet Explorer 4.0 and above display all the attributes applied to an element, even if they're from different styles, as long as the styles don't conflict. If they do conflict, browsers prioritize styles depending on how they're defined.

Here's an example to help you get the idea. You define a custom style called `.headline` as red and centered, and you apply it to a selection of text. Then you decide that you want that text to be bold, so you apply the bold tag independently by selecting it from the Property Inspector. You have now used two different types of styles. Because they don't conflict, all of them take effect and your text becomes bold, centered, and red. If, however, you decide that you want this text aligned left, instead of centered, and you apply left alignment directly from the Property Inspector, you have a conflict.

If a direct conflict exists, custom styles overrule regular HTML tag styles. The browser also gives priority to the attribute of the style that's inserted closest to the text. This can get really hard to juggle if you're applying defined styles, trying to keep track of standard HTML tags, and then trying to sort out how the browser prioritizes them. It gets worse with time, too, because these styles and priorities are sure to change and evolve. Your best bet is not to apply conflicting styles. Either go back and redefine an existing style, apply regular HTML tags individually, or create a new style. Remember that you can use the Duplicate option from the Edit Style Sheet dialog box to create a new duplicate style, and then make minor alterations.

Applying Styles

Defining styles is the complicated part. Applying them after you've defined them is easy. You simply select the text that you want to affect and choose the predefined style that you want to apply.

To apply a style, follow these steps:

1. **Highlight the text to which you want to apply a style.**

2. **Select the style that you want to apply from the list that appears in the white area of the CSS Styles panel.**

   The style is automatically applied to the selection. If the Style panel is not visible, choose Window➪CSS Styles to open it.

You can also apply a custom style by selecting the text that you want to change, choosing Text⇨CSS Styles, and choosing a style from the submenu.

Editing an Existing Style

You can change the attributes of any style by editing that style. This is a major advantage of Cascading Style Sheets: You can make global changes to a page or even to an entire Web site by changing a style that you applied to multiple elements with an external style sheet. Be aware, however, that everything you defined with that style changes.

Remember that you can also create new styles by duplicating an existing style and then altering it. Then you can apply that new style without affecting elements that are already formatted on your pages with the original version of the style.

The Edit Style Sheet dialog box, shown in Figure 8-15, includes the following options:

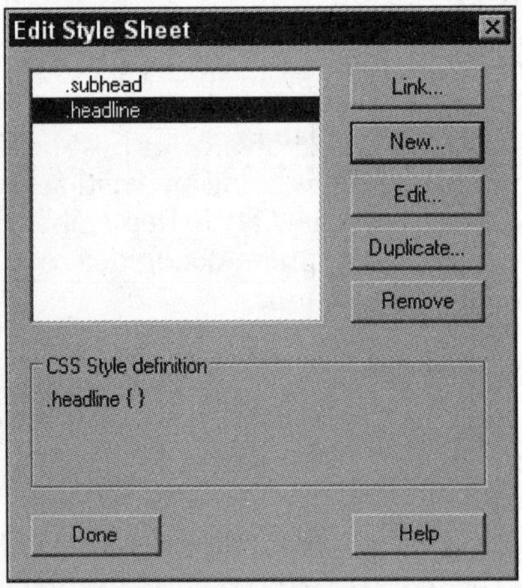

Figure 8-15:
The Edit
Style Sheet
dialog box.

✔ **Link:** Enables you to link to or import an external style sheet (a separate text file that defines a style) so that you can apply it to the page or even to the entire site that you're working on. You can find more information on external styles in the section "Using External Style Sheets" later in this chapter.

✔ **New:** Enables you to define one of three types of style sheets (Custom CSS Styles, HTML Tag Styles, and CSS Selector Styles). You can find these explained in detail in the section "Defining styles" earlier in the chapter.

✔ **Edit:** Enables you to change an existing style. For more information, see the steps following this bulleted list.

✔ **Duplicate:** Creates a copy of a selected style that you can then redefine as any one of the three style options.

✔ **Remove:** Enables you to delete a defined style.

The Undo feature doesn't work with the Remove option in the Edit Style Sheet dialog box. Before you select the Remove button, make sure that you really want to get rid of the style.

Duplicating a style with a new name and deleting the old one is a quick way to disable an unwanted style without losing the code. This way you don't have to recreate it should you ever want it back.

To edit an existing style, follow these steps:

1. **Choose Text⇨CSS Styles⇨Edit Style Sheet.**

   Alternatively, you can click the Open Style Sheet icon in the bottom-right corner of the CSS Styles panel.

2. **Select the style that you want to change in the Edit Style Sheet dialog box and click the Edit button.**

   The Style Definition dialog box for that style appears.

3. **Choose a category that you want to change, such as Type or Background, from the Category panel; then specify the style changes you want to make.**

   You can find descriptions of all the style options in the section "Defining styles" earlier in this chapter.

4. **When you've made all the changes you want, click OK.**

   The style automatically redefines to reflect your changes. At the same time, all elements that you defined with that style automatically change.

Using External Style Sheets

Up to now, you've been using CSS only in the context of internal style sheets. Internal style sheet information is stored in the HTML code of the document you are working on and only applies only to that document. If you want to create styles that you can share among documents, you need to use external style sheets. External style sheets enable you to create styles that you can apply to pages throughout a Web site by storing the style sheet information on a separate text page that can be linked to from any HTML document.

External style sheets are where you can realize the greatest time savings. You can define styles for common formatting options used throughout an entire site, such as headlines, captions, and even images, which makes applying multiple formatting options to elements faster and easier. Big news- and magazine-type Web sites often use external style sheets because they need to follow a consistent look and feel throughout the site, even when many people are working on the same site. Using external style sheets also makes global changes easier because when you change the external style sheet, you globally change every element to which you applied the style throughout the site.

Creating and Editing an External Style Sheet

You create external style sheets almost exactly the same way you create internal style sheets, except external style sheets need to be saved in separate text files. When you use Dreamweaver to create an external style sheet, Dreamweaver automatically links the style sheet to the page that you're working on. You can then link it to any other Web page in which you want to apply the style definitions.

To create an external style sheet, follow the same steps for creating an internal style sheet, except that in the New Style dialog box, select New Style Sheet File instead of This Document Only. When you click OK, you're prompted to save the style sheet somewhere on your drive as an external file.

To link an existing external style sheet to the current page, follow these steps:

1. **Select <u>W</u>indow⇨<u>C</u>SS Styles.**

   The CSS Styles panel appears.

2. **Click the Attach Style Sheet icon in the CSS Styles panel (the first button on the bottom right).**

   The Select Style Sheet dialog box appears, prompting you to identify the location of the external style sheet.

3. **After you select the external file name, click the Select button (Open button on a Mac).**

   The dialog box disappears and the external CSS file is automatically linked to your page. Any styles that you've defined in the external style sheet now appear in the CSS Styles panel. Because you've established a link on this page to the external style sheet, the styles in the external style sheet always appear in the CSS Styles panel whenever you open this file.

4. **To apply a style on your page, select the text you want to apply the style to and click the appropriate style in the CSS Styles panel.**

Changing Style Sheet Preferences

Style sheet preferences are available by choosing Edit➪Preferences and clicking the CSS Styles category. Dreamweaver is so good at taking care of things for you, however, that you should leave style sheet preferences alone unless you really know what you're doing. The only change you can make in style sheet preferences controls whether or not Dreamweaver writes styles using *shorthand* (a more concise way to write the code that creates a style). If you're experienced at writing the HTML code for style sheets and prefer using shorthand, you may want to make this change because it makes editing styles manually easier. I don't recommend it, however, because some older browsers don't correctly interpret the shorthand. And Dreamweaver does such a good job of creating styles for you that you shouldn't need to edit them yourself.

Part IV
Making It Cool

The 5th Wave   By Rich Tennant

Rothman
Paint Drying Equip.
TV Test Pattern Design
Sap Buckets

"Maybe it would help our Web site if we showed
our products in action."

In this part . . .

Bring your Web pages to life with the interactive features made possible by Dynamic HTML. Add animation, sound, and video by linking a wide range of multimedia files to your Web pages. And finally, use HTML forms to create search engines, online shopping systems, and so much more. This part arms you with the information you need to tackle these tasks. You also get a bonus chapter on Fireworks, Macromedia's image design program for the Web, which is fully integrated with Dreamweaver MX.

Chapter 9

Adding Interactivity with Dynamic HTML and Behaviors

Dynamic HTML *(DHTML)* has received so much hype and attention that you'd think you could do anything with it, including your laundry. Well, DHTML isn't quite powerful enough to take over your domestic duties, but it does add a range of functionality to a Web page that has been impossible with HTML alone. In fact, DHTML is kind of like HTML on steroids. You can use other technologies, such as Java, Shockwave, and Flash, to make interactive animations, but you can also create DHTML animations right within Dreamweaver, without the need to learn or buy another animation program.

DHTML is really about using advanced scripting techniques to create precise positioning of elements and dynamic content, which is impossible with HTML alone. *Dynamic content* means that you can create and alter page content *after* the page has been loaded in the browser. JavaScript has been used by designers to add dynamic effects to Web pages for a while, but with DHTML, you can actually affect the attributes of HTML tags, which means that you can create many more kinds of effects and make them happen more quickly.

The biggest drawback of DHTML is the same you find with any new Web technology — browsers are not consistent about support so some of the cool things you can do with DHTML don't work in all browsers and therefore are not widely used on the Internet. Dreamweaver does include features to make it easier to design pages that work in various browsers, especially if you use limited features of DHTML.

You should also know that you are getting into some of Dreamweaver's most complex Web design features in this chapter. All in all, DHTML deserves most of its hype because it takes Web page design to another level of interactivity and multimedia without compromising download times. The rest of this chapter shows you how to use layers to position elements precisely on your page and apply behaviors to add powerful, preset actions and interactivity. Chapter 10 covers how to create even more advanced DHTML features, such as using Dreamweaver's Timeline to create animations.

Understanding DHTML

DHTML is exciting because it adds so many possibilities to Web design — from global style formatting with Cascading Style Sheets to fast-loading animations and other interactive features made possible with the addition of layers and timelines. (Check out Chapter 8 to find out more about Cascading Style Sheets, and see Chapter 10 for more on timelines.)

One way in which DHTML brings dramatic improvements to Web design is by providing more precise design control. Using DHTML, you can actually position text blocks and images exactly where you want them on a page by specifying their distance from the top and left side of a page — something sorely missing in HTML. Dreamweaver refers to these as Top and Left, but in DHTML, they're officially called X,Y coordinates. One of the greatest limitations of HTML is the inability to stack elements on top of each other. In DHTML, a third positioning option — the Z coordinate — adds this capability, making it possible to layer text, images, and other elements.

DHTML also enables you to use a scripting language, such as JavaScript or VBScript, to control many of the elements or attributes of elements on a page. This means that you can dynamically change the size or color of text, the alignment of an image, or any other attribute of an HTML tag. When I say that you can change those dynamically, I mean that you can make those changes happen automatically, after a page loads, or you can assign the action to be triggered by an event, such as the click of a mouse by a visitor to your page. What is unique in DHTML is that the entire page doesn't have to reload for these changes to take effect; the action affects only the specified element or text on the page — and it can happen really fast because the page doesn't have to reload.

Designers have been using JavaScript to create some of these effects for a while. For example, you've probably seen sites where images change when you move a cursor over them. That trick, called a *rollover* effect, is just one that DHTML takes a step farther by adding many more events and actions to the arsenal of design tools. DHTML is, however, much more complicated to write than regular old HTML. Even HTML frames, which are complex by many Web design standards, look relatively simple when compared to JavaScript and the kind of code that you have to write to create DHTML. This is where Dreamweaver really shines — Macromedia has successfully created a WYSI-WYG (what-you-see-is-what-you-get) design environment that you can use to create DHTML, even if you're not a JavaScript programmer.

Three powerful features in Dreamweaver make creating DHTML features possible: layers, behaviors, and the timeline. Layers and behaviors are covered in this chapter, and you'll find step-by-step instructions for using them. Timelines are covered in Chapter 10, also with detailed step-by-step instructions. But before you get into each section, it's helpful to understand what each feature accomplishes and how they can all work together to create dramatic effects.

To enable precise positioning of elements, DHTML uses what's called *layers*. Think of a layer as a container. For this example, think of the container as a ship. Then break down *behaviors* as events and actions. For example, the ship hitting an iceberg is an event the same way in which clicking a graphic to cause text to change on a page is an event. The ship sinking could be considered an action the same way in which a graphic moving across a page is an action. Finally, think of a *timeline* as the ship's schedule. The ship leaves port at a certain time and passes the islands at another time, all on schedule. If you could control the ship's fate, you could determine its sinking at a certain time interval as well. The timeline in Dreamweaver enables you to control the actions and events on your page over time, giving you the power to create a precise schedule of events and actions and control the experience of your viewers. You can use these to add many features, such as an animation of a boat that moves across your Web page when a user clicks an image of a helm.

Working with Layers

Think of a layer as a transparent box or a container that you can use to hold images, text, and other elements. This box is handy because you can manipulate all of its contents together, move them on top of another layer, or make them visible or invisible as a unit. If you're familiar with Adobe Photoshop, you may be familiar with the general concept of how layers work. DHTML layers in Dreamweaver are very similar; you can move them around to position elements exactly where you want them, use them to overlap elements on a page, or turn them on and off to control visibility. If you're new to layers, you may want to use the following numbered steps to experiment a little with creating layers, adding images and other elements, and moving them around.

By using the positioning controls, you can place layers in exact locations on a page for precise design control. You can treat each layer as if it's a separate page that can be manipulated independently and can contain anything from text to images to plug-ins to tables, and even other layers.

Creating layers

To create a layer, follow these steps:

1. **Choose Insert⇨Layer.**

A box, representing an empty layer, appears at the top of the page.

Alternatively, you can click on the Draw Layer button in the Common Insert panel and then click and drag to create a new layer anywhere in the work area (see Figure 9-1).

2. **Click anywhere along the outline of the layer box to select it.**

   When you hold the mouse over the outline of the layer, the cursor turns to a four-pointed arrow (a hand on the Macintosh); clicking with this cursor selects the layer. When the layer is selected, eight tiny, black, square handles appear around the perimeter of the box, indicating that it has been selected.

3. **Click and drag any of the handles to resize the layer.**

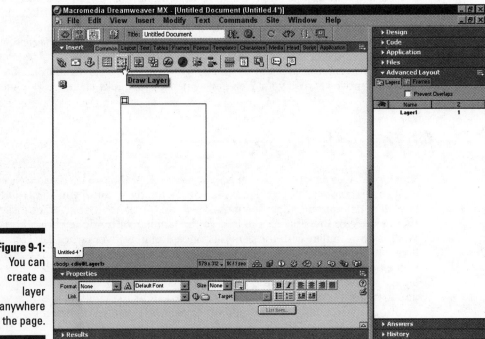

Figure 9-1:
You can create a layer anywhere on the page.

Adding elements, resizing, and repositioning layers

Remember that layers are like containers; to make a layer useful, you have to put something inside of it. You can place pretty much anything that you can place into a document within a layer. To add images or text to a layer, follow these steps:

1. **Click to insert your cursor inside the layer.**

   A blinking cursor appears inside the layer box.

2. **Choose Insert⇨Image.**

   The Select Image Source dialog box appears.

3. **Browse your drive to locate the image file that you want to insert; after you locate the image file, click the filename of the image to highlight it.**

4. **Double-click the filename or click the Select button (Open button on Macintosh) to insert the image.**

   The image appears inside the layer.

5. **Click inside the layer again to insert your cursor and enter some text.**

   As you can see in Figure 9-2, I typed *Layers are easy to create, but they don't work in all browsers* next to an image I inserted.

6. **Highlight the text and format it by using the text formatting options in the Property Inspector or by selecting the appropriate formatting options from the Text menu.**

   Formatting text inside of layers is just like formatting text inside a regular Dreamweaver document. In this case, I chose Heading 1 for the text.

Figure 9-2:
You can insert images and text inside layers just like you would insert them inside a document.

7. Select the image and use the Property Inspector to make any desired formatting changes to it.

Formatting images inside of layers works the same way. In this example, I chose Align⇨Middle from the Align option in the Property Inspector to achieve the positioning shown.(*Note:* If you're having trouble getting your text the way you want it, you may need to add a break tag by hitting the Enter key to insert desired space.)

8. Click the tab that appears at the top-left of the layer area or anywhere along the border to select the layer.

You know that you've successfully selected the layer when you see the selection *handles* — the little black squares that appear at the corners and in the middle of each side (refer to Figure 9-2) — again.

9. Click any handle and drag to resize the layer.

As a general rule, always size a layer so that its contents just fit within its boundaries, which makes positioning the layer on the page easier.

10. To move a layer, click the little tab that appears at the top-left of the layer when it is selected and use it to drag the layer to any place on the page.

Because layers use exact positioning, you can move them to any precise location on a page, and they display in that exact location in browsers that support DHTML, such as Navigator 4 and Internet Explorer 4 and above.

If you refer to Figure 9-2, you can see that the Property Inspector displays the Layer coordinates in pixels when the layer is selected: L (for left), T (for top), W (for width), and H (for height). In addition to using the click-and-drag method to move a layer, you can change a layer's position by entering a number in the position boxes, L (number of pixels from the left edge of the page), and T (number of pixels from the top of the page). Likewise, you can resize the layer by typing in new coordinates for width and height directly into the Property Inspector. The Property Inspector displays these options only when the layer is selected.

11. Name your layer by typing a name in the Layer ID text box in the top-left corner of the Property Inspector.

When you create a new layer, Dreamweaver automatically names your layers for you, starting with Layer1, Layer2, and so on. It's a good idea to change the name to something more descriptive by entering a new name in the Layer ID field. This is especially true if you're working with a lot of layers on a page. Keeping track of them by name makes them much easier to manage. Remember that you must select the layer first in order for its properties to appear in the Property Inspector.

Stacking layers and changing visibility

A powerful feature of layers is their maneuverability — you can stack them on top of each other and make them visible or invisible. Later in this chapter, in the section on adding behaviors, I show you how to use these features in combination with behaviors to create animations and other effects. Here, I help you get the hang of moving layers and changing layer visibility.

To stack layers, simply drag one layer on top of another. Unlike images, layers give you complete layout control on the page by including the ability to overlap one another. To overlap images, simply place each image within a separate layer like in the previous exercise and then move one layer so that it overlaps the other one. To control the order in which layers overlap, Dreamweaver provides two options: the Z index, available from the Property Inspector, and the Layers panel, shown in Figure 9-3, which you can access by choosing Window⇨Others⇨Layers.

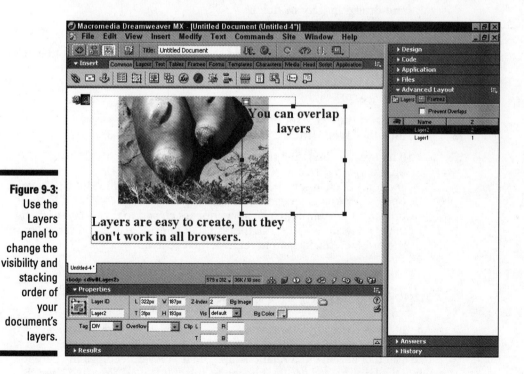

Figure 9-3:
Use the Layers panel to change the visibility and stacking order of your document's layers.

To stack layers and change their order and visibility, follow these steps:

1. **Select the layer by clicking anywhere on the border outline of the layer.**

2. **Click the small tab in the top-left corner of the layer and drag the layer to reposition it.**

   You can use drag-and-drop to move the layer anywhere on the page, including on top of another layer. When the layer is where you want it, release the mouse button.

   Using the 4-sided arrow cursor (or hand cursor on the Macintosh) that appears when you hover your cursor over the selected Layer's border, you can click and drag the layer anywhere else on the page without having to click the tab at the top left of the layer.

3. **Choose <u>W</u>indow⇨<u>O</u>thers⇨<u>L</u>ayers to open the Layers panel.**

   The Layers panel lists any layers that appear on your page. If you're familiar with layers in Adobe Photoshop or Macromedia Fireworks, you may find some similarities here, such as the eye icon to control layer visibility and the ability to drag layers around in the panel to reposition them.

4. **Reposition the layers by clicking the layer name in the Layers panel and dragging it up or down.**

   The layer order changes in the Layers panel.

   Layers are automatically named Layer1, Layer2, and so on, as they're created. You can rename a layer by double-clicking the name to select it, using the Delete key to remove the name, and then typing a new name in its place.

5. **Click on the eye icon to the left of any layer in the Layers panel to turn the layer visibility on or off (refer to Figure 9-3).**

   If no eye appears, then the visibility is set to default, which usually means on, except in the case of nested layers. (I cover nested layers in the next section.) Click in the visibility column to view the eye icon. If the eye is open, a layer is on, meaning that it's visible on the screen and in the browser. Click until the eye icon appears closed to turn a layer off and make it invisible — it's still there; it just doesn't display on screen or in the browser. Click again to remove the eye icon.

Nesting layers: One happy family

Another way to position layers on a page is by nesting them. A *nested layer* is essentially a layer that's invisibly tied to another layer, where the layers maintain a kind of parent-child relationship. The first layer becomes the parent while the layer nested within it becomes the child layer. The child layer then uses the upper-left corner of the parent layer as its orientation point for positioning instead of using the upper-left corner of the document because it is nested *within* the parent layer. Even if the layers are on different areas of the page, they still retain this parent-child relationship. When you move the first layer around on the page, the nested layer moves along with it. You can also think of this scenario as an owner walking his dog on a leash — where the owner goes, the dog has to follow, even though the dog can still move independently of its owner within the confines of the length of the leash.

If you were to nest another layer into the child layer, that would then make the child layer both a parent and a child. The new layer then uses the upper-left corner of its parent layer (in this case both a parent and a child) as its orientation point. The first layer in the nested chain still retains control over all the child layers, meaning that they will move when you move the parent.

Dreamweaver enables you to manage large numbers of layers in a document by nesting — in fact, this is one of the best reasons to use nested layers. Instead of trying to keep track of loads of different layers scattered all over your page, you can group them into more easily manageable "family units." Then, you can easily move a whole family around as one unit.

Furthermore, you can make a whole family visible or invisible by clicking the eye icon of the parent layer in the Layers panel if the child layer's visibility has been set to default (no eye icon in the Layers panel). When the child layer's visibility is set to default, it inherits the visibility of its parent layer, enabling you to show and hide whole families at a time. As you experiment with layers and start using a lot of them on your page, this becomes almost essential. Be aware, though, that when a child layer is set to either visible (eye icon on) or invisible (eye icon off) in the Layers panel, the child layer will be unaffected by the visibility setting of its parent layer. The child layer must be set to default to inherit the visibility properties of its parent.

To create a nested layer, follow these steps:

1. **Choose Insert⇨Layer.**

   A box representing the layer appears at the top of the page. Dreamweaver automatically names this Layer1.

2. **Move the cursor into the Document window and drag any of the corners of the box to resize the layer.**

3. **Place the cursor inside the first layer, and choose Insert⇨Layer to create a second layer inside the first.**

4. **Position the second layer anywhere on the page by dragging the small tab on the top left of the layer box or clicking and dragging anywhere on the layer's border.**

   Nested layers do not need to physically reside inside their parent layer; they can be placed anywhere else on the page or they can be stacked on top of each other.

5. **Click Layer2 in the Layers panel to select it.**

   The Layers panel lists each layer separately. Dreamweaver automatically names them Layer1, Layer2, and so on as you create them. If the Layers panel is not visible, choose Window⇨Layers to open the Layers panel. (If the Layers panel is already open, choosing Window⇨Layers will close it.)

When a layer is selected, the layer attributes are visible in the Property Inspector, as shown in Figure 9-4. You can use the Property Inspector to change the name of a layer and alter its size and other attributes. All the Layer attributes are described in the next section, "Setting layer options."

TIP

Another way to create a nested layer is to simply place your cursor inside any layer and choose Insert⇨Layer. When you do this, the new layer becomes a child of the first layer. You can then reposition the child layer as needed by dragging it elsewhere on the page.

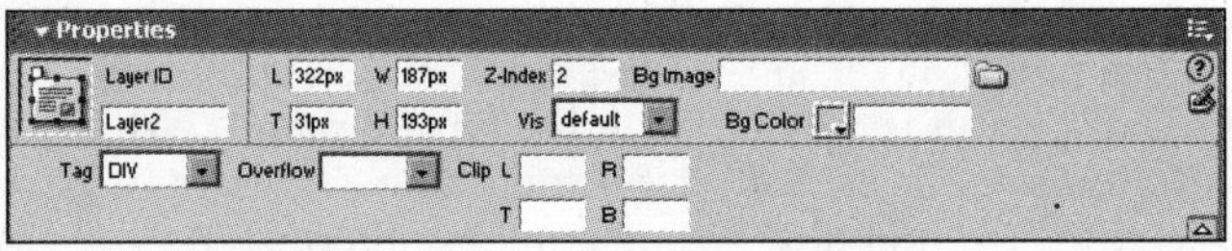

Figure 9-4:
When a
Layer is
selected,
you can use
the Property
Inspector to
edit its
attributes.

Setting layer options

Like other HTML elements, layers come with many options, such as height and width. Dreamweaver makes these options available in the Property Inspector when you select a layer (refer to Figure 9-4).

The following list describes the layer options and what they control:

✓ **Layer ID:** In the top-left corner of the Property Inspector, an unmarked text box lies just under the words *Layer ID* where you can enter a name to identify the layer. Use only standard alphanumeric characters for a layer name (don't use special characters like spaces, hyphens, slashes, or periods).

✓ **L (Left):** This value specifies the distance of the layer from the left side of the page or parent (outer) layer. Dreamweaver automatically enters a pixel value when you create or move a layer with drag-and-drop. You can also enter a numeric value (positive or negative) to control the positioning.

✓ **T (Top):** This value specifies the distance of the layer from the top of the page or parent (or outer) layer. Dreamweaver automatically enters a pixel value when you create or move a layer with drag-and-drop. You can also enter a numeric value (positive or negative) to control the positioning.

✔ **W (Width):** Dreamweaver automatically specifies the width when you create a layer on a page. You also have the option of entering a numeric value to specify the height. In addition, you can change the default measurement of px (pixels) to any of the following: pc (picas), pt (points), in (inches), mm (millimeters), cm (centimeters), or % (percentage of the parent's value). Don't put any spaces between the number and the measurement abbreviation.

✔ **H (Height):** Dreamweaver automatically specifies the height when you create a layer on a page. You also have the option of entering a numeric value to specify the height. In addition, you can change the default measurement of px (pixels) to any of the following: pc (picas), pt (points), in (inches), mm (millimeters), cm (centimeters), or % (percentage of the parent's value). Don't put any spaces between the number and the measurement abbreviation.

✔ **Z-Index:** This option determines the position of a layer in relation to other layers when layers are stacked. Higher-numbered layers appear on top of lower-numbered layers, and values can be positive or negative.

Changing the stacking order of layers is easier to do by using the Layers panel than by entering specific Z-index values. For more on using the Layers panel to change the order of layers, see "Stacking layers and changing visibility" earlier in the chapter.

✔ **Vis:** This visibility setting controls whether a layer is visible or invisible. You can use this setting with a scripting language, such as JavaScript, to dynamically change the display of layers.

You can choose from the following visibility options:

- *Default:* The default option in most browsers is the same visibility property as the parent's value.

- *Inherit:* This option always uses the visibility property of the layer's parent.

- *Visible:* This option always displays the layer, regardless of the parent's value.

- *Hidden:* This option always makes the layer transparent (invisible), regardless of the parent's value. Hidden layers take up the same space as visible layers.

You can dynamically control visibility by using the JavaScript behaviors covered in "Attaching behaviors" later in this chapter.

✔ **Bg Image:** With this option, you can select a background image for the layer in the same way that you would select a background image for a Web page. Click the folder icon to select an image or enter the name and path in the text box.

✔ **Bg Color:** Use this option to fill the background of a layer with a solid color. Click the color square to open a color palette, from which you can select a color. If you want the layer background to be transparent, leave it blank.

✔ **Tag:** This enables you to choose between using CSS layers (<DIV> or <SPAN> tags) or Netscape layers (<LAYER> or <ILAYER> tags). As a general rule, you should use CSS layers (Dreamweaver uses the <DIV> tag as the default setting). To find out more about the difference, see the sidebar "Netscape layers versus CSS layers."

✔ **Overflow:** These options determine how the contents of a layer are displayed if they exceed the size of the layer. (Note that this option applies only to CSS layers.)

You can choose from the following Overflow options:

- *Visible:* This option forces the layer size to increase so that all its contents are visible. The layer expands down and to the right.

- *Hidden:* This option clips off the edges of content that don't fit within the specified size of a layer. Be careful with this option; it doesn't provide any scroll bars.

- *Scroll:* This option adds scroll bars to the sides of a layer regardless of whether the contents exceed the layer's size or not. The advantage of this option is that scroll bars don't appear and disappear in a dynamic environment.

- *Auto:* If you select this option, scroll bars appear only if the layer's contents don't fit within the layer's boundaries.

✔ **Clip:** This option controls what sections of the contents of a layer are cropped if the layer isn't large enough to display all the contents. You should specify the distance from the L (Left), T (Top), R (Right), and B (Bottom). You can enter values in px (pixels), pc (picas), pt (points), in (inches), mm (millimeters), cm (centimeters), or % (a percentage of the parent's value). Don't add any spaces between the number and the measurement abbreviation.

The following options apply only to Netscape layers and appear only if you select LAYER or ILAYER from the Tag option. To find out more about the difference between Netscape layers and CSS layers, see the sidebar "Netscape layers versus CSS layers."

✔ **Top, Left or PageX, PageY:** Use these options for positioning the layer.

✔ **Source:** This option enables you to display another HTML document within a layer. Type the path of the document or click the folder icon to browse and select the document. Note that Dreamweaver doesn't display this property in the Document window.

✔ **A/B:** This option specifies the position of layers on the Z index, which controls the stacking of layers.

Netscape layers versus CSS layers

Netscape was the first to bring layers to the Web. However, it pushed the limits on its own and didn't wait for a standard. Unfortunately for Netscape (and for those of us sorting out DHTML), the result is that today you have two different ways to create layers — the Netscape layer tag, which consists of the <LAYER> and <ILAYER> tags, and the CSS positioning option *(CSS-P)*. In this chapter I really only cover CSS positioning, though later you do see some of the options for working with Netscape layers in the event that you want to use them in Dreamweaver.

I recommend (as do many others, including Macromedia) that you avoid Netscape's <LAYER> and <ILAYER> tags because the W3C (the committee that officially sets standards for the Web) and Microsoft Internet Explorer don't support them. Fortunately, Netscape did agree to adopt the standard proposed in the HTML 4.0 specification from the W3C, so some semblance of a standard is now emerging. If you use the <DIV> and <SPAN> tags, you can reach a broader audience because both Navigator 4 and Internet Explorer 4 and above support these tags. If you use Dreamweaver, you don't have to worry about this. The <DIV> tag is the default, although you can change it in Preferences.

If, for some reason, you choose to use the <LAYER> tag, you see additional options in the lower-right corner of the Property Inspector when you select the layer.

Converting layers to tables: Precise positioning for older browsers

If you want to achieve precise pixel-perfect positioning of elements on a Web page, layers are the easiest way to do it. You can achieve precision layout control using layers in a way that can't be done with regular HTML. Unfortunately, layers work only in version 4.0 and above browsers.

What if you want to use the precision layout features allowed by layers but also want to support a wider audience of pre-4.0 browser users? And bear in mind that if a visitor to your page is using an older browser that doesn't support layers, the contents of the layer won't be visible at all.

If you're still not sure if you should use layers, you may be pleased to learn that Dreamweaver offers a compromise. You can have the ease of using layers to design your page and then use tables in your final design because Dreamweaver includes a feature that enables you to convert a layout you created using layers into an HTML page that uses tables. By building a layout using layers and then converting it to tables, you can easily (with a single command) create a version of your page that works in older browsers.

To convert a page that uses layers to a page that uses tables only, yet maintains the same page layout, choose Modify➪Convert➪Layers to Table.

Dreamweaver rebuilds the page with a table structure that mimics the layers' layout using table cells to control positioning. (*Note:* If you haven't saved your page already, Dreamweaver prompts you to do so before it completes this task because it can dramatically alter the original page design.)

Suppose, for example, that you need to go back later and alter the layout — editing a table for exact positioning is not an easy task! Don't worry, converting the table to layers, which can be easily edited for exact positioning, is also just a command away. Choose Modify⇨Convert⇨Tables to Layers and the table layout converts to a layers layout where you can easily reposition elements with pixel level precision. After you're done, convert to tables again and voilà! — you've achieved exact positioning without requiring a 4.0 or above browser.

Dreamweaver's Layers to Table conversion feature isn't perfect because you can do things with layers that you can't do with tables, such as move a layer across the screen, causing text or images to fly in from the left or right (this is something you find out about in the Timeline section in Chapter 10 that's really cool about layers, but impossible to recreate in tables). Some designers use the Layers to Table conversion feature to create multiple pages and then direct visitors to the best design, even if they have to alter the tables version to make it look okay without all the DHTML features. Just make sure to use the Save As feature to save your converted page under a new name so you have both versions.

Working with Behaviors

Some of the coolest features used on the Web today are created by using Dreamweaver behaviors, which use a scripting language called JavaScript. These behaviors are really just built-in scripts — some of which use DHTML and some of which don't — that provide an easy way to add interactivity to your Web pages. You can apply behaviors to many elements on an HTML page, and even to the entire page itself. Writing JavaScript is more complex than writing HTML code, but not as difficult as writing in a programming language such as C, C++, or Java. (No, Java and JavaScript are not the same. Read Chapter 12 for more on Java applets and how they differ from JavaScript.) Dreamweaver takes all the difficulty out of writing JavaScript behaviors by giving you an easy and intuitive interface that doesn't require you to ever touch the complicated code behind the scenes.

In this section, I show you how surprisingly easy Dreamweaver makes it to apply a whole range of behaviors that you can use to create dynamic effects. Using the behaviors options, you can make images change when viewers pass their cursors over them (swapping images), and you can create animations that start when a visitor clicks an image or other element on a page. Combining the power of behaviors with layers opens up a range of tricks that look great on a page and load very fast. Add to that the power of the timeline, described in the next chapter, and you can make this happen automatically. The timeline enables you to trigger behaviors after a specified amount of time and to set one behavior to happen before another.

Attaching behaviors

If you've always wanted to add cool interactive features, such as making something flash or pop up when users move their cursors over an image or click a link, you're going to love the *behavior* feature in Dreamweaver. To fully appreciate what Dreamweaver can do for you, you may want to open the HTML Source window (available under the Window menu) before and after attaching a behavior just to see the complex code required to create behaviors. If you don't like what you see, don't worry; you can close the HTML Source window and just let Dreamweaver take care of the code for you.

When you use behaviors in Dreamweaver, you don't have to write any code at all. Instead, you use a couple of dialog boxes, and with a few clicks of your mouse, you get interactive effects. You can attach behaviors to a page, a link, an image, or almost any other element on a page simply by selecting the element, specifying the action or event that triggers the behavior, and then choosing the behavior from the Behaviors panel.

The following steps show you how to apply a behavior to an element, such as an image. Behaviors add lots of interesting capabilities to your pages. The one I demonstrate here opens a new browser window with a new Web page when the user clicks the image.

To add a behavior to an element on a page, follow these steps:

1. **Select an image or other element on a page by clicking it.**

    You can select any image, text, or layer on a page and apply a behavior to it.

    To attach a behavior to the entire page, click the <BODY> tag in the tag selector at the left end of the Status Bar at the bottom of the document window.

2. **Choose <u>Window</u>⇨<u>B</u>ehaviors to open the Behaviors panel.**

    You can also click the Behaviors button on the Launcher bar to open the panel.

3. **At the top left side of the Behaviors panel, click the plus sign (+) and choose the Open Browser Window behavior from the pop-up menu (see Figure 9-5).**

    The Open Browser Window dialog box appears, enabling you to specify the parameters for the new browser window.

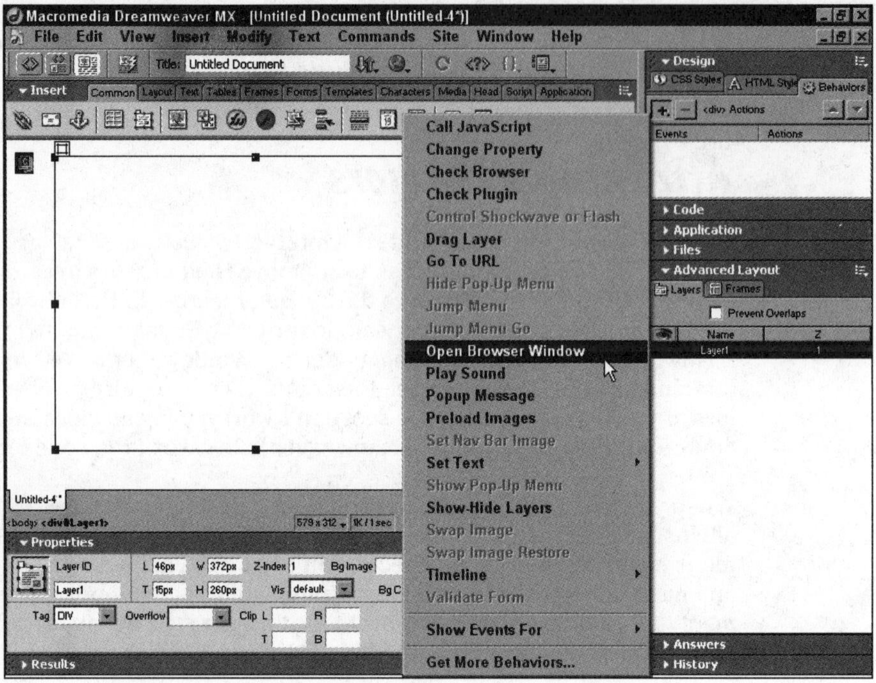

Figure 9-5:
Selecting a
behavior
from the
Behaviors
panel.

You can choose any of the behaviors listed on the pop-up menu. If an action is grayed out on the list in the pop-up menu, it means that the action won't work with the file or element that you selected. The Control Shockwave Action, for example, works only if you select a Shockwave file. After selecting the behavior, a dialog box specific to the behavior always appears enabling you to specify the parameters for each behavior.

4. In the dialog box associated with the action, specify the parameter options to control how you want the behavior to work.

Each behavior allows you to enter specific parameters to define how the behavior acts. In Figure 9-6, I set the Open Browser Window so that it opens the file ball_game.html into a new browser window. The new window's display area is only 150 pixels wide by 350 pixels high when it opens. You can choose any pixel dimensions you like by entering the height and width in the appropriate fields in this dialog box. The other parameters for this behavior control which elements of the browser — such as the navigation bar, title bar, menu bar, and so on — are present in the new window when it opens. You can use this behavior to completely customize the new window that opens up when the behavior is executed.

5. After you have specified the parameters for the behavior, click OK.

The dialog box goes away, and the Open Browser Window behavior now appears in the Behaviors panel under the Actions category.

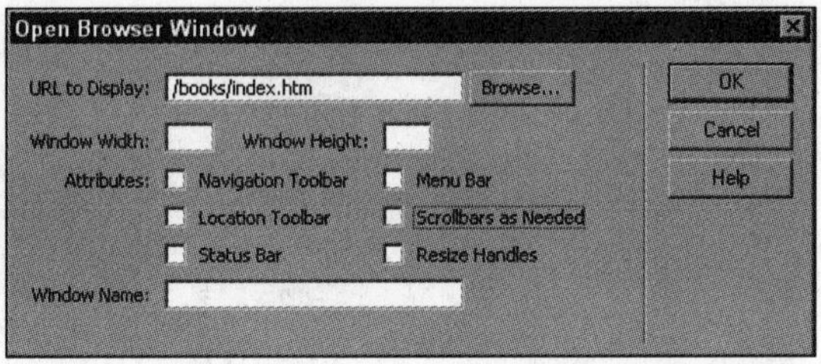

Figure 9-6:
Select an
action
from the
Behaviors
panel and a
dialog box
offers you
different
options for
controlling
the
behavior.

Figure 9-6:
Select an
action
from the
Behaviors
panel and a
dialog box
offers you
different
options for
controlling
the
behavior.

Open Browser Window

URL to Display: /books/index.htm   Browse...   OK

Window Width: [ ]   Window Height: [ ]   Cancel

Attributes: ☐ Navigation Toolbar ☐ Menu Bar   Help
☐ Location Toolbar ☐ Scrollbars as Needed
☐ Status Bar   ☐ Resize Handles

Window Name: [   ]

6. **To change the event that triggers your behavior, click the small downward-pointing triangle to the right of the Events category in the Behaviors panel.**

   This opens the Events drop-down list, from which you can select various events to trigger the behavior. I selected the onClick event, which causes the behavior to execute when the user clicks the image.

   An *event* is an action that a user takes on your Web page to trigger the behavior that you insert. Dreamweaver lists various events based on the target browsers that you selected for your behavior. For more information about events and what each one accomplishes, see the section "About Events" later in this chapter.

7. **To test the action, choose File⇨Preview in Browser, and then select the browser that you want to test your work in.**

   This opens the page in whatever browser you choose so that you can see how it really looks in that browser. If you get an error message from your browser about a filename after you try to preview the page, you need to go back and enter a name in the Name field of the Property Inspector for the page element you applied the behavior to (for example, image, layer, and so on). Click the element to display its properties in the Property Inspector and enter the name in the Name field and try again. Giving the element a "name" is usually necessary before the behavior can work properly.

TECHNICAL STUFF

If you're using Behaviors, try to avoid starting your filenames with a number or using a slash mark, which is never a good idea for a filename but is particularly problematic when applying Behaviors (more so with JavaScript than Dreamweaver). Your safest option is to avoid using slashes anywhere in the name or numbers at the beginning of a filename (you can use numbers anywhere else in the name).

Adding new behaviors to Dreamweaver

If you know how to write JavaScript, you can also add your own behaviors to the list of choices in Dreamweaver. You can find instructions for creating and adding new actions in the Dreamweaver Exchange section of Macromedia's site at www.macromedia.com/exchange/dreamweaver. You can also find new behaviors created by Macromedia, as well as other developers, that you can download free of charge and then add to Dreamweaver.

To automatically go to this site to get new behaviors, click the plus sign (+) in the Behaviors panel and select the Get More Behaviors option at the bottom of the drop-down menu. This launches your default Web browser and connects you to the Dreamweaver Exchange section of the Macromedia Web site if you are online.

Many event options, such as onMouseDown, onMouseOver, and onMouseOut, are available only if the element is linked to a URL. Dreamweaver helps you get around this by automatically adding the link tag when you choose one of these events for an element that isn't linked. Dreamweaver doesn't link the element to an external URL, though; instead, it places a hash sign in place of a filename or URL. The hash sign specifies a link to the current document instead of another document. This makes kind of a fake link, one that doesn't really go anywhere but allows you to attach an event that normally requires a link. Make sure that you don't delete the hash mark (#) from the Property Inspector or the HTML code. This is how it looks:

```
<a href="#">
```

You can replace the hash mark with a URL if you want the element to open another page. If you leave it as a hash mark, the event triggers the action without opening a new URL.

About events

Events in interactive Web-speak are things that a user does to interact with your Web page. Clicking an image is an event, as is loading a page in the browser or pressing a key on the keyboard. There are many more events available as well when you define your behaviors. Different browser versions support different events (and the more recent the browser version, the more events available), so based on which browser version you have selected as your target browser in the Behaviors panel, different events will be displayed in the events pop-up menu. To see the list of available events for specific browsers, click the plus (+) sign in the Behaviors panel to select a behavior. After selecting the behavior, the event appears in the Behaviors panel below it under the Events column. To the right of the event is a small triangle, which reveals a list of available events for that behavior when clicked. Notice that if you scroll to the bottom of the list of events, the final option says Show Events For. Use this submenu to select which browser version you want to design for, which increases or decreases the number of events you can select from the list. Remember to try and target the widest possible audience when you design behaviors; this usually means selecting either 3.0 and later browsers or 4.0 and later browsers.

The following list describes some of the more commonly used events, ones that can be experienced by the majority of Web users (4.0 and above browsers, Netscape, and Internet Explorer).

- ✔ **onAbort:** Triggered when the user stops the browser from completely loading an image (for example, when the user clicks the browser's Stop button while an image is loading).

- ✔ **onBlur:** Triggered when the specified element stops being the focus of user interaction. For example, when a user clicks outside a text field after clicking in the text field, the browser generates an onBlur event for the text field. OnBlur is the opposite of onFocus.

- ✔ **onChange:** Triggered when the user changes a value on the page, such as selecting an item from a pop-up menu, or when the user changes the value of a text field and then clicks elsewhere on the page.

- ✔ **onClick:** Triggered when the user clicks an element, such as a link, button, or image map.

- ✔ **onDblClick:** Triggered when the user double-clicks the specified element.

- ✔ **onError:** Triggered when a browser error occurs while a page or image is loading. This can be caused, for example, by an image or URL not being found on the server.

- ✔ **onFocus:** Triggered when the specified element becomes the focus of user interaction. For example, clicking in a text field of a form generates an onFocus event.

- ✔ **onKeyDown:** Triggered as soon as the user presses any key on the keyboard. (The user does not have to release the key for this event to be generated.)

- ✔ **onKeyPress:** Triggered when the user presses and releases any key on the keyboard; this event is like a combination of the onKeyDown and onKeyUp events.

- ✔ **onKeyUp:** Triggered when the user releases a key on the keyboard after pressing it.

- ✔ **onLoad:** Triggered when an image or page finishes loading.

- ✔ **onMouseDown:** Triggered when the user presses the mouse button. (The user does not have to release the mouse button to generate this event.)

- ✔ **onMouseMove:** Triggered when the user moves the mouse while pointing to the specified element and the pointer does not move away from element (stays within its boundaries).

✔ **onMouseOut:** Triggered when the pointer moves off the specified element (usually a link).

✔ **onMouseOver:** Triggered when the mouse pointer first moves over the specified element.

✔ **onMouseUp:** Triggered when a mouse button that has been pressed is released.

✔ **onMove:** Triggered when a window or frame is moved.

✔ **onReset:** Triggered when a form is reset to its default values, usually by clicking the Reset button.

✔ **onResize:** Triggered when the user resizes the browser window or a frame.

✔ **onScroll:** Triggered when the user scrolls up or down in the browser.

✔ **onSelect:** Triggered when the user selects text in a text field by highlighting it with the cursor.

✔ **onSubmit:** Triggered when the user submits a form, usually by clicking the Submit button.

✔ **onUnload:** Triggered when the user leaves the page, either by closing it or focusing on another browser window.

Adding a rollover image behavior to swap images

Rollover images are some of the most commonly used interactive elements on Web sites today. With rollovers, you can swap an image on the page when the mouse passes over it, giving users visible feedback as they interact with your site. You've seen this effect on Web site navigation menus in which moving your mouse over a menu choice makes it appear highlighted. In the past, creating a rollover image required that you know how to code in JavaScript, and even then took lots of time to do. With Dreamweaver behaviors, the same JavaScript code is generated automatically behind the scenes far more easily and in only a fraction of the time.

To create a rollover (swapping) image in Dreamweaver, follow these steps:

1. **Click to place your cursor on the page where you want the rollover to appear.**

   Rollover effects require at least two images., one for the initial state and one for the rollover state. You'll probably want to make a special set of images to use with your rollover behavior. They don't have to have the same exact dimensions, but you may get strange scaling effects if you don't. Rollovers are often used on navigation buttons, where one is a brighter color or there is some other change in the image that is noticeable when a visitor rolls a cursor over the image.

2. **Choose Insert⇨Interactive Images⇨Rollover Image to open the Insert Rollover Image dialog box.**

The Insert Rollover Image dialog box appears, as shown in Figure 9-7.

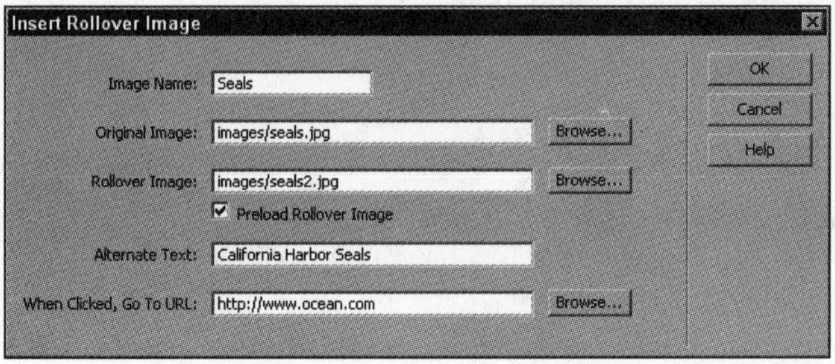

Figure 9-7:
In the Insert
Rollover
Image
dialog box,
you can
specify the
original and
rollover
images.

3. **Name your image in the Name field of the dialog.**

   In order to apply a behavior to an element, such as an image, the element must have a name so that the behavior script can reference it. Names also enable you to swap images in other locations on the page by using their names as a reference ID.

4. **Specify the first image you want visible in the Original Image text file. (Use the browse button to easily locate the image.)**

5. **Specify the second image, the one you'll want visible when visitors move their cursors over the first image. (Use the browse button to easily locate the image.)**

6. **Select Preload Rollover Image if you want the image to be loaded into the browser's cache even before it becomes visible to a visitor.**

7. **In the When Clicked, Go To URL section, enter a URL or browse to locate another page you want to link to on your site. If you don't specify a URL, Dreamweaver automatically inserts the # (anchor tag reference).**

8. **Click OK.**

   The images are automatically set up as a rollover.

Attaching multiple behaviors

You can attach multiple behaviors to the same element on a page (as long as they don't conflict, of course). For example, you can attach one action that is triggered when users click an image and another when they move their cursor over the image. You can also trigger the same action by more than one event. For example, you can play the same sound when a user triggers any number of events. You can't, however, attach multiple actions to a single event.

To attach additional behaviors to an element, follow the same steps in "Attaching behaviors" earlier in this chapter and then click the plus sign again and select another option from the pop-up menu to add another behavior. Repeat this as many times as you want.

Editing a behavior

You can always go back and edit a behavior after you create it. You can choose a different event to trigger the behavior, choose a different action, and add or remove behaviors. You can also change the parameters that you have specified.

To edit a behavior, follow these steps:

1. **Select an object with a behavior attached.**

2. **Choose Window⇨Behaviors to open the Behaviors panel.**

   You can also click the Behaviors button in the Launcher bar.

   Here are some options that you can choose from in the Behaviors panel:

   - To change an event, choose a different one from the Events drop-down menu in the Behaviors panel while the action is selected.

   - To remove an action, click the action in the Behaviors panel to select it and then click the minus sign located at the top of the pane. The action disappears.

   - To change parameters for an action, double-click the action, change the parameters that you want to affect in the Parameters dialog box, and then click OK.

   - To change the order of actions when multiple actions have been set, select an action, and then click the Up or Down buttons to move it to a different position in the list of actions.

Browser issues

Figuring out which browser to target when you start working with behaviors can be frustrating — the most powerful behaviors work only in Internet Explorer 5, but not everyone has access to that browser. Dreamweaver provides an alternative that strives to give you the best of both worlds. To take advantage of it, design your pages for Internet Explorer 5 and then convert them to a copy that works in 3.0 browsers when you're done. You then have two pages to which you can direct viewers. Dreamweaver can easily convert your pages for you and includes a script that can automatically direct viewers to the correct page based on the browser that they use. You can add the script to a page by using the Check Browser behavior and selecting the onLoad event in the Behaviors panel.

Choosing a target browser

Because behaviors are a newer development on the Web, only the latest browser versions support the majority of the events and actions available in the Behaviors Inspector. But Dreamweaver offers a couple of ways to accommodate browser differences. You can choose to limit yourself to the most basic behaviors by selecting Netscape Navigator 3, or you can choose the browser with the most options (Internet Explorer 5). These choices ensure that your pages work in the browsers that you've chosen. (If you choose one of the most advanced browsers, such as Internet Explorer 5.0, your pages may not work at all in other browsers.)

Using Extensions and the Package Manager

Extensions let you easily add new features to Dreamweaver simply by downloading them from a Web site or by creating your own new extensions, which you can share with others. Extensions are kind of like behaviors except that they are even more powerful — you can actually alter the menu system in Dreamweaver, adding new features by adding new menu items. With extensions, you can do things like change background colors, add a list of state zip codes or country codes, instantly embed QuickTime movies, or connect to backend databases with a simple menu command. The idea behind extensions is that anyone with a little bit of scripting ability can create new ways to customize Dreamweaver and share their creations with the Dreamweaver community. The place to go to find out more about extensions and to download them (mostly for free) is the Macromedia Exchange for Dreamweaver site at www.macromedia.com/exchange/dreamweaver.

After you log in to the Exchange for Dreamweaver site (membership is free), you're welcome to download and install any of the scores and scores of extensions — they grow every day as new developers are constantly creating new ones. You can search for extensions by category or simply browse the ever-growing list.

To install an extension, download it first from Macromedia's Exchange site or any other source (there are many sites with free extensions now on the Web) and then use the Extensions Manager, a utility included in Dreamweaver to install the new extension. Extensions that you download from the site are saved as files on your computer with an . mxp extension. The Extensions Manager makes installing and removing these files in Dreamweaver a breeze. To run the Package Manager and install an extension:

1. **Select Commands⇨Manage Extensions.**

   The utility launches.

2. **Select File⇨Install Extension within the Package Manager; then browse your drive to select the new Extension.**

   After installing, you see brief instructions on how to use the extension.

3. **Simply switch back to Dreamweaver, and you're ready to use your new extension.**

Chapter 10

Creating Advanced DHTML Features

• •

In This Chapter

▶ Working with timelines

▶ Using behaviors together with a timeline

▶ DHTML options for multiple browsers

• •

*I*f you read Chapter 9 before you turned to this chapter, you found out how to work with layers to achieve absolute positioning and add interactive elements to your site with behaviors. In terms of what DHTML can do, though, you still have only scratched the surface.

In this chapter, you'll find out how to animate DHTML layers and escape the world of static Web pages by adding the components of time and motion to your pages. Using a Dreamweaver feature called the *timeline*, you can create animations by changing the size, position, visibility, and stacking order of layers and their contents over time, frame by frame. For example, you can put a logo on your page that comes in from off-screen and scrolls across the page when viewers first load your page. Then, when they click your logo, it spins around and shoots off the page. Timelines let you build this kind of interactivity into your site without having to hand-edit the complex code that makes it all work.

Although the code for creating animated layers is quite complex, Dreamweaver simplifies it all with a very easy-to-use and intuitive interface. In addition, timelines can easily be integrated with behaviors, allowing for some really cutting-edge effects to further enhance the interactivity of your pages.

Using a Timeline

As the name implies, a timeline enables you to control actions over time, making it possible to create animations and automatically trigger behaviors. If you're familiar with other animation programs, such as the Macromedia products Flash or Director, you can figure out the timeline feature in Dreamweaver without much trouble. If you're completely new to timelines, you may find this a bit confusing at first. But hang in there; it's not that tough.

The steps in this section introduce you to the timeline options and explain the features that you can create. To work with timelines, you need to have a basic understanding of how DHTML layers work. If you don't, you may want to go back and read the section on layers in Chapter 9.

Only Dynamic HTML provides the functionality that makes a timeline necessary, so use the timeline feature only if you're designing DHTML to create something that happens over time, either automatically when a page loads, or as a result of some action, such as a visitor clicking an image.

DHTML is not supported by all browsers, which means that the animations and effects you create with the timeline work only in the most recent versions of browsers that support DHTML.

Timelines work by defining a series of frames that change over time. The elements in the frames (such as images or layers) can change in a variety of ways — from moving to a new location to being replaced by another layer or image. Thus, you can use timelines to create animations by loading a series of images, one after the other, or by moving them around the page. You can also define a trigger for an action, such as starting a behavior after a series of other actions occur.

You create timelines using the Timelines panel, available by selecting Window⇨Others⇨Timelines (see Figure 10-1). The timeline is basically a grid showing *channels* (running vertically) and *frames* (running horizontally). If you look closely at Figure 10-1, you can see that an object named Layer 1 occupies the first channel and that it has a duration of 22 frames.

Figure 10-1:
Using frames to represent time, the Timelines panel allows you to control objects and events over time.

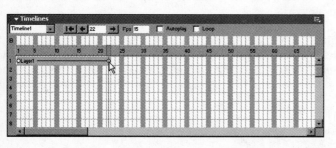

Understanding the Timelines panel controls

Before you get into using the timeline, take a few minutes to review the various components of the Timelines panel. Starting at the top and going from left to right, the Timelines panel features these controls and options:

- **Timeline name drop-down list:** You can have multiple timelines on one page, and assigning each a name allows you to manage them more easily. You give a timeline a name by typing it into the first field.

  Although Dreamweaver automatically names the timelines for you, starting with timeline1, it's best to use a more descriptive name to make it easier to manage multiple timelines. The timeline drop-down list enables you to select which of the timelines appear in the Timelines panel.

- **Rewind:** Represented by a left-pointing arrow with a vertical line, this button returns the playback to the first frame in the timeline.

- **Back:** Represented by a left-pointing arrow, this button moves the playback to the left one frame at a time. You can click and hold the Back button to play the frames backward continuously.

- **Current frame indicator:** Represented by a number field between the Back and Play buttons. The number listed in this field represents the frame that the playback head is currently located in.

- **Play:** Represented by a right-pointing arrow, the Play button moves the playback to the right one frame at a time. You can click and hold the Play button to play the frames forward continuously. When you reach the last frame, the playback loops and continues at the beginning of the timeline.

- **FPS:** This field represents the number of frames per second *(fps)* that play in the timeline. The default setting of 15 frames per second is a good rate for most browsers on Windows and Macintosh systems. Browsers always play every frame, even if they can't achieve the frame rate that you specify.

- **Autoplay:** Checking this box causes a timeline to begin playing automatically when the page loads in the browser. (Otherwise, the timeline can be triggered only by an event such as a mouse click, for example.)

- **Loop:** Checking this box causes the timeline to repeat while the page displays in the browser window. When you check the Loop box, the Go To Timeline Frame action is added. If you want to control the number of loops, you need to double-click the marker that is added to the Behavior channel (as I explain in the next bullet). This action opens the Behavior Inspector, where you can edit the parameters to define the number of loops.

✔ **Behavior channel:** Just below the controls across the top of the Timelines panel, the Behavior channel has a B to the left of it and displays behaviors that should execute at a particular frame in the timeline. See the section later on in this chapter called "Inserting behaviors into a timeline to trigger actions" to see how this works.

✔ **Frame numbers:** The numbers (listed in increments of five) along the bar that separates the Behavior channel from the Animation channels indicate how many frames each bar occupies. The number of the current frame is displayed between the Back and Play buttons at the top of the Timelines panel.

✔ **Animation channels:** This area is where the animation bars appear. In Figure 10-1, they are represented by Rows 1 – 9. Each row represents a different channel, which is kind of like a layer. You can create multiple animations by using multiple channels.

✔ **Playback head:** Indicated by a red vertical marker, which shows the active frame in the timeline (the one that currently displays on the page). In Figure 10-1, it is located at Frame 22.

✔ **Animation bars:** These blue bars appear in the timeline when you add an object. Each bar shows the duration of an object in number of frames over time. You can have multiple animation bars and control multiple objects in one timeline. In Figure 10-1, the animation bar is indicated by the horizontal bar titled Layer1.

✔ **Keyframes:** Represented by a circle within the animation bar, keyframes are frames in an animation that indicate properties, such as the position of an image on a page. In Figure 10-1, Layer1 has only two keyframes, a start frame and an end frame, each represented by circles at the beginning and end of the animation bar.

The best way to understand timelines is to compare them to frames in a cartoon animation. A cartoon animator creates an animation by drawing many versions of a single image that change slightly over time, frame by frame. In the same way, the timeline gives you frames to work with, in which objects move over time. The more frames your animation uses, the smoother it plays and the longer it takes to play through.

One of the advantages of timelines is that they can help automate the animation process. By using keyframes, also known as *tweens*, Dreamweaver can automatically fill in intermediate frames between a starting and ending frame by calculating intermediate values. For example, if you set a keyframe for an image positioned at the top of a page and then set a second keyframe for the same image positioned lower on the page, the timeline draws the image moving from the first keyframe to the last automatically, saving you the time of having to draw each frame individually. For this reason, working with timelines saves an enormous amount of time when building DHTML animated effects. For instructions on setting keyframes and an example of how this works, try the step-by-step example in the next section, "Creating timelines."

You can use the HTML Source window to view the JavaScript code that Dreamweaver creates when you use a timeline. You can find the code in the MM_initTimelines function, inside a <SCRIPT> tag in the <HEAD> of the document. If you choose to edit the HTML source of a document that uses timelines, be careful not to change anything controlled by the timeline. Just make sure you don't change anything between the opening tag:

```
<script language="JavaScript">
```

and the closing tag:

```
</script>
```

unless you are really familiar with how to write and edit JavaScript.

Creating timelines

In the following steps, I create a timeline that causes two layers to automatically move into position when a page loads and demonstrates how keyframes work.

To create a timeline with keyframes, follow these steps:

1. **Start by creating a layer and filling it with either text or an image.**

   Creating and positioning layers is covered in detail in Chapter 9.

2. **Position the layer where you want the animation sequence to begin by selecting it and then clicking the layer marker (the small box in the top-left corner of the layer) to drag it around on the page to the correct position for the beginning of the sequence.**

   If you're using multiple layers and want to change the position of other layers on the page in your animation, you can get them into their starting positions for the beginning frame of the animation as well.

   If you want to position a layer off the visible page, it's impossible to manually drag it completely off. However, you can still move it off the page by typing a negative number in the text boxes marked L (for left) or T (for top) in the Property Inspector for the layer. This is a great trick when you want to have a layer start off-screen and then slide into position as part of the animation sequence. Controlling the position of a layer by changing these numbers, rather than by using the drag-and-drop technique, also provides greater control over precise positioning.

3. **Choose Window⇨Others⇨Timelines.**

   The Timelines panel opens.

4. **Click the layer that you want to add to the timeline to select it and choose Modify⇨Timeline⇨Add Object to Timeline.**

You can also just click and drag the layer (or a selected image) from the document window into the Timelines panel to create a new animation bar.

A bar appears in the first channel of the timeline. The name of the layer or image appears in the bar (like the bar in Figure 10-1 labeled Layer1).

5. **Click to select the blue dot that represents the ending keyframe at the right end of the animation bar.**

Dots on the timeline represent keyframes. All objects in the timeline have a beginning and ending keyframe.

6. **With the keyframe still selected, go back and select the layer in the main document window and move it to a different position by clicking and dragging it to another location on the page.**

The position of the layer on the page is now different in the final keyframe than it is in the first keyframe. By changing the physical location of the layer in the final keyframe, Dreamweaver automatically creates an animated sequence of frames to fill in the gaps between the first and last keyframe layer positions. A line appears on the page between the new location of the layer and its original location in Keyframe 1, indicating the path of the layer over time, as shown in Figure 10-2. By clicking the Rewind or Play buttons at the top of the Timelines panel, you can see how the layer moves along this path frame by frame.

7. **To increase the duration of the animation, click the keyframe circle in the Timeline panel and drag it farther to the right, or drag it to the left to shorten it.**

This lengthens and shortens the animation bar and controls the amount of time that elapses while the timeline moves the element from the first keyframe to the second.

8. **If you want to add a bend or curve to the animation motion, you just need to add another keyframe and change the layer position associated with the new keyframe. Click any frame in the middle of the animation bar so that the playback head moves to that frame and choose Modify⇨Timeline⇨Add Keyframe.** You can also right-click the frame where you want to add the keyframe and select Add Keyframe from the pop-up menu.

A new keyframe circle appears in the frame you selected. You can add as many keyframes as you like and use them to control the location or other features of the element. In the example in Figure 10-3, I added a new keyframe at frame 13.

9. **After adding the keyframe, it is automatically selected in the animation bar. With the new keyframe circle still selected, move the layer on the page to the position that you want it to be in at that particular point in the animation sequence.**

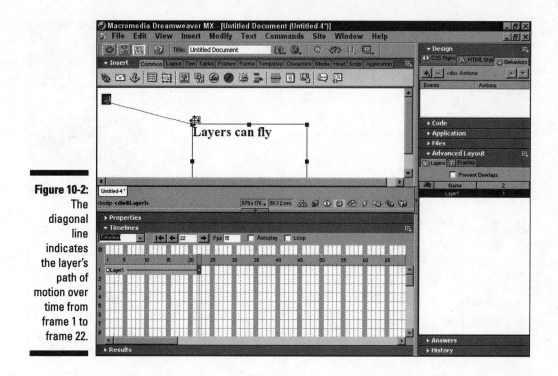

Figure 10-2:
The diagonal line indicates the layer's path of motion over time from frame 1 to frame 22.

For example, if you wanted a layer to move across the page on a curved path instead of a straight one, you could add a keyframe like the one in Step 8. Then position it, as shown in Figure 10-3, in a place on the page that would cause the motion of the layer to move to a third location as it progresses from the first keyframe to the last one.

10. Click to place a check mark in the Autoplay option in the Timelines panel.

Clicking the Autoplay option ensures that the animation begins right after the page loads. Otherwise, the animation won't take place until you define another event to trigger it. (See the section later in this chapter called "Using a behavior to trigger a timeline animation" for information on other ways to trigger the animation.)

11. To preview the animation, click and hold down the Play button or select File⇨Preview in Browser.

By pressing the Play button, you can get a preview of how the animation runs. The Preview in Browser command shows you how the rest of the world will see the animation.

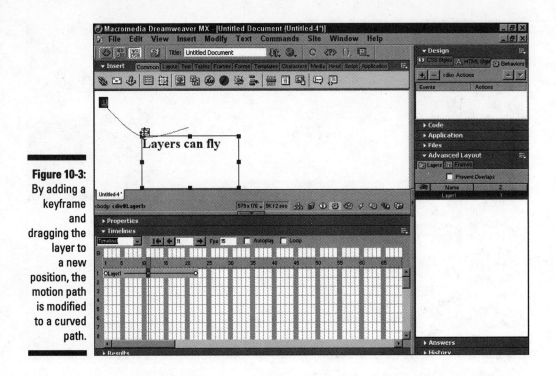

Figure 10-3:
By adding a
keyframe
and
dragging the
layer to
a new
position, the
motion path
is modified
to a curved
path.

By following these same steps, you can add additional layers to the timeline causing simultaneous actions. You can also click and drag the animation bars to stagger frame sequences. In Figure 10-4, you see two layers,
each represented by a different animation bar in the timeline. Notice
that the two animation bars are staggered and that, as the layers move
across the page, one progresses ahead of the other. In this example,
Layer1 stops animating at frame 22 while Layer2 continues to frame 60.

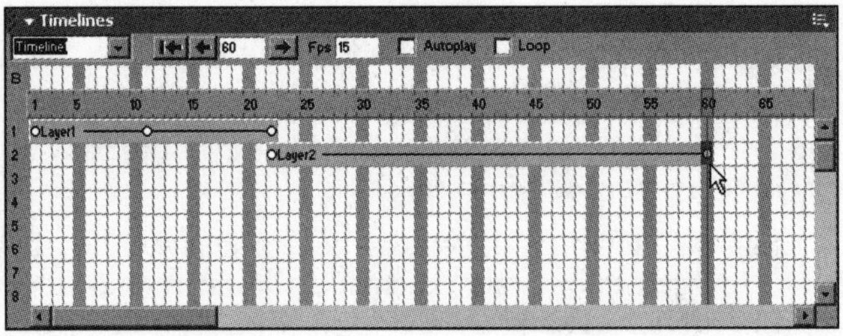

Figure 10-4:
Controlling
multiple
layers is
easy; each
bar in the
timeline
controls a
different
layer.

Recording a layer's path

In the steps in the preceding section, you see how to use keyframes to allow Dreamweaver to automatically generate in-between frames for an animated sequence by changing the position of the layer at each keyframe. Another way to create animations is to record a layer's path on the page simply by dragging it around manually. Suppose that you want your logo to circle around some text as it moves across the page or maybe follow a particular path that requires too many keyframes to generate. The Record Path of Layer feature can help you accomplish this.

To record a layer's path, follow these steps:

1. **Select the layer whose movement you want to record; then click and drag it to the position where you'd like the animation to begin.**

2. **With the layer still highlighted, choose Modify⇨Timeline⇨Record Path of Layer (see Figure 10-5).**

   If not already visible, the Timelines panel appears.

3. **Click and carefully drag the layer onscreen to define the animation path that you want it to take from beginning to end.**

   As you drag the mouse around, a gray line appears onscreen indicating the path of the layer. The timeline also automatically generates new keyframes represented by dots on the timeline. The slower you drag, the closer the keyframes.

4. **When you're finished drawing, release the mouse button. The path has now been recorded and the keyframes generated automatically.**

A note about frame rates and animation speed

You can increase the speed of your animation by increasing the frame rate in the *fps* (frames per second) indicator in the Timelines panel. Fps settings, however, can be deceiving. They are more dependent on the speed of the computer being used to view the page and the Internet connection speed than they are on an accurate frame rate per second.

The browser always plays every frame regardless of the fps setting, so speed can vary widely. For this reason, it's often best to stick with the default frame rate of 15 fps or at least stay close to it.

In order to increase or decrease the speed of your animation, it's more effective to lengthen or shorten the number of frames in your animation by dragging the last frame in the timeline in or out. To slow the animation, add more frames by dragging right; to speed up the animation, decrease the number of frames by dragging left.

You can also make your animations appear smoother by increasing the number of frames in the timeline rather than by increasing the frame rate.

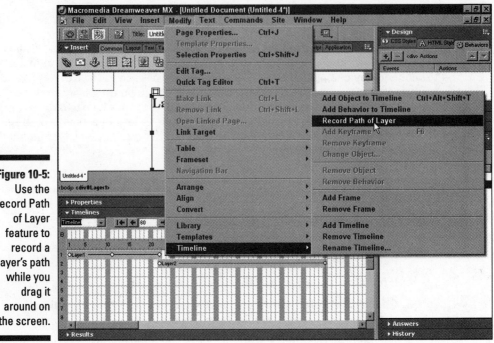

Figure 10-5:
Use the
Record Path
of Layer
feature to
record a
layer's path
while you
drag it
around on
the screen.

Playing your animations

When you create time-based animations, it's important that you control the time that these animations occur — right after the page loads, for example, or perhaps only after a certain event occurs.

When you create a timeline in Dreamweaver, you create an action that will occur, but you still need an event to trigger it — to define *when* it will occur. In order for the timeline to execute automatically after the page loads, you need to check the Autoplay option in the Timelines panel. Checking the Autoplay option adds an onLoad event handler in the <BODY> tag of your HTML. This tells the browser to begin playing the animation immediately after the page loads. After checking the Autoplay option, you can preview your animation in the browser by choosing File⇨Preview in Browser. You can also instruct the timeline to continue playing by selecting the Loop option. The Loop option tells the animation to continue to play over and over, rather than to stop after it has reached the last frame of the animation.

In the event that you don't want to play your animation directly after the page loads — for example, if you want to have it play only if the user clicks a certain button — leave the Autoplay button unchecked. You can then add a behavior that instructs the timeline to begin whenever you specify. In the next section, you see how to use timelines and behaviors together in this manner.

Using behaviors with a timeline

Just as you can attach behaviors to text and images, you can also insert behaviors into a timeline for even greater interactivity on your pages (for more about behaviors, see Chapter 9). You can use behaviors to trigger animations, meaning that you can start, stop, or even jump to any frame in a timeline by linking it to a behavior, or you can also execute behaviors anywhere along the timeline. This means that the behavior can be attached to any element, such as text, images, or even other layers, to control when and how the timeline animation occurs or to generate other interactive elements at a given point in time.

Using a behavior to trigger a timeline animation

Sometimes you don't want an animation to occur immediately when a page loads, but only after the user does something, such as clicking a logo. These steps show you how to start a timeline animation using a behavior.

To trigger the timeline that you just created by clicking an image link, follow these steps (these steps assume that you've already created a timeline on your page, as I describe earlier in the "Creating timelines" section):

1. **First, insert and position the image on your page that you want to trigger the timeline action.**

2. **Select Window⇨Behaviors to bring up the Behaviors panel (see Figure 10-6).**

3. **With the image selected in the document window, click the plus sign (+) in the Behaviors panel to access the Behaviors pop-up list.**

   The list of available behaviors appears for this object.

4. **Click the plus sign in the Behaviors panel to display the list of actions. Scroll down to Timeline and select Play Timeline from the submenu (see Figure 10-7).**

   The Play Timeline dialog box appears with a drop-down list box containing the available timelines on your page. The names appearing in this list reflect the names applied to various timelines in the name text box of the Timelines panel. If you haven't already created a timeline on your page, the drop-down list will be empty.

5. **Select the appropriate timeline from the drop-down list.**

   The Play Timeline action will appear in the Actions column of the Behaviors panel, and the trigger — the default is Onload — will appear in the Events column.

Figure 10-6:
You can add
a behavior
to play a
timeline.

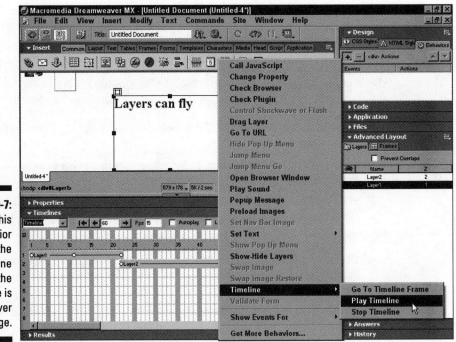

Figure 10-7:
This
behavior
will play the
timeline
when the
mouse is
moved over
the image.

You can also specify that behaviors are triggered by other events, such as onClick, which means a user clicking the image triggers the action, initiating the timeline animation. You may want to turn off the Autoplay option by unchecking it in the Timelines panel so that the animation plays only when the image is clicked, not when the page loads.

Besides using a behavior to start an animation, you can also have it stop the animation or jump to a specific frame in the animation. Both of these actions are available as submenus of the Timeline action in the Actions pop-up list (available by clicking the plus sign) in the Behaviors panel.

Inserting behaviors into a timeline to trigger actions

You can also add behaviors to keyframes, which triggers actions from within a timeline animation, or add behaviors to a specific frame in the Behaviors channel in the Timelines panel. These kinds of behaviors are triggered when the animation reaches a certain frame in the timeline rather than requiring an external event such as a mouse click. So far, I've been animating a bouncing ball in this chapter. But to make this animation more realistic, I want to make it look like the ball gets a little squished at the top and bottom when it bounces. I can get this effect by *swapping* the round ball image with a second image that shows the same ball with a little squish on each side at the appropriate frame, and this is accomplished by adding a behavior to the timeline that swaps the ball image at a certain keyframe. You can create similar effects by swapping any images at any point in a timeline sequence.

To add a swap image action to the timeline, follow these steps:

1. **Click to select the image inside the layer (select only the image, not the layer, by carefully clicking the image itself) and drag the image into the Timelines panel to create a second animation bar.**

   This animation bar is labeled with the word *Image* instead of *Layer*.

2. **Create a new keyframe at the point where you want the images to swap.**

   To do so, click anywhere in the image animation bar and choose Modify⇨Timeline⇨Add Keyframe (you can also add a Keyframe by typing the shortcut F6).

3. **With a keyframe circle selected in the image animation bar, use the Property Inspector to change the image source.**

   You can type in the name of another image or click the folder icon to browse for an image.

4. **Select the next keyframe and change the image source again.**

Don't overestimate your viewer's browser

Too many Web designers overestimate their audiences. Most of us who build Web sites are quick to upgrade, downloading new browser versions and installing plug-ins as soon as they're released. But many people on the Web don't know how to upgrade their browsers, or they just can't or don't bother.

Employees at big corporations are usually on networks where upgrading a browser means upgrading the entire system. Technical support staff are often slow to do the upgrade because they're busy with so many other tasks. Home users are often intimidated by the prospect of downloading anything off the Internet, so they're likely to stick with whatever browser they got when they first set up their connection to the Net.

Slowly, things are improving. Users are getting more sophisticated and software is getting easier to use. But for now, if you want to reach the broad audience on the Web, you need to design a Web site that works in a variety of browsers. Fortunately, Macromedia understood that problem when it developed Dreamweaver and included a number of features to help make it easier to design your site so that it takes advantage of high-end browsers while still being accessible to older browsers. Make sure that you take advantage of these features, such as the Target Browser options, Browser Check features, and the 3.0 Conversion features that enable you to easily create a second page that works in older browsers. You can find out more about all of these options in "Ensuring That Your Pages Work in Older Browsers" in this chapter.

5. Repeat Steps 2 and 3 if you want to change the image at any other keyframe.

6. To preview the animation, click and hold down the Play button.

7. When you're finished, you can choose Window⇨Others⇨Timelines to close the Timelines panel.

Another way to add a behavior to the timeline is to click any frame in the Behavior channel of the Timelines panel (the row at the top of the Timelines panel labeled with a B) and select a behavior from the Actions list in the Behaviors panel. This causes the behavior to execute when the playback head of the timeline reaches the frame that the behavior has been applied to.

Time-based layer animations are made possible by DHTML, and Dreamweaver makes it easy for anybody to animate layers by using the timeline. You can do an endless number of things with a timeline, from scrolling credits and flying logos to elements that come in off-screen and appear when needed. Use your imagination and have fun with the timelines in Dreamweaver. And be sure to check out www.dhtmlzone.com, Macromedia's Web site for DHTML tips and information, for more ideas on how to work with DHTML on your Web pages.

Ensuring That Your Pages Work in Older Browsers

You may love all the Dreamweaver features described in this chapter and in Chapter 9 because they make creating dynamic, interactive elements for your Web pages easy. Unfortunately, most of these features can be viewed only by the latest browsers, and many people on the Internet still use older browsers. By "older browsers," I mean any version of Microsoft Internet Explorer or Netscape Navigator earlier than version 4.0, although even with the newer browsers you may run into trouble because they don't support DHTML features the same way.

So that you can easily compensate for browser differences as you design your Web pages in Dreamweaver, the folks at Macromedia included features for targeting different browsers. When you choose a target browser in the Behaviors Inspector, you get a list of behavior options that work only in the browser that you select. This list allows you to know which behaviors work with which browsers. To expand your options, Dreamweaver includes a number of other features for targeting different browsers.

The Check Browser action

One way to deal with the problem of browser incompatibilities is to create two or more different versions of your site. To decide which browser sees which site, you can use the Check Browser action in the Actions list of the Behaviors panel, as shown in Figure 10-8. This action automatically sends users to different URLs depending on the version of browser they are using, so you can create a fancy version of your site for new browsers and a simpler version for older browsers. This action even allows you to send Netscape and Internet Explorer users to different URLs, so you can design different pages for each browser's capabilities. The best way to use this action is to select the <BODY> tag using the HTML tag selector in the document's status bar and then choose the Check Browser action in the Behaviors panel (click the plus sign to access the list of actions).

Applying this behavior to your page causes a browser-detect script to determine the type of browser that your visitor uses when the page first loads. After loading, the visitor is either directed to a different URL based on that detection or kept on the same page. For example, you can send all visitors using Netscape 3 or lower to one page in your site and users of Internet Explorer 5 to another page. To ensure that the oldest browsers see the simple page instead of trying to interpret fancy code that they don't understand, it's best to insert this behavior in the basic version of the page and then redirect the newest browsers to the alternate fancy pages. Of course the only problem with this solution is that you have to create more than one site, one for older browsers and one or more for the newer browsers, and that can turn into a lot more work.

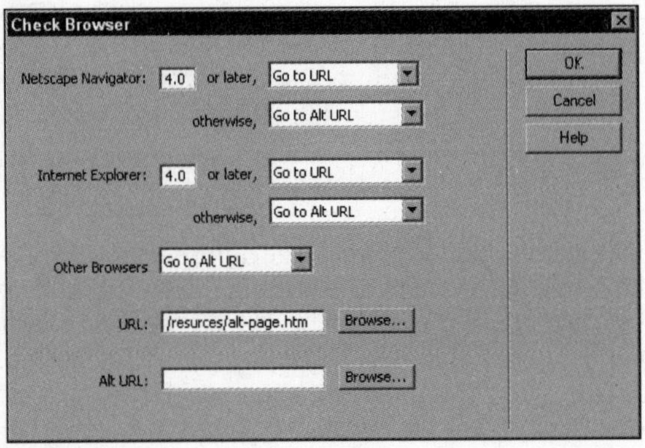

Figure 10-8:
The Check Browser dialog box lets you direct users to different URLs based on which browser they are using.

The Convert to 3.0 Browser Compatible command

Because Web designers often have to create alternate versions of their fancy pages for older browsers, Macromedia added another feature when they developed Dreamweaver. The Convert to 3.0 Browser Compatible command automates creating a second page that can display in older browsers. The 3.0-level browser is considered by most Web designers as a minimal target that virtually everyone surfing the Web will be able to view. Here's how it works: You create a page by using all the latest features that you want, such as layers and Cascading Style Sheets, and then run the conversion option. Dreamweaver automatically creates a second page that works in 3.0 browsers yet looks largely the same.

This isn't a perfect solution, but it's a great step toward making maintenance of dual sites easier. The problem is that you can't have the same features in the 3.0 version that work in the 4.0 and later version, and advanced features don't all convert down to less advanced features gracefully. For example, if you have an animated timeline that moves your buttons across the page, you lose the animation in the 3.0 conversion, but at least you can see your buttons. Still, you may have to tweak the converted page a little to get the buttons to the best location on a static page.

The 3.0-conversion process does the best job it can and works well for most CSS *(Cascading Style Sheets)* options because it converts applied styles back to individual formatting options. For example, if you've applied a headline style that is Helvetica, bold, and centered, Dreamweaver changes the formatting from the headline style to the individual tags for those three formatting options.

When you convert a file to 3.0-compatible using the Convert to 3.0 Browser Compatible command, Dreamweaver creates a copy of the original file and changes the code, often altering the design. Here are some of the changes that you can expect:

✔ Layers change to tables in an effort to preserve positioning. The table displays the layers in their original locations.

✔ HTML character styles replace CSS markup.

✔ Any CSS markup that can't be converted to HTML is removed.

✔ Timeline code that animates layers is removed.

✔ Timeline code that doesn't use layers, such as behaviors or changes to the image source, is preserved.

✔ The timeline is automatically rewound to frame 1, and all elements are placed in a static position on the page in the location specified in the first frame of the timeline.

You may have to reposition some of your elements after this conversion to ensure that they look good on a static page.

To convert a file that you designed with 4.0 or higher browser options to be 3.0 browser-compatible, follow these steps:

1. **Choose File⇨Convert⇨3.0 Browser Compatible.**

   The Convert to 3.0 Browser Compatible dialog box appears.

2. **Choose the conversions options that you want.**

   You can convert layers to tables or CSS styles to HTML markup. I recommend that you do both.

3. **Click Continue.**

   Dreamweaver opens the converted file in a new, untitled window.

4. **Choose File⇨Save and save the page with a new name.**

Dreamweaver also includes a Layer to Tables option that automates the process of converting a 4.0-compatible file that uses layers to a 3.0-compatible file with the same positioning offered by layers and DHTML. See Chapter 9 for more information on how this works.

I like to keep all these pages in their own folder so that I can easily keep track of them and they don't clutter the rest of my Web site structure.

If you maintain a site with two sets of pages (one for 4.0 browsers and another for 3.0 and older), don't forget that you have to update both sets every time you make a change.

Designing for multiple browsers is a key element to good Web design. Dreamweaver makes it easy to create lots of features that don't work in older browsers. Make sure that you also take advantage of the features that can help you ensure that your pages reach as broad an audience as possible.

Converting to XML

In addition to browser compatibility, Dreamweaver's Convert feature also enables you to convert an HTML page into XML. The eXtensible Markup Language is increasingly important on the Web, and if you work with XML, you'll appreciate that Dreamweaver is starting to support XML development.

XML is not a mark up language, it's a meta-markup language that can be used to store and organize data so that it can be tailored to meet a broad range of needs. XML is a subset of SGML, but it retains much more of the power of SGML than HTML did, while still being streamlined enough to be efficient on the Web. Because XML does not have a fixed set of tags and elements, XML enables developers to define the elements they need and apply those elements where they need them. That's what the X in XML is all about, it's *eXtensible*. You can adapt it to fit your content, whether you are a stockbroker, publisher, or astronomer.

XML is built on a solid foundation of rules and standards, and it is officially endorsed by the W3C, so it has the potential to solve many of the problems caused by conflicting standards in other formatting options available today. The rules dictate such crucial issues as where tags appear, which names are legal, and what attributes can be attached to which elements. These strict standards make it possible to develop XML parsers that can handle any XML document without limiting the ultimate flexibility of the kind of content or how it will be displayed. It also features rules for syntax and link checking, comparing document models, and datatyping, as well as checking to see if a document is well formed and valid. And XML uses Unicode as its standard character set, so it supports the broadest range of languages, special characters, and symbols, including Arabic, Chinese, and Russian.

One of the most significant differences between XML and HTML is that XML can be used to describe the type of content, not just specific formatting. That enables content to be stored and shared in a way that makes it easy to publish in multiple formatting styles. For example, instead of describing a headline as font size 5, Helvetica, bold, and the body of a document as font size 3, Times, you can simply describe the headline as a headline and the text as the body of the document. XML then allows you to apply a style sheet (or multiple style sheets) to that content so that the headline and body can be formatted on the fly. This is done with Cascading Style Sheets and XML's Extensible Style Sheets. The separation of the formatting from the content description is what enables the same content to be efficiently sent to a wide range of partners who can each apply their own formatting or to a broad range of viewing devices, such as Web browsers, Palm Pilots, and cell phones, which require different formatting.

If you want to know more about XML, consider reading *XML For Dummies* (published by Hungry Minds, Inc.).

Chapter 11

Roundtrip Integration: Fireworks and Dreamweaver

In This Chapter

▶ Fireworks as an image-editing program

▶ Roundtrip graphics editing

▶ Using other image editors besides Fireworks

▶ Inserting and editing Fireworks HTML

*I*n this chapter, I discuss some of the special features in Dreamweaver that integrate with Fireworks, Macromedia's image creation and editing program. If you're not familiar with Fireworks, you may want to have at look *Fireworks 4 For Dummies,* published by Wiley Publishing, Inc., to find out more about this excellent program. If you don't own or have access to Fireworks, you may just want to skim through this chapter as most of it is specific to using Fireworks and Dreamweaver together as a pair, but there's still relevant info for integrating other image editors with Dreamweaver

If you don't have Fireworks, you can download the free 30-day trial from this address: www.macromedia.com/software/fireworks/trial.

Unlike Dreamweaver, Fireworks is primarily a graphics tool. Because Dreamweaver doesn't have any native graphics capabilities, Fireworks (or programs like it — see Chapter 5) enables you to create images from scratch and edit them or work with existing images and prepare them for usage on the Web. However, Fireworks goes a lot further than most graphics programs because it's one of the very first image-editing programs designed specifically for the special needs of the Web. Using Fireworks, you can automate your workflow, *optimize* graphics (compress and prepare them for Web use), and create sophisticated animations, fancy *rollovers* (images that change when you hover the mouse pointer over them), and special effects in a fraction of the time that it used to take. Fireworks can even generate HTML and output Web pages all by itself! But more importantly for you, Fireworks integrates especially well with Dreamweaver, allowing roundtrip graphics editing back and forth between the two programs. Normally when you work with Dreamweaver and another graphics editor, it takes many steps to create and edit images back and forth between the two programs — one of the most time-consuming parts of building and maintaining a Web site. *Roundtrip graphics editing* simply gives you a lot of shortcuts, making the trips back and forth between the two programs a whole lot quicker and easier.

Dreamweaver to Fireworks: Image Editing

Suppose that you've got a logo on your Web page and your client suddenly wants it in a different color. Normally this would mean launching another image-editing program, tracking down the logo, opening it, editing it, saving it, switching back to Dreamweaver, and then re-importing the logo onto your page. Whew, that's a lot of steps. Using the special integration features between Dreamweaver and Fireworks, though, greatly simplifies the entire process — a few clicks of the mouse can replace all of those other time-consuming tasks.

The following steps show you how to select an image in Dreamweaver, automatically open it in Fireworks, edit it, and update the image back into Dreamweaver with just a few mouse clicks.

To launch Fireworks directly from Dreamweaver and edit an existing image, follow these steps:

1. **In Dreamweaver, select a .gif or .jpg image you want to edit.**

2. **In the Properties Inspector, click the Edit button, as shown in Figure 11-1.**

   The Find Source dialog box appears asking if you want to edit an existing document for the source of the file that you selected.

3. **Click one of the options in the Find Source for Editing dialog box.**

   Clicking Yes lets you select a different file from the actual optimized image file on your page. For example, you can select a PNG version of the optimized graphic (which may have been the original file from which you exported the optimized Web version of the graphic on your page). Clicking No opens the source file that you selected in Dreamweaver (the actual GIF or JPEG file that's linked on the page).

   If you click No, Fireworks launches with the GIF or JPEG image that you selected. If you click Yes, Fireworks allows you to pick an alternate image and launches by opening the alternate image in a new document. If you created the original image in Fireworks, the alternate image will be a PNG file. PNG is the Fireworks native file format. For more information, take a look at the sidebar in this chapter on PNG files. If you created the original image in another graphics program, for example, PhotoShop, your source file is a PSD. Fireworks does support most .PSD files created in PhotoShop 6 or higher.

Because the source file of the image used on your Web page was probably optimized earlier, editing an optimized GIF or JPEG image usually doesn't give you the best image quality results after you edit, re-optimize, and re-export it back into Dreamweaver. Going back to the original, pre-optimized version of the graphic gives you the option to start again from scratch. By clicking Yes in the Find Source for Editing dialog box, you can select a different file from the optimized source graphic. If you exported the image from a PNG file, you can select the PNG instead, edit a higher quality version of the file, and export it without suffering extra image degradation.

After clicking Yes or No, the image document opens in Fireworks.

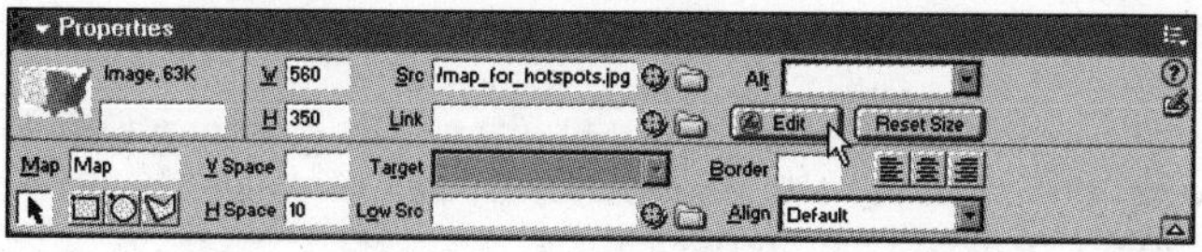

Figure 11-1:
The
Properties
Inspector
displays an
edit button
whenever
an image is
selected.
Click this
button to
launch your
image editor
of choice.

4. **Make the edits that you need to make to the image within Fireworks.**

   You can make any changes or edits to the image using any of the tools in Fireworks as well as using the Optimize panel to change the optimization settings for the file.

5. **When you're finished editing the image, click the Done button in the Fireworks document window (see Figure 11-2).**

   After clicking the Done button, the Fireworks document fades to the background, and the Dreamweaver document automatically comes into view. The image automatically updates on the page, reflecting the recent edits without requiring any other action on your part other than saving the document.

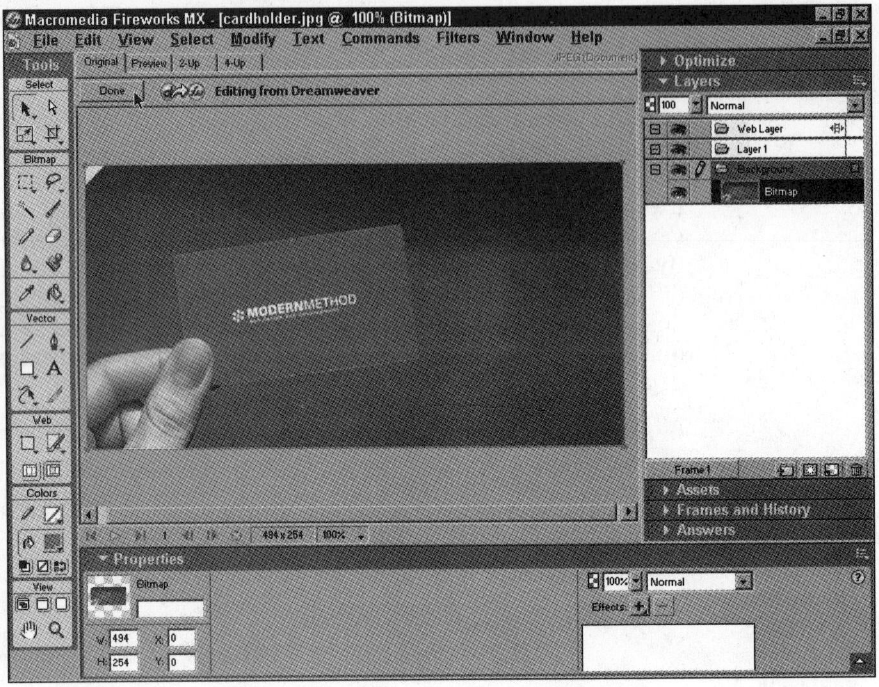

Figure 11-2:
Clicking the
Done button
in Fireworks
automatic-
ally updates
the image in
Dream-
weaver
without any
further
steps.

After you press the Done button in Fireworks, you can't undo any changes you make to the image files by selecting the Undo command. The changes are permanent.

Using an Image Editor Other Than Fireworks

When you click the edit button in the Properties Inspector (as in Step 2 in the previous example), Dreamweaver tries to launch Fireworks as the default editing application. But what if you don't use Fireworks or don't own a copy? Fear not, you can achieve a somewhat less-automated workflow with most any other graphics editor. You just need to change the preferences in Dreamweaver to specify which program you prefer to use instead of Fireworks.

To designate a different application as the Dreamweaver external image editor, follow these steps:

1. **In the Dreamweaver menu bar choose Edit➪Preferences and select the File Types/Editors category.**

PNG: Portable Network Graphics files

Fireworks uses the PNG *(Portable Network Graphics)* format as its native file format. PNG is kind of similar to the PSD format used by Adobe Photoshop in that it retains the highest quality possible for the graphic without suffering any of the degradation in image quality that usually occurs when a GIF or JPEG is generated. The Portable Network Graphics format was actually created long before Fireworks, and it is one of the few graphics formats, in addition to the GIF and JPEG formats, that can be viewed from within a Web browser. Because the PNG format allows for the many extra features that Fireworks offers, Macromedia chose it as the native format for Fireworks.

The PNG file format was originally created as a potential replacement for the GIF format because it offered far greater image quality, compression levels, and numerous other

features lacking in GIFs. PNG files offer a multitude of improvements over GIF, including resolution up to 48 bits (as opposed to 8 bits in GIF), better compression, built-in *gamma correction* (the capability to adjust to the different brightness levels between PC and Mac monitors), and greater levels of transparency.

All in all, PNG is a much more modern and feature-rich file format. Although PNG files represent a marked improvement over GIF files, they haven't seen widespread use on the Web yet due to limited native browser support and a lack of tools capable of generating the PNG format.

For more information about PNG files, take a look at the PNG home page at www.libpng.org/pub/png/ or the W3C's PNG page at www.w3.org/Graphics/PNG.

The Preferences dialog box for File Types/Editors appears, as shown in Figure 11-3.

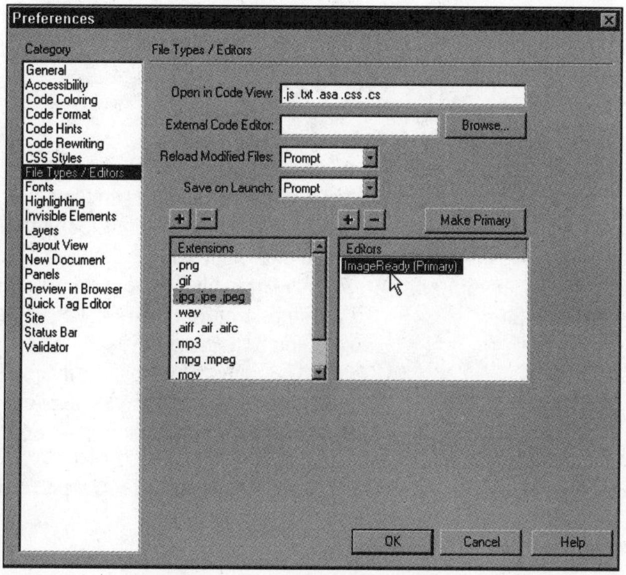

Figure 11-3: You can specify other image editors besides Fireworks.

2. **Select the .gif format in the Extensions list on the left side of the dialog box.**

   For each file format you can specify one or more external editors, in addition to a primary editor.

3. **In the Editors list on the right, click the plus sign (+) to add an editor for all your GIF files.**

   A standard browse dialog box appears asking you to find the program to assign as the editor for this file type.

4. **Browse your drive until you locate the graphics application you want to assign; then click Open.**

   After you click Open, the application appears in the list of image editors on the right.

5. **Click the Make Primary button to make this your primary editor. You can add as many editors to the list as you want, but you can assign only one primary editor for each file type.**

6. **Repeat Steps 2 through 5 for the .jpg extension and any other extensions you want to assign to other graphics editors.**

After you've assigned your program of choice as your primary external editor, clicking the Edit button in the Properties Inspector (refer to Figure 11-1) whenever you select an image automatically launches that program instead of Fireworks. Also, any other programs that you assign as image editors but not as primary editors appear in a pop-up menu if you right-click an image (Ctrl+click on the Mac), as shown in Figure 11-4.

Adobe ImageReady: Appreciating the other white meat

Although Fireworks does the whole roundtrip thing with Dreamweaver and it makes the most sense to use Fireworks instead of another image editor the connection between these two is so fluid, a growing number of Web designers are instead choosing to use Adobe ImageReady, which comes bundled with PhotoShop.

Although both programs perform many of the same functions in similar ways, the one major setback I see with Fireworks is that most designers already know how to use PhotoShop.

ImageReady looks, acts, and feels like PhotoShop, while performing most of the things that Fireworks can do. Many critics of Fireworks reason, "Why spend time learning a new program and figuring out how to do what you already know how to do (and perhaps, do *well*) in another program?" Fireworks, however, offers something that ImageReady has yet to bring to the table: roundtrip graphic editing and seamless integration with Dreamweaver. Both are excellent programs, and the choice is up to you.

Figure 11-4:
You can add
a whole lot
of image
editors to
your
preferences
and they will
all appear in
this pop-up
menu when
you right-
click an
image.

Because Fireworks is a companion tool to Dreamweaver, you can automatically update an image directly from Fireworks into Dreamweaver when you click the Done button in Fireworks. Note, though, that this won't work with any other image-editing program. You can open a file in that other program by clicking the Edit button in Dreamweaver, but you'll still need to save the edited graphic and re-import the image into Dreamweaver manually. Only Fireworks offers one-click automatic image updating back to Dreamweaver.

Dreamweaver to Fireworks: Optimizing an Image

Suppose that logo on your page looks fine, but you decide that it is taking too long to download and needs to be compressed a bit more. Earlier you learned how to easily edit a file in Fireworks from within Dreamweaver. In this example, I show you how to re-optimize an image in Fireworks from within Dreamweaver when all you need to do is change the optimization/compression settings but not make any actual alterations to the image.

To optimize an image in Fireworks from within Dreamweaver, follow these steps:

1. **Select the image in Dreamweaver.**

2. **Choose Commands⇨Optimize Image in Fireworks, or right-click the image (Ctrl+click on the Mac) to access this from a pop-up menu (refer to Figure 11-4).**

   The Find Source dialog box appears asking if you want to edit an existing document for the source of the file that you selected.

   The default setting for this command is for Dreamweaver to ask if you want to open an existing file each time you launch Fireworks. You can change the default by selecting Always Use Source PNG or Never Use Source PNG from the pull-down menu in this same dialog box.

3. **Click one of the options in the Find Source dialog box.**

   As explained earlier in the chapter, clicking Yes enables you to select a different file from the actual optimized image file on your page, such as the one from which you exported the optimized Web version of the graphic used on your page. Clicking No opens the source file that you selected in Dreamweaver (the actual GIF or JPEG file that is linked on the page) and displays the optimization dialog box within Fireworks.

   Whichever option you click, the image opens in Fireworks in the Optimize dialog box, ready to export.

4. **Apply the new optimization settings in Fireworks Optimize panel (see Figure 11-5).**

   You can change the bit depth and quality settings of the file to achieve a smaller file size and then preview the changes within Fireworks preview panel. You can also crop the image, but you can't make any other image edits in this window.

5. **Click Update.**

   The file is automatically updated in Dreamweaver with the changes that you just applied. If you selected a PNG file to edit (you clicked Yes in the dialog box), the original PNG file is not altered, only the resultant GIF or JPEG file.

   After you press the Update button in Fireworks, you cannot undo any changes you make to the image files by selecting the Undo command. The changes are permanent.

I have to admit, the coolest feature of Fireworks optimization by far has got to be the Size Optimize Wizard. You just type in your target size and the wizard tries to bring down color and quality proportionally to achieve the size you specified. While the settings usually require a bit more tweaking after running this command, the wizard does a great job of doing the groundwork.

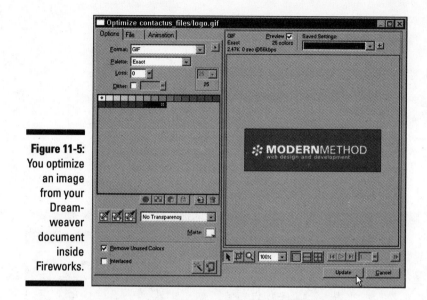

Figure 11-5:
You optimize
an image
from your
Dream-
weaver
document
inside
Fireworks.

Inserting Fireworks HTML

One of the niftiest features of Fireworks is that you can automatically generate tables and HTML files when cutting up images for your Web designs. This feature is great for slicing graphics where you need to use complicated tables to hold the pieces all together. The only question is, after you generate this HTML code from Fireworks, how do you get it onto your Dreamweaver page? Before Dreamweaver, you had to copy and paste the HTML manually. Now you can easily insert the HTML and associated images with just the click of a button.

To insert a Fireworks generated table with sliced images into Dreamweaver follow these steps (this example assumes you know how to use Fireworks to slice up images and generate HTML tables, and you have already output an HTML file from within Fireworks):

1. **Choose Insert⇨Interactive Images⇨Fireworks HTML.**

   The Insert Fireworks HTML dialog box appears (see Figure 11-6).

2. **Click the Browse button to select the HTML file to import; click Open when you've located it.**

   Dreamweaver inserts the table and associated images from the Fireworks document (see Figure 11-7).

Figure 11-6:
You can insert HTML code created by Fireworks directly into Dreamweaver.

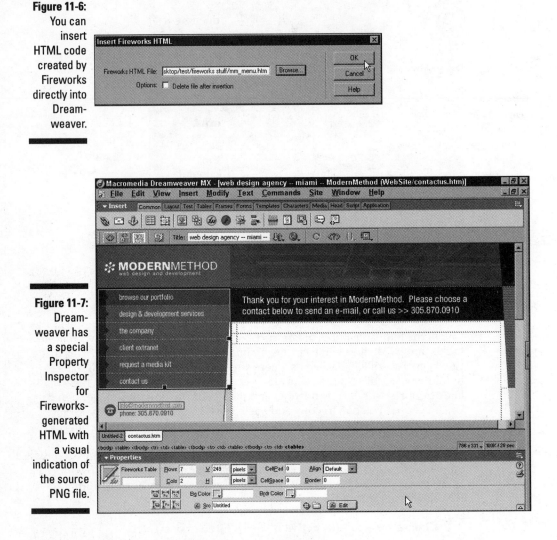

Figure 11-7:
Dreamweaver has a special Property Inspector for Fireworks-generated HTML with a visual indication of the source PNG file.

Editing Fireworks HTML

After you insert Fireworks HTML into Dreamweaver, some special options become available in the Properties Inspector, allowing you to easily edit the images and associated code back in Fireworks. Looking at Figure 11-8, you see that the Property Inspector adds a few items that appear only when you insert a Fireworks HTML table. One is an indicator of the source PNG file for the images, in this case a navigation bar with multiple buttons, and the other is an Edit button, which lets you edit the table in Fireworks.

To edit an existing Fireworks table in Dreamweaver, follow these steps:

1. **Select the table in the Dreamweaver document.**

   Fireworks-generated HTML imported into Dreamweaver becomes kind of an "object" that you can distinguish by dotted lines representing the top-level table of the imported HTML/graphics. You must select this "object" in order to display the options in the Properties Inspector (as shown in Figure 11-7).

2. **Click the Edit button to launch Fireworks.**

   You are asked to find the original PNG file corresponding to the inserted HTML/graphics if it can't be found. After locating the PNG file, the graphic appears within a Fireworks document window.

3. **Make any edits or adjustments to the Fireworks document.**

4. **Click the Done button in the Fireworks document window (see Figure 11-8).**

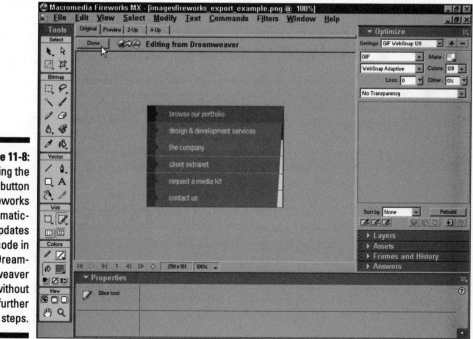

Figure 11-8:
Clicking the Done button in Fireworks automatic-ally updates the code in Dream-weaver without any further steps.

The HTML code is re-output and the graphics and table code are automatically updated in Dreamweaver!

If you are interested in learning more about Macromedia Fireworks, definitely check out *Playing With Fire: Tapping the Power of Macromedia Fireworks*, by Linda Rathgeber, published by Wiley Publishing, Inc.

If you'd like to try Adobe ImageReady, Linda Weinman's book, *Photoshop 6 ImageReady 3 Hands-On Training*, is a great place to start.

Chapter 12

Showing Off with Multimedia

● ●

In This Chapter

▶ Integrating multimedia into your Web pages

▶ Adding Shockwave and Flash movies

▶ Creating Flash buttons and text

▶ Getting familiar with Java and ActiveX controls

▶ Using sound, video, and other multimedia files

● ●

*T*hose who live in this multimedia world, spoiled by CD-ROMs and music videos, are far from satisfied with flat, text-based Web sites. Most Web designers want the rich, interactive features that they know are possible, even with the limits of bandwidth. They want animation, sound, video — the features that bring life to other media. But HTML, even with the addition of Dynamic HTML features, just doesn't fulfill those desires.

That's where plug-ins come in.

Plug-ins are small programs that work in cooperation with a Web browser to play sound, video, and animation. They're called plug-ins because they're basically small applications that plug into the browser and extend its capabilities. Any company can create plug-ins for browsers to enable the browsers to display and use new technologies. Some plug-ins have become so popular that browser makers Netscape and Microsoft have built them into their latest browsers. Plug-ins that aren't so well known require viewers to download and install them on their computers to run with the browsers.

Well-known multimedia and plug-in technologies include Macromedia's Shockwave and Flash, Real Networks' RealAudio and RealVideo, and Apple's QuickTime, to name a few. In this chapter, I tell you about the various types of multimedia technologies and how to use Dreamweaver to place these files into your Web pages. I also give you tips about making your pages work best in multiple browsers and how Dreamweaver makes that easy for you.

Working with Macromedia Shockwave and Flash Files

Flash and Shockwave are currently among the most widely used plug-in technologies for the Web. Although there are similarities between the two, Macromedia provides a different plug-in for Shockwave and Flash media types. Anyone can download these plug-ins separately or get them all in one large plug-in package from the Macromedia Web site. The software that plays Shockwave and Flash is available as both a Netscape plug-in and an ActiveX control for Internet Explorer.

Dreamweaver can handle both Shockwave and Flash (I describe both in more detail later) media types as well as most other media types that use a Netscape plug-in architecture. Other plug-ins from Macromedia include the Authorware plug-in for viewing Authorware media files in the browser. Treat the other file types as you would any other technology not specifically described in this chapter. You can find more on that in the section "Working with Other Plug-In Technologies" later in this chapter.

What is Shockwave?

Macromedia Shockwave for Director enables you to display multimedia files created in Macromedia Director on a Web page. Director is the most popular program around for creating CD-ROMs and other types of multimedia titles, which means that the program has a large following and many people know how to use it. You can recognize a Shockwave file because it uses the extension .DCR. Shockwave is one of the best formats available for creating complex multimedia files — such as games — that include animation, sound, video, and other interactive features like the capability to shoot a target or drive a car. Shockwave has some very powerful capabilities, such as the Lingo programming language that enables complex interactive features, but it can also be a difficult program to learn, and an even harder one to master.

Although Shockwave for Director has become one of the most popular plug-ins on the Web, there's still a problem with file sizes. Most files created for CD-ROMs are huge by Web standards, and consumers are spoiled by the quality and speed of CD-ROMs. Because of the bandwidth limitations of the Web, developers who create Shockwave files face many limitations. Even though the process of converting Director files to Shockwave results in somewhat reduced file sizes, most developers still stick to small, simple files that download quickly. Still, a few developers create large, complex Shockwave files and hope that their users have the bandwidth, or patience, to enjoy them. As always, when creating high-bandwidth multimedia files, you need to consider the audience that you're targeting and the type of Internet connections that visitors are likely to be using when you decide on file sizes. For more information on creating Shockwave for Director files, visit `www.macromedia.com/software/director`.

What is Flash?

You've probably heard a lot about Flash but may be wondering what exactly it is and how it differs from Shockwave. Flash utilizes something called *scaling vector graphics*. This technology means that the graphics in Flash are based on mathematical descriptions that take up far less space than bitmapped graphics like the kind Shockwave uses. Vector graphics can be scaled up or down to fill any size browser window without affecting the image quality or the size of the file that's downloaded. Because of this ability to scale, Flash is perfectly suited for usage on the Web. Flash files can be recognized by their file extension .SWF. Although Shockwave now supports Vector graphics and Flash files can now incorporate bitmap files, Flash is better suited to creating smaller files than Shockwave so they download faster.

As a format that was designed specifically for the Web, Flash continues to win acclaim and widespread adoption because it enables users to create animations that download really fast. You can also produce scalable, interactive animations with synchronized sound. All that, and you still get smaller file sizes than with any other animation technology on the Web.

So with such great performance on the Web, why would anybody choose Shockwave over Flash? Well, Director is still a far more robust multimedia programming environment than Flash, allowing for much more complicated applications, particularly for games. If you don't have a need for a really high degree of interactive content and don't relish the steep learning curve of Director, Flash is a better bet. For more on why Flash files download more quickly than other file types, see the sidebar "Download Flash files in a flash."

Macromedia recently added a programming language to Flash called ActionScript. Although ActionScript is not as robust as Lingo, it's powerful enough to interact with database-driven Web pages and can be used to create complex Flash games. If you want to see an example, try out the Banja game at `www.banja.com`, which was built in Flash with a database backend.

Inserting Shockwave and Flash movies

In the following section, I assume that you have already created the Shockwave or Flash movie file and that it's ready to be placed into your Web page. If you don't have any movie files to use, you can find a sample Flash file on the CD-ROM accompanying this book — just look for the files with the .SWF extension. In the section following this one, I show you how to create Flash buttons and text directly within Dreamweaver.

Using the <OBJECT> and <EMBED> tags together for best results in multiple browsers

HTML supports plug-in file formats, such as Macromedia's Shockwave or Flash, through either the <OBJECT> or <EMBED> tag. Both accomplish the same thing, yet each one is designed only for a particular browser. If you're designing Web pages for the broader audience of the World Wide Web, your best option is to use both tags in your HTML because, unfortunately, Netscape and Microsoft have never agreed on a standard. You see, some time ago, the two largest browser makers went off in different directions, with Netscape creating the <EMBED> tag and Microsoft introducing the <OBJECT> tag to accomplish the same goal of displaying plug-in media. Today, the best way to handle the situation is to use both tags when you insert plug-in files.

You can use these HTML tags together because browsers ignore HTML tags that they don't recognize. That means that because Navigator doesn't support the <OBJECT> tag, Navigator doesn't display any file that is embedded using that tag. If there's nothing else in the code that the browser does support, it may just display ugly gray squares in place of the plug-in file — and nobody wants ugly gray squares on a Web page. By using the <OBJECT> and <EMBED> tags together, you can achieve the best designs for the most browsers. For example, you can use the <EMBED> tag options to link an alternate GIF or JPEG image that displays in place of the plug-in file if the browser doesn't support plug-ins or lacks the appropriate plug-in.

If you're writing the code yourself and want to design for optimal results in both browsers, make sure that you nest the <EMBED> tag within the <OBJECT> tag. You should write the tags in this order because browsers that support the <OBJECT> tag, such as Internet Explorer, also support the <EMBED> tag and need to see the <OBJECT> tag first. Browsers that don't support the <OBJECT> tag, such as Navigator, ignore it and read the <EMBED> tag. Here's an example of what the HTML code looks like when you use both tags in combination to embed a Macromedia Flash file:

```
<object classid="clsid:D27CDB6E-AE6D-11cf-96B8-444553540000"
    codebase="http://download.
    macromedia.com/pub/shockwave/cabs/flash/swflash.cab#version=
    5,0,0,0" width="250" height="350" vspace="0" hspace="0">

        <param name=movie value="flash-presentation.swf">

        <param name=quality value=high>

        <embed src="flash-presentation.swf" quality= high
    pluginspage="http://www.macromedia.com/shockwave/download/
    index.cgi?P1_Prod_Version=ShockwaveFlash" type="application/
    x-shockwave-flash" width="250" height="350" vspace="0"
    hspace="0">

        </embed>

</object>
```

Before you get too worried about how complex the code is, let me reassure you: Dreamweaver creates all of this for you. Just follow the steps in the rest of this chapter and Dreamweaver takes care of the rest. The code example here is just to show you what's happening behind the scenes and to provide an example for those of you who like to code these things by hand.

Download Flash files in a flash

Flash files are dramatically faster to download because Flash images are vector-based. *Vector-based* means that the images are made up of coded instructions to draw specific geometric shapes, filled with specific colors. This takes far less space than the individual pixel data needed for bitmapped images, such as those used in animated GIFs. As a result, Flash files can be significantly smaller than other types of images and animation files. An animated GIF that's 200K and takes a minute to download on a 33K modem may only be 20K when recreated as a Flash animation and take only a few seconds to download. In fact, whole animated cartoon movies that are 10 minutes or more in length can be viewed in Flash over a regular 56K modem. You can find lots more information about creating Flash files at `www.macromedia.com/software/flash`.

If you need help using Shockwave or Flash, check out these books: *Shockwave For Dummies,* 2nd Edition, by Greg Harvey and *Macromedia Flash MX For Dummies* by Gurdy Leete and Ellen Finkelstein (both published by Hungry Minds, Inc.).

To add an existing Shockwave or Flash movie file to a Web page by using Dreamweaver, follow these steps:

1. **Click to insert the cursor where you want the Shockwave or Flash movie to be displayed on your Web page.**

2. **From the Objects panel, click the button for either Insert Shockwave or Insert Flash (see Figure 12-1).**

   You can also choose Insert⇨Media⇨Shockwave or Insert⇨Media⇨Flash. The Select File dialog box appears in either case.

3. **In the dialog box, browse your drive to locate the appropriate movie file that you want inserted into your page.**

4. **Click to highlight the filename and then click the Select button.**

   After you click Select, the dialog box closes.

   Alternatively, you can also type the name and path to the movie file in the text field under Movie Source. The Shockwave or Flash movie is automatically inserted in the page.

   Dreamweaver doesn't display plug-in media files in the editor when first inserted. Instead, you see a small icon that represents the Shockwave or Flash movie file (refer to Figure 12-1). To preview your choice, click the green Play button on the left side of the Property Inspector (if the Property Inspector is not visible, click the Shockwave or Flash file icon to open it). If you preview the page in your browser, you can also see the Shockwave or Flash movie displayed in context.

Figure 12-1:
You can
insert many
different
multimedia
file types
into your
documents
by clicking
the
appropriate
icon in the
Objects
panel.

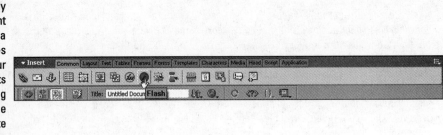

5. **With the Property Inspector panel visible, specify the width and height of the file in the text fields next to W and H.**

   You can set many options in the Property Inspector, but only the width and height are required. The next section tells you more about the other options.

Setting parameters and other options for Shockwave and Flash

Like most HTML tags, the tags that link Shockwave, Flash, and other plug-in files to Web pages have *attributes* (they're called *parameters* when used with the <OBJECT> tag). These parameters are even more important for plug-in files because you must set some of them — such as the height and width — for the file to work properly in a browser. Dreamweaver takes care of setting the height and width, but you may want to change some of the other settings. This section provides a list of attributes and parameters that you can change in the Property Inspector and what those attributes affect.

Don't worry about making sure that you specify property settings for both the <EMBED> and <OBJECT> tags. When you change options in the Property Inspector for either Shockwave or Flash, Dreamweaver automatically applies those changes to both the <EMBED> and <OBJECT> tags.

If you don't see all the options in the Property Inspector, click the expander arrow in the bottom-right corner to display the more advanced options.

Here are the Flash options in the Property Inspector, as shown in Figure 12-2:

- ✔ **Name field:** Use the text field in the top-left corner of the Inspector just to the right of the Shockwave icon if you want to type a name for your file. You can leave this blank or name it whatever you want. Dreamweaver won't apply a name if you leave it blank. This name only identifies the file for scripting.

- ✔ **W (Width):** Use this option to specify the width of the file. You can change the measurement by typing pc (picas), pt (points), in (inches), mm (millimeters), cm (centimeters), or % (percentage of the original file's value) immediately following the number. Don't put any spaces between the number and the measurement abbreviation.

- ✔ **H (Height):** Use this option to specify the height of the file. You can change the measurement by typing pc (picas), pt (points), in (inches), mm (millimeters), cm (centimeters), or % (percentage of the original file's value) immediately following the number. Don't put any spaces between the number and the measurement abbreviation.

- ✔ **File:** Use this text field to enter the name and path to the file. You can change this by typing in a new name or path or by clicking the folder icon to browse for a file.

- ✔ **Edit:** Enables you to launch the multimedia file in another program, such as Flash, where you can edit it without leaving Dreamweaver.

- ✔ **Reset Size:** Because Flash files can be scaled without losing any image quality, it's common to scale a Flash file on a Web page to a different size from the size it was created at. Clicking this button reverts the Flash file to the original size at which is was created.

- ✔ **Loop:** Checking this box causes the Flash file to repeat (or loop). If you don't check this box, the Flash movie stops after it reaches the last frame.

- ✔ **Autoplay:** This controls the Play parameter, enabling you to determine whether a Flash movie starts as soon as it downloads to the viewer's computer or whether a user must click a button or take another action to start the Flash movie. A check in this box causes the movie to automatically start to play as soon as the page finishes loading. If you don't check this box, whatever option you've set in the Flash file (such as onMouseOver or onMouseDown) is required to start the movie.

- ✔ **V Space (Vertical Space):** If you want blank space above or below the file, enter the number of pixels here.

- ✔ **H Space (Horizontal Space):** If you want blank space on either side of the file, enter the number of pixels here.

- ✔ **Quality:** This option enables you to prioritize the antialiasing options of your images versus the speed of playback. *Antialiasing,* which makes your files appear smoother, can slow down the rendering of each frame because the computer must first smooth the edges. The Quality parameter enables you to regulate how much the process is slowed down by letting you set priorities based on the importance of appearance versus playback speed.

You can choose from the following Quality options:

- **Low:** With this option, antialiasing is never used. Playback speed has priority over appearance.

- **High:** With this option, antialiasing is always used. Appearance has priority over playback speed.

- **Autohigh:** A somewhat more sophisticated option, Autohigh sets playback to begin with antialiasing turned on. However, if the actual frame rate supported by the user's computer drops below your specified frame rate, antialiasing automatically turns off to improve playback speed. This option emphasizes playback speed and appearance equally at first but sacrifices appearance for the sake of playback speed, if necessary.

- **Autolow:** With this option, playback begins with antialiasing turned off. If the Flash player detects that the processor can handle it, antialiasing is turned on. Use this option to emphasize speed at first but improve appearance whenever possible.

✔ **Scale:** Specify this option only if you use percentages for the Height and Width parameter. The Scale parameter enables you to define how the Flash movie displays within the boundaries of the area specified in the browser window.

Flash movies are scaleable. With the Scale option, you can specify the original dimensions in pixels or in percentages of a browser window in the W (width) and H (height) fields. This enables you to control how the Flash movie displays if a browser window is a different size from your original design. For example, if you always want your Flash movie to take up a quarter of the screen (no matter how large the screen is), set it to 25 percent; if you want it to always fill the screen, set it to 100 percent.

Because using a percentage can lead to undesired effects (such as cropping or distorting a file to make it fit), the following options in the Scale drop-down list enable you to set preferences about how a scaled Flash movie displays within the window:

- **Show all:** This option enables the entire movie to display in the specified area. The width and height proportions of the original movie are maintained and no distortion occurs, but borders may appear on two sides of the movie to fill the space.

- **No border:** This option enables you to scale a Flash movie to fill a specified area. Again, the original width and height proportions are maintained and no distortion occurs, but portions of the movie may be cropped.

- **Exact fit:** Using this option, the entire movie is visible in the specified area. However, the Flash movie may be distorted because the width and height proportions may be stretched or shrunk in order to fit the movie in the specified area.

✔ **Align:** This option controls the alignment of the file on the page. This setting works the same for plug-in files as for images.

✔ **BgColor:** This option sets a background color that fills the area of the file. This color displays if the specified height and width are larger than the file and during periods when the movie isn't playing, either because it's loading or it has finished playing.

✔ **Play button:** Click the green Play button to preview the Shockwave or Flash file directly in Dreamweaver. This button resembles a right-pointing arrow and is located on the left side of the Property Inspector in the lower half of the window.

✔ **Parameters:** This button provides access to a dialog box where you can enter additional parameters for the Shockwave movie.

Figure 12-2:
The Flash
options in
the Property
Inspector.

A word about Generator

Macromedia Generator is an advanced programming application for creating dynamic Flash applications that integrate with databases. For the most part, Generator is used to present dynamic graphics in realtime from a Database. Because Generator is a pretty high-level program, I won't devote time to it in this book, but you should know that Generator files are treated just like other media files in Dreamweaver. To insert a Generator file into a Dreamweaver document, choose Insert⇨ Media⇨Generator or click the Insert Generator button on the Common Objects panel.

If you want to see an example of Generator in action, check out the Discovery Channel Web site at www.discovery.com. The majority of moving images boxes and text on that site and pulled from a database using Generator.

Creating Flash Files from within Dreamweaver

Dreamweaver MX features the ability to create and edit simple Flash files from within Dreamweaver, which is really great because not only can you utilize Flash in your Web site without having to buy another program, but you don't have to learn another program, either. Though you can't create any really fancy Flash animations, this feature still allows you to create graphical text objects and cool Flash buttons using the familiar Dreamweaver interface. Dreamweaver includes a large library of existing Flash objects that you can use and, even better, because the Macromedia Flash Objects architecture is extensible, you can download new Flash styles from the Web or work with Flash developers to create new Flash objects for you to use in Dreamweaver.

Creating Flash text

With the Flash text object, you can create and insert a Flash (.swf) text movie into your document. Flash text movies allow you to utilize a vector-based text graphic in the font of your choice (*vector-based* means that the images are made up of coded instructions to draw specific geometric shapes). The great advantage to using Flash text is that you can utilize any fonts you want without worrying whether or not your audience has the same font on their computer. You can also set a rollover effect without the need to create separate images, and the size of the text can scale up or down without any effect on image quality or file size.

To insert a Flash text object follow these steps:

1. **Save your Dreamweaver document.**

   The document must be saved before you can insert a Flash text object.

2. **Click the Insert Flash Text icon in the Insert Media panel.**

   Or you can select Insert➪Interactive Images➪Flash Text.

   The Insert Flash Text dialog box appears, as pictured in Figure 12-3.

3. **Select the desired Text options including font, style, size, color, alignment, and so on.**

   To see the text previewed in your font of choice, check the box next to Show Font. The other options are defined here.

- **Rollover Color** indicates the color that the text should change to when the user rolls the mouse over the text. If you don't want a rollover effect, make the rollover color the same color.

- The **Link** and **Target** can be set for the text using the appropriate fields. The link is activated when the user clicks the text.

- Make the **Bg Color** (background color) the same as the background color of the Web page you're placing the text on.

- For **Save As,** always save the file with the .swf extension as you will actually be creating a Flash file. Browse your drive to indicate where you want to save the Flash file.

4. **When you're done selecting the appropriate options, click OK to insert the text.**

   You can also click Apply to see the effects in your Dreamweaver document before clicking OK.

   The dialog box closes and the Flash text is inserted on the page. To edit the text again or change any of the options, double-click the Flash text to open the dialog box.

If you're really interested in creating WYSIWYG Flash movies, check out Swish, a great little program that's reasonably priced, too. To learn more, visit www.swishzone.com.

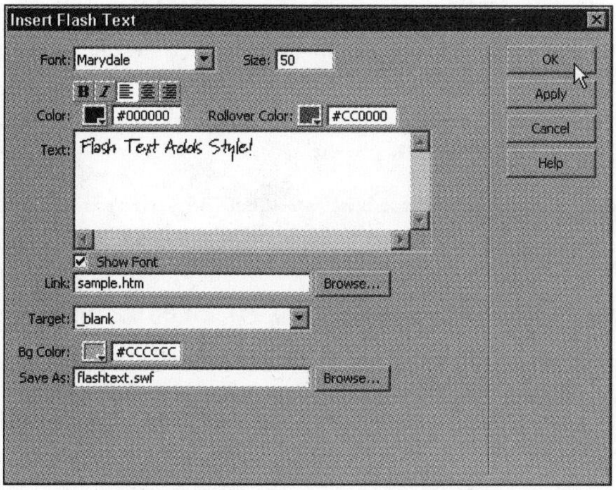

Figure 12-3:
The Insert
Flash Text
dialog box
lets you
create
and edit
interactive
Flash text
within
Dream-
weaver.

Insert Flash Text

Font: Marydale   Size: 50

B *I*

Color: #000000   Rollover Color: #CC0000

Text: Flash Text Adds Style!

☑ Show Font

Link: sample.htm   Browse...

Target: _blank

Bg Color: #CCCCCC

Save As: flashtext.swf   Browse...

OK
Apply
Cancel
Help

Creating Flash buttons

Even more exciting than Flash text are Flash buttons. Flash buttons are pre-created graphics that can be customized and used as interactive buttons on your Web sites. Like Flash text, Flash buttons are made up of vector graphics and can be scaled and resized without any degradation in quality. Dreamweaver ships with a library of over 50 button styles for you to use. You can also add styles by downloading them from the Web or creating your own in Flash.

To insert a Flash button follow these steps:

1. **Save your Dreamweaver document.**

   The document must be saved before you can insert a Flash button object.

2. **Click the Insert Flash Button icon in the Objects panel.**

   Or you can select Insert⇨Interactive Images⇨Flash Button.

   The Insert Flash Button dialog box appears, as shown in Figure 12-4.

3. **In the Style field, scroll to select the type of button you want to use.**

   You can view the currently selected choice in the Sample field.

4. **Select the appropriate options to customize your button.**

   Enter the text you want to use in the Button Text field or leave this blank if you don't want any text on the button. Select the other text options including font, style, size, color, alignment, and so on.

   Select the link, target, and background colors in the appropriate fields if applicable.

   Always save the file with the .swf extension as you will actually be creating a Flash file. Browse your drive to indicate where you want to save the Flash file.

5. **When you're done setting the options, click OK to insert the button.**

   You can also click Apply to see the effects in your Dreamweaver document before clicking OK.

   The dialog box closes and the button is inserted on the page. To edit the button again or change any of the options, double-click the button to open the dialog box.

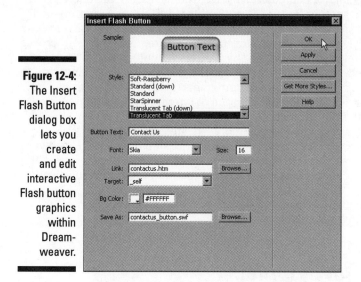

Figure 12-4:
The Insert
Flash Button
dialog box
lets you
create
and edit
interactive
Flash button
graphics
within
Dream-
weaver.

Adding new button styles

Because the Macromedia Flash Objects architecture is extensible, you can download new Flash styles from the Web or work with Flash developers to create new Flash objects for you to use in Dreamweaver. To get more styles from the Macromedia Exchange Web site, click the Get More Styles button in the Insert Flash Button dialog box. Clicking this button launches your Web browser and connects you to the Macromedia Exchange site where you can download more buttons (you must have a live Internet connection for this to work).

Because Macromedia developed Flash as open source, you can create Flash files with a variety of programs including Adobe Illustrator, which has an export to SWF option. A great site for learning more about the latest in Flash development is www.openswf.org.

Working with Java

Java is a programming language, like Pascal, Basic, C, or C++, that you can use to create programs that run on a computer. What makes Java special is that it can run on any computer system and can display in your browser. Usually, if you create a program in a computer language, you have to create one version for the Macintosh, another for the PC, and a third for UNIX. But Java, created by Sun Microsystems, is platform-independent so that developers can use it to create almost any kind of program — even complex programs like word processors or spreadsheets — that work on any type of computer without having to customize the code for each platform. Normally, programs also run independently of each other. But with Java, the programs (also called *applets*) can run within a Web browser, allowing the program to interact with different elements of the page or with other pages on the Web. This has made Java very popular because it provides a way to add more sophisticated capabilities to Web browsers regardless of which operating system the Web browser is running on. You can embed Java applets in Web pages, you can use Java to generate entire Web pages, or you can run Java applications separately after they download.

To find out more about Java, check out *Java 2 For Dummies* by Barry Burd (published by Hungry Minds, Inc.).

Inserting Java applets

To insert a Java applet in your Web page, follow these steps:

1. **Click to insert the cursor where you want the applet to display on your Web page.**

2. **From the Objects panel, click the button for Java applets (the button looks like a little coffee cup).**

   Alternatively, you can also choose Insert⇨Media⇨Applet.

   The Insert Applet dialog box appears.

3. **Use the Browse button to locate the Java applet file that you want inserted in the page.**

4. **Click to highlight the filename, click the Select button, and then click OK to close the dialog box.**

   You can also type in the name and path to the file in the text box under Java Class Source. The applet automatically links to the page.

   Dreamweaver doesn't display applets in the Dreamweaver work area. Instead, you see a small icon that represents the applet (the icon looks like the coffee cup icon you see in the Objects panel). To view the applet on your Web page (the only way to see the applet in action), preview the page in a browser, such as Navigator 4.0 and higher or Internet Explorer 4.0 and higher, that supports applets.

5. **Double-click the Applet icon to open the Property Inspector.**

   You can set many options in the Property Inspector. If you want to know more about these options, read on.

If you're having trouble viewing Java applets, it may be because you are using an older version of Internet Explorer. Microsoft and Sun have fought long and hard about Java standards, and as a result, native Java support was stripped from earlier versions of Internet Explorer. To view Java applets in older Microsoft browsers, you have to download Microsoft's Virtual Machine or Sun's Java Runtime. If your visitors are using an old version of Internet Explorer, you should prompt them to go to the Windows Update site to get a newer version.

Setting Java parameters and other options

Like other file formats that require plug-ins or advanced browser support, Java applets come with the following options (see Figure 12-5):

- **Applet Name:** Use this field in the top-left corner if you want to type a name for your applet. Dreamweaver does not apply a name if you leave this field blank. This name identifies the applet for scripting.

- **W (Width):** This option specifies the width of the applet. You can change the measurement by typing pc (picas), pt (points), in (inches), mm (millimeters), cm (centimeters), or % (percentage of the original file's value) immediately following the number. Don't put any spaces between the number and the measurement abbreviation.

- **H (Height):** This option specifies the height of the applet. You can change the measurement by typing pc (picas), pt (points), in (inches), mm (millimeters), cm (centimeters), or % (percentage of the original file's value) immediately following the number. Don't put any spaces between the number and the measurement abbreviation.

- **Code:** Dreamweaver automatically enters the code when you insert the file. Code specifies the content file of the applet. You may type in your own filename or click the folder icon to choose a file.

- **Base:** Automatically entered when you insert the file, Base identifies the folder that contains the applet. You may type in your own directory name.

- **Align:** This option determines how the object aligns on the page.

- **Alt:** This option enables you to specify an alternate file, such as an image that's displayed if the viewer's browser doesn't support Java. That way, the user doesn't see just a broken file icon. If you type text into this field, the viewer will see this text; Dreamweaver writes it into the code by using the Alt attribute of the Applet tag. If you use the folder icon to select an image, the viewer sees an image; Dreamweaver automatically inserts an `<IMG>` tag within the open and close tags of the applet.

- **V Space (Vertical Space):** If you want blank space above or below the applet, enter the number of pixels that you want.

✔ **H Space (Horizontal Space):** If you want blank space on either side of the applet, enter the number of pixels that you want.

✔ **Parameters:** Click this button to access a dialog box in which you can enter additional parameters for the applet.

You can find lots more information in *Java 2 For Dummies* by Barry Burd (published by Hungry Minds, Inc.).

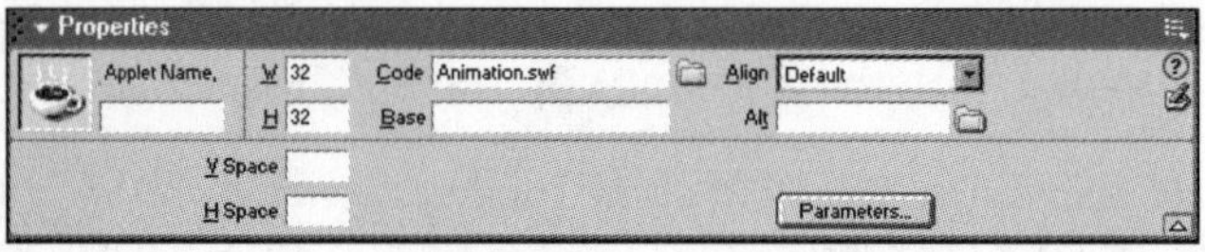

Figure 12-5:
The
Property
Inspector
lets you
specify
options for
Java
applets.

Using ActiveX Objects and Controls

Microsoft ActiveX objects and controls are reusable components similar to miniature applications that can act like browser plug-ins. Because they work only in Internet Explorer on the Windows platform, they haven't been widely accepted on the Web. As a result, no clear standard for identifying ActiveX objects and controls exists. Still, Dreamweaver supports using ActiveX and provides some flexibility so that you can set the parameters for the ActiveX control that you use, should you decide to use them.

The ActiveX Property Inspector provides the following options (see Figure 12-6):

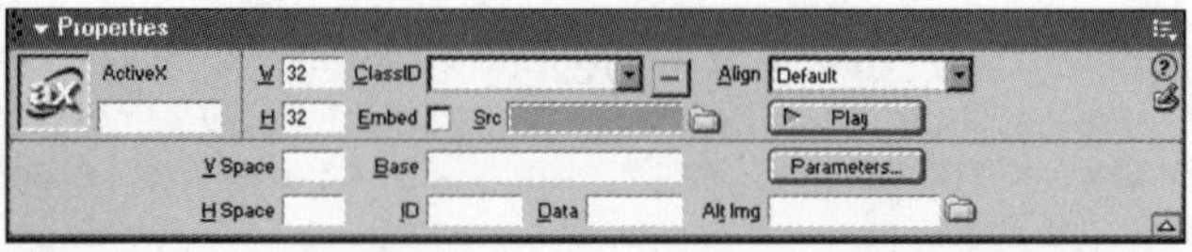

Figure 12-6:
The
Property
Inspector
lets you
specify
options for
ActiveX
objects and
controls.

✔ **Name text field:** Use the text field in the top-left corner of the Property Inspector just to the right of the ActiveX icon if you want to type a name for your ActiveX object. You can leave this blank or name it whatever you want. Dreamweaver does not provide a name if you leave it blank. This name identifies the ActiveX object only for scripting purposes.

✔ **W (Width):** You can specify the measurement of an ActiveX object by typing pc (picas), pt (points), in (inches), mm (millimeters), cm (centimeters), or % (percentage of the original file's value) immediately after the number. Don't put any spaces between the number and the measurement abbreviation.

✔ **H (Height):** You can specify the measurement of an ActiveX object by typing pc (picas), pt (points), in (inches), mm (millimeters), cm (centimeters), or % (percentage of the original file's value) immediately following the number. Don't put any spaces between the number and the measurement abbreviation.

✔ **ClassID:** The browser uses the ClassID to identify the ActiveX control. You can type any value or choose any of these options from the drop-down list: RealPlayer, Shockwave for Director, and Shockwave for Flash.

✔ **Embed:** Checking this box tells Dreamweaver to add an <EMBED> tag within the <OBJECT> tag. The <EMBED> tag activates a Netscape plug-in equivalent, if available, and makes your pages more accessible to Navigator users. Dreamweaver automatically sets the values that you've entered for ActiveX properties to the <EMBED> tag for any equivalent Netscape plug-in.

✔ **Src (Source):** This option identifies the file to be associated with the <EMBED> tag and used by a Netscape plug-in.

✔ **Align:** This option specifies how the object aligns on the page.

✔ **Parameters:** Click this button to access a dialog box in which you can enter additional parameters for the ActiveX controls.

✔ **V Space (Vertical Space):** If you want blank space above or below the object, enter the number of pixels that you want.

✔ **H Space (Horizontal Space):** If you want blank space on either side of the object, enter the number of pixels that you want.

✔ **Base:** This option enables you to specify a URL for the ActiveX control so that Internet Explorer can automatically download the control if it's not installed in the user's system.

✔ **ID:** This option identifies an optional ActiveX ID parameter. Consult the documentation for the ActiveX control you're using to find out which parameters to use.

✔ **Data:** This option enables you to specify a data file for the ActiveX control to load.

✔ **Alt Img:** This option enables you to link an image that displays if the browser doesn't support the <OBJECT> tag.

JavaScript is not Java

JavaScript, a scripting language that many people often confuse with Java, has little in common with Java other than its name and some syntactic similarities in the way that the language works. To be more accurate, think of JavaScript as a much-simplified relative of Java with far fewer capabilities. Unlike Java, though, you can write JavaScript directly into HTML code to create interactive features, but you can't use it to create standalone applets and programs as you can in Java. You won't get the complex functionality of Java, but JavaScript is a lot easier to use and doesn't require a plug-in.

JavaScript is often used in combination with other multimedia elements on the page, such as images or sound files, to add greater levels of interactivity. Dynamic HTML also uses JavaScript and is covered in Chapters 9 and 10. In these chapters, you can read about how to use Dreamweaver to apply behaviors and other features created by using JavaScript together with HTML.

Working with Other Plug-In Technologies

So many plug-ins, so little bandwidth. You can find literally hundreds of plug-ins available for Web pages. Some of them give you fabulous results, such as sound, video, a variety of image formats, and even three-dimensional worlds and animations. But with plug-ins — perhaps more than with any other technology on the Web — you have to be very careful. Web page visitors aren't usually excited about having to download a new plug-in, even if you as a Web site creator are excited about deploying it. Indeed, many visitors are scared off by the idea and others are just plain annoyed, while others lack the hardware or software requirements to run them. Don't risk doing that to your viewers unless you have a compelling reason.

If I visited your site, I wouldn't be happy if you sent me off to get a plug-in just so I could see your logo spinning around in all its three-dimensional splendor. On the other hand, if your site features interactive games or a three-dimensional environment with chat capability targeted for users with those interests, I may be quite happy to get a plug-in that enables me to experience something as interesting as a multi-user game or interactive environment. Make sure that you let your users know what they're in for before you send them off on a plug-in adventure. You're also wise to stick to the better known plug-in technologies — such as QuickTime, RealAudio, RealVideo, and the Shockwave/Flash suite — because users are more likely to already have them or appreciate the benefit of getting them because they know that they can use them on other sites.

Inserting Netscape Navigator plug-ins

Because Netscape invented the idea of browser plug-ins, most plug-ins use Netscape's original specifications to create new browser plug-ins. In most cases, Netscape Navigator plug-ins also function in Internet Explorer. Some of the more popular plug-ins include RealAudio, RealVideo, Quicktime, and Beatnik, as well as Flash and Shockwave, which are also considered Navigator plug-ins.

To use Dreamweaver to insert a Netscape-compatible plug-in file other than Flash or Shockwave into your Web page, follow these steps:

1. **Click to insert the cursor where you want the file to display on your Web page.**

2. **From the Objects panel, click the button for Netscape Plug-Ins (the button looks like a puzzle piece).**

   You can also choose Insert⇨Media⇨Plugin.

   The Select File dialog box appears.

3. **Browse your drive to locate the plug-in media file that you want inserted in your page and click to select it.**

4. **Click the Select button and then click OK to close the dialog box.**

   You can also type in the name and path to the file in the text field under Plug-In Source. The file is automatically inserted in the page and you see a small icon that represents the file (the icon looks like the puzzle piece icon in the Objects panel).

5. **Double-click the plug-in icon to open the Property Inspector.**

   You can set many options in the Property Inspector. If you want to know more about these options, continue reading the next section.

6. **Preview the plug-in.**

   Dreamweaver doesn't display plug-in files in the editor unless the plug-ins are installed on your computer and you click the green Play button in the Property Inspector. To view the plug-in file in Dreamweaver, click the Play button in the Property Inspector and it displays in the Document window.

Setting Netscape plug-in parameters and other options

You can specify the following settings in the Plug-In Property Inspector (see Figure 12-7):

✔ **Name text field:** Use the text field in the top-left corner of the Property Inspector just to the right of the plug-in icon if you want to type a name for your plug-in file. You can leave this blank or provide any name you want. Dreamweaver does not provide a name if you leave this field blank. This name identifies the file only for scripting purposes.

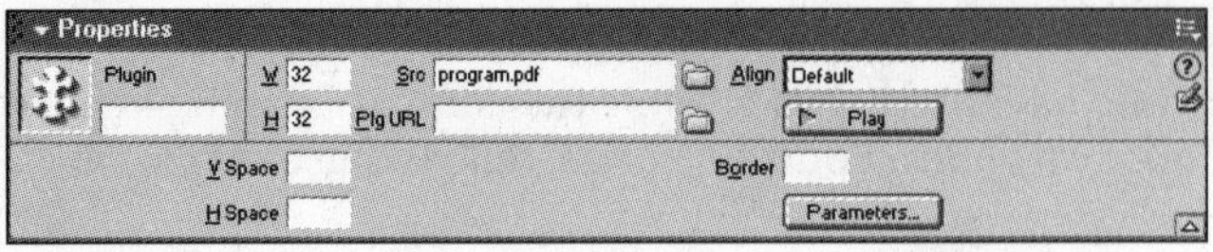

Figure 12-7:
The
Property
Inspector
lets you
specify
options for
Netscape
plug-ins.

✔ **W (Width):** You can specify the measurement of any Netscape plug-in by typing pc (picas), pt (points), in (inches), mm (millimeters), cm (centimeters), or % (percentage of the original file's value) immediately following the number. Don't put any spaces between the number and the measurement abbreviation.

✔ **H (Height):** You can specify the measurement of any Netscape plug-in by typing pc (picas), pt (points), in (inches), mm (millimeters), cm (centimeters), or % (percentage of the original file's value) immediately following the number. Don't put any spaces between the number and the measurement abbreviation.

For most plug-ins, the height and width tags are required. However, in some cases, such as sound files that don't display on a page, you can't specify height and width.

✔ **Src (Source):** This option specifies the name and path to the plug-in file. You can type in a filename or click the folder icon to browse for the file.

✔ **Plg URL:** This option enables you to provide a URL where viewers can download a plug-in if they don't already have it.

✔ **Align:** This option enables you to specify how the element aligns on the page.

✔ **Alt:** Here, you can provide alternate content that displays if the viewer's browser doesn't support the <EMBED> tag. You can link an image as an alternative or simply type text that displays in place of the plug-in file.

✔ **Play button:** Click the green Play button (the right-pointing arrow on the left side of the Property Inspector) to preview the media file. The media plug-in must be installed either in Dreamweaver (in the Configuration/ Plugins folder) or in one of the browsers on your computer for it to preview in Dreamweaver.

✔ **V Space (Vertical Space):** If you want blank space above and below the plug-in, enter the number of pixels that you want.

✔ **H Space (Horizontal Space):** If you want blank space on either side of the plug-in, enter the number of pixels that you want.

✔ **Border:** This option specifies the width of the border around the file.

✔ **Parameters:** Click this button to access a dialog box in which you can enter additional parameters for the plug-in file. To enter a parameter, click the plus (+) button and enter the parameter name in the parameter column as well as the corresponding value in the value column. See the documentation for the plug-in media type that you're using for information on the parameters that it utilizes.

If you want to add these kinds of multimedia files to your site, but you don't know how to create them yourself, here are two great sites that provide ready-to-use pre-made Flash files:

✔ **Flash Kit** (www.flashkit.com): Flash Kit is mainly an open-source Web site where you can download pre-made, fully-editable Flash source files to enhance your existing Flash animations or to use as a starting point for new animations.

✔ **We're Here Forums** (www.werehere.com): We're Here Forum also provides Flash source files for download and use. This site also offers sound loops and links to other Flash resources.

Chapter 13

Forms Follow Function

● ●

In This Chapter

▶ Discovering what forms can do

▶ Creating forms

▶ Making forms work

▶ Integrating forms into dynamic sites

● ●

Many powerful and interactive Web sites are adorned with HTML forms. Whether they create a simple text box that provides the interface to a search engine or a long registration form that collects valuable consumer information from visitors, HTML forms are a crucial part of any sophisticated site these days.

The HTML tags used to create forms — from radio buttons to drop-down lists — are a different kind of tag designed to work in conjunction with more complex programming on your server. In the past, this was done almost exclusively with *CGI* (Common Gateway Interface) scripts. Today CGI has been largely replaced with a more direct way to interface with the server, made possible by technologies like ASP, PHP, JSP, ColdFusion, and so on. These programs are now generally referred to as *server-side applications,* or ASPs if they are big applications (not to be confused with the programming language ASP). To learn more about CGI , visit www.pcwebopedia.com/TERM/C/CGI.html.

To better understand how Web forms work, think of the elements that make up a job application on paper. There are little boxes where you can fill in your address and areas where you check off items. These traditional elements from paper forms can be created in HTML with tags that allow site visitors to submit information to your Web server and receive information back from the server. Elements, such as checkboxes, radio buttons, and editable text boxes, can be created instantly with different types of tags. Just like a person has to manually process forms when received by people, a program needs to reside on your server to collect the information from a form when it is filled out on a Web page. This processing is handled by a program on your server, which requires some programming beyond HTML. Technologies like CGI and programming languages like ASP are most commonly used to create interactive forms

Understanding how CGI scripts work

Think of CGI scripts as the engine behind an HTML form and many other automated features on a Web site. CGI (or Common Gateway Interface) scripts are programs that are usually written in a programming language, such as Perl, Java, C, or C++. These scripts are much more complex to create than HTML pages, and these languages take much longer to learn than HTML. CGI scripts reside and run on the server and are usually triggered by an action that a user makes, such as clicking the Submit button in an HTML form.

A common scenario with a script may go like this:

1. The user loads a page, such as a guest book, fills out the HTML form, and clicks the Submit button.

2. That action triggers the CGI script on the server to gather the data entered into the form, format it, place it in an e-mail message, and send it to a specified e-mail address.

In Dreamweaver, you can easily create HTML forms and the Submit buttons that go with them — you can even use the new code editor in Dreamweaver MX to write CGI and other scripts — but you have to know a programming language to do so. If you know Perl, JAVA, C, or C++, writing most simple CGI scripts isn't that hard. But if you don't know one of these programming languages, you're probably better off hiring someone else to do it for you or downloading ready-made scripts from the Web. If you search the Web for CGI scripts, you can find that many programmers write them and then give them away for free. Be aware, however, that you still have to install these scripts on your server and almost always have to alter the programming code at least a little to tailor them to work with your unique system. You may also need to contact your Internet Service Provider *(ISP)* to help you load the script on the server because many commercial service providers won't give you access to do it yourself.

Many ISPs make basic CGI scripts (such as guest-book forms and simple shopping-cart systems) available to their customers as part of membership. This is an easy way to get scripts for your Web site and may even be worth changing ISPs for if your current ISP doesn't offer the scripts you want. Most ISPs that offer CGI scripts provide instructions for using them on their Web sites. These instructions include the location of the script on the server. You must include this information in your HTML form so that the Submit button triggers the proper script. You can find more information about setting your HTML form to work with a script in the section "Creating HTML Forms" later in this chapter.

Whether you want to create a simple guest book or a complicated online shopping cart system, you need to know how to set up the text areas, radio buttons, and drop-down lists that make up an HTML form. Fortunately, Dreamweaver makes creating forms easy by including a special toolbar on the Objects panel to provide quick access to common form elements.

In this chapter, I introduce you to the kinds of forms commonly used on the Web and show you how to use Dreamweaver to create them. I also explain a little about the CGI scripts, ASPs and other database systems, required to process forms. Forms are a key element in database-driven sites. You'll find information about creating dynamic sites using Dreamweaver's UltraDev features in Chapters 14, 15, and 16.

Setting up secure commerce systems

Many shopping-cart systems link to *secure commerce systems*. By using encryption technology, secure commerce systems encode data (such as credit card numbers and customer addresses) that's entered into a form, making it difficult for anyone to steal the information as it travels over the Internet. These systems often connect to financial systems, such as Verisign's Payflo Pro and Checkfree, that can process orders online, immediately approve or deny a credit card, and transfer funds to the appropriate bank account for the amount of the transaction. To make this easier for businesses, many ISPs now offer e-commerce solutions, designed to help you coordinate all of these requirements. Check the Web site of your service provider to find out more.

Appreciating What HTML Forms Can Do for You

Forms follow function, to paraphrase the old saying. On the Web, forms are an integral part of the function of many interactive features. By using forms, Web designers can collect information about users — information that they can then use in a variety of ways. Forms are commonly used to create shopping cart systems, guest books, contact forms, chat rooms and discussion areas, and search engines.

Creating HTML Forms

The basic elements of HTML forms — radio buttons, check boxes, text areas, and so on — are easy to create with Dreamweaver, as I demonstrate in the sections that follow. But remember, your form won't work unless it links to a script. Although Dreamweaver doesn't provide any scripts, it does make linking your HTML forms to a script or database easy. You need to know where the script resides on the server to set this link. The name and location of the script depend on your server, but for the purposes of showing you how to link to a script with Dreamweaver, assume that the script you need to link to is called guestbook.pl (the .pl indicates that the script was written in Perl) and that the script is located in a folder on the server called cgi-bin (a common name for the folder that holds these kinds of scripts).

The following steps walk you through linking any form to this sample script. To use these steps with a different script, simply change the name of the script and the name of the directory location to reflect your system. Start with an open page — either a new page or one you want to add a form to.

1. **Choose Insert⇨Form.**

   You can also select the Form icon from the Forms Insert panel, as shown at the top of Figure 13-1. This handy option reveals all the form elements that you may want to add as you create your form.

   A blank form in Dreamweaver shows up as a rectangle outlined by a red dotted line, like the one in the main page area of Figure 13-1. This dotted line is used by Dreamweaver to indicate that an area is defined as a form in the HTML code.

2. **Click the red outline to select the form and display the form options in the Property Inspector, shown in the bottom of Figure 13-1.**

3. **Type a name in the Form Name text box.**

   You can choose any name for this field. The name is used by scripting languages, such as JavaScript, to identify the form.

4. **Type the directory name and the name of the script in the Action text box.**

   Using the sample script I describe earlier, you can type **/cgi-bin/ guestbook.pl** to specify the path to the Perl script in the cgi-bin directory. You can only use the folder icon in the Property Inspector to set this link if you have a copy of the script on your computer in the same relative location in which it resides on the server. If you're not the programmer, or you don't know much about the script, you'll probably have to ask your system administrator or Internet Service Provider for this information (ISPs that offer scripts for their Web clients often include instructions with this information on their Web sites).

5. **In the Property Inspector, use the Method drop-down list box to choose Default, Get, or Post.**

   The Get and Post options control how the form works. The option you use depends on the kind of CGI script that you use on your server. Get this information from your system administrator, programmer, or Internet Service Provider.

6. **Choose Insert⇨Form Object⇨Button.**

   Use this step to insert Submit, Refresh, and/or Clear buttons needed to complete the task.

These are just the preliminary steps that you need to take to create a form. When you establish the boundaries of a form, as represented by the dotted red line that appears after Step 1, Dreamweaver creates the code that goes in the background of your form and enables it to interact with a script on your server. The rest of this chapter shows you how to add various form elements, such as text boxes, radio buttons, and drop-down list boxes.

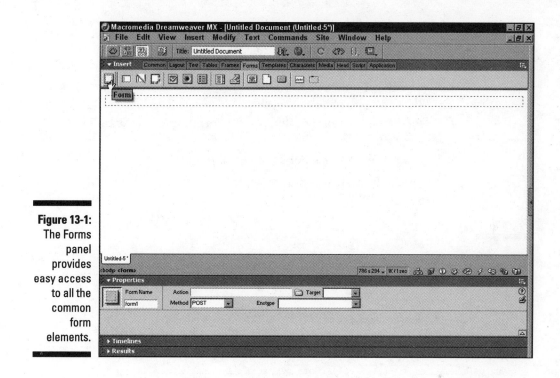

Figure 13-1:
The Forms
panel
provides
easy access
to all the
common
form
elements.

Comparing radio buttons and check boxes

Radio buttons and check boxes make it easier for viewers of your site to fill in a form. Instead of making users type in a word, such as *yes* or *no,* you can provide radio buttons and check boxes so that the user can simply click a box or button.

What's the difference between radio buttons and check boxes? *Radio buttons* enable users to select only one option from a group. Thus, radio buttons are good for yes/no options or options in which you want users to make only one choice. *Check boxes,* on the other hand, enable users to make multiple choices, so they're good for "choose all that apply" situations when users may make multiple choices.

Creating radio buttons

To create radio buttons on a form, follow these steps:

1. **Click your form to select it.**

   If you haven't yet created a form, follow the steps in the previous section, "Creating HTML Forms."

2. Click the Radio Button icon on the Forms Objects panel.

You can also choose Insert⇨Form Object⇨Radio Button. Either way, a radio button appears inside the form's perimeter.

3. Repeat Step 2 until you have the number of radio buttons that you want.

4. Select one of the radio buttons on the form to reveal the radio button's properties in the Property Inspector, as shown in Figure 13-2.

5. Type a name in the RadioButton text box.

All radio buttons in a group should have the same name to enable the script to identify the response and limit selections to one button.

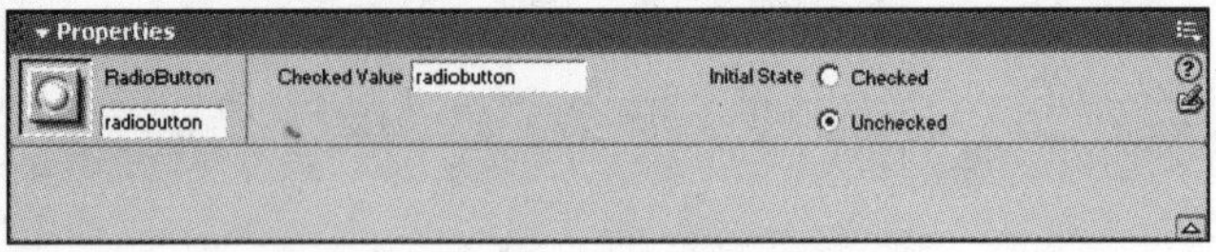

Figure 13-2:
Radio buttons are best for multiple choice options when you want to restrict users to only one choice.

6. Type a name in the Checked Value text box.

Each radio button in a group should have a different Checked Value name so that the CGI script can distinguish them. Naming them for the thing they represent is usually best — "yes" when the choice is yes and "no" when it's no. Or, in the case of the example in Figure 13-2, each radio button is named for the ice cream flavor that the button represents. This name is usually included in the data that you get back when the form is processed and returned to you (often in an e-mail message). How the data is returned depends on the CGI script. If you're looking at the data later, it's easier to interpret if the name means something that makes sense to you.

7. Choose Checked or Unchecked next to Initial State.

These two buttons determine whether the radio button on your form appears already selected when the Web page loads. Choose Checked if you want to preselect a choice. A user can always override this preselection by choosing another radio button.

8. **Select the other radio buttons one by one and repeat Steps 5 through 7 to specify the properties in the Property Inspector for each one.**

Creating check boxes

To create check boxes, follow these steps:

1. **Click your form to select it.**

   If you haven't yet created a form, follow the steps in the section "Creating HTML Forms."

2. **Click the CheckBox icon on the Forms Objects panel.**

   You can also choose Insert⇨Form Object⇨CheckBox.

3. **Repeat Step 2 to place as many check boxes as you want.**

4. **Select one of the check boxes on your form to reveal the check box properties in the Property Inspector, as shown in Figure 13-3.**

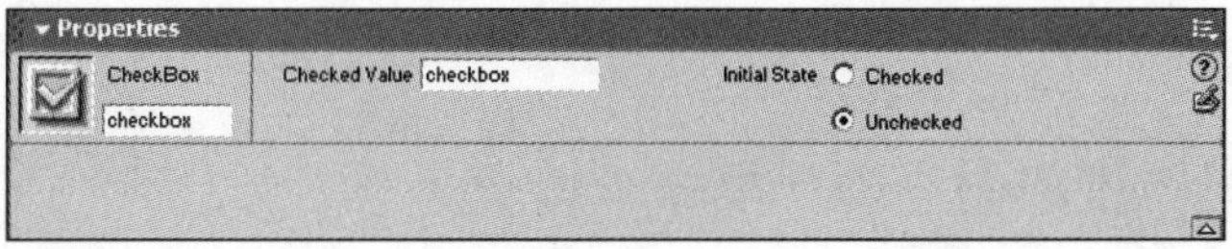

Figure 13-3:
Check boxes are best for multiple choice options that enable users to select more than one option.

5. **Type a name in the CheckBox text box.**

   You should use a distinct name for each check box because users can select more than one check box, and you want to ensure that the information submitted is separated and can be associated with each individual check box.

6. **Type a name in the Checked Value text box.**

Each check box in a group should have a different Checked Value name so that the CGI script can distinguish them. Naming them for the thing they represent is usually best. As with radio buttons, the Checked Value is usually included in the data you get back when the form is processed and returned to you. If you're looking at the data later, it's easier to interpret if the name means something that makes sense to you.

7. **Choose Checked or Unchecked next to Initial State.**

This option determines whether the check box appears already selected when the Web page loads. Choose Checked if you want to preselect a choice. A user can always override this preselection by clicking the text box again to deselect it.

8. **Select the other check boxes one by one and repeat Steps 5 through 7 to set the properties in the Property Inspector for each one.**

9. **After you have completed all of the other elements on your form, choose Insert⇨Form Object⇨Button.**

Use this step to insert Submit, Refresh, and/or Clear buttons needed to complete the task.

Adding text fields

When you want users to enter text, such as a name, e-mail address, or comment, use a text field. To insert text fields, follow these steps:

1. **Click your form to select it.**

If you haven't yet created a form, follow the steps in the section "Creating HTML Forms."

2. **Click the Text Field icon from the Forms Objects panel.**

You can also choose Insert⇨Form Object⇨Text Field. A text field box appears.

3. **On your form, click to place your cursor next to the first text field and type a question or other text prompt.**

For example, you may want to type *Address:* next to a text box where you want a user to enter an address.

4. **Select the text field on your form to reveal the text field properties in the Property Inspector, as shown in Figure 13-4.**

5. **Type a name in the TextField text box.**

Each text area on a form should have a different text field name so that the CGI script can distinguish them. Naming them for the thing they represent is usually best. In Figure 13-4, you can see that I named the

Address option *Address.* Many scripts return this name next to the contents of the text field a visitor enters at your Web site. If you're looking at the data later, it's easier to interpret if the name corresponds to the choice.

6. **In the Char Width box, type the number of characters you want users to be able to type in the field.**

   This determines the width of the text field that appears on the page. The size you make this should be determined by the amount of information you expect your user to enter.

Figure 13-4:
Use the Text
Field option
to create
form fields
in which
users can
enter one or
more lines
of text.

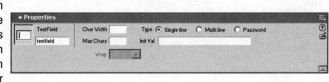

7. **Type the maximum number of characters that you want to allow in the Max Chars box.**

   If you leave this field blank, the user can type as many characters as they choose. I usually limit the number of characters only if I want to maintain consistency in the data. For example, I like to limit the State field to a two-character abbreviation. Again, the size you make this should be determined by the amount of information you expect your user to enter.

   You can set the Char Width to be longer or shorter than the Max Chars. You may choose to make these different if you want to maintain a certain display area because it looks better in the design, but you want to enable users to add more information if they choose to. That way, if users type more characters than can display in the area, the text scrolls so the users can still see the end of the text they were typing.

8. **Next to Type, choose Single Line, Multi Line, and/or Password.**

   • Choose **Single Line** if you want to create a one-line text box, such as the kind I created for the Name and Address fields in Figure 13-4.

   • Choose **Multi Line** if you want to give users space to enter text, such as the box I created for Comments in Figure 13-4. (Note that if you choose Multi Line, you also need to specify the number of lines that you want the text area to cover by typing a number in the Num Lines field, which appears as an option when you choose Multi Line.)

- Choose **Password** if this is a text line in which you ask a user to enter data that you don't want displayed on the screen. This causes entered data to appear as asterisks.

9. **In the Init Val text box, type any text that you want displayed when the form loads.**

   For example, you can include the words *Add comments here* on the form in the text field under Comments. These words were typed in the Init Val field of the Property Inspector for the Comments text field. Your users can delete the Init Value text or leave it and add more text to it.

10. **Select the other text areas one by one and repeat Steps 5 through 9 to set the properties in the Property Inspector for each one.**

Netscape Navigator and Microsoft Internet Explorer do not support text fields in forms equally. The differences vary depending on the version of the browser, but the general result is that a text field displays larger in Navigator than in Internet Explorer. Unfortunately, there is no perfect solution to this problem, but you should test all your forms in both browsers and create designs that look okay even when the text fields display differently.

When you want to give users a multiple-choice option but don't want to take up a lot of space on the page, drop-down lists are an ideal solution. To create a drop-down list using Dreamweaver, follow these steps:

1. **Click your form to select it.**

   If you haven't yet created a form, follow the steps in the section "Creating HTML Forms."

2. **Choose the List/Menu icon from the Forms Objects panel.**

   You can also choose Insert➪Form Object➪List/Menu. A drop-down list appears.

3. **Click to place your cursor next to the List and enter a question or other text prompt.**

   In Figure 13-5, I use the example *What is your favorite sport?*

4. **Select the field that represents the list on your page to reveal the List/Menu properties in the Property Inspector, as shown in the bottom of Figure 13-5.**

5. **Type a name in the List/Menu text box.**

   Each list or menu on a form should have a different name so that you can differentiate the lists when you sort out the data.

6. **Next to Type, choose Menu or List.**

   This determines if this form element is a drop-down menu or a scrollable list. If you choose List, you can specify the height and control how many items show at once. You can also specify if a user can select more than one item. If you choose Menu, these options aren't available.

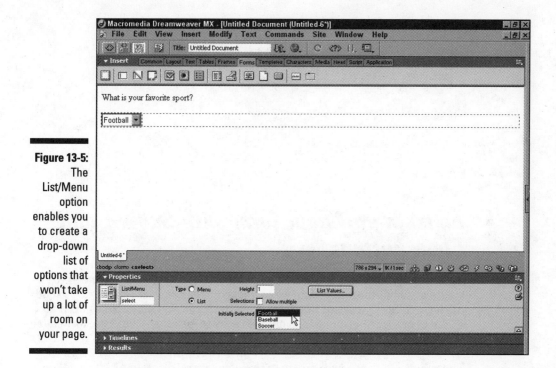

Figure 13-5:
The List/Menu option enables you to create a drop-down list of options that won't take up a lot of room on your page.

7. **Click the List Values button in the top-right corner of the Property Inspector.**

   The List Values dialog box opens (refer to Figure 13-6), and you can enter the choices that you want to make available. Click the plus sign (+) to add an Item Label; then type the label text you want in the text box that appears in the dialog box. Item Labels are displayed in the menu or list on the Web page in the order that you enter them. Use the minus sign (–) to delete a selected option. Use the tab key to move the cursor to the Value side of the dialog box, where you can enter a value. Values are sent to the server and provide a way of including information that you don't want displayed in the drop-down menu. For example, if you enter *football* as a label on the left, you may enter American as a value on the right to distinguish American football from soccer, which is often called football in other parts of the world. If you don't enter a value, the label is used as the only identifier when the data is collected.

8. **Click OK to close the dialog box.**

   Note that unless you have a CGI or other program connected to this form it will not execute, even if you've created the form itself correctly.

Finishing off your form with Submit and Clear buttons

In order for your users to send their completed forms to you, you need to create a Submit button, which, when clicked, tells the user's browser to send the form to the CGI script that processes the form. You may also want to add a Cancel or Clear button, which enable users to either not send the form at all or erase any information they've entered if they want to start over.

These buttons are easy to create in Dreamweaver. To create a button, follow these steps:

1. **Click your form to select it.**

   If you haven't yet created a form, check out the steps in the section "Creating HTML Forms." I suggest that you also enter a few fields, such as radio buttons or text fields. There's not much point in having a Submit button if you don't collect any data that needs to be submitted.

2. **Click the Button icon from the Forms Objects panel.**

   You can also choose Insert⇨Form Object⇨Button.

   A Submit button appears, and the Form Property Inspector changes to reveal button properties. You can change this to a Reset button or other kind of button by altering the attributes in the Property Inspector, as shown in the remaining steps.

3. **Select the button you just added to display the button properties in the Property Inspector, as shown in Figure 13-7.**

4. **Click either the Submit Form or Reset Form button next to Action.**

   A Submit button invokes an action, such as sending the user information to an e-mail address. A Reset button clears all user input.

5. **In the Label text box, type the text you want to display on the button.**

   You can type any text you want for the label, such as Search, Go, Clear, or Delete.

So, there you have it! Now that you know how to use Dreamweaver to create the basic elements of HTML forms, you can develop more intricate forms for your Web site. But remember, none of these forms will work without a CGI script or other program behind it to execute when the information is entered.

Using jump menus

Many designers use jump menus as navigational elements because they can provide a list of links in a drop-down list without taking up a lot of room on a Web page. You can also use a jump menu to launch an application or start an animation sequence.

To create a jump menu, follow these steps:

1. **Click your form to select it.**

   If you haven't yet created a form, follow the steps in the section "Creating HTML Forms." Note that you don't need a Submit button to make a jump menu work, but adding one may make the action step clearer to users.

2. **Click the Jump Menu icon from the Forms Objects panel.**

   You can also choose Insert⇨Form Object⇨Jump Menu.

   The Insert Jump Menu dialog box opens.

3. **In the Text area under Menu Items, type the name you want to display in the drop-down list.**

Choose the plus sign (+) to add more items. As you type items in the Text field, they're displayed in the Menu Items list, as shown in Figure 13-8.

4. **Use the Browser button to locate the page you want to link to or enter the URL for the page in the When Selected, Go to URL text area.**

You can link to a local file or enter any URL to link to a page on another Web site.

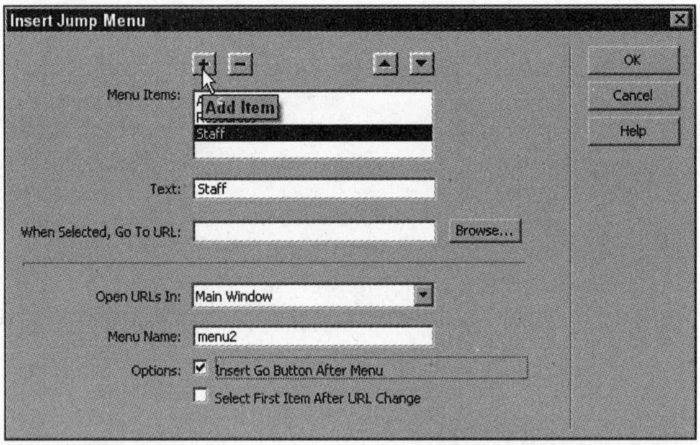

Figure 13-8:
When you create a jump list, items you type in the Text box are displayed in the Menu Items drop-down list, and you can specify the URL it should link to using the Browse option.

Insert Jump Menu

Menu Items: Add Item / Staff

Text: Staff

When Selected, Go To URL: Browse...

Open URLs In: Main Window

Menu Name: menu2

Options: ☑ Insert Go Button After Menu
☐ Select First Item After URL Change

OK
Cancel
Help

5. **Use the Open URLs In field to specify a target if you're using frames.**

If you're not using frames, the default is Main Window. Then when the user selects an option, the new page replaces the page he is viewing.

6. **Use the Menu Name field if you want to enter a unique identifier for this menu.**

This option can be useful if you have multiple jump menus on a page. You can use any name you want.

7. **Use the Insert Go Button After Menu option if you want to force users to click a button to activate the selection.**

If you don't add a Go button, the linked page loads automatically as soon as the user makes a selection. The Go button is really just a Submit button — it's just usually labeled a Go button in a Jump menu.

If you don't use a Go button, there is no way a user can return to the same option again, even if they go back to that page or the drop-down list is still visible because it's in a frame. The Go button lets you get around this and keeps all options available.

Other form options in Dreamweaver

As if all of the features I describe earlier in this chapter aren't enough, Dreamweaver includes a few specialized form options for facilitating interactivity, adding images, and even hidden fields. The bulleted list here explains how you can use each of these options:

- ✔ **File Field icon:** Enables you to add a Browse option to a form so users can upload files from their local computers to your server. The button enables users to upload images or text files, but it works only if your server is set up to handle this kind of upload from a browser. Check with your system administrator if you're not sure.

- ✔ **File Field feature:** Enables users to contribute their own materials to your Web site. For example, *The Miami Herald* has a "Build your own Web site" system that enables readers to create their own individual sites. Many Web sites now provide this service to users. They are generally template-based systems that walk readers through a series of forms where they choose designs and enter text that they want to appear on their Web pages. But most people want to be able to add more than just text to their sites — they want to add their own images, such as logos and photos. That's where a File Field becomes necessary. By using this form option, you can enable readers to browse their own hard drives for a file and then automatically upload it to your server where it can be linked to their pages.

  File Field is a complex feature that requires a sophisticated CGI script and special server access to work. If you aren't a programmer, you may need assistance to use this option on your site.

- ✔ **Image Field icon:** Makes it simple and easy to add an image to your form.

- ✔ **Hidden Field icon:** Inserts text that doesn't display to the user but may be used by a script or other application that processes the form.

Making your forms look good

The best way to get your form fields to line up nicely is to use an HTML table. You may want to use a table to align a form by putting all of your text in one row of cells and all of your text fields in an adjacent row. You may also want to place all of your radio buttons in the cells on the left and the text they correspond to in the cells on the right. (Chapter 6 shows you how to create HTML tables and how to use them to align information in your forms.) You can also use images and table border to make tables look better.

Part V
Working with Dynamic Content

The 5th Wave By Rich Tennant

"See? I created a little felon figure that runs around our Web site hiding behind banner ads. On the last page, our logo puts him in a non lethal choke hold and brings him back to the home page."

In this part . . .

The most dramatic change in Dreamweaver MX is the inclusion of Macromedia's creation tools for dynamic, database-driven Web sites. In this part, you'll discover the benefits of creating a dynamic site, find out how to work with a database on the Web, and follow step-by-step instructions to build your first dynamic site.

Chapter 14

Building a Dynamic Web Site: Getting Started

In This Chapter

▶ Defining a dynamic Web site

▶ Going over the basic terminology

▶ Exploring what you'll need to build a dynamic Web site

*O*nce upon a time, I used to farm out a lot of Web design work to programmers because I just didn't have the time to sit and learn all about databases and servers and ASP programming in order to finish a project on a tight deadline. Then, as if through some cosmic connection (or maybe it was market demand), the folks at Macromedia released Dreamweaver UltraDev 4, which introduced a whole new level of integration to the world of Web development. I occasionally refer to it as my "developer-in-a-box." With the release of Dreamweaver MX, Macromedia makes these features even more robust and versatile.

I still give a hearty helping of work to the programmers, but Dreamweaver has definitely allowed me to take care of more of this business on my own.

The new Dreamweaver MX packs in all the UltraDev features, allowing you to write code and insert "developer speak" using buttons and simple on-screen instructions. With just a few clicks (and some patience while you take in all the nuances of what makes it work), you can create anything from a search engine for your Web site to an completely searchable online catalog with thousands of products. In this chapter, you discover what a dynamic Web site and a database are and the many ways in which, through a dynamic Web site, you can display and edit information contained within a database. I also show you what you need to have in place in order to create a dynamic Web site. Some of the more advanced features of Dreamweaver MX are beyond the scope of this book, so I recommend other resources that you may find useful. Then, in Chapters 15 and 16, I go step-by-step through a reconstruction of the various dynamic features on a real world Web site.

ON THE CD

I've included a sample database on the CD-ROM to help you along with this chapter.

Understanding the Dynamic Web site

In the earlier chapters in this book, you find information about the features of Dreamweaver that allow you to build a Web site. In this chapter, and the two that follow it, you discover what it takes to make your Web site *dynamic*.

A dynamic Web site is usually connected to a *database,* which allows the Web site visitor to retrieve information relevant to his or her requests. The visitor (or sometimes a Web site administrator or content editor) can also make changes to the information that is displayed through a series of simple steps without ever leaving the Web browser. A good example of a dynamic Web site is a search engine on a Web site. You can type in what you want to find and get instant results with information from within that site that is relevant (ideally, anyway!) to your search request.

A dynamic Web site has many advantages besides the ability to create a site-wide search. Let's say you have a Web site where you sell 32 health and wellness supplements. On a *static* Web site you would actually have to create 32 pages, one for each product. With a database in place however, you create just *one* page that contains special code where the product name, image, description and any other pertinent information goes. The special code then communicates with the database, grabs each product's information from the database, and creates a page for each of those products on the fly.

Dynamic Web sites also allow changes and updates to be made with very little effort. Through a Web browser, users can add or remove products and make changes to existing products without knowing much about databases or programming. They simply enter the information on a form in a Web browser and click submit — the new information appears instantly the next time the page is loaded. Usually, you would limit the ability to make these changes to a few people on your staff. You don't necessarily want your customers making price changes or altering product descriptions, but you might want to make it easy for your sales staff to make changes, even when they are out in the field. This can be controlled by setting up different levels of access to your site. That way, customers can search information, and staff with special access and the right password, can actually makes changes, but the system you use to do both of these things is essentially the same.

Not all Web sites need to be dynamic. A 3-page personal Web site can be static and run effectively. However, if the Web site includes hundreds of pages, and is mainly similar content — for example, a news Web site, or an online catalog — going dynamic may be your best bet. I want to make clear that for a Web site of that magnitude there is a significant amount of setup and pages involved before a data entry person can make those quick and easy updates. It could take the programmer a lot more time to set up a simple content-management form than it would to create a couple of static pages. The big payoff (in both time and money) comes down the line when it is time to update those pages.

Talking the Talk: Key Concepts

Before jumping into your first dynamic Web site, there are a few concepts you should become familiar with, as they'll play an integral role in this show.

Exploring a database

A database is collection of information compiled in one or more *tables* with *fields* organized in columns, and *records* in rows. What? Okay, picture a mail order catalog, such as Pottery Barn. (Indulge me, it's my favorite.)

The catalog itself is the *database*. It contains a collection of information about various products. Each product is a *record* in the database. In this case, a particular product has an item number, a price, and a color — each of those is a *field*. A record in a database consists of a complete set of all the fields in the database. Taking it a step further, within the catalog, the various products are organized in categories often because they have something in common (furniture, rugs, bedding, wall décor). Each category is a *table* — a grouping of various records from a database that have something in common.

This is not the same kind of table discussed in Chapter 6, where you find out how HTML tables are used to format information, much like you'd use a spreadsheet program, such as Excel. Database tables aren't used for formatting, they are for grouping and organizing content.

How it works on the Web

Let's take this concept to the Web. It works in much the same way. Say you go to www.penpal.net, to find a new penpal. You can search by location, age, gender, and interests, so you enter: "Paris," "25," "female," and "writing." After you click OK, a list of potential penpals that match your requirements appears right before your eyes. (See Figure 14-1.)

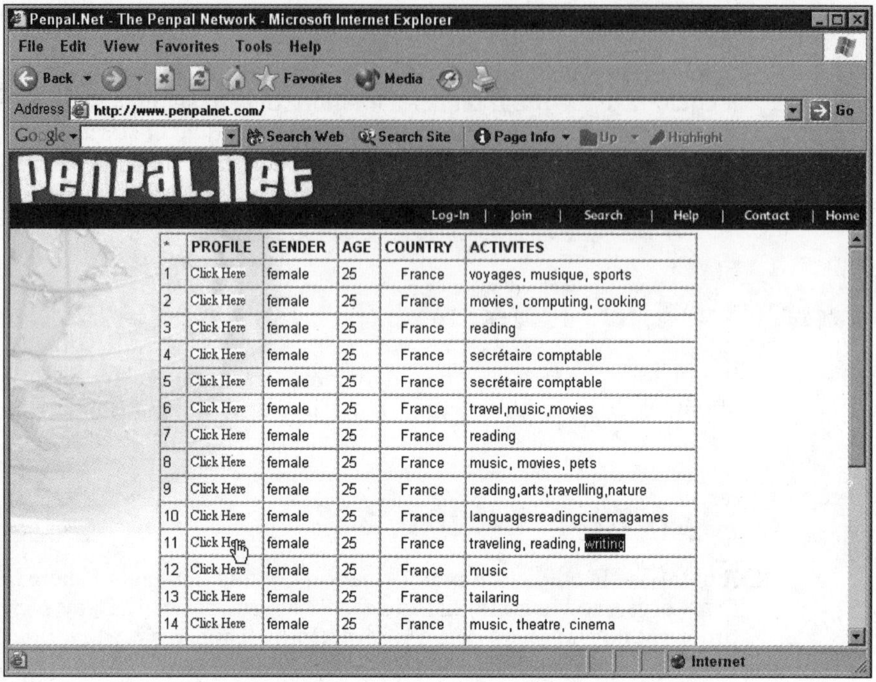

Penpal.Net - The Penpal Network - Microsoft Internet Explorer
File Edit View Favorites Tools Help
Back Favorites Media
Address http://www.penpalnet.com/
Go
Search Web Search Site Page Info Up Highlight
penpal.net
Log-In | Join | Search | Help | Contact | Home
* PROFILE GENDER AGE COUNTRY ACTIVITES
1 Click Here female 25 France voyages, musique, sports
2 Click Here female 25 France movies, computing, cooking
3 Click Here female 25 France reading
4 Click Here female 25 France secrétaire comptable
5 Click Here female 25 France secrétaire comptable
6 Click Here female 25 France travel,music,movies
7 Click Here female 25 France reading
8 Click Here female 25 France music, movies, pets
9 Click Here female 25 France reading,arts,travelling,nature
10 Click Here female 25 France languagesreadingcinemagames
11 Click Here female 25 France traveling, reading, writing
12 Click Here female 25 France music
13 Click Here female 25 France tailaring
14 Click Here female 25 France music, theatre, cinema
Internet

Figure 14-1: The Penpal.net results page.

When you submitted your criteria, some specific code on that page matched your information with information in a database that lists other people looking for a penpal. It looked through every field (individual criterion), trying to find records (penpals) with fields that matched your request. If you wanted to, you could also list yourself as a potential penpal for others to find you, by entering your information and adding it to the database right from your Web browser!

Database applications

There are various applications made specifically for creating and managing databases including Microsoft Access, SQL Server, MySQL, FoxPro, and Oracle. Access is most commonly used by novices to create small databases (MDB files). Access is also commonly used to communicate visually with bigger databases such as MSSQL.

CROSS-REFERENCE

I use Access in Windows 2000 for all the examples in this and the next two chapters. If you'd like to dig deeper into the world of databases, I recommend the books *Database Development For Dummies* and *SQL For Dummies*, both by Allen G. Taylor, *Access 2002 For Dummies* by John Kaufeld, and *Oracle8i For Dummies* by Carol McCullough-Dieter (all published by Hungry Minds, Inc.).

Plugging in the data

Now that you've got the database basics covered, you need to provide a way for the Web site and the database to communicate. In the next section, I show you how to set up a Web server and an application server step-by-step so you can get started.

Setting up the Web server

While working with static Web sites — *static* meaning that the content is entered by hand and is not influenced by, nor interacts with, the person viewing the site — you may be used to previewing pages directly from your local hard drive. It's not that simple when the content is dynamic because Dreamweaver MX adds some special code that needs to be processed by a server before content is published to the viewer. Having a Web server is crucial when working with a dynamic Web site because you need to test your work along the way to make sure that you get the results you're shooting for.

A Web server can be defined as an actual system where a Web site is stored, or as the software on that system that provides the server functionality. In this case, the Web server I'm referring to is actually the software installed on a system, not an actual system.

Server Technologies Supported by Dreamweaver MX

There are five server technologies (or scripting languages) that Dreamweaver MX supports:

- Active Server Pages (ASP)
- ASP.NET
- ColdFusion
- JavaServer Pages (JSP)
- PHP (which stands for PHP: Hypertext Preprocessor — a recursive acronym, for your wordsmiths out there)

For the examples in this book, I use ASP in Microsoft Windows. In essence, all five work toward the same outcome — dynamic content on a Web page or Web site. They all provide the ability to generate HTML dynamically. Using server-side code, they can display information from a database and create

HTML based on whether certain criteria is met or specified by a particular user. The following sections provide more detail on each of these scripting languages.

ASP

ASP is a server technology that comes, at no additional cost, built into Windows 2000 and can be easily installed into Windows 98 and NT as well. Used in conjunction with Microsoft IIS or Personal Web Server, ASP is not a standalone programming language, as much of the code you'll write for ASP pages are in VB Script or JavaScript.

ASP.NET

ASP.NET is a relatively new server technology. It is not a revision of ASP 3.0, in fact it's almost like a complete overhaul of it. This latest installment of ASP is not what 3.0 was to 2.0 — they've done more than add new tags. The language is actually more similar to traditional programming languages like C++ where code is compiled. This suggests that applications written in ASP.NET will run faster than anything available today because Web servers will be working less. However ASP.NET is not as verbose as ASP 3.0, so it's a lot harder to read for novice programmers. ASP.NET is a Microsoft technology, but you won't find anything more than marketing-speak on the Microsoft Web site. A great site to learn more about ASP.NET in what more closely resembles plain English is www.4guysfromrolla.com.

ColdFusion

ColdFusion, owned by Macromedia, uses its own server and scripting language. Although ColdFusion is probably the easiest to learn, it is the least robust and offers up the slowest server performance. ASP pages typically run and load faster than ColdFusion pages.

JavaServerPages (JSP)

JSP is from Sun Microsystems. Its dynamic code is based on Java, which makes it possible to run the pages from non-Microsoft Web servers. JSP can be used on Allaire JRun Server and IBM WebSphere. Using JSP, you can create and keep the dynamic code separated from the HTML pages (by using Java Beans) or you can embed the JSP code into the page. Unless you're a hard-core programmer however, JSP is horribly complex.

PHP

PHP was originally a native to UNIX-based servers. However, you can now download Windows binaries from `www.php.net` to run Apache (a server software typically used with PHP) from any version of Windows. You can even configure PHP to run on Personal Web Server (although it's rather tricky). PHP's scripting language is based on C, Perl, and Java. A good thing about PHP is that you can get more functionality with it right out of the box than you can with ASP. For example, virtually every ASP add-on that is on sale at `www.serverojects.com` comes built-in standard or is available for free from PHP.net.

To recommend one technology over the other really wouldn't be fair because they all offer very similar functionality with slight variations in speed and efficiency. The most marketable language is ASP because of its widely used and mature features. If you dream of becoming a highly paid programmer, you can't go wrong with this one.

Check out these other Dummies and Hungry Minds titles: *Active Server Pages Bible* by Eric Smith, *ASP.NET For Dummies* by Bill Hatfield, *Java Server Pages For Dummies* by Mac Rinehart, *ColdFusion 4 For Dummies* by Alexis D. Gutzman, and *PHP 4 Bible* by Tim Converse (all published by Hungry Minds, Inc.).

Making the Data Connection

One of the reasons I'm using ASP specifically for the next few examples is that it is much easier to set up than any of the other technologies, and assuming that you are rather new at this, I wouldn't want to throw you into the deep end (. . . just yet).

In order to set up a *Web server* you need server software. A Web server, sometimes called an HTTP server, responds to requests from a Web browser by serving up Web pages based on those requests.

You'll also need to set up an *application server,* which helps the Web server to process specially marked Web pages. When one of these pages is requested by the browser, the Web server hands the page off to the application server, which processes it before sending the page to the browser.

For the examples in this book, I am using ASP, and server choices are Microsoft IIS or Personal Web Server (PWS). Either one of these will work both as a Web server and an application server. PWS runs with Windows 98 or NT, and you can install it from your Windows CD. If you've got Windows 2000 Server or NT 4, IIS is part of the package. If you can't find your CD, you can always download IIS or PWS for free from Microsoft's Web site.

At this point, if you're running Windows 98 SE, Windows 95, or Windows NT, make sure that you have PWS installed. If you are running Windows 2000 or Windows XP Professional, IIS is already in your system and all you have to do is make sure that it is started.

If you're running Windows 2000 or XP Professional, and IIS is not enabled by default, you can install it by going to Control Panel➪Add/Remove Programs➪ Add/Remove Windows Components. When the Windows Components screen appears, scroll down the list and make sure there is a check mark next to Internet Information Server.

IIS does not work on XP Home Edition. You must upgrade to XP Professional to use it.

To download and install Microsoft Personal Web Server, go to `www. microsoft.com` and search for "option pack." Click the bullet that says "Download Windows NT 4.0 Option Pack." If you're using Windows 98, choose Windows 95 from the list of operating systems — it's the same file — and follow the downloading instructions.

Setting up a DSN

DSN is short for Data Source Name. A DSN is basically a name associated with your database that helps you to keep your connection with the database intact even if the database were to change to a new location.

Although you don't need Dreamweaver in order to set up a DSN, you do need a DSN in order to get your dynamic Dreamweaver site to work.

In order to follow the upcoming examples, you need to make sure that your Access Database Driver is installed. Follow these steps to install the driver or to check that it is already there:

1. **In Windows 2000, choose Start➪Programs➪Administrative Tools➪ Data Sources (ODBC).**

   You see the ODBC Data Source Administrator dialog box (see Figure 14-2). Under the first tab (User DSN), you see MS Access Database and Microsoft Access Driver (*mdb).

2. **Click the System DSN tab.**

   You see a list of database connections.

3. **Click Add.**

   A list of drivers appears. (See Figure 14-3.)

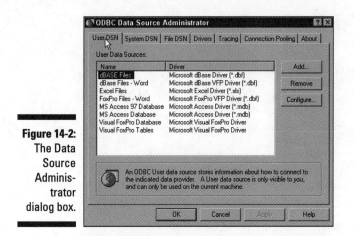

Figure 14-2:
The Data
Source
Adminis-
trator
dialog box.

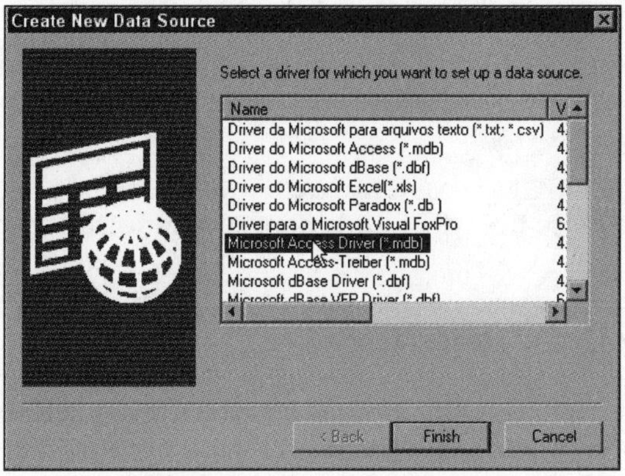

Figure 14-3:
The list of
drivers from
the Systems
DSN tab.

4. **Select Microsoft Access Driver and then click Finish.**

   The ODBC Microsoft Access Setup dialog box appears. (See Figure 14-4.)

5. **Next to Data Source Name, enter a name for your database (you can call it whatever you want as long as you remember what you called it). You don't *have* to type something in the Description area, but you can if you want to.**

   I'm going to use a sample database of products (products.mdb), based on the database used on www.metabolicnutrition.com for the next few examples. I'll call my database *products*.

6. **Click Select.**

   The Select Database dialog box appears.

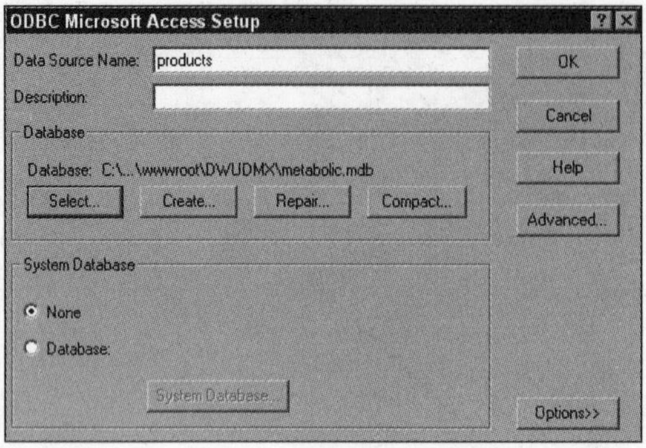

ODBC Microsoft Access Setup

Data Source Name: products

Description:

Database

Database: C:\...\wwwroot\DWUDMX\metabolic.mdb

[Select...] [Create...] [Repair...] [Compact...]

[OK]
[Cancel]
[Help]
[Advanced...]

System Database

● None
○ Database:

[System Database...]

[Options>>]

Figure 14-4:
The ODBC
MS Access
Setup dialog
box.

7. **Find the database you will be using and click OK.**

   As you can see, the path to the database is now listed under "Database" in the ODBC Microsoft Access Setup dialog box.

8. **You can click Advanced to fill out authorization information if your database will require a user name and password. Otherwise, don't worry about it.**

9. **Click OK on the ODBC Microsoft Access Setup dialog box to close it; then click OK to close the ODBC Data Source Administrator dialog box.**

Setting up in Dreamweaver MX

Creating the data connection in Dreamweaver takes a few quick steps. First you must set up your site's local information and remote site information, which I cover in Chapter 2 — check it out to get reacquainted if you're not already comfortable with this process.

For this example, I'm running the application server (IIS) on the same machine from which I run Dreamweaver, so I'll set up the connection locally.

If your IIS or PWS is enabled, when you go to your browser and type http:// localhost you will see a page confirming that your Web server is up and running.

For Mac Users

Setting up a data connection on a Mac is a little more complicated because you can't run a Web server or application server locally; you must be connected to a remote server. Ideally, you can connect your Mac to an NT server with permission to browse the Mac, and after you're networked, make the data connection. Dreamweaver MX includes information in the help files that specifically covers this process for Mac users.

Another suggestion is to download Apache's HTTP server, which is available for the new OSX. However, everyone using OS9 and under is out of luck.

Let's get started:

1. **Now that you've set up your new ASP site, click the Application panel to expand it, and click the Databases tab. (See Figure 14-5.)**

2. **Click the plus sign (+) and select Data Source Name (DSN) from the list.**

   You see the Data Source Name dialog box shown in Figure 14-6.

3. **Enter the name for the new connection.**

   I typed products and selected the products database I created earlier.

4. **Select your database from the list of DSNs, making sure you have indicated that Dreamweaver should connect using System DSN.**

   Of course, if you're going to use a remote application server, make sure that you have indicated that Dreamweaver should connect using DSN on the application server.

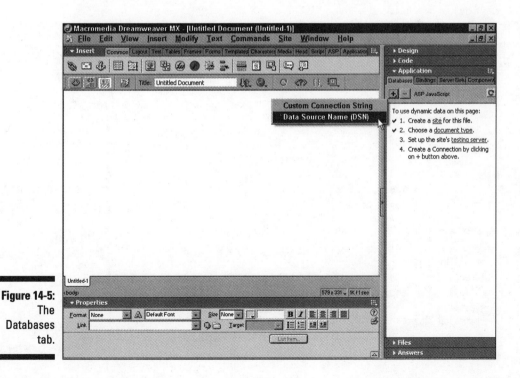

Figure 14-5:
The
Databases
tab.

Figure 14-6:
The Data
Source
Name
dialog box.

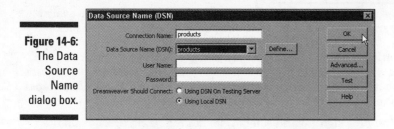

5. **Click the Test button.**

You get a pop-up message letting you know that the connection was made successfully, and you see your database listed in the Databases tab (see Figure 14-7).

On the Site tab in the Files panel, you also see a Connections folder on your local drive that contains an ASP file with the connection information for this database. Dreamweaver automatically references this file on any page you create that uses this database connection, saving you the need to insert by hand every time.

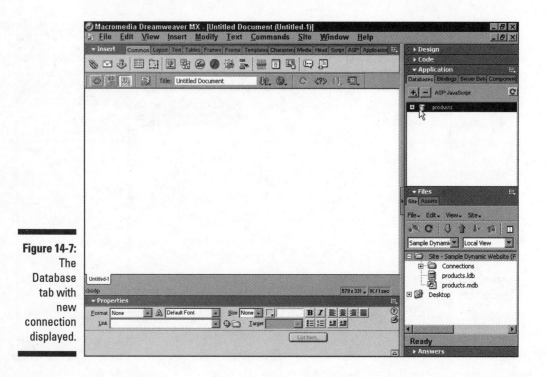

Figure 14-7:
The
Database
tab with
new
connection
displayed.

The ASP files in the Connections folder store necessary information that makes your page work correctly with the database. Remember to upload this folder when you upload your site files to the application server.

If your connection fails, check your DSN again, as well as your URL prefix for the application server. You can also check Dreamweaver's Help Index for other troubleshooting tips. Now you're ready to build a dynamic Web site. In the next few chapters, we'll get into more details so you can put these great Dreamweaver MX features to use on your site right away.

Chapter 15

Bringing Data into the Mix

• •

In This Chapter

▶ Taking a look at the panels

▶ Covering the Recordset basics

▶ Getting dynamic with your data

• •

*I*f you've never used the dynamic development capabilities of Dreamweaver, there are a few windows and inspectors that you want to get familiar with in the beginning of this chapter. In the rest of this chapter, you find out how these elements work together to create a Web site chock-full of dynamic features. For the purposes of illustration, each of the step-by-step exercises in this chapter is based on a Web site that sells nutrition products. Because the company already has all the product names, descriptions, and images in a database, it provides an ideal example of how you pull all of these elements together in a site that features products. If your site will feature another kind of data, don't worry — these steps show you how to use Dreamweaver to create any kind of dynamic site. Just apply the lessons and features explained in this chapter to your own data and you'll be creating your own dynamic site in no time.

I've included a sample database on the CD-ROM to help you along with this chapter.

Make sure your Application Server is running and that you save all the pages as ASP pages (*filename*.asp) so that the server parses the code correctly. For a quick reminder on how to set up the Application Server, refer to Chapter 14.

Exploring the Panel

In Dreamweaver, the most fundamental elements of creating a dynamic Web site are in the Application Explorer panel, which includes the Databases, Bindings, and Server Behaviors panels. In this section, I introduce you to the panels that will help you create your dynamic site.

The Bindings panel

The Bindings panel allows you to add and remove dynamic content data sources from your document. The number and kinds of available data sources can vary depending on whether you use ASP, JSP, or any other server technology (see Chapter 14 for a refresher on servers if you need to). A *data source* is where you get information to use on your dynamic Web page. An example of a data source is a recordset from a database, which you further explore in the next few sections of this chapter.

With the Bindings panel, you can access data sources in several ways. You can find out what data source objects you have available by clicking the plus (+) sign on the Bindings panel to get the Add Bindings pop-up menu (see Figure 15-1).

The Bindings pop-up menu includes

- **Recordset (Query):** A recordset stores data from your database for use on a page or set of pages. I explain recordsets in more detail in this chapter.

- **Command (stored procedure):** Store Procedures are reusable database items that contain SQL code and are commonly used to modify a database (insert, update, or delete records).

- **Request Variable:** Commonly used wherever there is a search involved, a Request Variable carries information from one page to another. When you use a form to submit data to another page, a request variable is created.

- **Session Variable:** Session Variables store and display infomration for the duration of a user's session (or visit). A different session is created on the server for each user and is kept in use either for a set period of time or until a specific action on the site terminates it (such as a log-out).

- **Application Variable:** Application Variables can be used to store and display information that must be present for all users and is constant throughout the lifetime of an application. These types of variables are commonly used for page counters, or date and time. Application variables are only available for ASP and ColdFusion pages, but not for PHP and JSP.

- **Get more data sources:** Use this option to open Dreamweaver Exchange in your browser. You can use Exchange to download extensions for Dreamweaver. For more information about extensions, see Chapter 16.

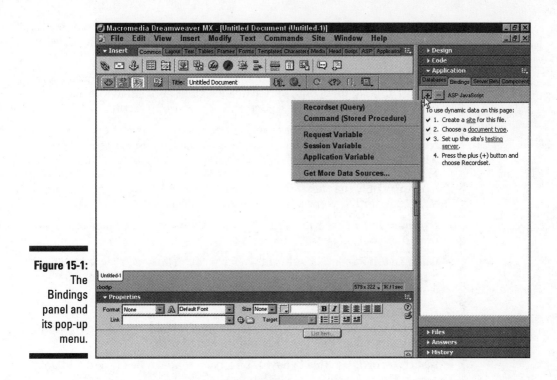

Figure 15-1:
The
Bindings
panel and
its pop-up
menu.

The Server Behaviors panel

Server Behaviors are server-side scripts that perform some type of action. Through the Server Behaviors panel you can add server-side scripts to your pages, like user authentication and record navigation, which you can read more about in this chapter and Chapter 16. Server behaviors available to you can vary depending on the server technology you use.

You can view the available server behaviors by clicking the plus (+) sign on the Server Behaviors panel to get the "Add Server Behaviors" pop-up menu (see Figure 15-2).

The Server Behaviors pop-up menu includes

- ✔ **Recordset (Query):** A recordset stores data from your database for use on a page or set of pages. I explain recordsets in more detail in this chapter.

- ✔ **Command (stored procedure):** Store Procedures are reusable database items that contain SQL code and are commonly used to modify a database (insert, update, or delete records).

✔ **Repeat Region:** This server object is used to display multiple records on a page. Repeat Region is most commonly used on tables or table rows. You can see more about this behavior later on in this chapter.

✔ **Recordset Paging:** If you have to display a large number of records, and are distributing them onto various pages, this set of behaviors allows you to navigate from page to page or from record to record.

✔ **Show Region:** With this set of server behaviors you can show or hide record navigation based on the records displayed. For instance, if you have "next" and "previous" on the bottom of every page and your user is on the first page or first record of the recordset, you can set a behavior to display only the "next" link. The same goes if the user is on the last page or record — you can set it to display "previous" only.

✔ **Dynamic Text:** The Dynamic Text option allows you to display information from your recordset anywhere on the page.

✔ **Go to Detail Page:** Using this behavior you can link each record in your repeated region to a detail page for that particular record. The behavior will also tell the detail page which record's information to display.

✔ **Go to Related Page:** You can use this behavior to link a particular dynamic page to another page that contains related information, passing the parameters of the first page to the related page.

✔ **Insert Record:** Use this behavior on a page that can be used to add new records to a database via a Web browser.

✔ **Update Record:** Use this behavior on a page to update existing records in a database via a Web browser.

✔ **Delete Record:** Use this behavior on a page to quickly delete a record from a database via a Web browser.

✔ **Dynamic Form Elements:** This set of server behaviors will turn text fields, list/menu fields, radio buttons, or check boxes into dynamic form elements, which you can set to display particular information from a recordset.

✔ **User Authentication:** The User Authentication set of behaviors allows you to log in a user, log out a user, check a user name against the information in your database, and restrict access to a page.

✔ **Edit Server Behaviors:** Use this option to customize or remove existing server behaviors. Unless you are very comfortable with SQL, I advise you not to mess with this option.

✔ **New Server Behaviors:** Use this option to create new server behaviors and add them to the list of existing behaviors. Again, this option is for the more advanced users who are comfortable with SQL.

✔ **Get More Server Behaviors:** Use this option to open Dreamweaver Exchange in your browser. You can use Exchange to download extensions for Dreamweaver. For more information about extensions, see Chapter 16.

The Databases panel

The Databases panel (see Figure 15-3) is new to Dreamweaver MX. You can create a Data Source Name (DSN) or a custom connection string by clicking the plus (+) sign. To see how you can create a Data Source Name using the Databases panel, refer to Chapter 14. The Databases panel also allows you to look at the databases on your application server without creating a recordset. In the Databases panel you can view your entire database structure within Dreamweaver — tables, fields, and stored procedures — without opening up the actual database.

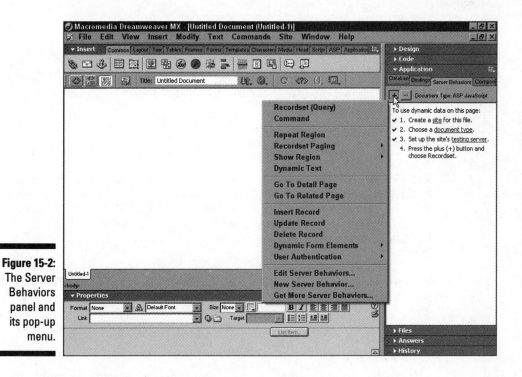

Figure 15-2: The Server Behaviors panel and its pop-up menu.

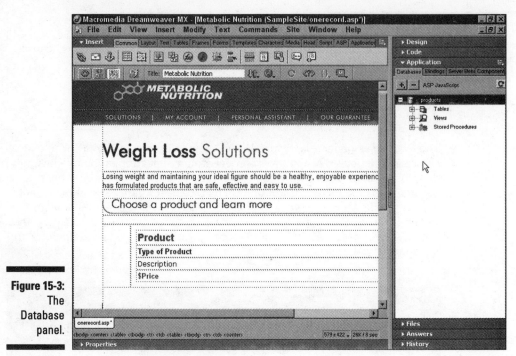

Figure 15-3:
The
Database
panel.

Creating a Recordset

The *recordset* stores data from your database for use on a page or set of pages by creating a query. A *query* gathers information from a database to be used on a page, using only the information in the fields you select for the particular query. The queries for a recordset are built with SQL (Structured Query Language), but you don't need to know SQL in order to get the job done. Dreamweaver writes it all for you.

With your recordset in place you will be able to display information from your database in various ways.

To define a recordset in Dreamweaver:

1. **Open the page that will use the recordset.**

2. **On the Bindings panel, click the plus sign and select Recordset (Query).**

   You see the Recordset dialog box, as shown in Figure 15-4.

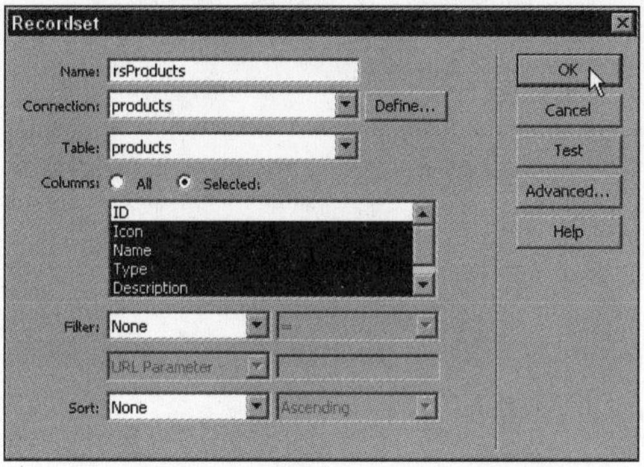

Figure 15-4:
The
Recordset
dialog box.

3. **Enter a name for your recordset.**

   Usually it is recommended that you add the letters *rs* to the beginning of the name to distinguish it as a recordset in your code, but it isn't necessary. Example: *rsProducts*.

4. **Select your connection from the Connections drop-down list.**

5. **Now choose a database table to collect the data for your recordset from the Table drop-down list.**

   You can select all the columns or only specific columns of data to be displayed.

6. **If you want the available information to be filtered to show only records that meet specific criteria, fill out the Filter area. If not, continue moving down the dialog box.**

7. **If you want the displayed records to be sorted in ascending or descending order, specify it in the Sort menu by selecting the field by which you want the records sorted (Product, Price, and so on).**

8. **To test the connection to the database, click Test.**

   You should see a screen with the data in the recordset (see Figure 15-5).

9. **Click OK to close the Test screen.**

10. **Click OK to complete the Recordset Dialog Box Information.**

    You can now see the recordset displayed in the Bindings panel (see Figure 15-6).

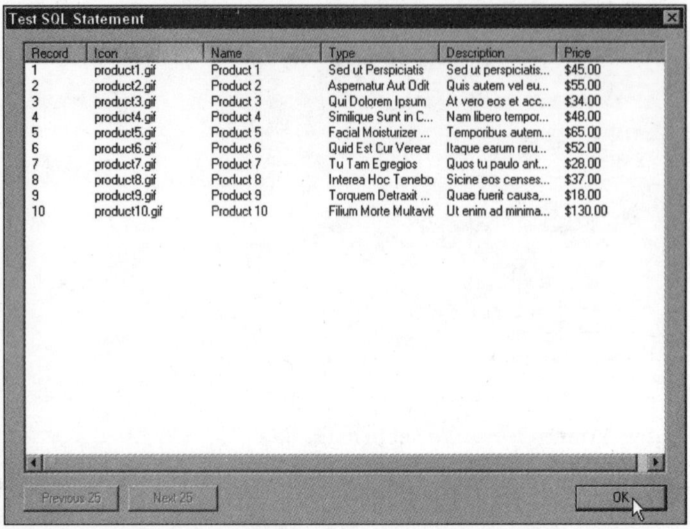

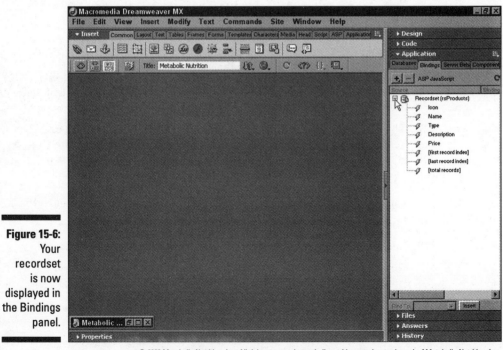

Figure 15-5:
A successful
test screen.

Figure 15-6:
Your
recordset
is now
displayed in
the Bindings
panel.

Using a Recordset on Your Page

Now that you've created a recordset, you can place the information on your page as you want. For this example, I'm going to make a basic list of all the products in the database, with a description, size, and price.

I have already built a page with a table showing the appropriate number of columns for all the dynamic text that I'm going to insert (see Figure 15-7).

After you have set up the document the way you want it, you can drag and drop each data source to its appropriate spot on the page.

1. **From the Bindings panel, select your first data source and drag it onto your page, dropping it where it's supposed to go.**

   The name of the dynamic text appears inside curly brackets. You can now format this piece of text any way you want, treating it as if it were normal HTML text (see Figure 15-8).

2. **Test the result by clicking the LiveData icon.**

   The first record of your database appears in place of the dynamic text code (see Figure 15-9).

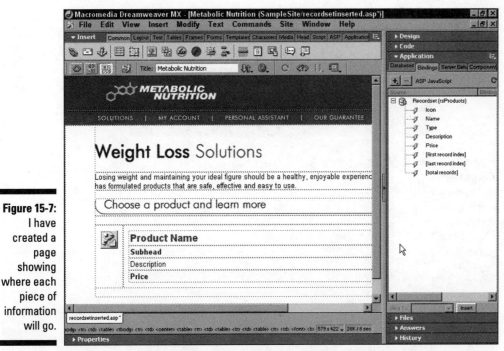

Figure 15-7:
I have created a page showing where each piece of information will go.

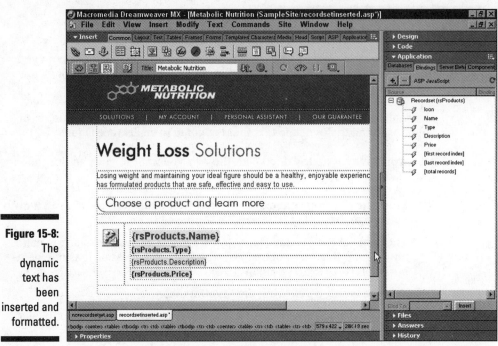

Figure 15-8:
The dynamic text has been inserted and formatted.

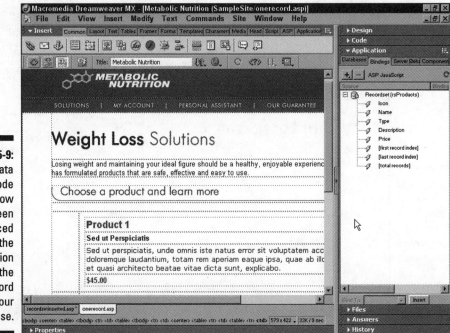

Figure 15-9:
The data source code has now been replaced with the information from the first record in your database.

Repeating a Region

You will probably want to show more than one record at a time on a page that's supposed to list all your products. You can do this by applying a server behavior to your region.

A *region* is any area of a page that displays information from a database on your page. After you have defined your region, you can apply a Repeat Region server behavior, which causes that area to be written to the page over and over, displaying every record in the database defined by your recordset until all records have been displayed. Repeat Region is most commonly used on tables or table rows.

To add a Repeat Region server behavior to your page:

1. **Select the area on your page that you would like to define as a region.**

2. **Click on the Server Behaviors panel, click on the plus (+) sign, and select Repeat Region.**

   The Repeat Region dialog box appears (see Figure 15-10).

3. **Select the number of records that you would like to show on the page and then click OK.**

4. **Click the LiveData button to see the results (see Figure 15-11).**

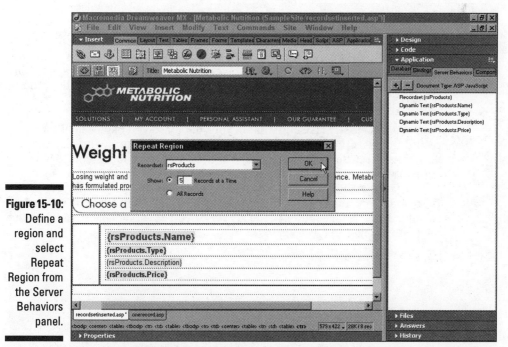

Figure 15-10: Define a region and select Repeat Region from the Server Behaviors panel.

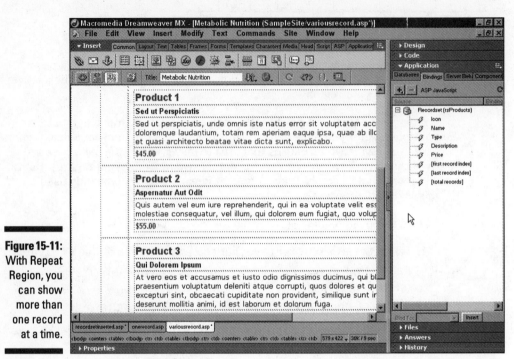

Figure 15-11: With Repeat Region, you can show more than one record at a time.

Adding a Dynamic Image

Whenever there is a dynamic Web site, images are usually involved, whether it is a catalog Web site or a news archive. There are various easy ways to bind an image to a recordset so that your images change depending on the other parts of the page that are bound to the same recordset.

First and foremost, make sure that in your database you have a field for each record that lists the actual path of the image for that record. For example, if your images resided in a folder called *images,* one level above your dynamic page, you would enter the following in the image field in your database: *images/imagename.gif,* remembering to replace the *imagename.gif* part with the actual filename for each image. It is equally important that you remember to upload your image folder to the server or you won't be able to preview the page with images in LiveData view.

If you've got that piece of the puzzle in place, the next step is to put a placeholder image in the spot that you would like an image to appear for all the records. You can use any of the images in your image folder as a placeholder. In the example I'm following, I use the image that pertains to the first record in my database.

Binding the Image

Now that you've got the placeholder image, there are two easy ways to bind images — with the Bindings panel or the Property Inspector.

Using the Bindings panel:

1. **Click the plus (+) sign to expand your recordset.**

2. **Click your placeholder image on the open document to select it.**

3. **Select the field in your recordset that contains the name of the image file.**

   In my example, I've called this field *icon*, but you can call it whatever you want.

4. **Click the Bind button at the bottom of the Bindings panel (see Figure 15-12).**

Using the Property Inspector:

1. **Click your placeholder image on the open document to select it.**

2. **Click the file folder icon in the Property Inspector next to the Image Source box.**

   The Select Image Source dialog box appears (see Figure 15-13).

3. **Next to Select File Name From, select the Data Sources option.**

4. **Select the field that contains your image information.**

5. **Click OK.**

After performing either of these two methods to bind your images to the page, click the LiveData view button to check out the results (see Figure 15-14).

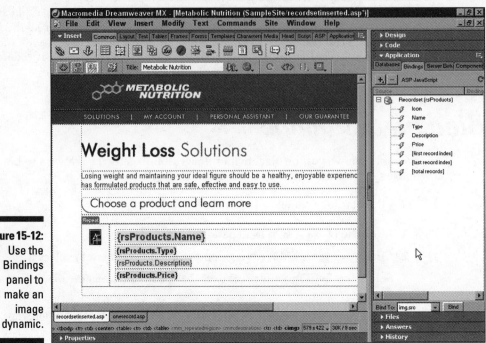

Figure 15-12:
Use the
Bindings
panel to
make an
image
dynamic.

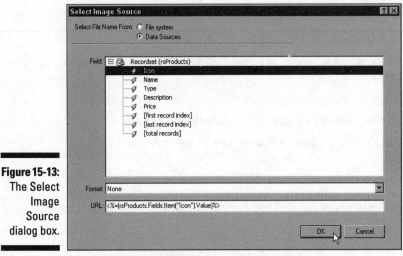

Figure 15-13:
The Select
Image
Source
dialog box.

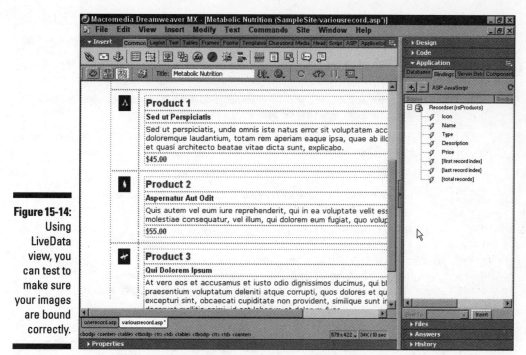

Figure 15-14: Using LiveData view, you can test to make sure your images are bound correctly.

Adding Navigation to a Dynamic Page

If your database contains many records, you may opt to show only a small number of records per page, so as to not overwhelm the user. Dreamweaver's Server Behaviors allow you to add navigation to your pages so that you can move forward or backward through records.

Define your Repeat Region and make sure that you did not select to show all records. You can add button images or text links at the bottom of the page to indicate some kind of navigation, such as "Previous Page" and "Next Page." With the buttons in place, you can activate them by using the Server Behaviors.

For example, to add the navigation movements for the Next and Previous buttons:

1. **Select the Previous Page button.**

2. **Expand the Application Building Explorer and select Server Behaviors.**

3. **Click the plus (+) sign and select Recordset Paging from the menu (see Figure 15-15).**

4. **From the submenu, choose the appropriate navigation movement (Move to Next Record or Move to Previous Record).**

   The Move to Record Dialog box appears, and in most cases you can just Click OK because the defaults will be right.

5. **Follow the same steps for the other button.**

6. **Choose File⇨Preview in Browser and select the browser you set up as your default preview browser.**

   You can now page through your records.

That's a pretty nifty trick. But did you notice that on the first page, the Previous Page button or link still appears, even though we both know there is no previous page? Not to worry — there is a server behavior that tells the navigation button when to show up.

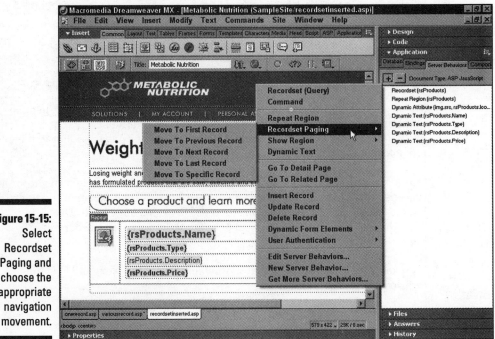

Figure 15-15:
Select Recordset Paging and choose the appropriate navigation movement.

1. **Click the button to select it.**

2. **Click the plus (+) sign on the Server Behaviors panel, and select Show Region from the menu (see Figure 15-16).**

3. **If you are working with the Previous Page button, select Show Region If Not First Record. If you are working with the Next Page button, select Show Region If Not Last Record.**

   The Show Region...Recordset dialog box appears. Usually the selected recordset is correct, so just click OK.

4. **Preview in your browser.**

   Notice that now when you're on the first page of records, the Previous Page button does not show, and when you're on the last page, the Next Page button does not show.

Now that you know how to add navigation to your recordsets, you can get really fancy and add buttons to go to the first or last record. So if you have, say, 100 pages of records, you can jump from page 1 to page 100 without having to click Previous Page or Next Page through countless other pages of records. The server behaviors for those two are Move to Record⇨Move to First Record and Move to Record⇨Move to Last Record. It's pretty useful stuff to know.

Figure 15-16:
Select Show Region and make the appropriate selection from the submenu.

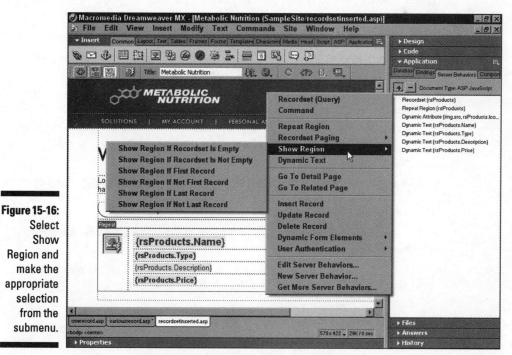

Creating a Master/Detail Page Set

A very common way to display information on a Web site is to show a list of records, such as a list of products, with a link to each individual record for more detailed information.

A master page displays a list of records and a link for each record. When a user clicks a particular link, a detail page appears with more information about that record. There are two types of master pages. The first type is a list of records determined by you. A user can't alter the list of records on this page, they can only click to view more information about those records displayed. The second type is a dynamically-created Master page. A good example of this type of master page is a search results page, where a user performs a search for specific records.

A detail page is the page that is displayed when a user clicks a particular link from a master page. This page can either display more information about a record (such as an online catalog), or it can be set up for administrative purposes, such as updating or deleting a record.

Creating a Master/Detail page requires just a few clicks of the mouse. Using the functions described earlier in this chapter, create a page that you will use to list all your products and prices. This is your master page. Next, create the page you will use as the detail page. Now you're ready to create the Master/Detail Page Set.

1. **Open the page you created to be the master page and choose Insert⇨ Server Objects⇨Master/Detail Page Set (see Figure 15-17).**

   The Insert Master/Detail Page Set dialog box opens. The top part of the dialog box is for defining the properties of the master page. The bottom part is for defining the detail page.

2. **Select the recordset from the drop-down list that you will use for your master page.**

3. **Next to Master Page Fields, use the plus (+) and minus (–) signs to add or remove fields that you want or don't want to display on the master page.**

4. **Select the field from which you want to provide a link to the detail page for each record.**

   For example, if you are listing a bunch of products, you can use the SKU number or the product name as the link to the detail.

5. **In the Pass Unique Key, usually the default is correct, if it is not, select the unique identifier that you want to pass on to the detail page.**

6. **Select the number of records you want to show at one time on the master page.**

   Remember that it's okay to show only a partial listing because you can add navigation to view more records.

7. **For the detail page, browse for the page you created to be the detail page in this set, or type in the filename in the text box.**

8. **Just like with the Master Page section, use the plus and minus signs to add or remove fields that you want or don't want to show on the detail page.**

9. **Click OK.**

Dreamweaver automatically adds all the necessary recordset information and SQL code for you to begin using your Master/Detail Page Set. Everything from navigation to record status is in there. You may want to rearrange and format the fields in a way that is more aesthetic because Dreamweaver just plops the stuff onto the pages, which looks really generic. For example, you can change the column labels to read in a friendlier way. You can also format the font, color and size, add padding to the table cells, and change the order of the columns.

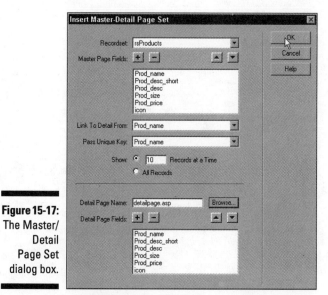

Figure 15-17:
The Master/
Detail
Page Set
dialog box.

Chapter 16

Using Forms to Manage Your Dynamic Web Site

Dynamic Web sites let you do a lot more than provide content and product listings to your Web site visitors. You can use Dreamweaver to create various types of forms that serve many useful purposes. Some examples include a login page so that users can register to use your Web site, a search page so users can search your Web site for specific information, or a data entry form to allow non-technical data-entry personnel to easily edit the content of a Web site.

Establishing User Authentication

One of the good things about a dynamic Web site is that you can retain a lot more control over it, from who can view it and how much they can view to who can edit it and how much they can edit. You can assign various users various levels of access depending on criteria that you determine. For example, you may have an employee directory online that all employees can access to obtain departmental information, title, and phone extensions. However, that directory also contains every employee's home phone number and home address, and you wouldn't want the entire company to have access to everyone's personal information, right? Dreamweaver's User Authentication Server Behavior enables you to create different levels of access that restrict the kind of information a user can see; in this example, you can make the personal information something only department managers may access.

In the first exercise for this chapter, you create a user login form that checks information against a database. I use a sample database of employees that contains the following fields:

- ✔ Employee number
- ✔ Password
- ✔ Last name
- ✔ First name
- ✔ Department
- ✔ Title
- ✔ Access level

If you want to use a pre-built database to complete this exercise, I have provided a sample database called employees.mdb on the accompanying CD. It was created using Access 2000.

After you have a database in place, create a page that contains a form with the following fields: a text box for User Name, a text box for Password, and a Submit button. Refer to Chapter 13 for more details on how to create a form.

Next, create a Data Source Name (DSN), database connection, and recordset that contains your employee number, last name, first name, password, department, title, and access level. Check out Chapters 14 and 15 if you need a quick review on this stuff.

Now that you've got everything in place, you're ready to add User Authentication to your form. For this exercise, I walk you through the setup for User Authentication on a company's employee directory. I use the employee number as the User Name.

1. **Select the form and click the plus sign (+) on the Server Behaviors panel (see Figure 16-1).**

   Selecting a form in Dreamweaver can be a little bit tricky sometimes, if you used a table to organize the form text boxes. A quick way to select the entire form is to click anywhere inside the form and then select the word "form" from the status bar at the bottom of the Dreamweaver window. This will select the entire form.

2. **From the menu, select User Authentication and select Log In User from the submenu that appears.**

   The Log In User dialog box appears (see Figure 16-2).

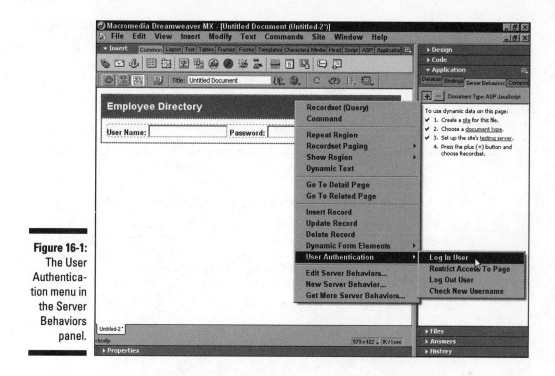

Figure 16-1:
The User
Authentication menu in the Server
Behaviors
panel.

3. In the Get Input From field, enter the form name.

It's good practice to name forms, especially if you have a page with multiple forms. Naming your forms makes each one easier to identify within the code.

4. Enter the name of the appropriate text box from your form next to Username Field and Password Field.

In my example, the user name field is called *user,* and the password field is called *pass.*

5. From the Connection and Table drop-down lists, make the appropriate selections.

6. From the Username Column and Password Column drop-down lists, select the fields in your database that will be used to verify the Username and Password provided by the user at login.

Because I'm using the employee number as the User Name, I selected that field as my User Name column, but if you have a specific User Name field in your database you would select *that* one instead.

7. Enter the name of the page where users will be redirected if the login succeeds.

In my example, the page is employees.asp, which will be the actual employee directory listing.

8. Next, enter the name of the page where users will be redirected if the login fails.

They can be redirected to the same login page, or you can create a secondary login page that looks like the first one but contains an error message saying something like, "That user name and/or password is incorrect. Please try again."

9. Finally, select Restrict Access Based on *User Name and Password*.

If you were restricting access only to certain users at a certain access level (say, Manager or Employee), you can define that in this area as well. The resulting effect is that only the users in the database whose access level matches what you specified are taken to the login success page. The rest are redirected to the login failed page.

10. Click OK.

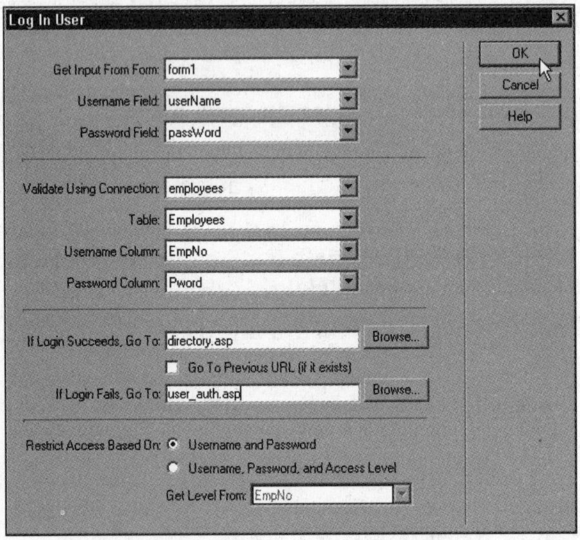

Figure 16-2:
The Log In
User dialog
box.

You can now preview this page in your browser and test the form by entering a user name and password from your database.

Easy Steps You Can Take to Secure Sensitive Information on Your Web Site

Here are some steps you can take that will help make your sensitive information more secure on the Web. Some steps are for the more advanced users, or those users more familiar with ASP and databases.

✔ Carefully choose the passwords you use, especially for your FTP, your database and the admin login area of your Web site. Too often people use common words, names, and number combinations as passwords that are easy for hackers to figure out. An effective password consists of mixed letters and numbers — the more random the better — and is case-sensitive whenever possible.

✔ Protect your development machine. Many Web site break-ins are inside jobs, where someone from within the company itself was able to obtain the sensitive information because he or she had access to the Web site files. If your development machine is on a network and you must grant access to it, grant only restricted access.

✔ On your Web server, turn Directory Browsing *off* so folders without an index page don't display everything that's in them. If you are not the administrator for your Web server, or don't know how to do this, ask a technical support representative at your hosting company to either walk you through it or do it for you. It's a fairly simple step.

✔ Pages that require authentication, such as employees.asp from the previous example, should have code on that page that kicks out users who didn't log in to get into that page. This way if someone happens to access the file without using the login page they'll be sent elsewhere. One of the easiest ways to do this is with a cookie — of the ASP variety, not chocolate chip! You can learn more about cookies and ASP in *Beginning Active Server™ Pages 3.0* by David Buser, et al. (published by Wrox Press).

✔ Don't use an access database for a serious Web site. Not only is it slow, it's simple to steal because it's typically a single file. Even if a person doesn't know SQL, he or she may be able to find it and read it off of your Web server.

✔ You can buff up database security by keeping it away from direct Internet access on a dedicated machine, allowing only your Web server to access that system through a local network infrastructure.

✔ Use SSL technology to encrypt sensitive information sent back and forth from the server.

✔ Don't copy and paste complex snippets of code that you found on the Web unless you absolutely trust the source and checked out all the stops. Sometimes this type of widely used code is easily picked out by hackers who are looking for it and know its specific vulnerabilities.

Please keep in mind that Dreamweaver's Login Authentication can be a pretty basic method of restricting access to a page if you only follow the basic steps outlined in this book. An amateur hacker could easily find your database, figure out passwords, or bypass the login page altogether to get to the information he or she wants. If you are building a site that contains sensitive information, and you are not very familiar with Web site security, consider hiring a consultant to advise you. At the very least, read up on the subject so you can get a better understanding of the security risks you may encounter. *Web Security, Privacy and Commerce* by Simson Garfinkel (published by O'Reilly & Associates) provides a very thorough look into the subject.

Searching for Database Records

With Dreamweaver, you can create a form to search for records on your database using specific criteria. This is pretty useful if you've got a large database. You wouldn't want to make your users read through pages and pages of listings, whether they are employee records or products or anything else). Providing a search form allows your users to quickly find the information they want.

In this next exercise, you discover a simple way to implement a database search on your dynamic Web site.

Setting up the search page

The search page is the simplest part to set up. All you need is a form with an Action that goes to the results page, a form text field, and a Submit button.

1. **First, create a new page that contains a form with the fields you would like your users to be able to search.**

   Check Chapter 13 to go over forms in more detail.

   I'm using the same employee directory database from the first exercise, so my text field is going to be *Lname*, which allows my users to search by employee last names.

2. **In the Action field in the Property Inspector, enter the name of the results page. (You create this page in the next example.)**

   My result page will be called *search_results.asp*.

3. **Save this page.**

Setting up the results page

The results page is a little bit more complex. The search actually takes place on this page, behind the scenes on the server, and what you see is only the result of that search. The text field that you determined in the search page is referred to as the *form variable* in the results page. That means that the information you entered in this form is going to be passed on to the results page in order for the search to take place.

1. **Create a new page that contains a table with a column for each field you would like to show in the results.**

2. **Create a connection and a recordset for this page using the database or table from which you want to bring in the results.**

   See Chapters 14 and 15 if you need more detailed information on how to do this.

3. **In the Recordset dialog box (see Figure 16-3), select the appropriate Connection and Table.**

4. **Next to Filter, select the column that corresponds with the field by which you want your users to search.**

5. **In the drop-down box directly below that one, select Form Variable, and then enter the name of the text field element from your search form in the text box next to it.**

6. **In the Sort By field, select the field by which you would like to sort your results.**

7. **Click OK.**

8. **Next, drag each field from your recordset to the appropriate column on the table in your results page. (See Figure 16-4.) You can review the steps to do this in Chapter 14.**

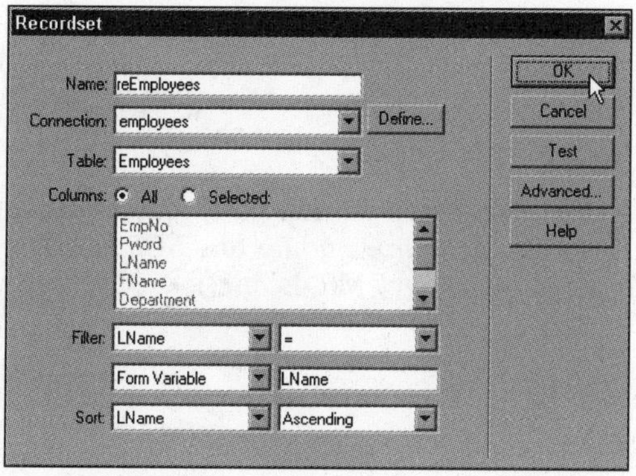

Figure 16-3:
The
Recordset
dialog box
prepared for
search
results.

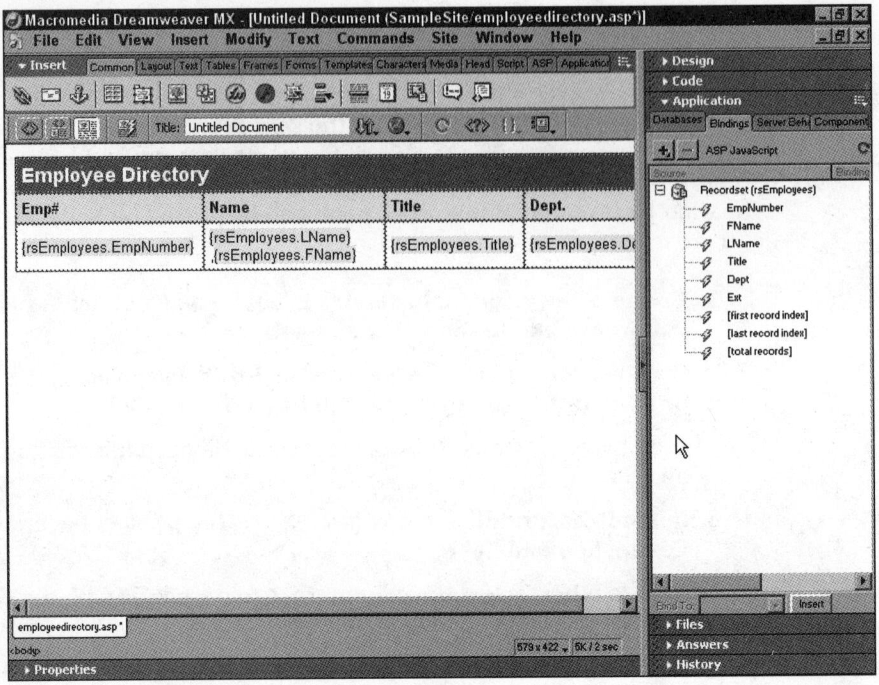

Macromedia Dreamweaver MX - [Untitled Document (SampleSite/employeedirectory.asp*)]

File   Edit   View   Insert   Modify   Text   Commands   Site   Window   Help

Insert | Common | Layout | Text | Tables | Frames | Forms | Templates | Characters | Media | Head | Script | ASP | Applicati2

Title: Untitled Document

Employee Directory

Emp#	Name	Title	Dept.
{rsEmployees.EmpNumber}	{rsEmployees.LName} {rsEmployees.FName}	{rsEmployees.Title}	{rsEmployees.D

▶ Design
▶ Code
▼ Application
Databases | Bindings | Server Beha | Component

ASP JavaScript

Source   Binding

⊟ 🔳 Recordset (rsEmployees)
      ◈ EmpNumber
      ◈ FName
      ◈ LName
      ◈ Title
      ◈ Dept
      ◈ Ext
      ◈ [first record index]
      ◈ [last record index]
      ◈ [total records]

Bind To: Insert

▶ Files
▶ Answers
▶ History

employeedirectory.asp*
<body>   579 x 422   5K / 2 sec
▶ Properties

Figure 16-4:
The Search
Results
page, ready
for action.

9. **Finally, transfer your pages to the server and open your search page in a browser. Try searching for one of the entries in your database. The search will find the entry and list it in your search results page, showing every field you have requested on that results page.**

   I searched for *Brooks*, and Figure 16-5 shows my search results.

That's it. Painless, right? This is a database search in its simplest form. The more advanced your understanding of Dreamweaver and the SQL language gets, the more complex that you can make your search forms. Users with a basic understanding of SQL can enhance this page to search using multiple criteria, filter out search results, sort by various fields, and even display only certain results depending on the Access level of the person performing the search.

If you would like to find out more about working with databases and SQL, I recommend *Database Development For Dummies* and *SQL For Dummies,* both by Allen G. Taylor (published by Hungry Minds, Inc.).

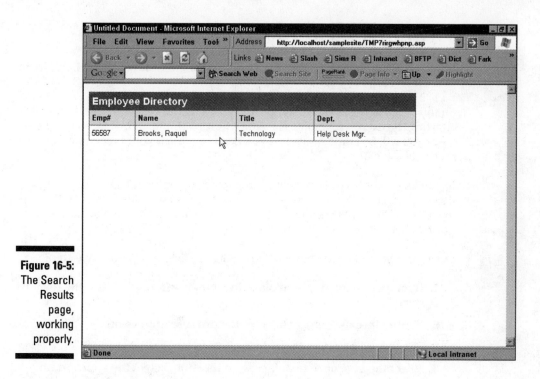

Figure 16-5:
The Search
Results
page,
working
properly.

Editing a Database from a Browser

Using forms is also an easy way to perform data-entry tasks on a database without having to open the database application. In fact, the person performing those tasks doesn't even need to know how a database works in order to use the form. All the work is done right on the browser window. Through the form, a user can add, update, or delete a record from the database.

Sticking to the employee directory example, let's say a manager wants to add a new employee and update some information in the directory for various employees who just received promotions. Using Dreamweaver, you can create a user-friendly interface where this manager can go to his browser, log in, and make those changes to the database. He can save his changes right there on his browser and view the updated information instantly, all without ever having to open a database application (such as Access).

You can secure content management pages (like those discussed in this section) from the public by using the authentication features of Dreamweaver covered at the beginning of this chapter.

Adding a record to your database

A record in a database (a row) consists of a complete set of all the fields in the database.

In this next exercise, you use a form to add a record to a database. Before starting the exercise, you must create a new page and connect it to the database you will be editing. Again, if you need to refresh your memory on how to do this, see Chapter 14.

If you have created your page, you are now ready to use Dreamweaver's Record Insertion Form Server Object. In one easy step, this Server Object creates a script that allows you to add a record to a database. It also creates the form that you use to make the addition.

A *server object* lets you create a more complex function in one easy step.

1. **Open your new page and place the cursor where you want the form to start.**

2. **Choose Insert⇨Server Objects⇨Record Insertion Form.**

   The Record Insertion Form dialog box opens (see Figure 16-6).

3. **Select the appropriate database connection, select the appropriate table from that database, and then enter the name of the page the user will be redirected to after the new addition has been made.**

4. **In the Form Fields section of the dialog box, verify that all the fields are displayed.**

   In the *label* column, you can change the actual name of the column by clicking a field from the list and editing the Label text. You can also determine what kind of form field and what type of formatting (numeric, text, and so on) will be used for each field. If any field should have a default value, you can define that in this dialog box as well.

5. **Click OK.**

You can now test your page (see Figure 16-7). Simply upload the page to your server, open it in your browser, and enter all the information for a new record. Click Insert Record. Did your new record show up in the database?

Remember to upload the Connections folder when you upload your site files to the application server, otherwise you will get an ASP "include file not found" error message.

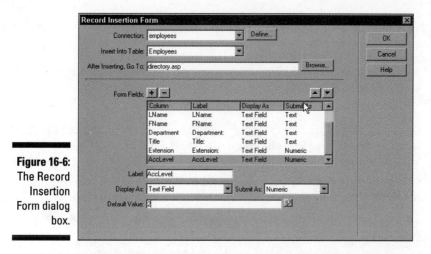

Figure 16-6:
The Record
Insertion
Form dialog
box.

When you created the database connection (refer to Chapter 14), a Connections folder was added to your site on the local drive. The ASP files in the Connections folder store necessary information that makes your page work correctly with the database. This type of file is typically called an *include file* because its contents can be referenced by the code in another page. Dreamweaver will automatically *include* the contents of this file on any page you create which uses this database connection.

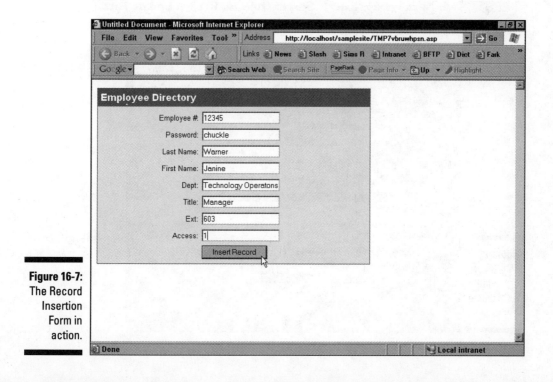

Figure 16-7:
The Record
Insertion
Form in
action.

Updating a record via a browser

To edit or *update* a record from a database, you first need to create a search form to search for the record you want to update. After you find the record, the Update Record form appears, which is where you perform the actual update.

1. **On a new page, start by creating a simple search form like the one in the first exercise in this chapter, with a text field element and a Submit button.**

2. **Select the text field on your page, and in the Properties panel replace *textfield* with a more descriptive name. For example, *mysearch*.**

   This helps to differentiate one text field from another on a page that contains multiple fields.

3. **Create a recordset, and filter by the field that you're using as your search criteria.**

   I'm using Employee Number (EmpNo) as my search criteria.

4. **From the drop-down list directly below the Filter list, select Form Variable. Next to Form Variable, type the name of the text field from your search form. In my case, I type *mysearch*.**

5. **Click OK.**

6. **Next, choose Insert➪Server Objects➪Record Update Form.**

   The Record Update Form dialog box opens (see Figure 16-8).

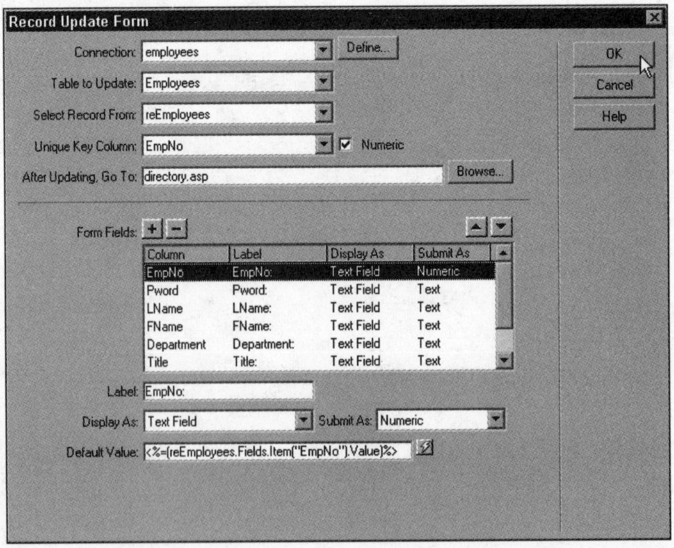

Figure 16-8: The Record Update Form dialog box.

7. **Select the appropriate connection and table.**

8. **Enter the name of the page you want to show after the update has been made.**

   I'm using employees.asp, which is my default employee directory page.

9. **Make sure that the field labels are correct, or rename them to what you want to be displayed on the update form. You can rename them later on your page, by selecting and replacing the text for each field directly on your page.**

10. **Click OK.**

    A new form appears on your page. You can format the look of the form (font, color, and so on) to make it match with the way the rest of your Web site looks.

11. **Finally, select the Server Behaviors Panel and click the plus sign (+). From the menu, select Show Region, and from the submenu, select Show Region if Recordset Is Not Empty.**

    This last step ensures that you don't get an error if there is no recordset that matches the criteria you enter into the search field.

Your Update form is now complete (see Figure 16-9).

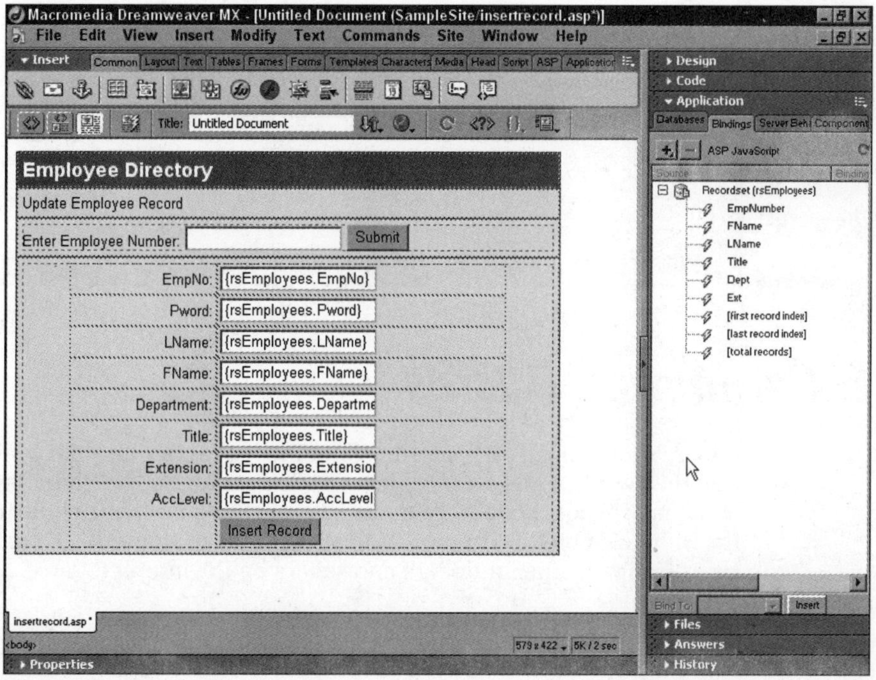

Figure 16-9:
The newly
created
Update
form.

TIP

Power users can take advantage of Dreamweaver's Expert mode to build more complex SQL queries on the spot.

Now you can test the new page by previewing it in your browser. Enter a value that you know exists in that field in your database and click Submit. The Update Record Form should now be populated with the information for that record. You can now make any changes to that record and click Update Record to save the changes to the database. The next time you view that record online, the changes will be there (see Figure 16-10).

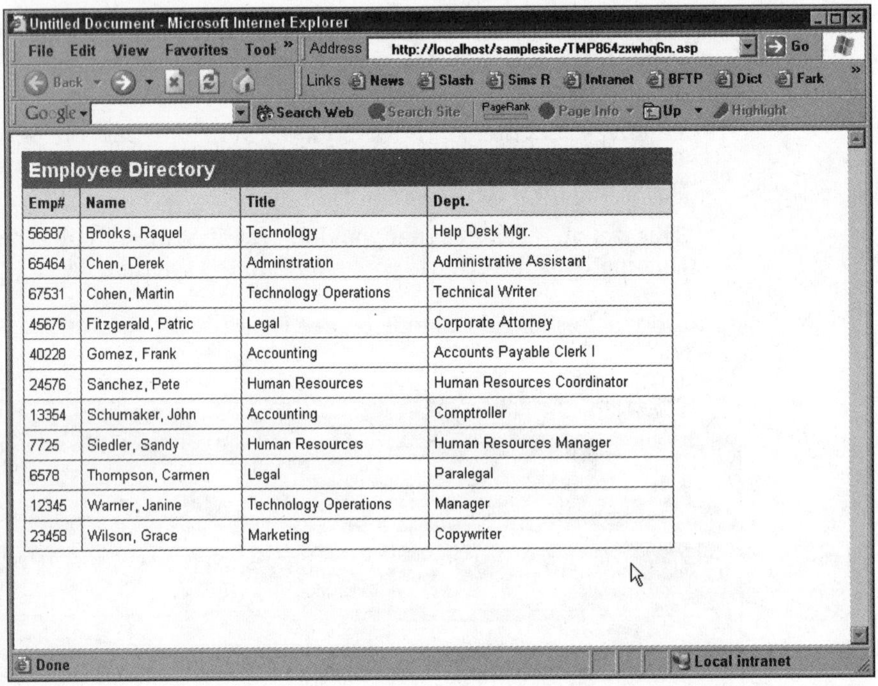

Untitled Document - Microsoft Internet Explorer

File   Edit   View   Favorites   Tool ˮ   Address   http://localhost/samplesite/TMP864zxwhq6n.asp   Go

Back   Links News   Slash   Sims R   Intranet   BFTP   Dict   Fark

Google   Search Web   Search Site   PageRank   Page Info   Up   Highlight

Employee Directory

Emp#	Name	Title	Dept.
56587	Brooks, Raquel	Technology	Help Desk Mgr.
65464	Chen, Derek	Adminstration	Administrative Assistant
67531	Cohen, Martin	Technology Operations	Technical Writer
45676	Fitzgerald, Patric	Legal	Corporate Attorney
40228	Gomez, Frank	Accounting	Accounts Payable Clerk I
24576	Sanchez, Pete	Human Resources	Human Resources Coordinator
13354	Schumaker, John	Accounting	Comptroller
7725	Siedler, Sandy	Human Resources	Human Resources Manager
6578	Thompson, Carmen	Legal	Paralegal
12345	Warner, Janine	Technology Operations	Manager
23458	Wilson, Grace	Marketing	Copywriter

Done   Local intranet

Figure 16-10:
The updated
record.

E-Commerce Basics

If there's one thing that's certain about most people who want a Web site, it's that they want to make money from it. The era of the "brochure" site is no more, my friends. People are hawking everything from fine china to soil from the Holy Land on the Internet (I kid you not about that one). E-commerce helps bring together shoppers and sellers on the Internet.

In the next few paragraphs, I tell you more about what an e-commerce Web site is and what you need to have in place in order to create a fully functional e-commerce site. However, if you're looking for information on how to create an e-commerce site right out of the box with Dreamweaver, stop here. It's not going to happen. I don't know why the powers that be over at Macromedia haven't included this feature yet. To be quite frank, I think this is really one of the only major flaws I could find with Dreamweaver. You *can* create an e-commerce Web site using Dreamweaver, but it will require an extension, which I go into in just a moment.

What puts the "e-commerce" into an e-commerce Web site?

An e-commerce Web site, in a nutshell, is a Web site that accepts real-time payments for goods and services. For example, if you're looking for a weight loss supplement you can log on to www.metabolicnutrition.com, browse offerings in their weight loss product line, and have one shipped to you overnight.

Not all e-commerce Web sites are the same — many companies have built customized tools to aid users in the shopping process. For example, Metabolic Nutrition also allows you to store your shipping information so that you don't have to key it in every time you order. It also has a virtual "personal assistant" that recommends products based on your health, age, diet, and lifestyle.

The cost of an e-commerce Web site is significantly more than the cost of building a regular Web site because there are several third-party costs that you have to figure into the whole. Here's a quick rundown of the minimal (traditional) e-commerce requirements:

- ✔ **A shopping cart:** A shopping cart is a series of scripts and applications that display items from your database, allow users to pick and choose which ones they want, and then collects payment and shipping information. Some Web-hosting accounts come with shopping carts included. Two popular ones are Miva Merchant (www.miva.com) and PDG Cart (www.pdgcart.com). There are also various Dreamweaver shopping cart extensions that are worth looking into. For example, PDG Cart offers a Dreamweaver extension that provides full integration with PDG's e-commerce capabilities with a price tag of about $400 for a lifetime license.

- ✔ **A merchant account:** This is literally an account with a bank or a financial institution that allows you to accept credit cards from your clients. Many merchant account providers also offer payment gateways and virtual terminals as a suite, which can save you money and time. Costs and transactions fees vary, as service providers set their own prices. OnlineDataCorp (www.onlinedatacorp.com) is a good one.

✔ **A payment gateway and virtual terminal:** A payment gateway is what ties your shopping cart to your merchant account. A virtual terminal is like an electronic bookkeeper and cash register in one — you can view your Web site transactions, issue refunds, and manage orders. The two most popular packages are Verisign's PayFlow Pro and PayFlow Link (www.verisign.com). PDG, mentioned previously, also supports payment from various services (www.pdgcart.com).

✔ **A secure site certificate:** This encrypts information between your Web site and the client's computer to protect the information from being stolen as you make your purchase online. This is commonly referred to as Secure Sockets Layer (SSL) technology. Verisign and Thawte's 128 bit certificates are popular picks. If you're on a shared Web-hosting account, you may be able to share the server's certificate to save money; however, this is often regarded as unprofessional, because the security certificate won't display your company name on it — shoppers who check it will see your Web-hosting company's name instead.

The definition of what a "traditional" e-commerce Web site is continues to change as new technologies and application service providers emerge. Services like Yahoo! Stores allow you to create a site without purchasing any of the previously mentioned items. PayPal.com offers all-inclusive e-commerce services with free shopping cart tools.

Pre-made shopping carts and e-commerce systems save you time and money up front, and buying one is the fastest way to get a business online. The downside of using a pre-made shopping cart is that you often can't make it look like an integral part of your Web site, meaning that you usually have limited control over the graphical elements on shopping-cart driven pages. Also, most shopping carts use their own database and give you limited access to the code (as a lot of it may be compiled CGI, which Dreamweaver can't read), so you may run into brick walls when trying to build new features that you didn't buy out of the box.

Considering the investment and risk, many companies prefer to hire a professional programming team to create a system from scratch that looks and functions exactly how they want it to. Amazon.com, for example, has spent millions on theirs to make it the incredibly smart and easy to use system it is today. But you don't have to break the bank — many very successful custom-built e-commerce Web sites were created for less than the cost of a used '93 Toyota Camry.

Extending Dreamweaver one feature at a time

At last count, a few minutes ago, there were 21 e-commerce-related extensions for Dreamweaver on the Macromedia Web site, from standalone shopping carts to a PayPal extension that allows shoppers to pay you via PayPal directly from your Web site.

However, e-commerce is just the proverbial ol' tip of the iceberg when it comes to extending Dreamweaver. At the Macromedia Exchange Web site, you can download an extension for just about any functionality you would like your Web site to have.

There are two ways you can add extensions to Dreamweaver. The first is by going directly to the Web site (`http://dynamic.macromedia.com/bin/ MM/exchange/ultradev/main.jsp`).

The other way to access Macromedia Exchange is through Dreamweaver itself. You must be connected to the Internet in order for this to work. This can be done from various points within the application:

- ✔ **From the Insert menu:** Choose Insert➪Get More Objects

- ✔ **From the Command menu:** Choose Command➪Get More Commands

- ✔ **From the Server Behaviors Panel:** Click the plus sign (+) and then select Get More Server Behaviors

- ✔ **From the Data Bindings Panel:** Click the plus sign (+) and then select Get More Data Sources

- ✔ **From the Behaviors Panel:** Click the plus sign (+) and then select Get More Behaviors

Once you are on Macromedia Exchange, if this is your first time there, you must register before downloading any extensions. Also, you need to make sure that your *Extension Manager* (which comes with Dreamweaver) is installed and running.

If you've registered and have the Extension Manager on your system, you can now search for extensions and download them to your system. You can also choose to download the extensions (.mxp files) onto your computer and install them using the manager, or you can choose to install them on the spot, which downloads and installs the extension from the Web without saving the installation file on your hard drive.

There are various ways in which you can run the Extension Manager for installing an extension. In Dreamweaver, you can click Command⇨Manage Extensions. You must have a document open. In Windows, you can go to Start⇨Macromedia Extension Manager⇨Macromedia Extension Manager. You can also launch it by double-clicking an .mxp file in Explorer.

When you open Extension Manager, you see all the extensions you have installed in your system. To view the description for any of these extensions, simply click it once, and any pertinent information will be displayed in the lower pane of the Extension Manager window.

Ready to add some extensions? Click File⇨Install New Extension and follow the simple prompts to have your new extension up and running in no time. Uninstalling is just as simple: Click File⇨Remove Extension, and voilà!

Part VI
The Part of Tens

The 5th Wave   By Rich Tennant

"I'm not sure I like a college whose home page
has a link to The Party Zone!"

In this part . . .

The Part of Tens features a chapter on ten Web sites that were created with Dreamweaver and do an exceptional job of showing off what Dreamweaver is capable of. These examples provide something to aspire to for all Web designers. Next, you get a chapter on ten great design and interface ideas to keep in mind as you build your Web site. Finally, you enjoy a chapter on ten timesaving tips that can make your work with Dreamweaver easier and more productive, including some great tips for getting the most out of the newest features of Dreamweaver MX.

Chapter 17

Ten Great Sites Designed with Dreamweaver

In This Chapter

▶ Dreamweaver sites provide great examples of Web design

▶ Filmmaker combines the power of Flash and Dreamweaver

▶ Online nutrition site takes e-commerce to new levels of integration

▶ Echo Medium shows its stuff on the Web

▶ . . . and a few more to look at, too

As the clear choice of many professional Web designers, Dreamweaver deserves credit for providing the development power behind many of the most popular sites on the Web. Taking the time to review some of these sites, and appreciate how they were created, is an ideal way to pick up good ideas for your own Web project.

Many of the sites featured in this chapter take advantage of the latest Web technologies, integrating Dynamic HTML, Flash, and more to create vivid animations and powerful interactivity.

The sites featured in this chapter provide an excellent overview of what you can do with Dreamweaver — and they're all great examples of what's possible on the Web today. Review the descriptions of these sites to find out what tools they used and then spend some time online, visiting each site to appreciate the full impact of their design, navigation, and other features.

You can connect directly to these Web sites by clicking the appropriate hyperlink in the HTML interface on the CD that accompanies this book.

Presenting Film and Photography

When F.M. Mashat, a photographer and filmmaker, decided to take his work online, he wanted more than just a static Web site. He wanted to create a site that had the look and feel of a major motion picture, yet still loaded quickly and was easy to navigate. He also had the challenge of presenting both of his talents — film and photography — in one site (see the opening page in Figure 17-1).

He found just what he was looking for in Francisco Rivera, a multi-talented Web designer, who drew on his experience with animation and the entertainment industry to help Mashat create a dynamic, almost cinematic site. (To find out more about Rivera, visit his site at www.balam.net.) This entire project was done in Flash, using Dreamweaver to pull it all together. The biggest challenges were keeping the image and film clips small enough that they would load quickly. In the case of the film clips, they opted to create three versions of each clip: one for very low bandwidth connections (and limited quality), another for faster modems, and finally one for visitors with high-speed connections that made the film look as good as possible on the Web.

Figure 17-1:
F.M.
Mashat's
site (www.
mashat.
com)
captures the
work of a
filmmaker
and photo-
grapher
with almost
cinematic
presen-
tation.

Selling Nutrition with Style

www.metabolicnutrition.com

Miami-based Web design firm ModernMethod did more than just create a beautiful Web site for Metabolic Nutrition (see Figure 17-2); they also helped the company improve product fulfillment and customer service by creating a next generation e-commerce solution. The site enables customers to interactively learn about products, get product recommendations from an automated personal assistant, quickly place orders, schedule automatic reorders, and securely manage their accounts.

The developers at ModernMethod used Dreamweaver to layout the templates for the product pages, relying on Dreamweaver's behaviors feature to easily create pop-ups. They also credit Dreamweaver with saving them tons of time setting up subtle roll-overs on the toolbar with the Swap Image behavior and Site Map feature.

This is a high-end project, powered by an Oracle database. The dynamic elements of the site were written in a text editor by their programmers, so the designers appreciated that Dreamweaver understood what PHP was and marked it with icons, making it easy to just wrap the design around the programming code. In case you're not sure what it is, *PHP* is a server-side scripting language for creating dynamic Web pages. This kind of programming code can get butchered in other Web design programs because they don't recognize what it is and try to alter the code.

The results: Metabolic Nutrition has enhanced their customer care capabilities dramatically. Customer service representatives can now process and modify orders more efficiently; marketing managers can more easily forecast trends with customized reports; and operations managers can watch inventory and process flow using bar codes. (To learn more about these talented developers, visit www.modernmethod.com.)

Although this data-base driven site was created with custom programming, we selected it as a model for this book and recreated many of the front-end site features using a simple Access database and Dreamweaver's UltraDev capabilities. You'll find detailed instructions about how Dreamweaver made that possible in Chapters 14, 15, and 16.

Figure 17-2:
The
Metabolic
Nutrition site
provides an
example of a
powerful
database-
driven
e-commerce
project
that not
only looks
great, but
improves
the com-
pany's ability
to manage
inventory
and serve
customers,
too.

Modern Web Design

www.modernmethod.com

The ModernMethod Web site shown in Figure 17-3 is essentially a self-promotional piece designed in Corel PhotoPaint and Flash and then pieced together with Dreamweaver.

Yanier Gonzalez, creative director, says, "Using Dreamweaver and other products from the Macromedia line makes creating big sites bearable. We use the Image Map and JavaScript Behavior tools extensively to allow our designers to get more done in less time and free our programmers to work on the hard stuff."

Figure 17-3:
Modern
Method has
been using
Dream-
weaver for
years on
their own
sites as well
as their
client's
sites.

Making Music on the Web

www.djtracyyoung.com

Tracy Young, a well-known DJ who has worked with a long list of high-profile artists, including Madonna, Cyndi Lauper, and Enrique Iglesias, wanted an interactive Web site to show fans and colleagues what she's really made of.

She hired ModernMethod (www.modernmethod.com) to redesign her site and add a hot Flash animation, message board, samples of her music, and a private press area (see the results in Figure 17-4).

The team at ModernMethod used Dreamweaver to piece together the Flash movies for the menu bar and to work around the static features of the site, such as the photo gallery. They also customized a pre-packaged message board system to look and feel like the rest of Tracy's site using Dreamweaver's sophisticated design tools.

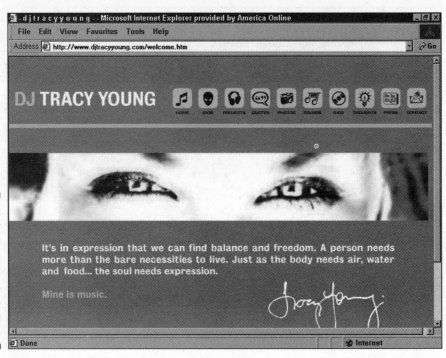

Figure 17-4:
DJ Tracy
Young's
Web site
comes alive
with Flash,
sound files,
and a photo
gallery.

So what does Tracy Young think of her new site? "It rocks!" (Don't you wish all *your* clients would say that about your work?)

Searching the Web, Spanish Style

www.terespondo.com

Whether you read Spanish and Portuguese or not, you can appreciate the sophisticated search engine and development work done on the Web site *Te Respondo* (translated: I respond to you), a leading Latin American pay-for-performance search engine.

The latest iteration of *Te Respondo* (shown in Figure 17-5) relies on a distributed search architecture that enables the site to accept millions of queries each month from other search engines in the South American market. Essentially, the company sells targeted placements in search results, but to make that work, they needed to be able to interact with a variety of other sites and come up with a design that adjusted to match the look and feel of each partner.

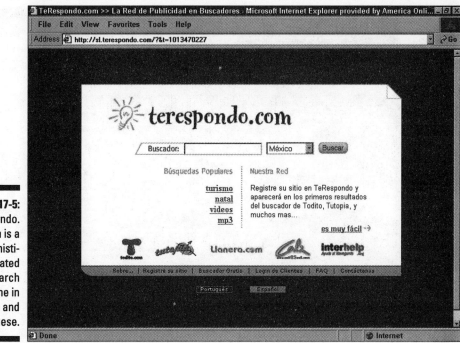

Figure 17-5:
Teresondo.
com is a
sophisti-
cated
search
engine in
Spanish and
Portuguese.

Challenges included making the system respond instantaneously when changes were made by the advertising manager, minimizing the opportunity for fraud, and absorbing extreme fluctuations in traffic. Behind the scenes, you'll find three high-end servers and lots of bandwidth, but what really makes it work is the programming and sophisticated design work.

The development team used Dreamweaver's design and programming features, in conjunction with a private label template system, to support three languages without duplicating code or turning designers into programmers. Today, that initial development work is paying for itself — and, thanks to Dreamweaver, the entire job of refreshing content is maintained by one junior-level designer.

Great Design Echos Across the Web

www.echomedium.com

Macromedia Dreamweaver was an essential part of the development of Echo Medium's corporate Web site at www.echomedium.com (see Figure 17-6). UltraDev was used in every step of the development process from design to conception.

Figure 17-6:
The Echo
Medium
Web site is
a state-of-
the-art
example of
advanced
Web design.

Initially, Dreamweaver was used to create the foundation in HTML and then used in the integration between Java Server Pages (JSP) and Echo Medium's legacy system. According to the designers, Macromedia Dreamweaver was especially helpful in its capacity for integration because it displayed files real-time in the preview window. It was also helpful with the deployment of JavaScript and DHTML functions.

Echo Medium has also used Macromedia Dreamweaver in online projects for their clients, which include Federal Express, Bacardi, Mexicana, Dewar's, and Unisa Shoes.

Cinemascope Photo Journey

www.cinemascope.com/photos

This site showcases photographer Andrew Peters's chronicle of his 1998 trip through five South American countries. Shooting with a conventional 35mm camera, Peters used a slide scanner to capture his images while combining Photoshop, ImageReady, Fireworks, and Dreamweaver to build his site. Dreamweaver was chosen because of its ease of use, templates, and style sheet features. Peters created a template for the site that allowed him to update global aspects of the interface easily while using style sheets to specify font size (see Figure 17-7). I like this site, in part, because Peters is not a "professional" photographer, and he created a site that looks fabulous. (See Chapter 4 for more on using Dreamweaver templates. Check out Chapter 8 to find out more about style sheets.)

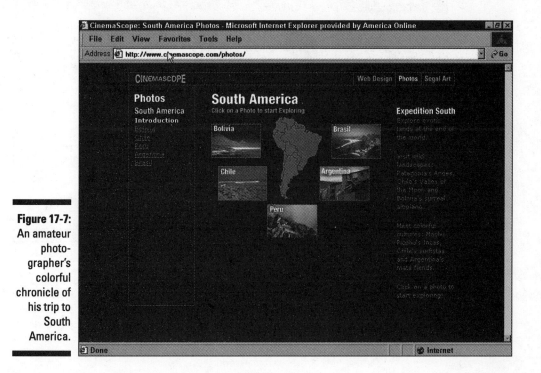

Figure 17-7: An amateur photographer's colorful chronicle of his trip to South America.

Biking through the Web

www.Big-Wheel.com

A local bike shop chain, Big Wheel, wanted to offer their product inventory of 10,000 plus items on the Web, and they wanted to integrate their Web site with their distributor's database (see Figure 17-8). Fortunately for them, the distributor was already online and they got the same design company to develop their site so it was easy, and more cost effective, to integrate their site with their distributor's database (J & B Distributors). The developers also created an administration system that enabled Big Wheel to manually edit their pricing and information and even make global changes to their entire database.

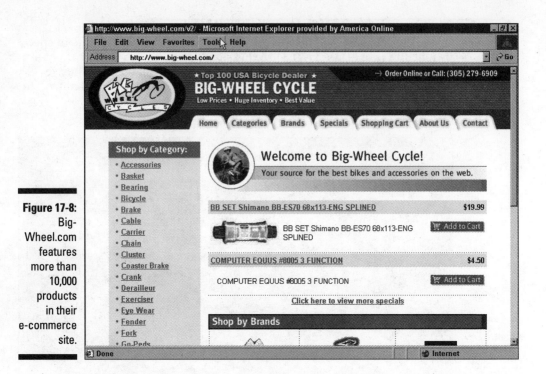

Figure 17-8:
Big-
Wheel.com
features
more than
10,000
products
in their
e-commerce
site.

The developers used Dreamweaver to layout the front end and were especially appreciative of Dreamweaver's Cascading Style Sheet (CSS) tool to handle several funky roll-overs for text links that unbold when selected. It's the little details that make for the best designs on sites like these. The rest of the site was built with custom PHP scripts and a MySQL database.

fabric8

www.fabric8.com

Fabric8 has been winning awards and accolades from all over the Web with its innovative and design-conscious clothing commerce site. Using Dreamweaver, the site's talented creator, Olivia Ongpin, employs DHTML, Shockwave, Flash, interactive audio, downloadable fonts, and many other cutting-edge technologies to deliver a fresh and exciting online experience.

Be sure to explore this site's deeper pages, and don't forget to look at its archives. Fabric8 has been developing great stuff since 1996 (see Figure 17-9). (To find out more about Flash and Shockwave, see Chapter 12. For more on DHTML, check out Chapters 9 and 10.)

Figure 17-9: fabric8 has been using Dreamweaver since it first came out and continues to make creative use of the Dreamweaver multimedia features.

Yours Truly

http://www.janinewarner.com

I would love to take credit for the design of my own Web site (see Figure 17-10), but the truth is that my talented co-author, Ivonne Berkowitz, developed my site using Dreamweaver's great features to create a complex design that is simple to update and maintain. (I can handle all of the technical development on my site, but Ivonne is a much better designer.)

The subtle animation she created on the front page made it possible for me to include quotes from two different sources, and the roll-over effects make the navigation buttons come alive. I use Dreamweaver to make regular additions to the site and handle site management when I want to add new sections or make more significant changes.

(Just for the record, I really do think Dreamweaver is the best Web design program on the market, and I can't imagine using anything else on my own site.)

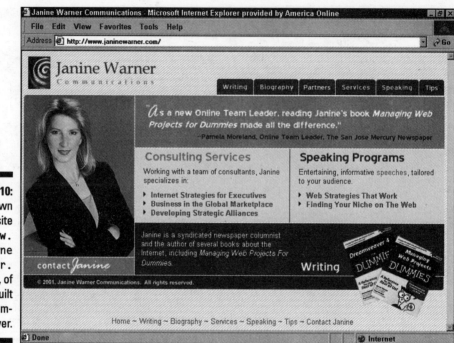

Figure 17-10: My own Web site at www. janine warner. com was, of course, built with Dream-weaver.

Chapter 18

Ten Web Site Ideas You Can Use

● ●

In This Chapter

▶ Making your Web site easy to read

▶ Designing for your audience

▶ Pulling it all together

▶ Following the rules

● ●

All good Web sites grow and evolve. If you start with a strong design and pay close attention to some basic rules about interface, navigation, and style, you have a better foundation to build on. The following design ideas can help you create a compelling Web site that grows gracefully.

Make It Easy

Creating a clear and intuitive navigational system is one of the most important elements in creating a Web site. Nothing is likely to frustrate your visitors more than not being able to find what they're looking for. Make sure that visitors can easily get to all the main sections of your site from every page in the site.

You can best do this by creating a set of links to each of the main sections and placing it at the top or side of every page. I call this set of links a *navigation row* or *navigation bar,* and it's a common feature on most well-designed sites. If the pages are very long, consider including a navigation bar, or footer, at the bottom of the page as well. Often the navigation bar at the bottom of the page is just a list of text links. The bottom of the page is also an ideal place to include basic contact information. A set of graphical icons can make this navigational element an attractive part of your design (see Chapter 7 for how to align navigation elements in table cells). Your goal is to make sure that viewers don't have to use the Back button in their browsers to move around your site.

White Space Is Not Wasted Space

One of the best design features you can add to a page is nothing at all (also known as *white space*). Understand that white space, in this case, is not always white; it's simply space that you haven't crammed full of text or images. It can be any color, but it's usually most effective if it's the color or pattern of your background. White space gives the eye a rest, something readers need even more often when they're staring at a computer monitor. You can use white space to separate one type of information from another and to focus the viewer's attention where you want it most. Some of the most beautiful and compelling designs on the Web use only a few well-thought-out elements against lots of white space.

Design for Your Audience

No matter how technically sophisticated a Web site is or how great the writing, most people notice the design first. Make sure that you leave plenty of time and budget to develop an appropriate and attractive design for your Web site. The right design is one that best suits your audience — that may or may not mean lots of fancy graphics and animations.

Think about who you want to attract to your Web site before you develop the design. A gaming Web site geared toward teenagers should look very different from a Web site with gardening tips or an online banking site for adults. Review other sites designed for your target market. Consider your audience's time constraints and attention span, and, most importantly, consider your audience's goals. If you design your site to provide information to busy businesspeople, you want fast-loading pages with few graphics and little or no animation. If you design your site for entertainment, your audience may be willing to wait a little longer for animation and other interactive features.

Back It Up

Make sure you have a system in place to back up your Web site. Always keep a copy of all the files that are on your server in a separate location and update it regularly to make sure you have the latest version of your site backed up at all times. Even the best Internet Service Providers sometimes have technical problems, so you should keep a backup of your site where you have easy access to it and can get it back online quickly if something ever does happen to delete any or all the files you have on the server.

Also keep a backup of your original source files, such as Photoshop images. For example, when you develop images for the Web, you usually start in a program like Photoshop, creating a high-resolution image that may include layers and other elements. Before the image goes on your Web site, those layers get flattened and the image gets compressed or reduced and converted into a GIF or JPEG. If you ever want to go back and alter that image in the future, you'll want the original source file before it was compressed and the layers were flattened. Whether you create your own images or you hire a professional designer, make sure you develop a system for saving all these original elements when they are created.

Be Consistent

As you lay out your Web page, keep related items physically close to one another. You want your viewers to instantly understand which pieces of information are related. Give elements of similar importance the same weight on a page. Distinguish different kinds of information by their design, location, and prominence. This kind of organization makes following information visually much easier for your viewers. You can find many other design tips in Chapter 4.

Make sure that all similar elements follow the same design parameters, such as type style, banner size, and page background color. If you use too many different elements on a page or within the same Web site, you quickly have a very "busy" design, and you may confuse your viewers. Defining a set of colors, shapes, or other elements that you use throughout the site is a good way to ensure a consistent style. Choose two or three fonts for your Web site and use those consistently as well. Using too many fonts makes your pages less appealing and harder to read.

Inconsistency can also weaken your brand. A clean, consistent Web site goes a long way in building a user's trust. Sapient, a business and technology consulting firm, did a study in 1999 on how visual alignments affect user attention, trust, and interest. They found being consistent with color schemes and type faces and keeping it simple made a significant difference.

Small and Fast

Despite all the promises that unlimited bandwidth was coming soon, the biggest problem on the Internet is still speed. Making sure that your pages download quickly makes your viewers more likely to keep clicking. You may create the best design ever to grace the Web, but if it takes too long to appear on your viewers' screens, no one will wait around long enough to compliment your design talents.

If your page designs take a long time to download, here are a few likely reasons and suggestions for how to make them load faster: First, take a look at multimedia elements and consider reducing the size or at least offering users the option to skip large multimedia files, such as Flash introductions. You especially don't want to make users wait too long for the first page of your site. If you suspect that static images are the problem, consider compression methods and use a program such as Fireworks or ImageReady that are designed for optimizing images for the Web (you'll find more on how to do this in Chapters 5 and 11). Finally, use Dreamweaver's code cleanup feature to get rid of extra tags that can contribute to a heavier page. To use this, choose Commands⇨Clean Up HTML.

Accessible Designs

As you design your site, keep in mind that viewers come to your pages with a variety of computers, operating systems, and monitors. Ensure that your site is accessible to all your potential viewers by testing your pages on a variety of systems. If you want to attract a large audience to your site, you need to ensure that it looks good on a broad range of systems. A design that looks great in Navigator 4.0 and higher may be unreadable in Internet Explorer 3.0. And many people still use old browsers because they haven't bothered — or don't know how — to download new versions.

Accessible design on the Web also includes pages that can be read (actually, converted to synthesized speech) by special browsers used by the blind. Using the ALT attribute in your image tags is a simple way to ensure that all visitors can get the information they need. The ALT attribute specifies a text alternative that is displayed if the image doesn't appear. It's inserted into an image tag like this:

```
<IMG SRC="CAT.GIF" ALT="A picture of a black and white cat.">
```

Follow the Three Clicks Rule

The Three Clicks Rule states that no important piece of information should ever be more than three clicks away from anywhere else on your Web site. The most important information should be even closer at hand. Some information, such as contact information, should never be more than one click away. Make it easy for viewers to find information by creating a site map (as I explain in the next section) and a *navigation bar* — a set of links to all the main sections on your site.

Map It Out

As your site gets larger, providing easy access to all the information on your Web site may get harder and harder. A great solution is to provide a *site map,* which is a page that includes links to almost every other page in the site. The site map can become a busy page and usually appears best in outline form. This page should be highly functional — it doesn't matter if it looks pretty. Don't put lots of graphics on this page; it should load quickly and provide easy access to anything that your visitors need.

Late-Breaking News

One of the greatest challenges of any Web site is the ability to post new information quickly, especially under pressure or in times of crisis. Don't wait for an emergency to find out if you're prepared to update your Web site quickly, and don't think that because you manage a Web site for a business or a non-profit group, you don't have to worry about being able to send breaking news to the Internet.

With a little planning and key systems set up in advance, you can be prepared for events that require timely updates — whether it's an international crises or an embarrassing event that makes your CEO cringe and demand that the "real" story be told as soon as possible.

Here are a few steps you can take to be prepared for timely updates on your site:

1. **Make sure you can send new information to your Web site quickly.**

    Many Web sites are designed with testing systems that safeguard against careless mistakes, but these systems can add hours, or even days, to the time it takes to add new information to your Web site. Work with your technical staff or consultants to make sure you can update your site quickly if necessary. This may require creating a new section that can be updated independently from the rest of the site or being able to override the regular update system.

2. **Make it easy to update important sections of your site.**

    Consider developing a content management system that uses a Web-based form to post new information to your site. Such a system can be designed to change or add information to a Web page as easily as filling out an online order form. You will need an experienced programmer to develop a form-based update system. Many Web consultants offer this kind of service, and after it's developed, it can be used for others kinds of updates as well. For example, this method works if you are a real estate agent and need to change listings or you have a calendar of events. Password protection should be included so that you control access to the form. You get the added advantage that updates can be made from any computer connected to the Internet so you can update your Web site, even if you can't get back into your office.

3. **Identify key staff to be trained to update the site.**

   With the right systems in place, you do not need to have much technical experience to make simple updates to a site, but your staff will need some instruction and regular reminders. Make sure you also develop a schedule for retraining to ensure that no one forgets emergency procedures. Your most serious emergency could happen tomorrow or may not happen for years to come — you never know, so it pays to be prepared.

Chapter 19

Ten Timesaving Dreamweaver Tips

In This Chapter

▶ Making the most of Dreamweaver MX

▶ Saving time with shortcuts

▶ Designing for all Web browsers

▶ Integrating Fireworks for image development

▶ Making DHTML design easy

*E*ven the best programs get better when you know how to make the most of them. As I put this book together, I collected tips and tricks and gathered them into this handy list. Take a moment to check out these tips and save tons of time in developing your Web site. Most of these tips apply to both Macintosh and Windows users.

Trying the New Interface

If you loved Dreamweaver 4's interface, you can stick with it in Dreamweaver MX, but make sure you give the new Dreamweaver interface a chance. When you first turn on the program, you're given a choice between the two interfaces — the old and the new.

The old interface still has all the floating panels (called *palettes* in previous versions), which provide quick access to Dreamweaver's most popular features. But, as you may have found in previous versions, those floating panels can clutter up the design area and get in your way. You can still use the F4 key as a short cut to hide all visible panels at once and the F4 key again to get them back, but if you like that short cut, you may be even happier with the new interface. Dreamweaver MX enables you to lock each of the panels into the workspace, keeping it handy without overlapping with the design area. You can move the panels around and change the icons that are visible on each of them to ensure that your favorite tools are where you like them. Macromedia changed the interface based on tons of feedback from professional designers, and you're likely to find it a better option as well. Even better, you can still use F4 to hide palettes, even in their new docked mode, so you get the best of both worlds.

Creating Dynamic Web Sites

Don't be intimidated by all the new panels and options in Dreamweaver MX. Much of what has been added are the features that were previously reserved for Macromedia's UltraDev program. These include high-end programming features for creating dynamic, database-driven sites using ASP, JSP, and ColdFusion. If that's all new to you, take your time getting into these advanced features in Chapters 14, 15, and 16.

And don't worry — if you aren't creating a database-driven site, you don't need to learn these features, at least not yet. But rest assured they're ready for you when you want to take your site to the next level. Most of the best sites on the Web these days are dynamic and require a database and the power to connect it to the Web. That's why Macromedia integrated these features into Dreamweaver and made sure you had them handy because you're likely to need them sooner or later.

Splitting the View: Working in the Code

If you like to switch back and forth between the HTML source code and the WYSIWYG (What You See Is What You Get) design view in Dreamweaver, you'll appreciate the option split the window so you can view the HTML source and the WYSIWYG design area at the same time. To split the window, choose View⇨Code and Design or select the Show Code and Design Views button, located just under the Insert panel at the top of the work space.

Tabling Your Designs

HTML tables still offer the best way to create complex Web designs (because layers aren't supported by older browsers and even in new browsers they aren't supported consistently). Fortunately, Dreamweaver MX has made it easier than ever to create tables in its visual design area. In the Layout View, you can "draw" tables on a page, drag them into place, and even group cells in a nested table — without ever worrying about how many rows and cells you've created. You can even use this feature to create tables that change with the window size, a great technique for ensuring your designs work on all monitors. (Did you know people are surfing the Web with Palm Pilots and Pocket PCs these days?)

Choose View⇨Table View⇨Layout View to access Dreamweaver's special table creation environment. But then make sure to switch back to the Standard View where you'll find that editing and formatting your table is easier. You find cell and table layout options in the Objects panel when you select the table or cell. For more information about using Layout View and working with HTML tables, check out Chapter 6.

Designing in a Flash

Flash rocks! Macromedia's vector-based design and animation program, Flash, is one of the hottest programs on the Web today because it makes creating fast-loading images and animations that dynamically adjust to fit any screen size possible. Now that the Flash plug-in is built into most current browsers, Flash has become a standard, and Dreamweaver has made it easier than ever to add Flash buttons and text to your Web pages.

To add pre-made Flash buttons to your site, just click the Insert Flash Button option in the Media tab of the Insert panel. The dialog box makes it easy to choose a button design and edit the text that appears on the button, all from within Dreamweaver. You can even create your own buttons in Flash and add them to the list of available buttons.

You can add Flash Text the same way, by choosing Insert Flash Text from the Objects panel. For more on these integrated Flash features, read Chapter 12.

Making Fireworks with Your Images

The Dreamweaver integration with Fireworks, Macromedia's Web image program, makes it easy to edit images while you're working in Dreamweaver. Need to change the text on a button or create a new banner? Just use the edit image button in the Property Inspector to launch Fireworks and view the PNG source file; you can click the Edit button in the Property Inspector when an image is selected to edit it in Fireworks, and any changes you make to an image are automatically reflected in the Dreamweaver file. If you've always used another image program, such as Photoshop, this level of integration should at least get you to consider using Fireworks. It can save you a ton of time in your design work, especially when your pesky colleagues and clients are always asking for last minute changes. For more on using Fireworks and Dreamweaver in tandem, check out Chapter 11.

Finding Functional Fonts

Designers get so excited when they find out that they can use any font on a Web page. But, in reality, your viewers must still have the font on their computers for it to display. The more common the font, the more likely it is to display the way you intend. If you want to use a more unusual font, go for it — just be sure that you also include alternatives. The Dreamweaver Font List already includes collections of common fonts, and you can always create your own Font List by choosing Text⇨Font⇨Edit Font List.

And here's another tip: Windows is by far the most common operating system that people use to browse the Net. To ensure the best — and fastest — results for the majority of your users, list a Windows font first.

In an effort to make text easier to read on the Web, Adobe and Microsoft have both created fonts that are especially suited to computer screens. Visit their Web sites at `www.adobe.com` and `www.microsoft.com` respectively and search for Web fonts to find out more.

Differentiating DHTML for All Browsers

If you like pushing the technical limits of what works on the Web, don't overlook one of the most valuable features of Dreamweaver: the Convert option. This feature automatically converts your complex page designs that work only in 4.0 and later browsers into alternative pages that display in 3.0 browsers. The feature converts the CSS and DHTML tags into regular HTML style tags by converting CSS formatting into HTML formatting tags and recreating layers into HTML Tables.

To convert CSS and other features on a page, choose File⇨Convert⇨3.0 Browser Compatible. Beware that HTML is not capable of the complex designs you can create using DHTML, so your converted pages may not look as much like the original as you would like; for example, there is no way to do justice to a layer that moves across the screen in a static table cell. Chapter 10 walks you through the process in detail. The conversion isn't a perfect science, but it is a relatively easy way to ensure your pages are at least presentable in older browsers.

I've heard too many good designers say that users should upgrade their browsers and that they don't care about users who are so lame they're still using an old version of AOL. Here's a word of caution: It only takes one really important viewer to get you in trouble for not doing multi-browser designs. Beware that one of the most likely people to be using an older browser is the president of the company who is traveling with his laptop that he's never upgraded the browser on because he only uses it from hotel rooms on the road. Don't take the risk that your paying clients, your boss, or worse yet, your investors, are the ones with the old browsers. Make sure your designs work well for everyone — it's the sign of a truly high-end Web designer.

Directing Your Viewers

Creating multiple pages is the most fail-safe solution for making sure that all your viewers are happy when you use cutting-edge page designs filled with DHTML and CSS. That means you create two or more sets of pages: one that uses the latest features and one that uses older, more universally supported HTML tags. But how do you ensure that viewers get to the right pages? Use the Check Browser behavior.

The Check Browser behavior is written in JavaScript and determines the browser type used by each viewer who lands on your site. The behavior then directs users to the page design best suited to their browser version. To use this feature, choose Window➪Behaviors to open the Behaviors panel. You can also find this panel by clicking the Design panel in the top right of your screen and choosing the Behaviors tab.

Select the plus sign (+) to open the drop-down list of options and choose Check Browser. In the Check Browser dialog box specify what browser versions should be directed to what pages on your site. When users arrive at your site, they are automatically directed to the page of your choice, based on the browser type and version that you specify.

Keeping Frequently Used Items Handy

If you use the same element on multiple pages of your site, Dreameaver's Assets feature can help you keep them handy and organized. In this newest version, you'll find the Assets feature (also called the Library) in the Files Panel, under the Assets Tab. Use this feature to store images, text strings, and other elements you use regularly. This is an ideal place to store your company logo, navigation elements, and other frequently used items.

To store an element in the Library, simply drag it from any page into the Assets panel. To retrieve it, drag it from the Assets panel and place it on any page. This is just another great way to save time with Dreamweaver — because we can all use more time for dreaming . . . .

Appendix

About the CD

The CD-ROM that accompanies this book contains the following goodies:

- ✔ Shareware version of Expandable Language HTML Rename!, a filename conversion program that can save you hours of manual searching and replacing

- ✔ Lots of extra trial versions of software (see the "What You'll Find" section later in this appendix) that can help you become more efficient in many aspects of Web design

- ✔ Flash files for you to use when you try out Dreamweaver's plug-in features

- ✔ A few extra GIF and JPEG images for you to use while you're becoming familiar with building Web pages in Dreamweaver

- ✔ A bonus chapter that covers the basics of HTML

- ✔ A glossary that can help you become familiar with Web design and Dreamweaver lingo

System Requirements

Make sure that your computer meets the minimum system requirements shown in the following list. If your computer doesn't match up to most of these requirements, you may have problems using the software and files on the CD.

✔ A PC with a Pentium II or faster processor and 300+ MHz; or a Power Mac G3 OS computer or faster processor

✔ Microsoft Windows 98, 2000, NT, ME, or XP; or Mac OS system software 9.1, 9.2.1, or OS 10.1

✔ At least 64MB of available RAM on your computer; for best performance, we recommend at least 128MB

✔ A CD-ROM drive

✔ A sound card for PCs; Mac OS computers have built-in sound support

✔ A monitor capable of displaying at least 256 colors or grayscale

✔ A modem with a speed of at least 14,400 bps

If you need more information on the basics, check out these books published by Hungry Minds, Inc.: *PCs For Dummies*, by Dan Gookin; *Macs For Dummies*, by David Pogue; *iMacs For Dummies* by David Pogue; *Windows 95 For Dummies*, *Windows 98 For Dummies*, *Windows 2000 Professional For Dummies*, *Microsoft Windows ME Millennium Edition For Dummies*, all by Andy Rathbone.

Using the CD with Microsoft Windows

To install items from the CD to your hard drive, follow these steps:

1. **Insert the CD into your computer's CD-ROM drive.**

2. **Click the Start button and choose Run from the menu.**

3. **In the dialog box that appears, type** d:\start.htm.

   Replace *d* with the proper drive letter for your CD-ROM if it uses a different letter. (If you don't know the letter, double-click My Computer on your desktop and see what letter is listed for your CD-ROM drive.)

   Your browser opens, and the license agreement is displayed.

4. **Read through the license agreement, nod your head, and click the Agree button if you want to use the CD.**

   After you click Agree, you're taken to the Main menu, where you can browse through the contents of the CD.

5. **To navigate within the interface, click a topic of interest to take you to an explanation of the files on the CD and how to use or install them.**

6. **To install software from the CD, simply click the software name.**

   You'll see two options: to run or open the file from the current location or to save the file to your hard drive. Choose to run or open the file from its current location, and the installation procedure continues. When you finish using the interface, close your browser as usual.

Note: We have included an "easy install" in these HTML pages. If your browser supports installations from within it, go ahead and click the links of the program names you see. You'll see two options: Run the File from the Current Location and Save the File to Your Hard Drive. Choose to Run the File from the Current Location and the installation procedure will continue. A Security Warning dialog box appears. Click Yes to continue the installation.

Using the CD with Mac OS

To install items from the CD to your hard drive, follow these steps:

1. **Insert the CD into your computer's CD-ROM drive.**

   In a moment, an icon representing the CD you just inserted appears on your Mac desktop. Chances are, the icon looks like a CD-ROM.

2. **Double-click the CD icon to show the CD's contents.**

3. **Double-click** `start.htm` **to open your browser and display the license agreement.**

   If your browser doesn't open automatically, open it as you normally would by choosing File⇨Open File (in Internet Explorer) or File⇨Open⇨Location in Netscape (in Netscape Navigator) and select *Dreamweaver MX FD*. The license agreement appears.

4. **Read through the license agreement, nod your head, and click the Accept button if you want to use the CD.**

   After you click Accept, you're taken to the Main menu. This is where you can browse through the contents of the CD.

5. **To navigate within the interface, click any topic of interest and you're taken to an explanation of the files on the CD and how to use or install them.**

6. **To install software from the CD, simply click the software name.**

What You'll Find on the CD

The following sections are arranged by category and provide a summary of the software and other goodies you'll find on the CD. If you need help with installing the items provided on the CD, refer to the installation instructions in the preceding section.

Shareware programs are fully functional, free, trial versions of copyrighted programs. If you like particular programs, register with their authors for a nominal fee and receive licenses, enhanced versions, and technical support. *Freeware programs* are free, copyrighted games, applications, and utilities. You can copy them to as many PCs as you like — for free — but they offer no technical support. *GNU software* is governed by its own license, which is included inside the folder of the GNU software. There are no restrictions on distribution of GNU software. See the GNU license at the root of the CD for more details. *Trial, demo,* or *evaluation* versions of software are usually limited either by time or functionality (such as not letting you save a project after you create it).

Software programs

Acrobat Reader from Adobe Systems

For Mac and Windows. Freeware version.

This program lets you view and print Portable Document Format (PDF) files. Many programs on the Internet use the PDF format for storing documentation because it supports assorted fonts and colorful graphics.

To learn more about using Acrobat Reader, choose the Reader Online Guide from the Help menu, or view the Acrobat.pdf file installed in the same folder as the program. You can also get more information by visiting the Adobe Systems Web site at www.adobe.com.

ChangeAgent™ from Expandable Language

For Windows. Shareware version.

ChangeAgent makes fixing Web site problems quick and simple. ChangeAgent brings problems out into the open through its interactive display of broken links and unused files. It closely integrates problem discovery with problem investigation and repair, providing rich feedback exactly where it is needed. You can quickly discover the right fix for a problem and apply it on the spot.

HTML Rename!® from Expandable Language

For Mac and Windows. Shareware version.

This program started out as a simple utility and has grown beyond its creator's original vision. It's now a high-powered development tool perfect for converting Web sites from one platform to another by automating the process of renaming files without breaking links. To find out more, check out the site at www.xlanguage.com.

Illustrator from Adobe

For Mac OS and Windows. Tryout version.

Adobe's advanced vector-drawing program enables you to create complex images with powerful precision. To learn more, check out the Adobe Web site at www.adobe.com.

Photoshop from Adobe

For Mac OS and Windows. Tryout version.

The most popular and best respected photo manipulation program available, Photoshop is a must-have for any serious graphic designer and a great tool for developing Web graphics. To learn more, check out the Adobe Web site at www.adobe.com.

BrowserSizer from Apply This Software Inc.

For Windows. Freeware version.

You can use BrowserSizer to check the way your pages look in a browser on resolutions of 640 x 480, 800 x 600, 1024 x 768, and WebTV.

Flash from Macromedia

Trial version for Mac and Windows.

For more information about Flash, check out Macromedia's Web site at www.macromedia.com.

IrfanView from Skiljan Irfan

For Windows. Freeware version.

IrfanView is a freeware graphics viewer that supports many graphic and animation formats. For more information, visit www.irfanview.com.

Web browsers and plug-ins

Shockwave from Macromedia

For Mac and Windows. Commercial product.

Use this plug-in to view Director and Flash files. Visit the Macromedia Web site at www.macromedia.com for more information and program updates.

Note: If you don't have Netscape installed and are using IE 4.0, go to the Web site and download the ActiveX version of Shockwave.

Other Great Stuff

And here's some more for you.

Flash animations

One of the most dynamic elements you can add to a Web page is a Flash animation. But inserting them on a Web page in a way that works effectively on a variety of browsers can be complicated. Dreamweaver includes several features to help you include special code so that your Flash files play well on almost any computer on the Web. You'll find instructions about how to insert Flash files in Chapter 12, and you'll find a sample Flash file on the CD that you can use as you work through the step-by-step exercises.

Glossary

Don't forget to check out the glossary on the CD. It can be your first resource when you stumble across some Web-design lingo that you're just not sure about.

Bonus chapter on HTML

This bonus chapter walks you through the basics of HTML — a great introduction for beginners and a refresher course for those already familiar with HTML.

Web links document

I compiled all the Web addresses mentioned in this book and put them in one spot to make getting there extra easy for you.

Author-created material

For Windows and Mac.

All the examples provided in this book are located in the Author directory on the CD and work with Macintosh, Linux, Unix and Windows 95/98/NT and later computers.

Image files

To make it easy for you to follow along with steps to add images to your Web pages, I've included a couple of image files for you to use with exercises in Chapters 2, 5, and 11.

Sample databases

If you'd like to save some time when preparing for the exercises in Chapters 14, 15, and 16, you will find two small databases (both for Access 2000) on the CD for use with those exercises.

Troubleshooting

I tried my best to compile programs that work on most computers with the minimum system requirements. Alas, your computer may differ, and some programs may not work properly for some reason.

The two likeliest problems are that you don't have enough memory (RAM) for the programs you want to use, or you have other programs running that are affecting installation or running of a program. If you get an error message such as Not enough memory or Setup cannot continue, try one or more of the following suggestions and then try using the software again:

- **Turn off any antivirus software running on your computer.** Installation programs sometimes mimic virus activity and may make your computer incorrectly believe that it's being infected by a virus.

- **Close all running programs.** The more programs you have running, the less memory is available to other programs. Installation programs typically update files and programs; so if you keep other programs running, installation may not work properly.

- **Have your local computer store add more RAM to your computer.** This is, admittedly, a drastic and somewhat expensive step. However, if you have a Windows 95 PC or a Mac OS computer with a PowerPC chip, adding more memory can really help the speed of your computer and allow more programs to run at the same time. This may include closing the CD interface and running a product's installation program from Windows Explorer.

If you still have trouble installing the items from the CD, please call the Hungry Minds, Inc. Customer Service phone number at 800-762-2974 (outside the U.S.: 317-572-3994) or send e-mail to techsupdum@wiley.com. Hungry Minds will provide technical support only for installation and other general quality control items; for technical support on the applications themselves, consult the program's vendor or author.

Index

● *I* ●

Notes

Notes

Notes

Hungry Minds, Inc., End-User License Agreement

READ THIS. You should carefully read these terms and conditions before opening the software packet(s) included with this book ("Book"). This is a license agreement ("Agreement") between you and Hungry Minds, Inc. ("HMI"). By opening the accompanying software packet(s), you acknowledge that you have read and accept the following terms and conditions. If you do not agree and do not want to be bound by such terms and conditions, promptly return the Book and the unopened software packet(s) to the place you obtained them for a full refund.

1. **License Grant.** HMI grants to you (either an individual or entity) a nonexclusive license to use one copy of the enclosed software program(s) (collectively, the "Software") solely for your own personal or business purposes on a single computer (whether a standard computer or a workstation component of a multi-user network). The Software is in use on a computer when it is loaded into temporary memory (RAM) or installed into permanent memory (hard disk, CD-ROM, or other storage device). HMI reserves all rights not expressly granted herein.

2. **Ownership.** HMI is the owner of all right, title, and interest, including copyright, in and to the compilation of the Software recorded on the disk(s) or CD-ROM ("Software Media"). Copyright to the individual programs recorded on the Software Media is owned by the author or other authorized copyright owner of each program. Ownership of the Software and all proprietary rights relating thereto remain with HMI and its licensers.

3. **Restrictions on Use and Transfer.**

    (a) You may only (i) make one copy of the Software for backup or archival purposes, or (ii) transfer the Software to a single hard disk, provided that you keep the original for backup or archival purposes. You may not (i) rent or lease the Software, (ii) copy or reproduce the Software through a LAN or other network system or through any computer subscriber system or bulletin-board system, or (iii) modify, adapt, or create derivative works based on the Software.

    (b) You may not reverse engineer, decompile, or disassemble the Software. You may transfer the Software and user documentation on a permanent basis, provided that the transferee agrees to accept the terms and conditions of this Agreement and you retain no copies. If the Software is an update or has been updated, any transfer must include the most recent update and all prior versions.

4. **Restrictions on Use of Individual Programs.** You must follow the individual requirements and restrictions detailed for each individual program in the "About the CD" appendix of this Book. These limitations are also contained in the individual license agreements recorded on the Software Media. These limitations may include a requirement that after using the program for a specified period of time, the user must pay a registration fee or discontinue use. By opening the Software packet(s), you will be agreeing to abide by the licenses and restrictions for these individual programs that are detailed in the "About the CD" appendix and on the Software Media. None of the material on this Software Media or listed in this Book may ever be redistributed, in original or modified form, for commercial purposes.

5. **Limited Warranty.**

   (a) HMI warrants that the Software and Software Media are free from defects in materials and workmanship under normal use for a period of sixty (60) days from the date of purchase of this Book. If HMI receives notification within the warranty period of defects in materials or workmanship, HMI will replace the defective Software Media.

   (b) **HMI AND THE AUTHOR OF THE BOOK DISCLAIM ALL OTHER WARRANTIES, EXPRESS OR IMPLIED, INCLUDING WITHOUT LIMITATION IMPLIED WARRANTIES OF MERCHANTABILITY AND FITNESS FOR A PARTICULAR PURPOSE, WITH RESPECT TO THE SOFTWARE, THE PROGRAMS, THE SOURCE CODE CONTAINED THEREIN, AND/OR THE TECHNIQUES DESCRIBED IN THIS BOOK. HMI DOES NOT WARRANT THAT THE FUNCTIONS CONTAINED IN THE SOFTWARE WILL MEET YOUR REQUIREMENTS OR THAT THE OPERATION OF THE SOFTWARE WILL BE ERROR FREE.**

   (c) This limited warranty gives you specific legal rights, and you may have other rights that vary from jurisdiction to jurisdiction.

6. **Remedies.**

   (a) HMI's entire liability and your exclusive remedy for defects in materials and workmanship shall be limited to replacement of the Software Media, which may be returned to HMI with a copy of your receipt at the following address: Software Media Fulfillment Department, Attn.: *Dreamweaver MX For Dummies*, Hungry Minds, Inc., 10475 Crosspoint Blvd., Indianapolis, IN 46256, or call 1-800-762-2974. Please allow four to six weeks for delivery. This Limited Warranty is void if failure of the Software Media has resulted from accident, abuse, or misapplication. Any replacement Software Media will be warranted for the remainder of the original warranty period or thirty (30) days, whichever is longer.

   (b) In no event shall HMI or the author be liable for any damages whatsoever (including without limitation damages for loss of business profits, business interruption, loss of business information, or any other pecuniary loss) arising from the use of or inability to use the Book or the Software, even if HMI has been advised of the possibility of such damages.

   (c) Because some jurisdictions do not allow the exclusion or limitation of liability for consequential or incidental damages, the above limitation or exclusion may not apply to you.

7. **U.S. Government Restricted Rights.** Use, duplication, or disclosure of the Software for or on behalf of the United States of America, its agencies and/or instrumentalities (the "U.S. Government") is subject to restrictions as stated in paragraph (c)(1)(ii) of the Rights in Technical Data and Computer Software clause of DFARS 252.227-7013, or subparagraphs (c) (1) and (2) of the Commercial Computer Software - Restricted Rights clause at FAR 52.227-19, and in similar clauses in the NASA FAR supplement, as applicable.

8. **General.** This Agreement constitutes the entire understanding of the parties and revokes and supersedes all prior agreements, oral or written, between them and may not be modified or amended except in a writing signed by both parties hereto that specifically refers to this Agreement. This Agreement shall take precedence over any other documents that may be in conflict herewith. If any one or more provisions contained in this Agreement are held by any court or tribunal to be invalid, illegal, or otherwise unenforceable, each and every other provision shall remain in full force and effect.

Installation Instructions

The *Dreamweaver MX For Dummies* CD offers valuable information that you won't want to miss. To install the items from the CD to your hard drive, see the detailed instructions in the "About the CD" appendix.